MASONIC

SYMBOLS ILLUSTRATED

Dr. Cathy Burns

Sharing
212 E. 7th St. (Y)
Mt. Carmel, PA 17851-2211

TABLE OF CONTENTS

1. WHAT IS A SYMBOL?

What is a symbol? Webster tells us that a symbol is "something that stands for or suggests something else by reason of relationship, association, convention, or accidental resemblance; *esp:* **a visible sign of something invisible.**" [Emphasis mine throughout] This is important to know because when we see a symbol we now know that there is a meaning **BEHIND** what is actually being shown since a symbol is "a **visible** sign of something **invisible.**" A related word, symbolism, is "the use of conventional or traditional signs in the representation of **DIVINE BEINGS AND SPIRITS.**" This, too, is important because many of these symbols also represent gods and goddesses.

Since this book will be covering many occultic and Masonic symbols, a few quotes from Masons about symbols would be in order. Masonic author, George H. Steinmetz, shares the following:

"The symbols are *not* used in the commonly accepted meaning. It is 'NOT BY EXACT RESEMBLANCE'; there *IS* a more recondite [meaning occult or esoteric] interpretation, as we suspected; it is one of 'SUGGESTIONS OR ASSOCIATION *IN THOUGHT.*'

"There is a SECRET DOCTRINE in Freemasonry. That secret doctrine is **concealed,** rather than revealed, by the very lectures which, we are told, offer a 'rational explanation' of the ceremonies of initiation. If we were to accept these 'rational explanations' as final, and seek no further, Freemasonry would be a farce."[1] [Italics and caps in the original; Boldface added]

Carl Claudy, a Masonic writer, mentions that there are secrets inside secrets in symbolism. He wrote: **"CUT THROUGH THE OUTER SHELL AND FIND A MEANING; CUT THROUGH THAT MEANING AND FIND ANOTHER; UNDER IT IF YOU DIG DEEP ENOUGH YOU MAY FIND A THIRD, A FOURTH—WHO SHALL SAY HOW MANY TEACHINGS?"**

In an Eastern Star book we are told: "A symbol is a figure of something intellectual, moral or spiritual, a visible object, **REPRESENTING** to the mind the semblance of **SOMETHING WHICH IS NOT SHOWN** but realized by association with it."[2]

Albert Mackey, a well-known Mason, writes that a symbol is a "sensible image used to express an **OCCULT** but analogical signification."[3]

Another book reminds us that "An emblem is a figure or symbol which stands for **SOMETHING ELSE.**"[4] We are also told that there is a **HIDDEN MEANING** to these symbols, so what is presented to the candidate is not what is really meant. Eastern Star writer, Mary Ann Slipper, states "that everyone who becomes a member of the Order of the Eastern Star should be familiar with the **ESOTERIC meaning of every symbol used in the work....**"[5]

One *Short Talk Bulletin,* which was supposed to be read in the Lodge, says:

> "It may be asserted in the broadest terms that the **FREEMASON WHO KNOWS NOTHING OF OUR SYMBOLISM KNOWS LITTLE OF FREEMASONRY.** He may be able to repeat every line of the ritual without an error, yet, if he does not understand the meaning of the ceremonies, the signs, the words, the emblems and figures, he is a **MASONIC IGNORAMUS.**"[6]

Throughout this book we will be looking at numerous symbols and we'll discover some of the **HIDDEN MEANINGS** behind these symbols. We will also see how various **symbols represent pagan gods and goddesses.** Additionally, we'll learn how **many emblems conceal and shroud sexual connotations under the guise of symbolism.** Charles G. Berger explains:

> "At first, in art, the sex organs were represented by pictures of them, but as man developed and ideas of morals changed, such representations seemed offensive or crude, and they were therefore **GRADUALLY MODIFIED UNTIL THE SYMBOLS COULD SCARCELY BE RECOGNIZED AS SEXUAL** in origin. **OTHER EX-PLANATIONS AND MEANINGS WERE INVENTED**

FOR THE MASSES, who were not supposed to understand the **TRUE MEANINGS.** Thus, **SYMBOLS CAME TO HAVE TWO MEANINGS,** the esoteric and the exoteric. The **ESOTERIC** meaning was the true or original meaning, **UNDERSTOOD BY ONLY A FEW** and closely guarded by them. The exoteric meaning was the invented, or modified, explanation intended for the many. The sacred mysteries, which are often mentioned in connection with many ancient religions and which were closely guarded by the initiate, concerned esoteric meanings in the religions of previous times. These sacred mysteries very often were merely continuations of the simpler forms of early sex worship carried on by a select few."[7]

The Migration of Symbols also states: "Without doubt the symbols that have attracted in the highest degree the **veneration** of the multitude have been the **representative signs of gods, often uncouth and indecent....**"[8]

Is this really the way we want Him—no longer King of Kings and Lord of Lords, but just another "guest" at the table?

Since the sexual nature of many symbols is now concealed under other guises, the average person no longer realizes the vulgarity behind many of them. Many organizations, however, use particular symbols and logos **INTENTIONALLY**—knowing **PRECISELY** what is being represented thereby. Multitudes of occultists, New Agers, witches, and Satanists understand the meanings of the symbols they use. On the other hand, many people are using these same symbols (or variations of them) today without knowing what they really represent. Hopefully, this book will show numerous symbols and explain the esoteric meaning of many of them so that the average person can be more aware of what is being portrayed behind some of the emblems being used.

We must remember that even though many leaders are aware of symbology, not every one who uses these symbols in their logos, etc., are familiar with the pagan connotations behind them. For example, we cannot just assume that everyone who wears a pentagram is evil and knows that this emblem is used extensively in Satanism and witchcraft. Many people do not know this and they "innocently" wear Satanic and pagan symbols. We must be careful not to accuse everyone who uses these symbols as being an occultist or New Ager. Of course, if we know that a particular group is an occultic association then the symbol that they use should not be taken lightly. Many of the people who design the logos know **exactly** what they are doing. We will cover many of these logos in this book and give their own explanations about the particular meaning behind the design selected.

Some people try to make some of the occultic symbols into "Christian" symbols such as saying that the pentagram represents the five wounds of Christ or that the triangle is a symbol of the Trinity. We cannot do this for the Bible says in Deuteronomy 4:15-19, 23:

> "Take ye therefore good heed unto yourselves; for ye saw no manner of similitude on the day that the Lord spake unto you in Horeb out of the midst of the fire: Lest ye corrupt yourselves, and make you a graven image, the similitude of any figure, the likeness of male or female, The likeness of any beast that is on the earth, the likeness of any winged fowl that flieth in the air, The likeness of any thing that creepeth on the ground, the likeness of any fish that is in the waters beneath the earth: And lest thou lift up thine eyes unto heaven, and when thou seest the sun, and the moon, and the stars, even all the host of heaven, shouldest be driven to worship them, and serve them, which the Lord thy God

hath divided unto all nations under the whole heaven....Take heed unto yourselves, lest ye forget the covenant of the Lord your God, which He made with you, and make you a graven image, or the likeness of any thing, which the Lord thy God hath forbidden thee."

God does not want us to make **ANY** image of Him in any way. "Forasmuch then as we are the offspring of God, we ought not to think that the Godhead is like unto gold, or silver, or stone, graven by art and man's device" (Acts 17:29).

When the Israelites went into pagan nations, the Lord instructed them to "overthrow their altars, and break their pillars, and burn their groves with fire; and ye shall hew down the graven images of their gods, and destroy the names of them out of that place. Ye shall not do so unto the Lord your God" (Deuteronomy 12:3-4; See also Deuteronomy 7:5).

Deuteronomy 7:25-26 says:

"The graven images of their gods shall ye burn with fire: thou shalt not desire the silver or gold that is on them, nor take it unto thee, lest thou be snared therein: for it is an abomination to the Lord thy God. Neither shalt thou bring an abomination into thine house, lest thou be a cursed thing like it: but thou shalt utterly detest it, and thou shalt utterly abhor it; for it is a cursed thing."

Although there are numerous symbols given throughout this book, this is definitely not an exhaustive itemization. Many, many other symbols could have been included but because of time and space considerations, they were left out. The symbols included here, however, should give you a good start in being able to identify many occultic logos that are appearing today.

2. YIN/YANG SYMBOL

The yin/yang symbol can be seen almost any place one looks. It is used in logos, on book covers, in the New Age movement, in the martial arts, and so forth. "Yin and yang are considered to be opposites. Yin represents eternity, dark, feminine, left side of the body, etc. Yang is its opposite and represents history, light, masculine, right side of the body, etc."[1] "Yang is male, positive, and represented by the Sun. Yin is female, negative, and represented by the Moon,"[2] says Paul E. Desautels in *The Gem Kingdom.*

"The symbol itself dates back at least to the fourth century B.C., and has been identified with the Eastern philosophical religions of Confucianism, Buddhism, and Taoism. In the Western world it has long been adopted into the symbolism of myth, magic, astrology, and witchcraft."[3]

A book, *Black Magic, White Magic,* explains the Yin-Yang like this:

"Another ancient magical sign called the yin-and-yang first appeared sometime before the 3rd century B.C. in China. This emblem became a favorite of **SORCERERS** and mystics throughout the Orient because it, too, embodies so many possible meanings."[4]

One well-known witch, Sybil Leek, who is called the "mistress of the occult," proclaims that the Yin-Yang theory is:

"...an idea that inspired such things as Chinese boxing, breath control [used in yoga, meditation, etc.], the use of special herbs, and some rather erotic sexual exercises designed to nourish the Yang with the Yin."[5]

She adds: "Crucial to Taoism is the idea of Yin and Yang."[6]

"According to the ancient Chinese philosophers, in the beginning was Tao. But then Tao separated into the two prime principles, yang and yin. And from the many combinations of yang and yin everything else that is in the world has emerged.

"Yang and yin produced the 'five elements', which are metal, wood, fire, water and earth. Everything in life is in a constant state of flux; in fact, the only thing that you can be sure of is that it will change."[7]

Another book states:

"The Yang-Yin symbol is one of the easiest to recognize and understand. It represents the two opposite, conflicting forces found in every action, and which are responsible for the dynamic universe....The Yang and Yin operate in the universe primarily through the agency of the five elements: Earth (Saturn), Water (Mercury), Metal (Venus), Wood (Jupiter), and Fire (Mars). These elements under the guidance of the five planets form, with the Sun and Moon, the seven rulers. Each of the elements may also be Yang or Yin, so that combinations of all these could produce broad number possibilities (sic) and astrological alternatives. Each, of course, has its symbol which can be, and often was, incised into jade."[8]

The concept of yin and yang (also called Tai-gi-tu), likewise plays an important role in many other occult practices. For instance, the *Dictionary of Mysticism* states the following about the practice of shu shu:

"**Shu shu:** The ancient Chinese system of magic, divination and occult practices, including astrology, dream interpretation, the art of coordinating human affairs by the active and passive principles of the universe *(yin yang)* and the Five Elements *(wu hsing),* fortune telling by the use of the stalks of the divination plant and the tortoise shell, and miscellaneous methods such as dream interpretation, the regulation of forms and shapes of buildings, etc."[9] [Emphasis in the original]

Of course, many of the Chinese exercises, medical practices, etc., are also based on the theory of yin and yang. In *Health: A Holistic Approach* we find:

"The techniques of *acupuncture, acupressure,* and *moxibustion* apply needle, pressure, or thermal (heat) stimulation respectively to meridian points to effect a change in the orderly flow of Chi through the meridians. This treatment helps to re-establish the yin-yang balance by initiating normal energy flow in stagnant meridians. The choice of meridian points to be stimulated is arrived at by using specific laws derived directly from the five-element theory and knowing the order of Chi distribution in the meridians. The five-element theory is the practical, tangible application of the complementary opposites—yin and yang.

"The Chinese system of *physiotherapy*, or therapeutic exercises, is represented primarily in the practice of *T'ai Chi Ch'uan*, which is a system of exercises performed in close coordination with regulated breathing. The exercises are comprised of thirty-seven movement patterns, the composition of which is regulated by the principles of yin and yang."[10] [Emphasis in the original]

"The philosophy of T'ai Chi Ch'uan is rooted in Taoism, which advocates natural effort, and in the I Ching, or Book of Changes. The movements and inner teachings are derived from the complementary relationship between Yin and Yang, two fundamental forces that create and harmonize the Universe by their interaction.

"The interaction of Yin and Yang is vital to the practice of T'ai Chi Ch'uan since physically and mentally the practitioner is continually shifting between empty and full and soft and hard to achieve a proper and evolving equilibrium."[11]

In fact, t'ai chi came to be "represented by the circle divided into the light and the dark, yang and yin."[12]

Other interrelated techniques dependent upon yin/yang are zone therapy, polarity therapy, macrobiotics, Shiatsu, Jin-Shin, Do-In, the martial arts (such as Kung Fu, Chi Kung, Karate, T'ai Chi), etc.

Palmistry, the **occult** practice of foretelling the future by reading the hand, is also based on the theories of **yin** and **yang** and the **Five Elements.** In another **OCCULT** book, *The Chinese Art of Healing*, written by a **BUDDHIST monk,** the author explains how the ancients relate **massage,** which **includes REFLEXOLOGY,** to the **Five Elements** and to **palmistry.** He states:

> "The thumb, for example, was associated with the spleen, which belonged to the **earth element,** the index finger with the large intestine (**metal element**)...and so on....The form of **massage** known as 'from the water element to the earth element,' reminds us of **OCCULT** concepts of this kind.

> "According to Oriental **MAGICIANS,** the palm of the hand contains the secrets of life. There was also an ancient Chinese school of thought which maintained that the palm of the hand was a replica of **Yin** and **Yang** and could provide information about illness and good health and one's entire fate."

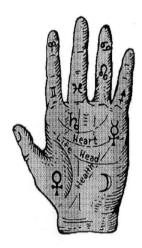

(For more information on Reflexology, see my booklet entitled "Hidden Dangers of Reflexology." It can be obtained through Sharing by writing to the address in the back of this book.)

Masonry also uses the concept of yin and yang in their symbolism but it is in a disguised form. Albert Pike states that the black and white pavement symbolizes "the Good and Evil Principles of the Egyptian and Persian creed. It is the warfare of Michael and Satan, of the Gods and Titans, of Balder and Lok; between light and shadow, which is darkness; Day and Night; Freedom and Despotism...."[13]

Masons also use the two triangles to represent this idea of opposites. In the *Short Talk Bulletin,* a pamphlet which is to be read in the Lodges, we are told that the triangles "are symbolic of good and evil, day and night, the Chinese **YANG AND YIN,** etc."[14]

The two triangles joined together to form a hexagram indicate sexual union. This same viewpoint is also associated with the yin/yang. In *Our Phallic Heritage* we are told:

"But since union of the sexes is necessary to produce offspring, both sexes were represented in most religions. In the crudest forms of worship, representations of the genitalia of both sexes, or of the sex organs in union, were worshiped. Such was the worship of the phallus-kteis in Greece and Egypt, the lingam-yoni in India, the massebasher of Syria, the yoseki-inseki in Japan, the **YANG-YIN** in China, and the baal-peor of the Canaanites in the Bible."[15]

Masonic author, George Oliver, states:

"Thus the monad and duad were the phallus and kteis of the Greeks, the lingam and yoni of the Hindoos (sic), the woden and friga of the Goths, and **YANG AND YIN** of the Chinese, and indeed, of the creative and destructive powers of every country under Heaven."[16]

This thought is reiterated in *Myths and Symbols in Indian Art and Civilization:*

"Lingam and yoni, Shiva and his goddess, symbolize the antagonistic yet co-operating forces of the sexes. Their Sacred Marriage (Greek: *hieros-gamos*) is multifariously figured in the various traditions of world mythology. They are the archetypal parents, Father and Mother of the World, themselves the first-born of the pairs of opposites, first bifurcation of the primal, cosmogonic reality, now reunited in productive harmony. Under the form of Father Heaven and Mother Earth they were known to the Greeks as Zeus and Hera, Uranos and Gaia, to the Chinese as T'ien and Ti, **YANG AND YIN.**"[17] [Italics in the original; Boldface and caps added]

One catalog that sells statues of gods and goddesses as well as many other occultic items states:

"At once the most sacred and the most mysterious path to higher consciousness, Tantra refers to the Divine Union of Opposites. Taoists refer to these energies as *yin* (from *yoni*, the active principle) and *yang* (the recumbent principle)."[18]

Since there is some yin (female) in the yang (male), which is represented by the little dot, and some yang in the yin, the concept of bisexuality is also symbolized. Charles Berger remarks:

"Sometimes efforts were made to make gods bisexual. Hermaphrodite is the best example of this. He was the son of Hermes and Aphrodite and embraced Salmaco, a nymph, who called upon the gods to make them inseparable. The gods heard the plea, and formed of the two a perfect being who possessed the characteristics of both sexes. From this mythical being comes the term *hermaphrodite*. Omphale was a queen of Lydia and the task-mistress of Hercules. She is represented with a lion's skin and a club, male symbols, while Hercules wears her gown and spins for her. Omphale is thus represented as double-sexed, as is Hercules by his dress and his work. The name Omphale is a bisexual name, coming from 'Om,' the Universal Mother, and from *phallus,* the male organ. Likewise, Janus of the Greeks not only had opposite faces but was double-sexed, or hermaphroditic."[19] [Emphasis in the original]

The New Age movement looks favorably on homosexuality. In fact, in alchemy, the androgyne (meaning male and female in one body) was considered to be "the image of human perfection and wholeness. By some ancient traditions, the original and perfect form of the human being....A fashionable look among some celebrities."[20] "Bly, Nin, and Jung tell us that each individual must achieve inner marriage of their masculine and feminine natures to encounter true equipoise."[21]

The assumption of yin/yang also leads to homosexuality. In one issue of the *Whole Life Times* was a letter from David Lang. He wrote:

"For example, macrobiotic theory explains homosex-uality as a yin-yang imbalance caused (or at least aggravated) by excess consumption of yin foods (such as raw fruit) on the part of males and excessive ingestion of yang foods (such as animal flesh) on the part of females."[22]

Texe Marrs explains:

"Homosexuality and bi-sexuality are accepted, even encouraged by the New Age teacher. The unholy doctrine of reincarnation and the principle of *yin/yang* are perfect excuses and rationale for homosexuality and other forms of sexual immorality. If you are a homosexual or a lesbian in this lifetime, New Age teachers believe that it is probably because you were a person of the opposite sex in a previous incarnation or past life. The residue and influence of that past life is simply retained within your brain and consciousness.

"The *yin/yang* principle, also called *unity, integration* or *polarity,* holds that a person is born with both masculine and feminine traits. A man supposedly could have been a man 250 times and a woman 250 times in previous incarnations, and the memory of those past life experiences are said to remain as indelible traces of consciousness. Thus, we are each a combination of male and female, masculine and feminine. The New Age encourages children and adults to appreciate and practice the harmony of opposites, teaching the individual to merge the two selves, man and woman."[23]

Many of the gods and goddesses of paganism are shown to have dual sexual natures. Mercury, called the "male-female," was an androgyne.[24] Even much symbolism contains this dual nature. For instance:

"The serpent's head and neck is distinctly a masculine symbol, but the serpent is sometime symbolized with its tail in it mouth [oroboros], the body forming a circle which is feminine. Also, the mouth is feminine, while the tail, which is in the mouth, is masculine. Thus for two good reasons the serpent with its tail in its mouth represents both sexes. Sacred fire was often prepared on religious occasions by rotating a realistic wooden representation of the phallus in a wooden representation of the kteis, rotating being done by an apparatus resembling a bow. The cornucopia, or horn of plenty, was double sexed in symbolism. The horn was masculine and the inside was feminine. The fruit inside symbolized productiveness of the female."[25]

"The four-limbed cross generally had a different meaning, and represented the male and the female in unison, in the act of creation. From time immemorial a perpendicular line or object has been used to symbolize the phallus, and a horizontal line the kteis or vulva. The surface of water, a female element in creation, was horizontal, and women were practically in the horizontal position in the act of creation. Prostitutes were spoken of as 'women who made their living horizontally,' and the term was applied to women who were kept in their own room by some wealthy man. Coitus has been called 'horizontal exercise.' *Horizontales* (horizontals) is one of the names which the French apply to women who sell love favors, women of easy virtue. The four-armed cross was an easy figure to make, being an intersection of two straight lines at right angels, and it became a symbol of man's most lofty and most holy activity, expressing the reverence for the act. Some of the Asherahs of the Bible represented Baal in union with Astoreth. The results of the union between the sexes resulted in a new life. Separately, man and woman were incomplete, important, and barren, but in their union they became a perfect soul, realizing the immortality of life."[26]

We'll cover the symbols mentioned above (the oroboros, cornucopia, and swastika) in more detail later.

One particular group that knows the sexual implications of the yin/yang and intentionally uses it as their official symbol is The Sex Information and Education Council of the United States (SIECUS).[27] This group promotes extensive sex education in schools. SIECUS Position Statements reveal the following:

"It is the position of SIECUS that contraceptive services should be available to all—including minors who should enjoy the same rights of free and independent access to...contraceptive care as do others....It is the position of SIECUS that the use of explicit sexual materials (sometimes referred to as pornography) can serve a variety of important needs in the lives of countless individuals...."[28]

Another group using the yin/yang (knowingly or unknowing) is the Girl Scouts. "On page 66 of the *Girl Scout Badges and Signs* book, the yin/yang symbol is used to represent the World in My Community proficiency badge. In the *Junior Girl Scout Handbook*, yoga exercises are explained. The theme for their 1987 program was 'The Year of Magic.'"[29]

The I Ching (Book of Changes) is another occult practice that incorporates the use of the yin/yang. Geoffrey Parrinder writes: "The *yin-yang* dualism entered into Confucian orthodoxy by its incorporation into the *I Ching*—a late compilation from, and rational arrangement of, earlier works on **DIVINATION.**"[30]

William Spear teaches astrology and macrobiotics and has been using the I Ching for 20 years.[31] He states:

"Taoism, inseparable from the philosophy of the I Ching, is based on the complimentary yet antagonistic principles of Yin and Yang which mutually create and destroy each other by the ceaseless rearrangements of their relationship. The basic rule they obey is life's only certainty: change."[32]

One ad for a book by Diane Stein on the I Ching (also called Kwan Yin) tells us: "*The Kwan Yin Book of Changes* is a wonderful book, finding admirerers (sic) with not only **NEW AGERS, AND FEMINISTS, BUT OTHERS SUCH AS PAGANS, DIVINA-TION FANS, GODDESS WORSHIPPERS,** and those involved with Eastern philosophy."[33]

Of course Diane Stein isn't the only pagan who uses the I Ching. A witchcraft magazine, *Circle Network News,* gives an extensive ritual to be used in connection with the I Ching. Part of the instructions are:

> "An altar should be set up in the middle of a room facing north....Lay the stalks in the middle of the altar along with the I Ching book that you are going to use and your I Ching journal. Include on the altar other ritual tools and symbols that you feel you need. Be sure to include burning incense.

> "Ritually purify yourself and the space with techniques of your choosing. Ground and center. Call the quarters and Spirit in a fashion that feels appropriate....

> "Once you have determined the hexagram, draw it in your journal. Look it up within the text of your I Ching book....

> "When you feel complete with your answer and have recorded all relevant information in your journal, pay respects to the I Ching in whatever way you feel comfortable....**Thank the spirit helpers [demons!] and the quarters for helping with your work."**[34]

New Ager, Jeffrey S. Stamps, likes to use the yin/yang in a slightly different form. He calls his symbol the "Emergent Tao." He explains:

> "The ridgepole symbolizes the line of the roof, thus separating heaven from earth. As a line, the ridgepole is

unity, yet it generates duality—'above and below, a right and left, front and back—in a word, the world of opposites.'...

"As a symbol of change, tao, too, may change. To compress my thought of many pages to a single symbol, I offer *Emergent Tao*....This symbol extends the traditional t'ai chi symbol of the circle with a ridgepole dividing the complements of yin and yang. I have added the spiral curves between the outer circle and the two inner circles. With these lines, the symbol clearly expresses emergence and levels: the circle of the whole (n) and the 'higher' (n+1) and 'lower' (n-1) smaller circles/levels. Emergent tao expresses the essence of Holonomy: complements, levels, and unitary process."[35]

Emergent Tao

The yin/yang symbol is quite appropriate today for humanists, New Agers, witches, Satanists, etc. As Michael Tierra, a proponent of the yin/yang theory, states: "The Yin/Yang theory is a teaching method and does not define anything absolute."[36] There are seven laws concerning the yin/yang, one of which is: "2. Everything changes."[37]

This is an important item to notice. The idea that "everything changes" does not agree with the Bible. There we find that Jesus Christ is the same yesterday, today, and forever (Hebrews 13:8). He doesn't change. James 1:17 also states: "Every good gift and every perfect gift is from above, and cometh down from the Father of lights, with whom is **NO VARIABLENESS,** neither shadow of turning." Malachi 3:6 tells us: "I am the Lord, I **CHANGE NOT."**

Another law is: "3. All antagonisms are complementary."[38] Again, this is contradictory to Scriptures. This would make Jesus and Satan complementary to each other! What blasphemy!

Yet another law is: "6. The extreme of any condition will produce signs of the opposite."[39] Again applying this to Christ would mean that because He is the extreme in goodness, mercy, compassion, etc., that He will produce signs of hate, injustice, unconcern, etc. This also would make Satan eventually become kind, loving, obedient, and so forth. The Bible warns: "Woe unto them that call evil good, and good evil: that put darkness for light, and light for darkness; that put bitter for sweet, and sweet for bitter! Woe unto them that are wise in their own eyes, and prudent in their own sight!...Which justify the wicked for reward, and take away the righteousness of the righteous from him!" (Isaiah 5:20-21, 23).

In addition to the seven laws of yin/yang, there are twelve theorems. One of these is: "8. Nothing is solely Yin or Yang; everything involves polarity."[40] This is stating that nothing is entirely good or entirely evil. This again contradicts the Scripture for in Habbakkuk 1:13 we find that God is "of purer eyes than to behold evil and canst not look on iniquity." The Bible also tells us that there is no truth in Satan (John 8:44). Obviously, the yin/yang theory is not consistent with God's Word.

We'll cover the sinister aspects of the hexagram later, but it's interesting to note that *An Illustrated Encyclopedia of Traditional Symbols* tells us that the hexagram is affiliated with the "Chinese **OCCULT** symbol of ying (sic) and yang."[41] The connotations, therefore, of the hexagram also apply to the yin/yang symbol.

There are probably hundreds upon hundreds of groups that have used the yin/yang in their logo or symbolism. Some groups probably do so innocently, but I believe the majority of them know exactly what they are doing and what the symbolism means. On the following pages are just some of the ways in which the yin/yang is being used.

For more information on Exploris (pictured above), see the excellent article by Mrs. Peggy Cuddy in the June 1998 issue of <u>Christian Conscience</u>.

3. THE CIRCLE

The circle is the symbol of the universe.[1] Eastern Star writer, Sarah Terry, mentions that the circle "is derived from the **SUN**."[2] Masonic author, J. S. M. Ward, explains that the circle also symbolizes God.[3] A *Treasury of Witchcraft* states that "the circle that the magician draws on the ground...[is] to enforce demons to appear."[4] Shortly we'll discover who the god of Masonry is, so it will be evident which god the circle represents.

One particular symbol that is prevalent in Masonry utilizes the circle but a point is added inside the circle. It is called the "point within the circle." Harold Percival in his Masonic book tells us: "The point and the circle are the same, the point is the infinitesimally small circle and the circle is the point fully expressed."[5] Since the point and the circle are the same, let's look at what Masons tell us about this specific symbol.

In the *Masonic Quiz Book* we find that this symbol "is from the Egyptian and is a symbolic sign for the **SUN** and the god **OSIRIS**."[6] Albert Mackey, a 33° Mason, reveals that:

> "The point within the circle is an interesting and important symbol in Freemasonry....The **SYMBOL IS REALLY A BEAUTIFUL BUT SOMEWHAT AB-STRUSE ALLUSION TO THE OLD SUN-WORSHIP,** and introduces us for the first time to that modification of it, known among the ancients as the **WORSHIP OF THE PHALLUS**."[7]

While some Masons are now trying to distance themselves from Mackey, he is nevertheless a **HIGHLY RESPECTED**

MASON and is still looked up to today by many "higher" level Masons. In one *Short Talk Bulletin* about Mackey, lodge members were told: "Never did he read into a Masonic symbol a meaning which is not actually there,"[8] so we have every reason, then, to accept his interpretation that the point within a circle actually represents the phallus.

Albert Churchward, a Mason, says that: "The **POINT WITHIN A CIRCLE IS ONE OF THE HIEROGLYPHIC SIGNS OF THE SUN-GOD, RA....**"[9]

The point within the circle represents other gods in other mythologies. In India the dot or the point within the circle represents **SHIVA**[10] and in Egyptian mythology it represents **HORUS**[11] or **OSIRIS.**[12] The Druids used the point within a circle as the emblem of their Supreme God who was **ODIN.**[13] Masons, by the way, admire the Druids and some of them even claim that Masonry came from Druidism. Of course, the Druids were occultic priests, practiced astrology, and offered human sacrifices.

So, like all the other symbols which we have looked at, we find that the circle and the point within the circle refer to a pagan god. Also, like the previous symbols, the point within the circle has a sexual connotation.

In one *Short Talk Bulletin* entitled "Point Within a Circle," which was to be read in Lodge meetings, we are told that this symbol is connected with **SUN WORSHIP.** This pamphlet states:

> "'It was believed in India that at the general deluge everything was involved in the common destruction except the male and female principles or **ORGANS OF GENERATION,** which were destined to produce a new

race and to repeople the earth when the waters had subsided from its surface. The female principle, symbolized by the moon, assumed the form of a lunette, or crescent, while the male principle, symbolized by the sun, assumed the form of the lingam (or Phallus) and placed himself erect in the center of the lunette, like the mast of a ship. The two principles in this united form floated on the surface of the waters during the period of their prevalence on the earth, and thus became the progenitors of a new race of men.'...

"The Indian interpretation makes the **POINT THE MALE PRINCIPLE, THE CIRCLE THE FEMALE;** the point became the sun and the circle the solar system which ancient peoples thought was the universe because the sun is the vivifying, the life-giving principle, for all that lives."[14]

Albert Pike writes that Isis and Osiris:

"the Active and Passive Principles of the Universe, were commonly symbolized by the generative parts of man and woman....The Indian lingam was the union of both, as were the boat and mast and the point within a circle: all of which expressed the same philosophical idea as to the Union of the two great Causes of Nature, which concur, one actively and the other passively, in the generation of all beings...."[15]

The point within a circle has been employed in some rather unique ways. For instance, one Masonic book states: "The sign of the infamous Mafia or Cosa Nostra is not the 'black hand,' as many believe, but the familiar dot within a circle."[16] We are further informed that:

"Because the true purposes of Illuminism were so shocking, Weishaupt constantly encouraged the **SECRETIVE** nature of the order. No member was ever allowed himself to be identified as an Illuminati. The words Illuminism or Illuminati were never to be used in correspondence, but were to be replaced by the astrological symbol for the sun, a circle with a dot in the middle."[17]

Weishaupt, you'll probably recall, was a Mason and the founder of the Illuminati.

Another thing we need to look at is a circle surrounding the inverted five-pointed star. In *The Question of Freemasonry* we learn: "The inverted five-pointed star **within a circle** is the **highest form of satanic expression, representing Baphomet,** the God of Mendes, or the embodiment of Lucifer as god."[18] In fact, the **PENTAGRAM ENCLOSED WITHIN THE CIRCLE IS A SIGN FOR THE GOD AND GODDESS.**[19]

Actually, any occult symbol is considered to be even more powerful whenever a circle is used around another occultic symbol.[20]

4. THE TRIANGLE

The triangle is a very important symbol to the Masons and Eastern Star members. When a new Eastern Star Chapter is established, the Officers-elect are to form an equilateral triangle around the Altar.[1] The Altar itself "is shaped in the form of a triangle. Traditionally, one angle is directed so that it points toward the East."[2] The pentagram itself is made up of triangles.[3] Of course, like the pentagram, the triangle can be used in two different positions and each position has a special significance. A triangle, with one point down, represents the deity and is called the "Deity's Triangle" or the "Water Triangle."[4] With one point up it is called the "Earthly Triangle," "Pyramid Triangle," or the "Fire Triangle,"[5] and this emblem symbolizes "the PERFECT or DIVINE MAN."[6] [Emphasis in the original]

Manly P. Hall, a 33° Mason, boasts: **"MAN IS A GOD IN THE MAKING...."**[7] George H. Steinmetz, another Masonic writer, brags:

> "'Be still—and know—that I am God.'"...'THAT *I* AM GOD'—the final recognition of the All in All, the unity of the Self with the Cosmos—the cognition of the DIVINITY OF THE SELF!"[8] [Emphasis in the original]

Joseph Fort Newton, a well-known Mason, claims that the Third Degree of Masonry testifies "to the profoundest insight of the human soul—that God becomes man that man may become God."[9]

This theme of godhood or the divinity of man can be found in book after book written by Masons, New Agers, witches, and

Satanists.[10] Masonic author, J. D. Buck, states: "It is far more important that **MEN SHOULD STRIVE TO BECOME CHRISTS** than that they should believe that Jesus was Christ".[11]

Arthur Edward Waite writes that "the Master-Builder of the THIRD DEGREE does actually rise as Christ...."[12] [Emphasis in the original]

In a book written by a 32° Mason, Charles H. Vail, entitled *The Ancient Mysteries and Modern Masonry,* we find:

"The consummation of all this was to **MAKE THE INITIATE A GOD,** either by union with a Divine Being without or by the realization of the Divine Self within....

"**MAN IS LIKE GOD IN THAT HE BECOMES A GOD.**"[13]

This theme of godhood or the divinity of man has to also be the object of the Eastern Star since no one can become an Eastern Star member without having a close relative who has received the third degree of Masonry. It is that degree which is claimed to make a Mason a **"DIVINIZED MAN."**[14]

There is more symbolism involved in the triangle, though. The triangle with one point up just happens to be the symbol for Set and Shiva. In *Signs and Symbols of Primordial Man,* written by Albert Churchward, a Mason, we find that this **TRIANGLE** with the one point facing upward, was the **SYMBOL FOR SET** (or Sut)![15] In India, the triangle is "the caste mark of the followers of **SHIVA**...who wear it on their forehead."[16] Another Masonic writer, J. S. M. Ward, adds:

"With the point upwards the **EQUILATERAL TRIANGLE STANDS FOR SHIVA THE DESTROYER,**

and signifies the flame which rises upwards from the funeral pyre toward Heaven. This symbol is familiar to us [the Masons] in several degrees, notably the Thirtieth degree."[17]

There's no contradiction here, for Set is the Egyptian devil and Shiva is the Indian god of destruction. Both names, **SET AND SHIVA,** are also listed in *The Satanic Bible* as another name for **SATAN!**[18] Furthermore, Helena Petrovna Blavatsky affirms: "Now, we have but to remember that Siva [Shiva] and the Palestinian Baal, or Moloch, and Saturn are identical...."[19] So, then, when the Masons and Eastern Stars tell us that the triangle represents the deity, we now know **WHICH** deity is being worshiped by the symbolism of the triangle.

Another clue as to which deity is being worshiped may be found in Alice Bailey's book, *Discipleship in the New Age.* She claims: "It might be said symbolically that 'the point of the triangle is based in the courts of Heaven (Shamballa) and from that point two streams of power pour forth....'"[20] Shamballa is the mythological place where the "Lord of the World," Sanat Kumara or Shiva (who is actually Satan), is supposed to live![21] Bailey is looking forward to the time when "there can be the inauguration of a new phase of activity in Shamballa. This will enable the Lord of the Word to become the ruler of a Sacred Planet, which, up to date, has not been the case."[22]

Interestingly, Bailey reminds us that Masonry emanates from Shamballa.[23] Lynn Perkins, a Masonic author, also agrees. He mentions that Shamballa "has a bearing on the ancient origins of Freemasonry and upon its future in the coming Aquarian Age...."[24] He adds:

"Shambhala,—the legendary and mystical home of the Great Masters of the Wisdom...out of which Ancient and Modern **FREEMASONRY** sprang...is the site of 'the Great White Lodge' of Initiate Masters, which, as a Brotherhood of Mystics and **OCCULTISTS,** is a prototype, an original model, of which every Masonic Lodge is a more or less perfect physical and spiritual replica....That **MASONS OF TODAY ARE NOT AWARE OF THE EXISTENCE AND SIGNIFICANCE OF THE ESOTERIC**

TRADITION, that encompasses the whole purpose and Destiny of every living Soul, is no proof that it does not exist."[25]

Yet another meaning for the triangle has to do with a sexual reference. Without going into detail, I'll just mention that it represents the male and female generative organs. When the two triangles are joined together to form a hexagram (discussed elsewhere in this book), it depicts sexual union between the male and female.

Masonic author, R. H. MacKenzie, states:

"TRIANGLE.—An important symbol in Masonry. 1. The equilateral triangle was adopted by all ancient nations as a symbol of Deity, and was regarded as the most perfect of figures. It constantly recurred in Craft Masonry as well as in the Royal Arch. 2. The right-angled triangle was also regarded as an important figure. Among the Egyptians the base represented **OSIRIS, OR THE MALE PRINCIPLE;** the perpendicular, **ISIS, OR THE FEMALE PRINCIPLE;** and the hypotenuse, **HORUS,** their son, **THE PRODUCT.**"[26]

John Yarker, a Mason, writes:

"The basis of the Masonic Jewel of a Master in the Chair is an old Egyptian symbol, for Plutarch informs us that a triangle whose base is 4, perpendicular 3, and hypotenuse of 5 parts, the square of which is equal to the square of those sides, containing the right angle, was an important emblem in Egypt, as a symbol of nature. The base figured **Osiris,** the perpendicular **Isis,** and the hypotenuse **Horus;** the originating and receptive principles, and the offspring of the two."[27]

Another Masonic writer, reveals:

"The triangle is found variously arranged throughout the Masonic system. In one instance we have the interlaced triangles, one black, the other white, the white triangle has its point up; the black triangle points down. Thus arranged it represents the union of the active and passive forces in nature; it represents the male and female elements. The interlaced black and white triangles represent the forces of darkness and light [yin/yang], error and truth, ignorance and wisdom and good and evil; when properly placed they represent balance and harmony."[28]

In *The Gods of India,* we find:

"The triangle with its apex upward is also taken to represent fire, identified with the male principle, the *linga* or phallus, symbol of Siva the Progenitor or of the Cosmic-Person (*purusa*)....Its numerical symbol is the number 3.

"The triangle pointing downward represents the force of inertia which pulls downward, and tends to suppress activity. It is associated with the element water, which always tends to come down, to equalize its level. It is the passive aspect of creation and thus is represented by the *yoni* or female organ, the emblem of Energy (Sakti) or Cosmic-Nature (*prakrti*). Other symbols associated with the element water are the arc of a circle, the crescent, and the wave. The corresponding number symbol is the number 2."[29]

R. Swinburne Clymer, in *The Mysteries of Osiris or Ancient Egyptian Initiation,* writes: "The Phallus or Lingam, and the Yoni, the male and female emblems of generation are found in the triangle and the tau...."[30]

The lesbians and gays like to make use of the triangle symbolism. One catalog catering to lesbians states:

"The Triangle is a symbol of Gay and Lesbian identity, community and pride. It says that we are Out, standing up, unifying across the breathtaking diversity of our kind, and that we are committed to our freedom and our lives. The triangle is also an ancient glyph for vulva, for the Feminine....The triangle was reclaimed by the Gay Liberation movement in the '70s as a symbol both of resistance to oppression ('Silence = Death') and of Lesbian and Gay pride."[31]

Below is a picture of a triangular card that "was designed especially for lesbians!"[32]

The Bible tells us in I Corinthians 6:9-10 that homosexuals shall not inherit heaven:

"Know ye not that the unrighteous shall not inherit the kingdom of God? Be not deceived: neither fornicators, nor idolaters, nor adulterers, nor effeminate, nor abusers of themselves with mankind, Nor thieves, nor covetous, nor drunkards, nor revilers, nor extortioners, shall inherit the kingdom of God."

Closely related to the triangle is the pyramid. One author writes:

"The *pyramid* has a close relationship in symbolic significance to the triangle. Indeed, the pyramid is shaped in triangular form. A number of New Age communities and groups, such as the Institute of Healing Sciences in New York, have erected pyramid-shaped structures. Some New Age churches display small pyramid replicas on their altars.

"New Agers believe in pyramid-power. Some wear miniature pyramids on chains to bring positive energy forces into their bodies; others make cardboard pyramids and place them into close proximity with foodstuffs, believing in the curative and preservative powers of pyramids."[33] [Emphasis in the original]

We can see that the triangle represents pagan gods and has a sexual connotation. When the upward triangle and the downward triangle are joined, it forms the hexagram or the six-pointed star. We will cover this symbol in the next chapter.

5. THE HEXAGRAM

The Hexagram is formed by uniting the Water Triangle with the Fire Triangle, which is called the Six-pointed Star, Star of David, Solomon's Seal, etc.

When the two triangles (the "Water Triangle" and the "Fire Triangle") are joined together into one symbol, it forms a six pointed star known as a double triangle, hexagram, Crest of Solomon, star of the microcosm and the Shield of David, among other names. It is even called the "talisman of Saturn."[1] Mary Ann Slipper remarks: "This six pointed star is used in masonic work and is also found in other well known secret orders."[2]

The Second Mile, an Eastern Star book, reveals that the "six pointed star is a very ancient symbol, and one of the most powerful."[3] It sure is a powerful symbol—to witches, sorcerers, and magicians![4] "The hexagram is used in magic, witchcraft, occultism and the casting of zodiacal horoscopes internationally and by all races."[5] "It was considered to possess mysterious powers,"[6] says *A Concise Cyclopaedia of Freemasonry.*

It is used as a "stand-by for **MAGICIANS AND ALCHEMISTS. The SORCERERS** believed it represented the footprint of a special kind of **DEMON** called a trud and used it in ceremonies both to **CALL UP DEMONS** and to keep them away."[7]

Former Satanist, Bill Schnoebelen, reminds us: "To the sorcerer, the hexagram is a powerful tool to invoke Satan...."[8] **A HEXAGRAM MUST BE PRESENT TO CALL A DEMON FORTH.** In fact, the word "HEX" comes from this emblem.[9]

Another meaning associated with the hexagram has to do with sexual union and reproduction. The triangle pointing downward "is a female symbol corresponding to the yoni"[10] and the "upward-pointing triangle is the male, the lingam...."[11] When the two triangles are interlaced, "it represents the union of the active and passive forces in nature; it represents the male and female elements."[12]

In *The Gods of India,* we find:

"The two complementary principles, the *linga* and the *yoni,* are graphically represented by the fiery triangle with upward apex and the watery triangle with downward apex. When the triangles penetrate one another to form the hexagon, this is taken to show the state of manifestation. When they part, the universe dissolves."[13]

The linga (or lingam) and the yoni are the male and female sexual parts.

A former witch reveals: "When the male triangle penetrates the female triangle it produces the six pointed crest of Solomon or hexagram, the most wicked symbol in witchcraft."[14]

The hexagram was also used for communication with the dead as E. A. Wallis Budge states: "Those who believed in the physical significance of the Hexagram taught that communication between the living and the dead was possible, and adopted the dogma of **REINCARNATION.**"[15]

A book entitled *Witchcraft, Magic and Alchemy,* links the hexagram to spiritualism.[16]

The Hexagram was also the sign used in the Royal Arch (in Masonry) and "with the Hindoos (sic) of Trimurti the Trinity in Unity, or Brahma, Vishnu and Shiva in one."[17] J. S. M. Ward adds:

Trimurti

"The [hexagram] with or without the circle, is strictly the sign of Trimurti, the Three in One, typifying the creative, preservative and destructive natures of the Deity. When Trimurti is depicted, which is seldom, it is as a three-headed man; one head is bearded, as with European mediaeval pictures of God the Father, while the heads which represent Vishnu and Shiva are devoid of a beard."[18]

Interestingly, this hexagram:

"...certainly has three sixes. It contains a six, within a six, within a six: 666. (Count the sides of each triangle facing the clockwise direction, the sides facing the counterclockwise direction, and the third six—the sides of the inner hexagon.)"[19]

There is still another meaning of the hexagram. One Masonic author states:

"In one instance we have the interlaced triangles, one black, the other white, the white triangle has its point up; the black triangle points down....The interlaced black and white triangles represent the forces of darkness and light, error and truth, ignorance and wisdom and good and evil; when properly placed they represent balance and harmony."[20]

Another Masonic pamphlet affirms that these triangles that make up the hexagram "are symbolic of good and evil, day and night, the Chinese **YANG AND YIN,** etc."[21] We've already covered the yin/yang symbol, so we can see that the hexagram is not a good symbol and does not have a favorable connotation. It is used to call up demons, communicate with the dead, describe sexual acts, and represent false and pagan gods (such as Brahma, Vishnu, and Siva).

The Bible tells us in Philippians 4:8:

"Finally, brethren, whatsoever things are true, whatsoever things are honest, whatsoever things are just, whatsoever things are pure, whatsoever things are lovely, whatsoever things are of good report; if there be any virtue, and if there be any praise, **THINK** on these things."

Isn't there a big difference between what the Scriptures tell us to dwell on and what the occult promotes?

6. THE PENTAGRAM

Satanists and witches love the pentagram, and we are told that the pentagram is one of the main symbols of witchcraft and occultism. It has always been used in ritual magic and is used for divination, the conjuration of spirits and to summon demoniac help. In the *Dictionary of Mysticism,* we learn that the pentagram:

> "is considered by occultists to be the most potent means of conjuring spirits. When a single point of the star points upward, it is regarded as the sign of the good and a means to conjure benevolent spirits; when the **SINGLE POINT POINTS DOWN** and a pair of points are on top, it is a **SIGN OF THE EVIL (SATAN)** and is **USED TO CONJURE POWERS OF EVIL.**"[1]

Pentagram   *Inverted Pentagram*

"The **PENTAGRAM** is a very important symbol **USED IN CALLING DEMONS** and as an aid in the casting of spells. When

Book entitled <u>A Witch's Bible Compleat</u>

pointed skyward, the star symbolizes the power of witchcraft. Most Wiccans—(witches/warlocks) believe that their power comes from such elements as the earth, sky and wind."[2]

In fact, the Pentagram is called "The Great Rite" in witchcraft. Witches Janet and Stewart Farrar report:

> "The couple enacting the Great Rite are offering themselves, with reverence and joy, as expressions of the God and Goddess aspects of the Ultimate Source....They are making themselves to the best of their ability, channels for that divine polarity on all levels, from physical to spiritual. That is why it is called the Great Rite.... 'Ritual sexual intercourse,' says Doreen Valiente, 'is a very old idea indeed—probably as old as humanity itself.'...The Great Rite invocation specially declares that the body of the woman taking part is an altar, with her womb and generative organs as its sacred focus, and reveres it as such....The High Priestess then lays herself down towards the altar, and her arms and legs outstretched to form the **PENTAGRAM.**"[3]

Laurie Cabot, a **WITCH,** explains: "It really isn't that difficult to distinguish the Craft from Satanism. Witches wear the pentacle with the point up. **SATANISTS REVERSE IT WITH THE POINT DOWN....**"[4]

Witches' pentagram

It should be obvious by now that the occultists, New Agers, magicians, Satanists, and witches all claim the pentagram as one of **THEIR** symbols and hold it in high regard. "Symbols," we are told, "are representative of ownership."[5] In fact, Fred and Jill Buck from the Magi Craftsmen, announce: "The Pentagram is one of the most powerful symbols for the **NEW AGE**."[6] A witchcraft magazine was even entitled *Pentagram.*[7]

As is well-known, the pentagram (or five-pointed star) can be drawn in two ways—with one point facing up or with two points facing up (known as the inverted or Satanic pentagram).[8] "When pointing down, as on the front of the Satanic Bible, the star signifies the Church of Satan, symbolic of power from Hell."[9] Occultist and 33° Mason, Manly Hall, admits: "In symbolism, an **inverted figure always signifies a perverted power.** The average person does not even suspect the **occult** properties of emblematic **pentacles**."[10] As can be seen, this star is a crucial ingredient in the occult, Wicca (witchcraft), and Satanism and the fashion in which this star is placed is highly illuminating. Former witch, Mason, Mormon, and Satanist, Bill Schnoebelen, "emphasized that **TO THE MAGICIAN, THE INVERTED PENTAGRAM HAS ONE USE ONLY,** and that is to **CALL UP THE POWER OF SATAN** and bring the Kingdom of the Devil into manifestation on earth."[11]

An organization called the Continental Association of Satan's Hope (CASH) advertises that a **"POWERFUL SATANIC PENTAGRAM CAN NOW BE YOURS ABSOLUTELY FREE!"**[12] [Emphasis in the original] It goes on to explain:

> *"You will find the Satanic Pentagram invaluable and indispensable as you attempt to draw from the infernal power of our lord Satan! This extremely powerful amulet is the sign of the microcosm and is the summation of all the occult forces! In other words, there is no amulet or talisman more powerful or even close to as powerful as the Satanic Pentagram!"*[13] [Emphasis in the original]

Across the bottom of this ad are the words in large letters: "HAIL SATAN!"[14]

The pentagram also plays an important role in **MASONRY AND THE EASTERN STAR.** Granted, many Masons and Eastern Star women are unaware of the connotation of this star (especially in the manner in which it is drawn), but many in the higher echelons of Masonry **KNOW** all about the particular symbol.

Let's turn to a few Masonic writers to see what they tell us about the meaning of the pentagram and the position in which it is drawn. We'll start with a quotation from Manly Hall. He points out that:

"The **PENTAGRAM IS USED EXTENSIVELY IN BLACK MAGIC,** but when so used its form always differs in one of three ways: The star may be broken at one point by not permitting the converging lines to touch; it may be inverted by having one point down and two up; or it may be distorted by having the points of varying lengths. When used in **BLACK MAGIC,** the pentagram is called the 'sign of the cloven hoof,' or the **FOOTPRINT OF THE DEVIL.** The star with two points upward is also called the 'Goat of Mendes,' because the inverted star is the same shape as a goat's head. When the upright star turns and the upper point falls to the bottom, it signifies the fall of the Morning Star."[15]

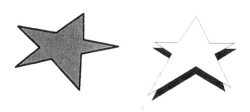

S. R. Parchment, in his book *Ancient Operative Masonry,* states that:

> "...the **PENTAGRAM** represents the liberated spirit. When the star is shown point upward, it is considered the symbol of the white magician who is able at will to leave the body [an out of the body experience] by way of the head; **WHEN DOWNWARD, BLACK MAGIC.**"[16]

One Masonic pamphlet to be read in the Lodges is the *Short Talk Bulletin,* (reprinted in 1982) entitled "Symbolism." It states: "The five-pointed star—point up—is a very ancient symbol of man, and was used by the old sages to designate the absolute sign of human intelligence. It refers to the spiritual element predominant in man, while the same figure with **TWO POINTS UP REFERS TO THE GOAT OF MENDES**—or that the beast is in the ascendant."[17]

Henry L. Stillson and William J. Hughan, in *History of Freemasonry and Concordant Orders,* describe the pentagram like this: "...when turned with one point down it represents EVIL, all that is opposed to the *good, pure,* and *virtuous;* in fine, it represents the GOAT OF MENDES."[18] [Emphasis in the original]

This star represents GOD, all that is *pure, virtuous,* and *good,* when represented with one point upward: but when turned with one point down it represents EVIL, all that is opposed to the *good, pure,* and *virtuous;* in fine, it represents the GOAT of MENDES.

The Seeker's Handbook states the following about the inverted pentagram:

> "Inverted, it presents the abstract figure of a goat's head and is generally taken to represent the exploitation and glorification of the animal drives and erotic forces, as encouraged in SATANISM."[19] [Emphasis in the original]

Obviously, the inverted pentagram is a sign for evil. It represented Satan and is used for invoking evil spirits.

The pentagram is known by several other names:

> "Celtic priests called it the **WITCH'S FOOT.** In the Middle Ages it became known in Britain and elsewhere in Europe as the goblin's cross, **DEVIL'S SIGN,** and the **WIZARD'S STAR.** Among the druids of Great Britain, it was the blasphemous sign of the Godhead."[20]

> "It is also Solomon's seal....In ancient times it was a magic charm amongst the people of Babylon."[21]

> "It was one of the most important symbols of the Pythagoreans, for whom its mathematical properties were most significant as the pentalpha, but who also fashioned it into trinkets to be used as talismen to ward off evil spirits, ill health, or misfortune. This symbolism persisted throughout the centuries of European history; in Germany, for example, it became the *Druttenfuss,* a **HEX SIGN** to prevent witches and goblins from entering barns and cottages."[22]

The pentagram is also sometimes called a pentacle or pantacle. Webster's Dictionary says that the pentacle (or pentagram) is a "5-pointed or sometimes 6-pointed star used as a **MAGICAL** symbol." Witches Janet and Stewart Farrar describe the pentagram like this: "a five-pointed star, one of the **MAIN SYMBOLS OF WITCHCRAFT AND OCCULTISM** in general."[23] A book on numerology agrees that the pentagram "is used in many ritualistic ceremonies including **witchcraft.**"[24]

Witchcraft books entitled <u>Witchcraft: Yesterday and Today</u> and <u>Secrets of a Witch's Coven</u>

One witchcraft magazine explains:

> "The five-pointed star is one of the world's oldest symbols and it has been used in many cultures since ancient times as an amulet to bring good fortune and ward off harm. Most **WICCAN** [witchcraft] **PRACTITIONERS ALSO WEAR IT** today as a symbol of their religion....In the Wiccan religion, the five points of the **PENTAGRAM REPRESENT THE FIVE ELEMENTS** of Nature—Earth, Air, Fire, Water, and Spirit—with the top point corresponding to Spirit, the unifying element....A Pentagram inscribed on a platter is called a Pentacle. Pentacles are used as ceremonial tools for the Element Earth and placed above windows and doorways to bless and protect a dwelling."[25]

Sybil Leek, a well-known **WITCH,** declares that the "pentagram has always been used in ritual **MAGIC** and in the **WITCHCRAFT** rites of healing."[26] New Ager Dick Sutphen agrees that the "pentacle holds an important place in ritual **MAGIC.**"[27] Another book on witchcraft mentions:

"The pentacle, the five-pointed figure, contained mystic symbols, used especially in **DIVINATION** and the **CONJURATION OF SPIRITS.** The pentalpha, a design formed by interlacing five A's, was also in similar use. To **SUMMON DEMONIAC HELP,** the pentagram was fashioned: a five-pointed geometric figure."[28]

International Imports produces an occult catalog. This company sells altar covers with pentagrams on them—a "circled pentagram for white magic occult work; **INVERTED PENTAGRAM FOR BLACK MAGIC RITUALS."**[29] Elsewhere this catalog advertises occult jewelry with a pentagram. It adds that the pentagram is the "most powerful of all occult talismans....It is alleged that it is more powerful than the cross...."[30] We are also told that the **INVERTED PENTAGRAM IS "A SIGN FOR EVIL."**[31] Gary Jennings, in his book, *Black Magic, White Magic,* reveals that:

> "...the most powerful and respected of all magical symbols was the pentagram—the figure of five sides and five angles....The belief was that if this figure were drawn with a single angle...**POINTING DOWN, THE SIGN REPRESENTED SATAN** and thus was **USED FOR INVOKING EVIL SPIRITS."**[32]

Since we have been informed several times by Masonic authors that the inverted (or Satanic) pentagram refers to the Goat of Mendes, let's take a look at what this goat represents. In *A*

Dictionary of Symbols we notice that the he-goat is associated with the devil.[33] Mendes was an "Egyptian god resembling Pan; he was worshipped in the form of a goat."[34]

Pan

One witchcraft organization, Nuit Unlimited Imports, sells a Goat of Mendes T-shirt. They mention that this goat is also known as Baphomet.[35] An occult catalog mentions that Baphomet is the "traditional symbol of Pagans, witches, Satanists and mystics."[36] The *Dictionary of Mysticism* admits: **"Baphomet:** In occultism, the Sabbatic goat, in whose form Satan was said to be worshipped at the Witches' Sabbath."[37] The Occult Emporium's catalog sells Baphomet wall plaques. They brag that the plaques are "in appropriate colors of each quarter, and the appropriate qabbalistic **Demonic** name in the circumference. **Officially approved by Rev. Yaj Nomolos, Church of SATAN."[38]** An earlier catalog stated that one particular **Baphomet was "worn by the Priest of Satan...."[39]**

Describing Baphomet, Nuit Unlimited Imports says this:

"...art work was drawn by Eliphas Levi, the foremost **OCCULT** authority of the 19th century. Symbols were included relating directly to ceremonial **MAGIC** and identified with Baphomet. Much of the same symbols carry forward as on the **DEVIL CARD** in the Thoth deck of Crowley.

"The **GOAT OF MENDES** itself is known as the 'GOD OF THE WITCHES'...."[40]

Levi's drawing of Baphomet shows his emphasis on sex, for he made Baphomet as an androgynous (meaning both male and female) figure.[41] Satan, like Baphomet, "is often pictured as a hermaphroditic deity, having a male phallus and the breasts of a woman."[42] "The winged staff between Baphomet represents the phallus."[43]

The goat is one of the symbolical animals of Hermetic magic, says Levi, and it is the "symbol of generation."[44] In a book on witchcraft, *The Complete Book of Witchcraft and Demonology,* we find a picture of Baphomet. The caption states that he is the "horned god of the witches, symbol of sex incarnate."[45] This picture, by the way, shows Baphomet making the Devil's triad with his right hand.

Starhawk, a witch, boasts:

"The God of the Witches is sexual—but sexuality is seen as sacred, not as obscene or blasphemous. Our God wears horns—but they are the waxing and waning crescents of the Goddess Moon, and the symbol of animal vitality. In

some aspects, He is black, not because He is dreadful or fearful, but because darkness and the night are times of power, and part of the cycles of time....

"The God of the Witches is the God of love. This love includes sexuality, which is also wild and untamed as well as gentle and tender. His sexuality is fully *felt,* in a context in which sexual desire is sacred, not only because it is the means by which life is procreated but also because it is the means by which our own lives are most deeply and ecstatically realized. In Witchcraft, sex is a sacrament, an outward sign of an inward grace."[46] [Emphasis in the original]

Eliphas Levi wrote:

"The star of the microcosm, or the **MAGIC PENTAGRAM,** that star wherein the human figure was represented by Agrippa, with the head in the ascending point and the four members in the four other points—the Burning **STAR, WHICH, WHEN INVERTED, IS THE HIEROGLYPHIC SIGN OF THE GOAT OF BLACK MAGIC,** whose head can then be sketched in the star with the two horns above, the ears on the right and left, and the beard below, sign of antagonism and blind fatality, the goat of lewdness assaulting heaven with its horns, a sign execrated even in the Sabbath by initiates of a superior order."[47]

He also said:

"The **PENTAGRAM WITH TWO HORNS IN THE ASCENDANT REPRESENTS SATAN,** or the goat of the

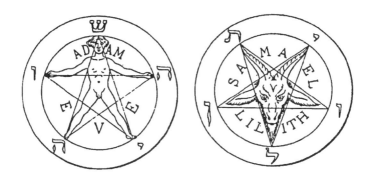

Sabbath....**IT IS THE FIGURE OF A HUMAN BODY** with the four members and a point representing the head; a human figure **HEAD DOWNWARD NATURALLY REPRESENTS THE DEMON,** that is, intellectual subversion, disorder and folly."[48]

Of course, one of the most sinister aspects of this star is its correlation with the god Set.[49] "Set was the ancient Egyptian god of evil. He was also known by the names Seth and Sutekh. He was a wicked and powerful god who often used witchcraft to achieve his aims."[50]

Set

Furthermore, the name **SET** (or Sut) is another name for **SATAN!** Proof of this can be found by turning to Masonic writer, Albert Churchward, in which he states: "Set or Sut, according to Plutarch, is the Egyptian name of Typhon—*i.e.* Satan of the Christian Cult."[51] John Yarker, another Masonic author agrees when he stated that **SET WAS "A DEVIL** identical with Typhon."[52] Yet another book, *Freemasonry and the Ancient Gods,* authored by Mason J. S. M. Ward, reveals that Set was "regarded as evil, because he represented darkness."[53] In *The Adelphi Quarterly,* a New Age magazine, we are notified: "The word 'Satan' comes from the Egyptian god of the underworld, Set or Seth."[54]

Further proof of the relationship between Set and Satan can be found in *The Satanic Bible,* written by Anton LaVey, the founder of the first Church of Satan. Under the enumeration of "The Infernal Names" for Satan is listed "Set."[55] On another page in this Satanic "bible," "Set" is described as the "Egyptian devil."[56] In *Treasury of Witchcraft* is included a listing of other names for Satan, one of which is Set.[57] Another New Age book (which praises Lucifer) describes Set as "the early Egyptian god of death, evil, and hell."[58] Additionally, occultist, New Ager, and Theosophist, Helen Petrovna Blavatsky, links Set and Satan together when she writes:

> "...Hermes, the god of wisdom, called also Thoth, Tat, Seth, Set and *Sat-an;* and that he was, furthermore, when viewed under his bad aspect, Typhon, the Egyptian Satan, who was also *Set.* "[59] [Emphasis in the original]

Thoth

In fact, knowing the abominable background of Set, it is no shock to discover that in "ancient Egypt, Set was worshiped with obscene, homosexual rituals."[60] We are told that the rituals performed for Set and Sirius were so horrible and debased "that later rulers of Egypt defaced their temples and obelisks and tried to drive them from the land."[61] In mythology we find that Set himself was involved in incest for he married his sister, Nephthys.[62] Set was also involved in adulterous affairs for he had at least two other consorts: Septet and Khekhsit.[63]

Set is likewise portrayed as the "Devil of Darkness,"[64] "Prince of Darkness,"[65] and "the Lord of the Underworld."[66] It is stressed that the "Underworld" of which Set is in charge, is not Hades, but Tartarus, for "Tartarus is the hell of the damned and it was of this world that Set was the Lord."[67] Set's symbol is the **INVERTED PENTAGRAM!**[68]

Michael Aquino "has written that Set is the oldest formulation of the being now called Satan, the embodiment of the sense of alienation and loneliness which man feels from the universe."[69] Aquino was a member of Anton LaVey's Church of Satan.[70] After leaving LaVey's church, he started his own organization called the **Temple of Set**[71] and his newsletter is entitled *The Scroll of Set.* The split between LaVey and Aquino was partially due to their individual conception of Satan. LaVey believed that Satan was just a symbol but Aquino contended that Satan, in the form of Set, was an absolute reality.[72]

Michael and Lilith Aquino

In spite of Aquino's beliefs and his status as a Satan worshipper, he was also a United States Army Lieutenant Colonel who served in Psy-Op operations.[73] When Aquino appeared on the Oprah Winfrey Show, he described Satanists as "very decent, very law-abiding people [with]...a very high set of personal ethics...[who have] nothing to do with evil."[74] Yet Aquino seems to contradict himself when he points out "that the essence of Satanism is an arrogant and hostile rebellion against universal law."[75]

Notice that Aquino uses a plain inverted pentagram (see picture on previous page). This symbol is **called Baphomet with or without the goat's head** drawn in it. For example see the advertisement for the two Baphomet pieces of jewelry. One has the goat's head and the other one has a snake wrapped about the pentagram but **BOTH** of them are referred to as Baphomet.

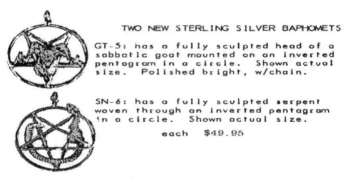

TWO NEW STERLING SILVER BAPHOMETS

GT-5: has a fully sculpted head of a sabbatic goat mounted on an inverted pentagram in a circle. Shown actual size. Polished bright, w/chain.

SN-6: has a fully sculpted serpent woven through an inverted pentagram in a circle. Shown actual size.

each $49.95

So, the pentagram really has a very evil connotation no matter how it is drawn. With one point up it represents Lucifer[76] and with two points up it depicts Satan.

The Bible tells us that the whole world lies in wickedness at the present time (I John 5:19), but there is coming a day when Satan will be bound. Revelation 20:1-3 states:

> "And I saw an angel come down from heaven, having the key of the bottomless pit and a great chain in his hand. And he laid hold on the dragon, that old serpent, which is the Devil, and Satan, and bound him a thousand years. And cast him into the bottomless pit, and shut him up, and set a seal upon him, that he should deceive the nations no more...."

The final victor will be Jesus Christ.

7. THE DREAM NET

The dream net (or dream catcher) is quite popular these days—especially for use in babies' cribs. However, this is **NOT** an innocent ornament. It is actually a **charm**. A *Dictionary of Mysticism* reports that a **charm is "any magic word, formula, incantation, object, sign or amulet supposed to possess occult power."**[1] Webster tells us that a charm is an "incantation," "the chanting or reciting of a **MAGIC SPELL,**" "an act or expression believed to have **MAGIC** power," **"AMULET."** An amulet is: "a charm (as an ornament) often inscribed with a magic incantation or symbol to protect the wearer against evil or to aid him." A **charmer is called an enchanter or a magician!** (As an aside, many people wear "charm bracelets" and think nothing of it, but they are actually wearing magical symbols which have a tendency to attract evil spirits!) In *Roget's Thesaurus* we find some interesting synonyms for charm. They are: enchantment, magic spell, spell, hex, amulet, and talisman. The verb form of "charm" means to bewitch or put under a magic spell. Do you want to wear any of these items or put a charm on your baby's crib?!

One witchcraft magazine, *Circle Network News,* in an article entitled "Amulets, Talismans & Charms," written by Selena Fox, a witch, explains the dream net like this:

> "This **CHARM,** from the Ojibway tribe in Minnesota, is made of sinew stretched over a small hoop of ash. It is designed to bring a good night's sleep, especially for children, and is hung horizontally over a child's cradleboard or crib. Tradition says that the air is filled with both good and bad dreams waiting to come to a sleeping child. This net allows good dreams to find their way to the child through the hole in the center, while bad dreams are caught up in the web where they dissolve in the dawn's light. Dream nets continue to be used by some Ojibway people today as in ancient times."[2]

One paper explaining the "Legend of the Dream Catcher" states:

> "Long ago when the world was young, an old Lakota spiritual leader was on a high mountain and had a vision.

> "In his vision, Iktomi, the great trickster and teacher of wisdom, appeared in the form of a spider.

> "Iktomi spoke to him in a sacred language that only the spiritual leaders of the Lakota could understand....

> "All the while the spider spoke, he continued to weave his web starting from the outside and working towards the center....

> "'If you believe in the great spirit, the web will catch your good ideas—and the bad ones will go through the hole.'

> "The Lakota elder passed on his vision to his people and now the Sioux Indians use the dream catcher as the web of their life.

"It is hung above their beds or in their home to sift their dreams and visions.

"The good in their dreams are captured in the web of life and carried with them...but the evil in their dreams escapes through the hole in the center of the web and are no longer a part of them.

"They believe that the dream catcher holds the destiny of their future."[3]

Without going into much comment on the above tale, most Christian researchers will recognize the occultic connotations throughout this little story. Notice the fantasy of a spider speaking, the use of visions, the "sacred language," and the idea that it is the dream catcher that holds each person's destiny rather than God.

Notice also the phrase "web of life." The idea of an etheric or planetary web was developed by Alice A. Bailey, an occultist, but initially expressed by Chief Seattle around 1854 in his supposed quote:

"This we know...the earth does not belong to man, man belongs to the earth. All things are connected, like blood which connects one family. Whatever befalls the earth befalls the children of the earth. Man did not weave the **web of life**—he is merely a strand in it. Whatever he does to the web, he does to himself."[4]

John Lash reveals that it is a "[k]ey idea in New Age philosophy of holistics, central to the new paradigm of GAIA, and major subject of study and exploration in geomancy."[5] [Emphasis in the original] Geomancy, by the way, is a form of **divination,** which is explicitly forbidden in the Bible. (See Deuteronomy 18:10-12; II Kings 17:17; Jeremiah 14:14; Ezekiel 12:24; 13:6-7; Acts 16:16.)

Returning to the story of the dream net, we find that the spider (Iktomi) was known as a **trickster.** How can you be sure that he didn't trick the people with his tale of the dream catcher? How can you be sure that the good dreams are caught and the evil ones are filtered out? A trickster is known for lying, deception, and mischief. Even if the story were true, the spider himself could not be trusted to be telling the truth!

Another catalog that sells lots of **occultic** materials states:

> "**THE DREAMCATCHER WEB** *Believe in its _mystical_ powers, and you may sleep more peacefully! Through the center _spirit_ hole flow your good dreams; trapped in the web are the 'bad,' which disappear with the morning sun.*"[6] [Bold and caps in the original; underlining added]

If you noticed carefully, even the descriptions of this dream net differ from place to place. Some people believe that the bad dreams are caught in the web and others believe that the good dreams are caught. Regardless of the discrepancies, this is not an item that any Christian would want in their home.

We do not need any "protection" from occult sources. Jeremiah 7:8 says: "Behold, ye trust in lying words, that cannot profit." All we need to do is to pray and ask the Lord to watch over our children and protect them and He will do it. Here are a few verses to ponder and remember:

"It is better to trust in the Lord than to put confidence in man" (Psalm 118:8).

"Blessed is that man that maketh the Lord his trust, and respecteth not the proud, nor such as turn aside to lies" (Psalm 40:4).

"What time I am afraid, I will trust in Thee" (Psalm 56:3).

"I will say of the Lord, He is my refuge and my fortress: my God; in Him will I trust" (Psalm 91:2).

"But let all those that put their trust in Thee rejoice: let them ever shout for joy, because Thou defendest them: let them also that love Thy name be joyful in Thee" (Psalm 5:11).

"Trust in the Lord with all thine heart; and lean not unto thine own understanding. In all thy ways acknowledge Him, and He shall direct thy paths" (Proverbs 3:5-6).

8. ELEMENTALS

Helena Petrovna Blavatsky, Theosophist, occultist, and New Ager, explains about the elementals. She writes:

"ELEMENTAL SPIRITS.—The creatures **evolved** in the four kingdoms of earth, air, fire, and water, and called by the kabalists gnomes, sylphs, salamanders, and undines. They may be termed the forces of nature, and will either operate effects as the servile agents of general law, or may be employed by the **disembodied spirits**—whether pure or impure—and by living adepts of **magic and sorcery,** to produce desired phenomenal results. Such beings never become men.

"Under the general designation of fairies, and fays, these spirits of the elements appear in the myth, fable, tradition, or poetry of all nations, ancient and modern. Their names are legion—peris, devs, jinn, sylvans, satyrs, fauns, elves, dwarfs, trolls, norns, nisses, kobolds, brownies, necks, stromkarls, undines, nixies, salamanders, goblins, ponkes, banshees, kelpies, pixies, moss people, good people, good neighbors, wild women, men of peace, white ladies—and many more. They have been seen, feared, blessed, banned, and invoked in every quarter of the globe and in every age. Shall we then concede that all who have met them were hallucinated?

"These elementals are the principal agents of disembodied but *never visible* spirits at **seances,** and the producers of all the phenomena except the subjective."[1] [Caps and italics in the original Boldface added]

One New Age catalog sells a tape on nature spirits. It asks:

"What is a nature spirit? Oral tradition and literature depict nature spirits as fairies, trolls, leprechauns and angels.

Become acquainted with the qualities and sensitives of these unusual, mysterious creatures, from primitive to complex. This myth-dispelling tape reveals interaction patterns between nature spirits and humans, touching on common conceptions of satanic and demonic-type beings as well. Safely guided through **meditations to contact nature spirits,** you will be captivated as you feel the joyful love abundant in their enchanting realm."[2]

In the November/December 1989 issue of *Connecting Link* was an article on elementals entitled "Helpers." This is an article dictated by a **SPIRIT GUIDE (demon).** Samuel (the spirit guide/ demon) says:

"There's a group that specializes in the earth. Another in air. Another in water. Another in fire. Another in spirit. The four basic elements, earth, air, water and fire work with specific things of earth. The elementals of spirit work specifically with that creation which has grown beyond simple form and are beings of spirits or humans. All of this group is called the angelic kingdom. It is also called the devic kingdom.

"Deva is a Sanskrit word which means 'the shining ones.'...Deva is shining one (sic) because it is describing light energy.

"There are very many names within each of these groups and the names that I am using here are your words. Every language has its own words. Legends, childhood stories, will have many differentiations or labels for specific aspects of energy. For instance, earth energy is under a great broad category I am calling gnomes. Under gnomes there are very many species. Each of those species has a particular work to do. And it is the work that is to be done that determines the particular species....

"Perhaps you would prefer to think of earth energy as fairies rather than gnomes. One is perhaps a prettier thought but the idea of a gnome I believe gives a picture that is more earthy....

"Earth elementals, for this, will be called gnomes. Now, of course, you've got pixies and brownies. You've got dryads. You've got all kinds of things in here—elves, leprechauns....

"The devic kingdom is here to help you....

"There is a water energy, that which works with the element of water. They are called undines. Again, these are light beings. The only body that these beings have are the bodies which your thoughts create and they create an actual thought form which these light beings are more than delighted to slip into to try to **communicate with you [spirit communication].**

"If you are convinced that sea spirits look like women with very pretty long hair and fishy tails, that's what you'll see. If you believe that leprechauns wear small green hats and small green suits and have pointed ears, they'll put that on. If you believe a fairy has lovely translucent wings and long flowing gowns, that is what you will see. Your expectations are creating the body through which that light can manifest in a more easy manner....

"Sylphs are the elementals of air. You go into a city in which the air is quite filled with debris. Perhaps you need to be the only one in the city wise enough to call upon the sylphs to give you an extra dose of pure air.

"The element of fire is perhaps the most powerful of the earth elements. It is often considered the purification element. It is changeable. It is beautiful. Those elementals which work with fire are called salamanders. When you need fire, you call upon the salamanders. When you need fire to stop, call upon the salamanders....

"They've got their own work to do, but they are affected by you. When you call them, consciously or not, they are going to do your bidding....[When you meditate and say, 'heal the planet,'—ed.] you are commanding legions."[3]

Some of these elementals are once again becoming popular. Take the troll, for instance. A few years ago the troll was a big fad for children. There were the "Treasure Trolls." One author wrote: "They're so ugly that they're cute, but are they as harmless as the (sic) look?"[4]

"Treasure Trolls come with a 'wishstone,' a crystal inserted in the belly button. Crystals are important to the New Age theology, as it is believed they possess a life force influence that can be tapped for healing purposes. The belly button is significant because it represents the umbilical connection, or the centre of the lifeforce.

"The gems on the Treasure Troll doll have an additional significance, one not lost on the imagination of children. They are wishstones, **talismans** that can make their every dream come true."[5]

Another author states:

"The cute-ugly trolls that have captivated American children epitomize today's delight in neo-paganism when joined to popular ideals. While the trolls of Scandinavian fairy tales would uproot trees, enslave beautiful women and turn people into stone with cruel spells, today's monsters are environmentally correct. Note how one troll-maker disguises the evil and makes myth sound like truth:

"*There was a time when waters were clean and forests were untouched, when ancient legends spoke of Guardians of the Earth...In Scandinavian lands, these mysterious creatures were TROLLS, and were known to guard what was left of the earth's natural treasures...Because they were rarely seen, people believed TROLLS no longer existed. Today, these nearly forgotten creatures are once again in our midst...working their earth magic to help humans.'* ('Troll Kidz' by Russ Berrie and Co.)"[6] [Emphasis in the original]

Of course, children aren't the only ones being attracted to these spirit beings. When an earthquake in October 1989 shook a span of the San Francisco's Bay Bridge, "help" was soon offered in the form of a **talisman**.[7] Webster tells us a talisman is "an object bearing a sign or character engraved under **astrological** influences and thought to act as a **charm** to avert evil and bring good fortune." The talisman put beneath the roadway was a troll with horned head and webbed feet. It is supposed to ward off evil spirits.[8] "The craftsmen plan to offer trolls to other structures damaged by the earthquake, and even to new high-rise office blocks. Meanwhile, troll T-shirts are selling well in San Francisco."[9]

What most people don't realize is that the "word **troll comes from the Old Norse word for demon** and is defined by some sources as a 'devil: a person of great wickedness or maliciousness.'"[10]

So, when your child brings home a troll, he or she has in actuality brought home a representation of a demon!! These demons are also disguised as gnomes, pixies, dwarves, leprechauns, and elves (as well as many other creatures). I'm sure you recall the Keebler elves. Of course, Santa has his elves, too. There's also Snow White with her seven dwarves and Cinderella with her fairy godmother. All these are **demonic representations** but they are presented in such a "cute" way that most people have no idea of the evil character behind these objects.

Another elemental spirit is known as a vetta. There are supposedly evil and good vettas. The vetta was introduced to a host of people during the 1994 Winter Olympics. "A CBS reporter described the event: 'We introduce you to the mythical beliefs of the Norwegian people. Popping out of the ground are the Vettas, mythical characters rooted in ancient Nordic folktales and sagas.'"[11] The reporter continued:

> "'We know them as gnomes, pixies, trolls....The vettas are an integral part of Norwegian beliefs...They are said to be knowledgeable and wise...and watch constantly over the activities of mankind. That's because these are good vettas as opposed to the evil vettas. They say that if you are good to the vettas and consult [them—Ed.] before you build your barn, [they—Ed.] will be good to you.'"[12]

In *The Seeker's Handbook* we are told that elementals are:

> "Nature-spirits who inhabit the four elements, widely described in folklore as visible to people of former times who lived in close communion with nature; for instance, leprechauns, fairies, and 'little people.' Specifically, gnomes (Earth), undines (Water), sylphs (Air), salamanders (Fire)— all **CREATURES WHO FIGURE STRONGLY IN**

**CEREMONIAL MAGIC AND PRACTICES OF NA-
TURE-WORSHIP, OR WICCA."**[13]

One occult/New Age organization states:

**"ELEMENTALS ARE USED IN HIGH MAGICK,
AND OCCASIONALLY IN WITCHCRAFT AND
OTHER MAGICAL TRADITIONS, TO GUARD
MAGICK CIRCLES AND ASSIST IN MAGICKAL**
(sic) **ACTS.**

"In *The Golden Dawn,* Israel Regardie explains how
to use elementals within rituals."[14]

"Occultists regard elementals as beings having
substance, but visible only to those who have inner sight;
some elementals are regarded benign, others as malignant."[15]

One organization that gained fame in the past 30 years is
Findhorn Community. It was founded in 1965 by Peter and Eileen
Caddy and Dorothy Maclean.

"[Maclean] made contact with the devas—nature spirits
said to be associated with various plant, species, or landscape
features....The first contact was made with a pea deva.
Maclean was told that the garden would succeed as they
cooperated with the devas by seeking their advice and
gaining their permission to rearrange the landscape. Some
like the pea deva were specific to a species, while others
like the landscape deva relate to more general aspects of the
garden itself. The garden's abundance became known
throughout the neighborhood and its noteworthy success
brought several other followers to the community.

"During the next several years the group continued to
follow Eileen's guidance and the advice of the devas
channeled through Maclean. Members also established
contact with other **theosophical and spiritualist groups.**

In 1965 Peter traveled to a gathering of spiritual groups organized by Sir George Trevelyan, author and head of the Wrekin Trust. They were visited in 1966 by Robert Ogilvie Crombie, an Edinburgh **spiritualist** who, as a result of his visit, contacted the elemental nature spirits who work with the devas. Crombie soon made contact with **PAN, THE GOD OF THE NATURE ELEMENTALS,** and brought what was seen as completeness to the efforts of the Caddys and Maclean. Findhorn residents began to think of themselves as an experiment in cooperation between devas, nature elementals, and humans."[16]

Pan

One person who worked with Findhorn was David Spangler. He wrote:

"**LUCIFER** works within each of us to bring us to wholeness, and as we move into a **NEW AGE,** which is the age of man's wholeness, each of us in some way is brought to that point which I term the **LUCIFERIC INITIATION,** the particular doorway through which the individual **MUST PASS IF** he is to come "fully" into the presence of his light and his wholeness."[17]

Later in his book, *Reflections on the Christ,* Spangler states: "**LUCIFER** came to give us the final gift of wholeness. If we accept it then he is free and we are free. That is the **LUCIFERIC INITIATION.** It is one that many people now, and in the days ahead will be facing, for **it is an initiation into the NEW AGE.**"[18] People who worship and adore Lucifer are also the ones who believe in elementals!

One elemental or nature spirit that most people would recognize is the leprechaun. You can see this elemental every St. Patrick's Day. You also see the leprechaun on boxes of **Lucky Charms** cereal. Also, take a good look at the name of the cereal— Lucky Charms. Notice the occult overtone. By the way, the word cereal comes from Ceres—the **GODDESS** of grain.[19]

Another popular creature is called a gargoyle. Although the gargoyle is not considered to be an elemental or a nature spirit, it is supposed to ward off evil. They "were thought to have protective, **SPIRITUAL** and **MAGICAL** qualities."[20] These creatures are appearing even in very prominent places. Dr. Dennis Cuddy states:

> "That the New Age New World Order will include all aspects of life, even athletics, is demonstrated in the closing ceremony of the Olympics, in which 'happy devils' dance and figures representing demons writhe on the stadium floor accompanied by eerie music. It is a message to the people of the world. It also reminds us of the rows of grotesque gargoyles or demons' heads that have recently been painted

on the southeast and northeast corridor walls of the Library of Congress' Thomas Jefferson Building Main Vestibule, **replacing** a group of our nation's founders kneeling in prayer which has been on the walls since 1897, when the building was constructed. A poster describing the future agenda of the Library of Congress said the Thomas Jefferson Building *'now undergoing renovation, will reopen in 1993....Following its renovation, the Thomas Jefferson Building will celebrate the HUMANISTIC legacy of the world.'*"[21] [Italics in the original; Caps and boldface added]

A Dictionary of Symbols says that the gargoyles are "Fabulous animals and monsters make their appearance in mediaeval religious art as symbols of the forces of the cosmos, or as **IMAGES OF THE DEMONIACAL AND DRAGON-INFESTED UNDER-WORLD....**"[22]

Annabel Wharton, a Duke art professor, reveals that:

"A general rise in interest in mysticism, the supernatural and primitive forms of Christianity...help account for the gargoyle fascination....

"'We're now in a period of eclecticism in which we're mixing various doctrines....'"[23]

Marisa Lobe, a woman who makes gargoyles, said "she was intrigued by the idea that **PAGAN RELIGIONS COULD BE**

BLENDED WITH CHRISTIANITY."[24] She "also makes leaf men, the tree spirits worshiped by the **Druids**...."[25]

Another artist, Hope Stewart, is "attracted to the **MYSTICAL AURA** that surrounds" the gargoyles and said that they "give the feeling of a house that **SPIRITS WOULD VISIT.**"[26]

Several years ago, a comic book was named *The Gargoyle.* Here's one quote from that book: *"I am the master of the shadows...and I claim that church as my own. I smell blood, the blood of the Lamb. He's here. DRIVE HIM OUT! (The Gargoyle* comic book, *Marvel Comics).*"[27] [Emphasis in the original]

In spite of the demonic implications of the gargoyle, one supposedly "Christian" magazine basically told parents not to worry if their child's Christmas list contained a gargoyle on it. Jolene L. Roehlkepartain said:

> **"If a satanic-looking gargoyle** appears on your teenager's Christmas list this year, don't scream. Many of the gargoyle reproductions are made into bookends, candlesticks, statues and even are on T-shirts. These gruesome, grotesque gargoyles are going to the top of most 15- to 30-year olds' Christmas lists as the latest in new fads.

> "Why the infatuation with these snarling figures? 'They are shocking, forbidden and mysterious,' said Mark Thomas, of The Alley, a Chicago gargoyle store. 'These gargoyles,' he says, 'are perceived to be good guys who defend your home from evil.'"[28]

Below is a list of some different kinds of nature spirits.

"Brownie: In the **OCCULT** lore of Scotland, the name given to dark-featured nocturnal nature-spirits which haunt country and farm houses; believed to be good-natured and bearers of good omen."[29]

"**Harpy:** In classical mythology, a monstrous, evil, rapacious and vengeful creature with the head and breasts of a woman, the body of a bird and the claws of a lion."[30]

"**Fay:** Fairy."[31] Also considered to be an elf.

Fairy: "A tiny imaginary being in human form, depicted as clever, mischievous, and possessing **MAGICAL** powers."

"**Sylph:** An *elemental*...of the element Air."[32] [Emphasis in the original]

"**Undine:** An *elemental*...of the element Water; undines are believed to appear usually in the shapes of women, but able also to assume the forms of fishes or snakes."[33] [Emphasis in the original]

"**Genie:** See: *Jinn*."[34]

"**Jinn, jinnee:** In Arab **OCCULTIC** terminology, one of a race of beings created out of fire, which inhabited the Earth before the advent of man. They can become visible or invisible at will, have many other superhuman and magic powers. Some *jinns* are

good and friendly to humans, others are malignant."[35] [Italics in the original; Caps added]

"Salamander: An *elemental*...of the element Fire."[36] [Emphasis in the original]

"Goblin: A mischievous nature-spirit."[37]

"Banshee: A nature-spirit believed in Ireland and Scotland to take the form of an old woman, to chant a mournful dirge under the windows of a house in which a person is to die soon."[38]

"Hatif: In pre-Islamic Arabic folklore, an invisible nature-spirit who can be heard by men as he gives advice and warnings."[39]

"Hobgoblin: A cheerful but very mischievous fairy or nature-spirit who delights in playing pranks on mortal beings."[40]

"Gnome: An *elemental*...of the element Earth."[41] [Emphasis in the original] The gnome is one "of a fabled race of dwarflike creatures who live underground and guard treasure hoards."

"Ifrit: A viciously malignant spirit, of hideous appearance, in Arabic folklore."[42]

"Satyr: One of a class of woodland deities of Greek-Roman mythology, represented by the Greeks as a human figure with a horse's ears and tail, and by the Romans as a human figure with a goat's ears, tail, legs and budding horns."[43]

"Seiktha: In Burmese folklore, a tree spirit, usually malignant."[44]

"**Pisky:** See: *Pixie.*"[45]

"**Pixie, pixy:** A fairy-like nature-spirit."[46]

"**Yazatas:** Nature-spirits or minor deities of Zoroastrianism."[47]

"**Wild-women:** Nature-spirits of German folklore."[48]

"**Triton:** In Greek mythology, a merman, son of Poseidon and Amphitrite."[49]

"**Nat:** In Burmese folklore, a nature-spirit of the forest."[50]

"**Troll:** A hideous, evil earth-**demon** of Teutonic mythology, living in caves."[51] The troll can be a dwarf or a giant who also lives in the hills and under bridges.

"**Water-sprite:** A nature-spirit of the water."[52]

"**Peri:** In Persian mythology, a fairy-like creature descended from a race of fallen angels."[53]

"**Tengus:** Evil tree spirits (Japan), human in form but hatched from eggs."[54]

"**Nenufaremi:** In **OCCULT** lore, a name for elementals...of the air."[55]

"**Sprite:** A nature-spirit; a ghost or spook."[56] Also: "A small or elusive supernatural being; an elf or a pixy."

"**Spunkie:** A malignant goblin which delights in attracting travellers who have lost their way, by letting them see a light, and lures them into a morass or over a precipice."[57]

"Spectre: A ghost or ghostly apparition."[58]

"Spook: A ghostly apparition."[59]

"Naiad: In **OCCULTISM,** a nature-spirit or elemental of rivers, lakes and springs."[60] A nymph.

"Oread: A nature-spirit of the mountains."[61] A nymph.

"Nereid: A sea nymph...as opposed to the *naiads,* the nymphs of sweet waters."[62] [Emphasis in the original]

Dryad: "A divinity presiding over forests and trees; a wood nymph."

"Oceanids: A nature-spirit or elemental...of the class of nymphs, dwelling in the ocean. In Greek mythology, the oceanids were the 4,000 daughters of Okeanos and Tethys."[63]

"Nymph; nympha: In occultism, little, graceful, gay female nature-spirits, usually friendly; they are generally regarded as water-spirits...but some authors place the *dryads* and *hamadryads*...in this class, too. Nymphs are regarded as long-lived, but not immortal, and possessing certain magical abilities."[64] [Emphasis in the original]

"Leprechaun: Nature-spirits of Irish **OCCULT** lore."[65] A leprechaun is from the race of elves and is supposed to be able to reveal hidden treasure to someone who is able to catch him.

"**Nivashi:** In the magic lore of the Gypsies of Southeastern Europe, a malignant water-spirit."[66]

"**Nix, nixie:** A nature-spirit of the water; a nymph."[67]

"**Kobold:** A mischievous nature spirit, living in caves and subterranean places."[68] A goblin.[69]

"**Ogre:** In **OCCULT** lore, and in the folklore of certain races, an evil nature-spirit of hideous appearance, at times a man-eating giant."[70]

"**Faun:** A nature spirit, half man, half goat, venerated as a rural deity by the ancient Romans. The Fauns were attendants of Pan."[71]

Elf: "A small, often mischievous creature considered to have **MAGICAL** powers."

Although some of these creatures may appear cute on the surface, all of them are nonetheless **demonic entities** that have their origin in the **occult** world. Many Christians bring these items into their home innocently, but they really have no place in a Christian's home since they are representations of demons.

These elementals are also considered to be **spirit guides,** spirit helpers, and familiar spirits.[72] The Bible clearly warns us about these things in numerous passages.

Leviticus 19:31: "Regard not them that have familiar spirits, neither seek after wizards, to be defiled by them: I am the Lord your God."

Leviticus 20:6: "And the soul that turneth after such as have familiar spirits, and after wizards, to go a whoring after them, I will even set My face against that soul, and will cut him off from among his people."

Deuteronomy 18:9-12: "When thou art come into the land which the Lord thy God giveth thee, thou shalt not learn to do after the abominations of those nations. There shall not be found among you any one that maketh his son or his daughter to pass through the fire, or that useth divination, or an observer of times, or an enchanter, or a witch, Or a charmer, or a consulter with familiar spirits, or a wizard, or a necromancer. For all that do these things are an abomination unto the Lord: and because of these abominations the Lord thy God doth drive them out from before thee."

See also: II Kings 21:6; 23:24; II Chronicles 33:6; Isaiah 8:19; Leviticus 20:27; I Samuel 28:3, 7-9; and I Chronicles 10:13.

9. TAROT AND PLAYING CARDS

With the resurgence of the occult and the New Age movement has come a new interest in the Tarot card deck. The *New Age Almanac* explains:

"The tarot, however, began to take on **OCCULT** associations and to be **USED PREDOMINANTLY FOR CARTOMANCY, DIVINATION, OR FORTUNE-TELLING** with cards. The person primarily responsible for the new developments in the tarot was a French Huguenot pastor, Antoine Court de Gebelin (1719-1784). In the 1770s, de Gebelin became active in Parisian **FREEMASONRY** circles and joined the Philalethes, a French **MASONIC OCCULT ORDER** derived from the teachings of Martines de Pasqually (d. 1774). He became an accomplished **OCCULT** scholar. This French **occult** perspective came to be an essential building block in the revolutionary thought that would bring down the French government in a few years.

"Through his social connections, de Gebelin discovered the tarot. He immediately saw in them **OCCULT SYM-BOLOGY,** and tied them to ancient Egypt. As ancient Egypt disintegrated, the priests developed playing cards to hide their wisdom from the profane and at the same time ensure their survival. He concluded that they had traveled to Rome, kept in the possession of the popes who took them to Avignon. From Avignon they were disseminated throughout Europe. De Gebelin published his speculations in 1781 in the eighth volume of his multi-volume study of the ancient world, *Le Monde primitif*, in which he begins to designate the occult symbology of the deck. De Gebelin is, for example, the one who originated the idea that the 22 Major cards were to be equated with the 22 letters of the Hebrew alphabet. In an essay by an unknown associate appended to his own account of the tarot, de Gebelin suggested that the **TAROT BE USED AS A METHOD OF DIVINATION.** The idea was adopted by a **fortune-teller** known only as Etteilla, who in 1783 published a book detailing a methodology for tarot cartomancy, and over the next decade authored a host of books and pamphlets on fortune-telling using the tarot and other means. Cartomancy with the tarot grew increasingly prevalent during the decades of post-revolutionary France.

"Etteilla's students passed the practice of fortune-telling with cards to Alphonse-Louis Constant (better known under his penname, Eliphas Levi). **LEVI, THE FOUNTAIN-HEAD OF MODERN RITUAL MAGIC, INTEGRATED THE TAROT INTO HIS MAGICAL TEACHINGS AND ALIGNED IT WITH THE MASSIVE BODY OF OCCULT SYMBOLISM.** Through Levi's very popular writings, the use of the tarot flowed into the **occult** groups which flourished in Europe at the end of the nineteenth century, and the **MASTERY OF THE SYMBOLISM OF THE TAROT BECAME A STANDARD PART OF THE TRAINING OF A MAGICIAN.** The most famous of the accomplished masters of the tarot in France was Dr. Gerard Encausse (1865-1916), who wrote several influential books on the tarot and who was most responsible for lifting up an idea first proposed by de Gebelin, but given some expanded treatment by J. F. Vaillant, of tying *The Tarot to the Bohemians* (1889), written under the pseudonym Papus.

"In England, the tarot was integrated into the symbolism of that most famous of **magical** orders, the Hermetic Order of the Golden Dawn. One degree of the order's program of advancement included the member's construction of a complete tarot deck. Two of the order's members would create the two most popular decks used in the twentieth century. Arthur Edward Waite (1857-1942) was the most scholarly member of the Golden Dawn. He was responsible for the English translations of several of Levi's works and he revised the first English translation of Papus' text. More importantly, with the help of an artist, Pamela Coleman Smith, he devised a new tarot deck complete with all 78 cards (i.e., both the major and minor cards), the first such comprehensive revision in more than one hundred years. He also authored an instruction book, *The Pictorial Guide to the Tarot* (1910), with which anyone could take a deck of cards and master their use as a basic fortune-telling instrument. It was the combination of the deck and the instruction book which gave the Waite deck its dominance in the field through most of the twentieth century.

"The second accomplished student of the tarot was **Aleister Crowley** (1875-1947), the order's nemesis. In 1909 Crowley began publishing the order's secrets, including their teaching on the tarot, through an independent journal, *The Equinox*. Crowley worked with Freida Harris in the design of a new tarot deck to which he composed a commentary much like Waite's *The Book of Thoth*. It was published in a limited edition in 1944, but the cards were not published until about 1960. Only after a new edition of *The Book of Thoth* appeared in 1969 did the Crowley deck begin to grow in popularity to rival Waite's deck. In choosing to name his deck after the Egyptian deity Thoth, Crowley asserted both his own preference for Egyptian **magical** symbolism and his belief in de Gebelin's claims as to the deck's Egyptian origin."[1]

A *Dictionary of Mysticism* states:

"**Tarot:** A deck of playing cards, based on a system of **occult** symbols arranged in a pattern of 78 cards; 22 of these are tarot cards ('major arcana'), the other 56 are suit cards ('minor arcana'). These cards can be used for **divination.** The term *tarot* is applied also to designate such divination."[2] [Italics in the original; Boldface added]

We are further informed by an **occult** organization that the "Tarot has often been interpreted as a **fortune telling** device, but, as Gareth Knight reveals, it is also a profound and powerful system of High Renaissance **MAGIC!**"[3]

Since we've already covered the yin/yang symbol and the I Ching, I think it is interesting to note that *The Occult Explosion* states: "The occidental **COUNTERPART TO THE I CHING IS THE TAROT CARD DECK.** The most widely-spread **OCCULT** tradition about the origin of the Tarot is that it was invented by a great international assemblage of esoteric scholars in Egypt...."[4] It adds: "Tarot and I Ching really have a lot in common...."[5]

What is even more intriguing is that the Tarot is really the ancestor of the standard playing card deck that is used today.[6] For instance one book on the Tarot reveals: "Even the common playing cards we know today are derived from the ancient tarot and vary widely due to their centuries of use as instruments of gambling."[7]

Stewart Farrar, a witch, indicates:

> "The Tarot consists of seventy-eight cards, and is clearly the ancestor of the bridge-player's pack. Fifty-six of them are divided into four suits—Cups (corresponding to Heart), Swords (Spades), Wands (Clubs), and Pentacles (Diamonds). Each suit has the Ace to Ten and the Knave— in between the Page and the Queen. (The Knight is sometimes called the Prince, and the Page the Princess.) The four suits represent the four **occult** elements—their usual allocation being Cups for Water, Swords for Air, Wands for Fire, and Pentacles for Earth...."[8]

In *The Occult: A History* we are told:

"Apart from the Greater Arcana [in the Tarot deck], there are also the fifty-six cards of the Lesser Arcana, the four suits that have become the ordinary playing cards of today, with its rods, (or wands), cups, swords and shekels (or pentacles) changing into clubs, hearts, spades and diamonds. It is worth observing in passing, that we have here two rod-shaped objects—wands and swords—and two circular objects—cups and money—and since one of the commentators mentions that wands and money were used in mediaeval methods of divination, it would not be inaccurate to see them as related to the yarrow stalks and coins of the I Ching. Each suit has a king, queen, knight and knave, as well as cards numbered from one to ten."[9]

In *Our Phallic Heritage* we find that the symbols used on the playing cards are actually sexual connotations. This book explains:

"The symbols used on playing cards are the diamond, heart, club, and the spade, which was often the acorn. In sex symbolism the diamond and heart were female symbols, and the spade and club were male symbols. The two colors represented the sexes; red symbolized the male, and black the female. In the Orient are found the yang-yin (male and female symbols), similar to the Northern Pacific Railroad trademark with these colors. Possibly coincidentally, remember that in certain sections of the cities there were the red-light districts, and they operated in the darkness.

"Both sexes are symbolized on each card by having a symbol of one sex and a color of the opposite sex. The trinity or complete family is seen in the three highest cards, which are the king, queen, and jack or knave. 'Knave,' like knabe in German, means 'boy.' Therefore, in cards, we have the father, mother and child, the natural trinity or perfect family. There are four suits to symbolize the male triad and female unit, forming the Arba-el, or the four gods. The thirteen cards in each suit represent the lunar months or menstruations in a year. They also represent the weeks in a season, and have been compared to the calendar, the colors red and black representing day and night; the four suits, the four weeks in a month, and four seasons in a year, or the four cardinal points of the compass; the twelve picture cards, the twelve months in a year; the fifty-two cards, the weeks in a year; and counting the jack as eleven, the queen as twelve, and the king as thirteen, the number of spots in the deck equals 364 and, with the joker, 365, the number of days in a year."[10]

I think it would be informative to give the history and the real meaning of ordinary playing cards. The following is taken from *The Gospel Standard.*

"The first deck of cards was made for Charles of France in the year 1392. King Charles was an insane man. It is not generally known by card players that cards have a secret meaning, but after the following statements were made public, the members of the gambling fraternity of professional gamblers declared that they are absolutely true.

"The *King* card represents the enemy of God, the devil. The *Ten* spot represents the spirit of lawlessness and is in direct opposition to the Ten Commandments of the Bible. Closely associated with the ten spot is the *Club* card. When cards were invented the club was the weapon of the murderer. In those days there were no revolvers or machine guns. The Club card stands for murder. The *Jack* represents the lustful libertine who lives on the gains of the prostitutes. It represents the moral leper. There is a game of cards called 'the brothel game' in which the players use the secret obscene language of the cards and converse with each other merely by dropping a card.

"Now we come to the part that is even more shockingly wicked. The *Queen* card represents the Virgin Mary, the mother of our Lord. In the secrets of cards she is called the mother of harlots. The *Joker* in card language represents our Lord Jesus Christ. Joker means fool! Jesus Christ is held up by the card players as a fool. And if this is not bad enough yet, the secret language of a deck of cards goes further and declares that Jesus (the Joker card) is the offspring of a lustful Jack, and the Queen mother, Mary.

"And there you have the true meaning of a deck of so-called innocent playing cards!"[11] [Emphasis in the original]

As a little extra note, I thought it was interesting to find out that the President of the U.S. Playing Card Company (from 1929-1930) and the President of Standard Playing Card Company (in 1898) was Benjamin C. Hawkes—a Mason.[12]

Many people play or gamble with the regular card deck but is any of this pleasing to Christ—especially in light of the blasphemy that is represented by these cards? Not only do the regular playing cards come from the occultic Tarot card background, but the meaning of the cards are an insult and offense to Christ and the Christian teaching of the Virgin Birth. Jesus did not have an illegitimate birth. Matthew states: "Behold, a virgin shall be with child, and shall bring forth a son, and they shall call His name Emmanuel, which being interpreted is, God with us" (Matthew 1:23). He was also named Jesus "for He shall save His people from their sins" (Matthew 1:21). He came to give His life as a sacrifice on our behalf so that we may have the privilege of receiving eternal life and having our sins forgiven.

I realize that many people had no idea what the cards which they were using meant, but now that you know, can you still use them?

10. HUMANIST SYMBOLS

The humanist movement has adopted a number of symbols for their association. One of these symbols is called the "Happy Man." This one, which was taken from an International Humanist and Ethical Union (IHEU) pamphlet, "is fast becoming the most universal humanist symbol."[1]

A slight variation of the IHEU's symbol is also used on the American Humanist Association's (AHA) literature. In a pamphlet by the AHA entitled "Statement Affirming Evolution As a Principle of Science," we find:

"For many years it has been well established scientifically that all known forms of life, including human beings, have developed by a lengthy process of **evolution.** It is also verifiable today that very primitive forms of life, ancestral to all living forms, came into being thousands of millions of years ago...

"Creationism is not scientific, but it is a purely religious view held by some religious sects and persons and strongly opposed by other religious sects and persons. Evolution is the only presently known, strictly scientific, and not religious explanation for the existence and diversity of living organisms. It is therefore the only view which should be expounded in public school courses on science, which are distinct from those on religion."[2]

Of course, the above statement is not true at all. Evolution **IS** associated with religion. In *Ancient Operative Masonry* we find: "It is the firm belief of students of **OCCULT SCIENCE** that through the slow process of **EVOLUTION,** the whole human family, save those who have elected to follow the left-hand path, shall attain self-mastery and finally **reach perfection.**"[3]

Besides, evolution **IS NOT** scientific. The reason evolution has to be propagated is because the humanist denies God. Without God no creation can take place. Therefore, since they do not believe in God, they are left to create or design their own **THEORY** of how the world began without God. They have failed miserably in their speculations but they continue to maintain that evolution is scientific in spite of having **NO PROOF** whatsoever. Remember the Bible says: "The fool hath said in his heart, There is no God" (Psalm 53:1; 14:1).

Humanist Manifesto signer, Corliss Lamont, said that all "entities are related to one another in respect to gravity, most of them are totally at any one time to most others in most ways. **Every thing has some relations with other things....**"[4] If this is the case, then how did a one-cell amoeba exist or survive when it was **ALONE** and could not be dependent on anything else? He also states:

"No matter how far back, in our analysis, we push the cause-effect sequences of the universe, we are certain to discover a **plurality of event-streams** that can be accurately described only in terms of a plurality of principles. There was no *one* event that started the universe going, and in fact no beginning at all."[5]

If there is a **PLURALITY** of events, then a **SINGLE** one-celled amoeba could never have existed alone and Lamont's theory of evolution is INVALID on HIS OWN statement!

Additionally, **HUMANISM ITSELF IS A RELIGION.** Although humanism is often denied to be a religion, the early documents from humanists clearly show that humanism is a religion. I believe the humanists today are trying to steer clear of the "religious" label because they are heavily involved in the education of children and religion is supposedly not allowed in the classroom. By hiding behind an erroneous (and deceitful) label, religious humanism has infiltrated the classroom as a religion while at the same time it repudiates it is a religion.

"In fact, the [former] president of the American Humanist Association, Lloyd Morain, has stated that **Humanism is '...a religion without God, divine revelation or sacred scriptures.'**

"The position that Humanism is a religion was confirmed by the U.S. Supreme Court in 1965, when it ruled in the case of U.S. vs. Seeger: 'A humanistic...belief that is sincerely professed as a religion shall be entitled to recognition as religious under the Selective Service Law.'

"And again, in the case of Torcase (sic) vs. Watkins, the Court ruled that: 'Among **religions** in this country which do not teach what would generally be considered a belief in the existence of God are Buddhism, Taoism, Ethical Culture, **Secular Humanism** and others.'

"So when Madlyn (sic) Murray O'Hair got the Supreme Court to remove the right of the children to open their school day with a simple prayer because she wished to separate 'Church and State,' what she was doing was substituting one religion for another: a belief in God with a belief in Humanism. Mrs. O'Hair knew this because she had been the editor of the magazine, *The Free Humanist,* and was elected to the Board of the American Humanist Association in 1965, and was elected in 1973 for a second four-year term."[6]

Humanist Manifesto I, written in 1933, plainly states that humanism is a religion. In 1973 *Humanist Manifesto II* was written. In the "Preface" to these Manifestos we find: "Humanism is a philosophical, **RELIGIOUS,** and moral point of view as old as human civilization itself."[7]

Also:

> "In 1933 a group of thirty-four liberal humanists in the United States defined and enunciated the philosophical and **RELIGIOUS PRINCIPLES** that seemed to them fundamental. They drafted *Humanist Manifesto I,* which for its time was a radical document. **It was concerned with expressing a general RELIGIOUS and philosophical outlook** that rejected orthodox and dogmatic positions and provided meaning and direction, unity and purpose to human life. It was committed to reason, science, and democracy."[8]

Humanist Manifesto I states: "In order that **RELIGIOUS HUMANISM** may be better understood we, the undersigned, desire to make certain affirmations which we believe the facts of our contemporary life demonstrate."[9] The Manifesto adds:

> "We therefore affirm the following:

> "*First:* **RELIGIOUS HUMANISTS** regard the universe as self-existing and not created.

> "*Second:* Humanism believes that man is a part of nature and that he has emerged as the result of a continuous process [evolution]....

"*Sixth:* We are convinced that the time has passed for theism, deism, modernism, and the several varieties of 'new thought.'...

"*Eighth:* **RELIGIOUS HUMANISM** considers the complete realization of human personality to be the end of man's life and seeks its development and fulfillment in the here and now. This is the explanation of the humanist's social passion.

"*Ninth:* In place of the old attitudes involved in worship and prayer the **HUMANIST FINDS HIS RELIGIOUS EMOTIONS** expressed in a heightened sense of personal life and in a cooperative effort to promote social well-being....

"*Twelfth:* Believing that religion must work increasingly to joy in living, **RELIGIOUS HUMANISTS** aim to foster the creative in man and to encourage achievements that add to the satisfactions of life.

"*Thirteenth:* **Religious humanism** maintains that all associations and institutions exist for the fulfillment of human life. The intelligent evaluation, transformation, control, and direction of such associations, and institutions with a view to the enhancement of human life is the purpose and program of humanism. Certainly religious institutions, their ritualistic forms, ecclesiastical methods, and communal activities must be reconstituted as rapidly as experience allows, in order to function effectively in the modern world....

"So stand the theses of **RELIGIOUS HUMANISM.** Though we consider the religious forms and ideas of our father no longer adequate, the quest for the good life is still the central task for mankind. Man is at last becoming aware that he alone is responsible for the realization of the world of his dreams, that he has within himself the power for its achievement. He must set intelligence and will to the task."[10]

The "Preface" to *Humanist Manifesto II* once again reiterates that **HUMANISM IS RELIGIOUS.**

> "Many kinds of humanism exist in the contemporary world. The varieties and emphases of naturalistic humanism include 'scientific,' 'ethical,' 'democratic,' **'RELIGIOUS,'** and 'Marxist' humanism. Free thought, atheism, agnosticism, skepticism, deism, rationalism, ethical culture, and liberal religion all claim to be heir to the humanist tradition."[11]

Isn't it interesting to note that the **same** person, Paul Kurtz, who edited the *Humanist Manifesto I and II* testified in an Alabama textbook hearing and said that humanism is "non-religious....It uses science, reason, and evidence to test theory"?[12] Of course, humanists believe that there are no absolutes and lying is okay. In fact, on "NBC's 'Today Show,' January 22, 1990, Dr. Michael Lewis of the New Jersey Robert Wood Johnson Medical School said, *'Lying is an important part of social life, and children who are unable to do it are children who may have developmental problems.'*"[13] [Emphasis in the original] You can tell Lewis doesn't believe the Bible for Revelation 21:8 tells us that **ALL** liars have their part in the lake of fire. Proverbs 12:22 states: "Lying lips are **abomination** to the Lord." (See also Proverbs 13:5 and Ephesians 4:25.)

Corliss Lamont, a humanist and signer of the *Humanist Manifesto II,* also reveals a little of the **RELIGIOUS** background behind the writing of this document. He remarks:

> "Approximately a hundred years after the founding of Unitarianism the more advanced members of this sect, most of them from the Middle West, started the movement known as **RELIGIOUS HUMANISM.** Dr. Curtis W. Reese, a Unitarian pastor, precipitated the discussions that led to **RELIGIOUS HUMANISM** by a challenging sermon at Des Moines in 1917 and an address at the Harvard Divinity School in 1920. Philosophers, teachers, writers, and clergymen quickly entered into the debate; and the result was the definite emergence of **HUMANISM IN RELI-GION,** eventually culminating in the *Humanist Manifesto* of 1933. This key document was initiated by three Unitarian **ministers:** L.M. Birkhead, Raymond B. Bragg, and Edwin

H. Wilson: and by two university teachers, Dr. A. Eustace Haydon, a professor of religion, and Dr. Roy Wood Sellars, a professor of philosophy. Dr. Sellars drew up the *Manifesto's* first draft, which served as the essential frame and basis for the final formulations....

"A large proportion of the Unitarian churches in the United States are acknowledgedly Humanist."[14]

Just in 1990, the American Humanist Association (AHA) held their annual meeting which was covered in the **"RELIGION"** section of the *St. Petersburg Times.*[15] As Dr. Dennis Cuddy writes:

"...the evidence that humanism constitutes a religion is, in fact, overwhelming. *Webster's New International Dictionary* has defined it as a 'contemporary cult or belief calling itself religious but substitutes faith in man for faith in God.'

"The AHA is described in the *Encyclopedia of American Religions* and former AHA president Lloyd Morain and his wife Mary (who was the director of the International Humanist and Ethical Union which has 4 million members) wrote a book titled *Humanism as the Next Step,* which declared that **'HUMANISM IS THE MOST RAPIDLY GROWING RELIGIOUS MOVEMENT IN AMERICA TODAY.'**

"The AHA also certifies counselors who have the legal status of ordained pastors, priests, and rabbis, and in at least the Supreme Court decision, secular humanism was listed as a non-theistic religion.

"Because humanism clearly constitutes a religion, the promotion of its values in our public schools is unconstitutional, and should therefore be prohibited."[16]

With churches like the Unitarian churches (and many, many others), we can see the prophecy of Amos 8:11 coming true: "Behold, the days come, saith the Lord God, that I will send a famine in the land, not a famine of bread, nor a thirst for water, but of hearing the words of the Lord." "For the pastors are become brutish, and have not sought the Lord: therefore they shall not prosper, and all their flocks shall be scattered" (Jeremiah 10:21). "Many pastors have destroyed My vineyard, they have trodden My portion under foot, they have made My pleasant portion a desolate wilderness" (Jeremiah 12:10). "Woe be unto the pastors that destroy and scatter the sheep of My pasture! saith the Lord" (Jeremiah 23:1).

Earlier we mentioned evolution as one of the items promoted by humanists. "Former Humanist of the Year Sir Julian Huxley said humanism's 'keynote, the central concept to which all its details are related, is evolution....'"[17] Of course, evolution is not the only thing that Humanists propagate. *Humanist Manifesto II* states:

> "*Sixth:* In the area of sexuality, we believe that intolerant attitudes, often cultivated by orthodox religions and puritanical cultures, unduly repress sexual conduct. The **RIGHT TO BIRTH CONTROL, ABORTION, AND DIVORCE SHOULD BE RECOGNIZED.** While we do not approve of exploitive, denigrating forms of sexual expression, neither do we wish to prohibit it, by law or social sanction, sexual behavior between consenting adults. The many varieties of sexual exploration should not in themselves be considered 'evil.' [This would include bisexuality, homosexual, bestiality, etc.] Without countenancing mindless permissiveness or unbridled promiscuity, a civilized society should be a *tolerant* one. Short of harming others or compelling them to do likewise, individuals should be permitted to express their sexual proclivities and pursue their life-styles as they desire."[18] [Italics in the original; Caps and boldface added.]

> "*Twelfth:* We deplore the division of humankind on nationalistic grounds. We have reached a turning point in human history where the best option is to *transcend the limits of national sovereignty* and to move toward the building of a world community in which all sectors of the human family

can participate. Thus we look to the development of a system of world law and a world order based upon transnational federal government. This would appreciate cultural pluralism and diversity."[19] [Emphasis in the original]

"Hence extreme disproportions in wealth, income, and economic growth should be reduced [redistribution is being advocated] on a worldwide basis."[20]

"At the present juncture of history, commitment to all humankind is the highest commitment of which we are capable; it transcends the narrow allegiances of church, state, party, class, or race in moving toward a wider vision of human potentiality. What more daring a goal for humankind than for each person to become, in ideal as well as practice, a citizen of a **WORLD COMMUNITY.** It is a classical vision; we can now give it new vitality. Humanism thus interpreted is a moral force that has time on its side. We believe that humankind has the potential intelligence, good will, and cooperative skill to implement this commitment in the decades ahead."[21]

"We believe in equal rights for both women and men to fulfill their unique careers and potentialities as they see fit, free of invidious discrimination."[22]

"In *Humanist Magazine* (November/December 1980) author Riane Eisler, author of *The Equal Rights Handbook,* says: 'It is absurd to say...that one is a humanist but not a feminist...feminism is the last evolutionary development of humanism, Feminism is humanism on its most advanced level.'"[23]

Not only is feminism humanism, so is Marxism. *"Karl Marx's own definition of Humanism reads: 'Humanism is the denial of God, and the total affirmation of man....Humanism is really nothing else but Marxism.'"*[24] [Emphasis in the original] He also said: "Communism begins from the outset with atheism...Communism, as fully developed naturalism, equals humanism."[25] Another

Communist, Leonid Brezhnev, stated: "Soviet society today is the real embodiment of the ideas of proletarian, socialist humanism."[26]

Brezhnev

Humanism, then, is really based on Feminism, Evolution, Atheism, and Communism.[27]

It is also quite obvious that Humanism certainly has infiltrated the classroom with its philosophy.

"John Dewey, the father of modern American education, signed the first *Humanist Manifesto,* as did C.F. Potter, who wrote in *Humanism, A New Religion* that 'education is thus a most powerful ally of humanism and every American public school is a school of humanism. What can the theistic Sunday schools...do to stem the tide of a five-day program of humanistic teaching?'"[28]

Dewey commented: "There is no God and no soul. Hence, there are no needs for the props of traditional religion. With dogma and creed excluded then immutable truth is also dead and buried. There is no room for fixed, natural law or permanent absolutes."[29]

Dewey, sad to say, was the leading educator named during 1924-1974 in the 1974 issue of *Saturday Review.* One individual who was polled remarked: "No individual has influenced the thinking of American educators more."[30]

Once again showing a connection to **RELIGIOUS HUMAN-ISM** and education, was an essay written by John Dunphy which won third place and was printed in the January/February 1983 issue of *The Humanist* (which is the mouthpiece for the American Humanist Association). The essay was entitled "A Religion for the New Age" and said:

"I am convinced that the battle for humankind's future must be waged and won in the public school classroom by teachers who correctly perceive their role as the proselytizers of a new faith: a religion of humanity that recognizes and respects the spark of what theologians call divinity in every human being. These teachers must embody the same selfless dedication as the most rabid fundamentalist preachers, for they will be ministers of another sort, utilizing a classroom instead of a pulpit to convey humanist values in whatever subject they teach, regardless of the educational level—preschool, day care or large state university. The classroom must and will become an arena of conflict between the old and the new—the rotting corpse of Christianity, together with all its adjacent evils and misery, and the new faith of humanism, resplendent in its promise of a world in which the never-realized Christian ideal of "love thy neighbor" will finally be achieved.

"...It will undoubtedly be a long, arduous, painful struggle replete with much sorrow and many tears, but humanism will emerge triumphant. It must if the family of humankind is to survive."[31] [Emphasis in the original]

Another humanist, Paul Blanshard, commented in *The Humanist:*

"I think the most important factor leading us to a secular society has been the educational factor. Our schools may not teach Johnny to read properly, but the fact that Johnny is in school until he is 16 tends to lead toward the elimination of religious superstition. The average child now acquires a high school education, and this militates against Adam and Eve and all other myths of alleged history."[32]

J. J. Blackham, the founder of the International Humanist and Ethical Union (IHEU) wrote in *The Humanist* that if schools would teach dependence on one's self, "they are more revolutionary than any conspiracy to overthrow the government."[33]

This is why the symbol of the humanist is the "Happy Man." Man is supposedly sufficient in and of himself. There is no God in humanist theology. As humanist Corliss Lamont states:

> "In the Humanist ethics the chief end of thought and action is to further this-earthly human interests in behalf of the greater glory of man. The watchword of Humanism is happiness for all humanity in this existence as contrasted with salvation for the individual soul in a future existence and the glorification of a supernatural Supreme Being."[34]

> "For his great achievements man, utilizing the resources and the laws of Nature, yet without Divine aid, can take full credit. Similarly, for his shortcomings he must take full responsibility. **HUMANISM ASSIGNS TO MAN NOTHING LESS THAN THE TASK OF BEING HIS OWN SAVIOUR AND REDEEMER.**"[35]

> "By laying stress on the beauty of Nature, Humanism becomes able to make one of the most powerful and persuasive of all affirmations....There is no heavenly Father in or behind Nature...."[36]

Humanism, then, simply is a religion of **SELF**. Man is the redeemer, man is the creator, man is all there is and all that really counts. The Bible tells us that the emphasis on self would take place in the last days. Paul wrote: "This know also, that in the last days perilous times shall come, FOR MEN SHALL BE LOVERS OF THEIR **OWN SELVES**" (II Tim. 3:1-2a). Christ came to redeem mankind from their selfish ways and desires. Isaiah 53:6 clearly says: "All we like sheep have gone astray. **WE HAVE TURNED EVERYONE TO HIS OWN WAY** and the Lord hath laid on Him the iniquity of us all."

As mentioned at the beginning of this chapter, the "Happy Man" is the most universal humanist symbol. I found it quite fascinating that the June 1998 issue of *The Emergence* (which is the newsletter put out by Benjamin Creme who is supposed to be the forerunner of the Maitreya) claimed: "Maitreya actually means **'The Happy One'**—the one who brings happiness to the world."[37] Seeing that humanism is a religion for the New Age and that Maitreya is the New Age "Christ," I think the correlation is noteworthy. Another New Age organization is the 3HO which stands for "Healthy, **Happy,** Holy."[38]

In *The Mystical Maze* we find this about the 3HO:

"A *kundalini* yoga sect founded by yogi Bhajan. This sect is based on *sikhism,* a mixture of Hinduism and Islam, and teaches both monotheism and reincarnation. Enlightenment is achieved within this cult through the awakening of the *kundalini* or 'serpent power' located at the base of the spine. Through various yoga techniques this mystic power coils its way up the spine eventually uniting with the mind to produce a state of altered consciousness or enlightenment."[39] [Emphasis in the original]

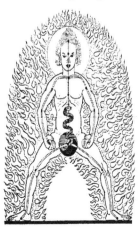

A brochure received directly from the 3HO mentions about the Summer Solstice they held in June 1987. It was on "White Tantric [sex] Meditation with Yogi Bhajan." They brag:

"It is said that only a few in any generation are fortunate enough to instruct their souls under the guidance of a master. Yogi Bhajan, master of Kundalini Yoga and White Tantric Yoga, has dedicated his life to helping people to see beyond their limitations and find their own creative potential. Daily meditations directed by Yogi Bhajan are the heart of the Summer Solstice experience. **White Tantric Meditation is a powerful means of establishing faith in the SELF,** trust in others and balance in personal relationships."[40]

Also during this "Summer Solstice" there were "classes in **KUNDALINI YOGA,** marriage and relationships, business and personal success, **NUMEROLOGY,** herbology, and the healing arts."[41] The 3HO "operates the Kundalini Research Institute, publishes the *Journal of Science and Consciousness for Living in the Aquarian Age,* and is listed in *The First Report and Directory NETWORKING.* "[42] According to the *Encyclopedia of Associations* (1998), there are 265,000 members in this organization and 108 centers in the U.S., Canada, and elsewhere.[43]

"Yogi Bhajan is the founder of the Sikh Dharma and its better known educational arm, the 3HO organization (Healthy, Happy, Holy Organization). Bhajan's full formal name is Siri Singh Sahib Harbhajan Singh Khalsa Yogi. Siri Singh Sahib is a title conferred on him by the center of Sikh religious authority in Amritsar. He was born Harbhajan Singh in Kot Harkan, Tehsil Wazirabad, India (now Pakistan) on August 29, 1929. Khalsa is an adopted last name that replaces the family name with which he was born. His family name indicates the subcaste of his family in the Hindu caste system, and Sikhism generally opposes that system....

"Bhajan worked as a customs official and Interpol officer from 1954 to 1969, when he came to the United States and founded the 3HO Foundation (1620 Preuss Rd., Los Angeles, CA 90035), which he has continued to direct. Under his leadership, the 3HO Foundation acts as a teaching and outreach organization which combines traditional Sikhism and yoga....

"Bhajan has been co-president of the World Parliament of Religions; cochairperson (sic) of the World Fellowship of Religions; director of the Unity of Man Conference; a member of the Interreligious Council of Southern California; and a member of the board of directors of the American Council of Executives in Religion....

"The core of Bhajan's teaching is a synthesis of Sikhism and a type of Kundalini yoga that he assembled from information gathered from many different teachers and practitioners in India and Pakistan."[44]

Yogi Bhajan even has live classes of Kundalini Yoga and Meditation on the Internet.[45] He states:

*"By better understanding the **SELF** and its mysteries, we gain tolerance and compassion for others. It is in this relaxed state that we can express our infinite potential for love, creativity, and freedom. It is here that we can begin to experience the oneness of all things and the love inherent in all creation."*[46] [Emphasis in the original; Caps and boldface added.]

Once again we can see the focus on **SELF**. Also, in the June 1998 issue of *Imprimis* we find that even art puts an emphasis on the human being. The article explains:

"From earliest times, the human figure has symbolized the unknown forces that govern the universe. It has also served as the vehicle for those powers mankind ardently reveres. In one form or another, it has been at the center of ritual throughout the world since prehistoric times, and it has been the medium through which the human and the divine communicated.

"The human figure embodies the universe of human existence and experience. It personifies all that is human and is, therefore, the one form in art with which we totally, uniquely, and immediately identify. That empathy derives from the fact that the figure is the complete expression of the beauty, mystery, and dignity of the human person, the quintessential form of life....

"The ancient Greeks were the first to establish standards of beauty for the human figure based on the perfection of physical development. They recognized that the body's design is a perpetual marvel of proportion, flesh, and organization....

"...the human figure has been the central theme in art and people's yearning for immortality its underlying principle."[47]

Yes, the Greeks did prize the human body—but they drew and sculpted their human figures in the nude.[48] In fact, says Terence D. McLean (in reference to the Greek Olympics), "...once in the stadium, everyone was required to be naked."[49]

"Olympic athletes served as models for those workmen who were fashioning idol Greek gods and goddesses for the people to worship! Thus, the gods and goddesses were endowed with spectacular physical gifts that resembled those of the Olympic athletes. And the legends built to support these idols were that the Greek gods were almost always immoral and promiscuous."[50]

Of course, this immoral behavior is fully condoned (and even sometimes supported and promoted) by the humanists. Remember (as mentioned earlier) that the *Humanist Manifesto II* says:

"While we do not approve of exploitive, denigrating forms of sexual expression, neither do we wish to prohibit it, by law or social sanction, sexual behavior between consenting adults. The many varieties of sexual exploration should not in themselves be considered 'evil.'...a civilized society should be a *tolerant* one. Short of harming others or compelling them to do likewise, individuals should be permitted to express their sexual proclivities and pursue their life-styles as they desire."[51] [Italics in the original]

A lot of this sexual tolerance (or a better word would be promiscuity) is also being taught in our schools. Remember, as was mentioned in the chapter on the yin/yang, that the Sex Information and Education Council of the United States (SIECUS) stated that contraceptive services should be available to minors. They added: "It is the position of SIECUS that the use of explicit sexual materials (sometimes referred to as **pornography**) can serve a variety of important needs in the lives of countless individuals...."[52] Again, the Bible warns about this in Jude 1:17b-19: "[T]he apostles of our Lord Jesus Christ...told you there should be mockers in the last time, who should walk after their own lusts. These be they who separate themselves, **SENSUAL,** having not the Spirit."

"In 1933, the Humanist Manifesto declared that 'social hygiene' (sex education) would be one of the paths of Humanism for the future. In 1961, Elysium, Inc. was incorporated to purvey **pornography** which would lead to the formation of SIECUS 'to solve the problem of pornography' by sex education in schools."[53]

A 1969 *Ankh* magazine says this about the Elysium Institute:

"The **ELYSIUM INSTITUTE** is a non-profit organization whose purpose is research and dissemination of information in the behavioral sciences relating to nudity and the 'body taboo' neuroses so prevalent in our culture. The Elysium Institute promotes self-acceptance and acceptance of others through a wholesome attitude towards the human body and its functions, both physical and emotional, and including man's sexuality."[54] [Emphasis in the original]

The "Elysium Credo" states (in part):

"We will implement this credo by aiding as many people as possible through sensitivity-awareness and psychotherapy programs, and through the experience of recreational activities in which nudity is enjoyed on a clothing-optional basis....

"Here, people experience benefits of unencumbrance from clothing in an appropriate setting....The casual acceptance of the naked self brings with it emotional freedom unknown to those uninitiated to social nudism. Benefits of freedom from clothing are enormous for children....A minister who recently visited Elysium Field remarked that, without effort on anyone's part, these children were getting the most wholesome sex education he could imagine."[55]

The SIECUS Circle informs us:

"SIECUS itself, in fact, maintains close liaison with the pornography cartel through its connection with Elysium Institute, located in Los Angeles. This hedonistic haven prides itself on the programs of nudism, sensitivity awareness, and group sex activities which it offers to its patrons. SIECUS is listed in the Elysium Institute Directory as pursuing the same objective as, and maintaining an exchange of information with, Elysium, as are also the Sexual Freedom League (of Berkeley); Castalia (Timothy Leary's "League for Spiritual Discovery"); the Institute for the Study of Non-Violence (whose co-director is Humanist Joan Baez); the Institute for Rational Living (headed by Humanist Albert Ellis); the University of Humanism; and the Underground Press (dedicated to the promotion of drug usage, sex, sensitivity training, and obscenity).

"The published aims of SIECUS and Elysium, which are amazingly similar in phraseology, have been compared on a point-by-point basis in a special newsletter published by a group of physicians opposed to SIECUS-style sex education. Particularly striking is the fact that Elysium Institute's publishing arm, Elysium, Inc., also prints *Nude Living, ANKH, Jay Bird,* and *Sun West*—magazines that feature totally unretouched male and female nudes in a variety of lewd and suggestive poses. The physicians' newsletter further discloses that, while Elysium, Inc., is entrenched in the field of pornography, it nevertheless wishes to retain some semblance of respectability, and thus assumes the fictitious name of "PANU-CO" when advertising certain obscene publications in its magazines."[56]

A few other names listed in the Elysium Institute Directory include: "the American Humanist Association; Esalen Institute; Kairos; the Sexual Freedom League;...Glide Urban Center; the Neo-American Church; and the Society For Human Abortion—to name just a few!"[57]

It is interesting to notice that both SIECUS and Elysium use the yin/yang as their logo. In fact, a magazine published by Elysium entitled *Nude Living* showed a yin/yang logo on the back cover of their magazine in order to advertise *Nude Living* and *Sundial*.[58]

Another logo that Elysium uses is the ankh.[59] The ankh is described elsewhere in my book.

I find it fascinating that "Elysium" was a term in mythology. It was supposed to be the sacred abode of the deities.[60] Elysium was also an "abode of **happiness.**"[61] (Remember the "Happy Man" symbol of the humanists?) Elysium was "opened to the favourites of the Olympians and the souls of the just."[62] (Remember the nudity of the Olympians?) Are all these items just "coincidental"?

There's one other fascinating bit of information about Elysium. The *Treasury of Witchcraft* says that "Elysium" was a name "Invoked in Roman Necromancy"![63] Necromancy, by the way, is communication with the dead.

Returning to the "Happy Man" symbol, observe the logo of the Communities in Schools of North Carolina. Doesn't it look like a variation of the "Happy Man"? Remember that our schools are filled with humanistic teachings, so this could be a very applicable logo.

Notice also the logo for *Holistic Education Review.* Their magazine states:

"**Holistic Education Review** aims to stimulate discussion and application of all **PERSON-CENTERED** educational ideas and methods. Articles explore how education can encourage the fullest possible development of **HUMAN POTENTIALS and PLANETARY CONSCIOUSNESS.** We believe that **HUMAN FULFILLMENT,** global cooperation and ecological responsibility should be the primary goals of education, and we will inquire into the historical, social, and philosophical issues that have prevented them from so becoming."[64]

The Holistic Health Association of the Princeton Area appears to use a "Happy Man" variation. This isn't surprising since they state that they integrate the best approaches from **HUMAN POTENTIAL therapies, HUMANISTIC psychology, parapsychology, meditation, visualization, biofeedback, psychotherapy, HUMANISTIC gerontology,** etc.[65]

The Society for Individual Liberty, a Libertarian group, also seems to utilize the "Happy Man."

Even the Youth for Christ group incorporates a design similar to the "Happy Man" in their logo. Is this just coincidental? After all, Dr. Siang-Yang Tan of Youth for Christ International was installed as a Professor of **PSYCHOLOGY** on April 28, 1998.[66] He "will this year be the President of Division 36 (Psychology of Religion) in the world famous American Psychological Association."[67]

Minirth/Meier New Life Clinics are steeped in psychology, so I guess it's not surprising to see that they also use a "Happy Man" variation.[68]

Sponsored by: NEW LIFE

1-800-NEW-LIFE

Additionally, the Payap University has an interesting logo. There is a 666 variation but if you carefully notice the center of this design, there appears to be a "Happy Man."

Below are a few more symbols used by humanists.

"Used by The American Humanist Association and The Fellowship of Religious Humanists, these circles were inspired by Edwin Markham's praise of tolerance: *He drew a circle that shut me out/Heretic, rebel, a thing to flout/But love and I had the wit to win/We drew a circle that took him in.*"[69] [Emphasis in the original]

"The overlapping circles symbolize the merger of Unitarians and Universalists; the lamp, knowledge and the appeal to reason. Used originally by the Unitarian Universalist Service Committee, it has been adopted widely by liberal churches."[70]

"A conventionalization of the universal man of Leonardo da Vinci; until recently used on the cover of *International Humanism*, this symbol has more recently been used by The American Ethical Union."[71]

"I.H.E.U. is the International Humanist and Ethical Union organized in Amsterdam in 1952 with 38 Humanist organizations from 23 countries related to it in 1970."[72]

"Among humanists the peace symbol symbolizes the global hope for a shared world at peace where all men may realize security, brotherhood and creativity."[73] This symbol is covered more thoroughly in the chapter on "Hand Signals."

Below are a few other possible representations of the "Happy Man" symbol.

Cocle
Good Luck Lady

A truly happy person is one who delights himself or herself in the Lord. Psalm 37:4-5 says: "Delight thyself also in the Lord; and He shall give thee the desires of thine heart. Commit thy way unto the Lord; trust also in Him; and He shall bring it to pass."

11. ANIMALS, BIRDS, AND INSECTS

Many animals are used to portray certain meanings. Obviously, not every animal you see has an occultic meaning connected to it. However, the occult world does make use of particular creatures and when they do so, there is a meaning behind it. For instance, let's look at the dolphins. *The Seeker's Handbook* states: "Dolphin stories are a part of planetary folklore."[1]

The dolphin was one of the emblems of the goddesses Ceres[2] and Demeter[3] and one of the favorite animals of the god Dionysus.[4] Melcarth, the god of the sea, is represented as riding on a dolphin.[5] Occasionally the god Apollo would assume the form of a dolphin.[6] Neptune is often portrayed seated in a chariot drawn by dolphins.[7] Eros (or Cupid) was "the boy on the dolphin."[8] The Nereids were fifty nymphs who rode on dolphins and bore tridents.[9] The *Handbook of Ornament* adds: "In symbolic representations he [the dolphin] is the companion of Nymphs, Nereids, and Tritons, and of Arion, Aphrodite, and Neptune, with whose trident he is often combined in ornament."[10] Below are some dolphins. Notice the trident variations on the crown and the tails.

Earlier we covered the Goat of Mendes (a portrayal of Satan). His consort was a dolphin goddess.[11]

A Dictionary of Symbols explains:

"**Dolphin** The figure of the dolphin can be seen in many allegories and emblems, sometimes duplicated....But the inverted arrangement, that is, with one dolphin pointing upwards and the other downwards, always symbolizes the dual cosmic streams of involution and evolution; this is what the 17th-century Spanish writer Saavedra Fajardo meant by 'Either up or down.' **The dolphin by itself is an allegory of salvation,** inspired in the ancient legends which show it as the friend of man. **Its figure is associated with** that of the anchor (another symbol of salvation), with **pagan, erotic deities** and with other symbols. The ancients also held that the dolphin was the swiftest of marine animals, and hence, when, among the emblems of Francesco Colonna, it is shown twined round an anchor, it comes to signify arrested speed, that is, prudence."[12]

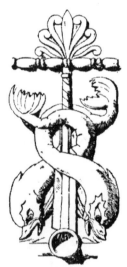

The renewed interest in dolphins took place in 1959 when psychologist John Lilly started doing dolphin research. He was convinced that dolphins were advanced spiritual beings. Many New Agers also feel that dolphins can be communicated with telepathically.[13] "In a 1987 interview Lilly said telepathy is, at least theoretically, the most effective way for human beings and dolphins to communicate...."[14]

Richard O'Barry trained dolphins for the television show *Flipper.* He said:

> "I worked with dolphins for seven or eight years. We had five of them on the *Flipper* show, and we did 120 half-hour TV shows and two features in three years. The few dolphins we had were asked to do so much, so many different tricks, that we were teaching them on the spot. At the end, I realized it was *all* psychic! No words were used; they just seemed to sort of understand, anticipate what you wanted them to do, and do it.... If you want to call it telepathy or whatever, it was very much a part of what was going on."[15] [Emphasis in the original]

Many groups have sprung up that offer workshops where one can swim with the dolphins, etc.[16] The Dolphin Data Base has a list of 3,000 organizations and people who are involved in dolphin projects with at least 300 of them attempting to make inter-species communication.[17] One group, the Dolphin Society Church:

> "trains persons in out-of-body traveling with dolphin and whale spiritual liberators. Through the practice, the Society's advertising claims, 'one can make friends, **spirit helpers** and lovers in the sea, visit alien star systems, learn healing, **levitation, teleportation** and shapeshifting.'"[18]

The *New Age Almanac* says:

"New Age fascination with dolphins stems from a romantic nature mysticism which is expressed in New Agers' concern with ecology and animal rights. Unlike benevolent alien visitors or wise Ascended Masters, whose existence is not supported by an abundance of evidence, there is no doubt dolphins do exist. Nor is their intelligence in doubt, although scientists concede the reach or limitations of their intelligence are unknown. For all of these reasons, dolphins continue to be a source of speculation and fascination for the New Age community."[19]

The dolphin was even incorporated into children's education in the classroom. A self-esteem program, Developing Understanding of Self and Others (DUSO), has a series of 42 guided imagery lessons. When the children relax and close their eyes, they are to imagine that they are journeying to faraway places. There they meet animals such as DUSO the dolphin.[20]

Another animal that became popular in the past decade was the goose. *The Continuum Encyclopedia of Symbols* claims:

"In Egyptian mythology, the goose plays an important role as the primeval goose that either laid the world egg or—according to different versions—was born from it. In Egypt, as in China, wild geese were also regarded as mediaries between heaven...and EARTH.—In Greece, the goose was sacred to Aphrodite and, in Rome, was sacred to Juno; it was regarded as a symbol of love, fertility, and maritial (sic) fidelity, yet also of vigilance....For the Celts, the goose was symbolically closely related to the SWAN and, like the swan, was thought to be a messenger from the spiritual world."[21] [Emphasis in the original]

The goose was sacred to the Goddess.[22] The Egyptian god Seb (also Geb or Keb) was called the "great cackler" and "the goose that laid the cosmic egg." He is sometimes depicted with a goose on his head and he sometimes takes on the form of a goose.[23] He is the God of the Earth but he also has authority in the Underworld.[24]

The cosmic egg (or world egg) is encountered in many cultures. It is "a symbol of the totality of creative forces—is thought to have been present at the primeval beginning, when it floated on the primeval waters and issued from itself the entire world and the elements, or initially at least heaven and earth."[25] It is also a symbol of perfection.[26] "In alchemy, the philosophical egg played an important role as a symbol of PRIMA MATERIA, from which the philosophical fire hatched the PHILOSOPHERS' Stone."[27]

[Emphasis in the original] Below is a picture of the world egg (portraying Providence) with a snake (representing time) entwined about it. Pike says: "The Serpent entwined round an Egg, was a symbol common to the Indians, the Egyptians, and the Druids. It referred to the creation of the Universe."[28] Also, below, is a drawing of Mercury in a philosophical egg.

Returning to the symbolism of the goose, we find in *Treasury of Witchcraft* that the goose was linked to the Indian god Brahma.[29] It is also an emblem of Horus, Osiris, and Isis, and associated with Mars, Priapus (a fertility god), and the goddess Bau.[30]

In *The Pagan Festivals of Christmas and Easter* we learn about the "Christmas goose":

> "Other Christmas customs are the 'Christmas goose' (or its equivalent in various parts of the world), and 'Christmas cakes.' Both were used in the worship of the Babylonian 'messiah.' The goose was sacred in many ancient lands: Rome, Asia Minor, India, Chaldea. In Egypt, the goose was a symbol for a *child,* ready to *die!* In other words, a symbol of the pagan 'messiah,' ready to give his life (supposedly) for the world. Blasphemy! A satanic mockery of the truth."[31] [Emphasis in the original]

The quail is important in China. There it:

"is a symbol of spring because it is a migratory bird that returns in the spring. It is **closely associated with fire, light and thus with the Yang principle.** Its annual coming and going also made the quail a **symbol of the alternating influence of the opposing forces.**"[32]

The butterfly is also quite popular today. It is used in the 24° of Masonry on the cordon. *A Bridge to Light* states that the cordon "is a broad, watered scarlet ribbon worn from right to left. On the front is embroidered in gold, a **winged-globe** and under it a **scarab,** under which is a brilliant **butterfly; all are symbols of immortality.**"[33]

Along with the symbolism of immortality, the butterfly represents reincarnation,[34] rebirth, and resurrection.[35]

The Japanese use the butterfly as a symbol of womanhood but two butterflies depict marital happiness.[36]

"To the Aztecs the butterfly symbolized the soul or the breath of life exhaled by the dying. A butterfly fluttering among the flowers represented the soul of the warrior who had fallen on the battlefield....Dead warriors accompanied the Sun on the first half of his visible journey, until midday. They then descended to earth in the shapes of hummingbirds or butterflies....

"Thus the Aztec fire-god wore a pectoral ornament called 'the OBSIDIAN butterfly.' Like flint, obsidian is a fire-stone and its use for the blades of sacrificial knives is well known. In 'the House of Eagles' or Warriors' Temple, the Sun was depicted as a butterfly.

"Symbol of daylight and the solar fire—and hence of the warrior's SOUL—the butterfly for the Mexicans was also a symbol of the 'Black Sun' which passed through the Underworlds during its nightly journey. It was thus a symbol of hidden chthonian fire and associated with ideas of sacrifice, death and resurrection. In Aztec carving, the butterfly became an alternative for the hand as the emblem of the figure FIVE, the number of the centre of the Earth....

"Similarly contemporary psychoanalysis sees the butterfly as a symbol of rebirth.

"In Classical antiquity it was a common belief that the soul left the body in the shape of a butterfly. Psyche is depicted as a little girl with butterfly-wings...."[37] [Emphasis in the original]

Sherry Hansen Steiger, a New Ager who has an interest in UFOs, evidently knew the meaning associated with the butterfly. She named her organization the Butterfly Center for Transformation.[38]

The phoenix is also making a comeback in today's society. The printer who produced *What Witches Do* was called **Phoenix**

Publishing Company. A television serial was called "Phoenix" which gave "us an extraterrestrial **shaman** and 'messiah' upon whom the salvation of the world may depend. He is endowed with awesome **psychic** powers, not the least of which are **levitation, psychokinesis and acute ESP.**"[39] "Both King Henry VII and his granddaughter, Queen Elizabeth I (Queen of England, 1558-1603), used the 'phoenix' as one of their badges."[40]

The January 9, 1988 issue of *The Economist* said that a new currency was coming. Its name will be the **phoenix.**[41]

Mason and occultist, Manly Palmer Hall, wrote a book entitled *The Phoenix: An Illustrated Review of **Occultism** and Philosophy.* Elsewhere he relates:

"Among the ancients a fabulous bird called the Phoenix is described by early writers such as Clement, Herodotus, and Pliny; in size and shape it resembled the eagle, but with certain differences. The body of the Phoenix is one covered with glossy purple feathers, and the plumes in its tail are alternately blue and red. The head of the bird is light in color, and about its neck is a circlet of golden plumage. At the back of its back the Phoenix has a crest of feathers of brilliant color. Only one of these birds was supposed to live at a time, with its home in the distant parts of Arabia, in a nest of frankincense and myrrh. The Phoenix, it is said, lives for 500 years, and at its death its body opens and the new born Phoenix emerges. Because of this symbolism, the **Phoenix is generally regarded as representing immortality and resurrection.**

"All symbols have their origin in something tangible, and the **Phoenix is one sign of the secret orders** of the ancient world and of the initiate of those orders, for it was common to refer to one who had been accepted into the temples as a man twice-born, or re-born. Wisdom confers a new life, and those who become wise are born again.

"The Phoenix symbol is important in another way, as an emblem among nearly all civilized nations of royalty, power, superiority, and immortality. The Phoenix of China is identical in meaning with the Phoenix of Egypt; and the **Phoenix of the Greeks is the same as the Thunder Bird of the American Indians.**"[42]

In yet another book by Hall we find:

"Farther south the thunderbird symbol merged with the quetzal and the serpent feathered with quetzal plumes. The quetzal was identical in meaning with the phoenix of Asia, North Africa, and the Near East. The feathered-serpent symbolism can be traced back to the hooded Nagas, or serpent gods of India, and to the winged serpents which occur in the writings and sculpturings of the Egyptians."[43]

The phoenix is also "the ancient symbol of human aspiration toward Universal good."[44] Barbara Walker, a radical feminist, reveals that the Egyptians and Phoenicians believed that the phoenix was the representation of a god who *"rose to heaven in the form of a morning star, like Lucifer, after his fire-immolation of death and rebirth...."*[45]

One former witch explains:

"The Phoenix, or *Bennu* is believed to be a divine bird going back to Egypt....This Phoenix destroys itself in flames and then rises from the ashes. Most occultists believe that the Phoenix is a symbol of Lucifer who was cast down in flames and who (they *think)* will one day rise triumphant. This, of course, also relates to the raising of Hiram Abiff, the Masonic 'christ.'"[46] [Emphasis in the original]

With the continual rebirth of the phoenix, it became a symbol of reincarnation[47] and eternity.[48]

E. A. Wallis Budge writes: "The **Morning Star was** the ferryman of OSIRIS, or the Soul of OSIRIS, i.e. the Benu (sic) bird, which the GREEKS identified with **the Phoenix."**[49] [Caps in the original; Boldface added] The sun god, who supposedly created all the other gods, was also pictured in the form of a Phoenix.[50]

One of the symbols in the 32° degree of Masonry is a triangle on which a raven, a dove, and a phoenix are displayed.[51]

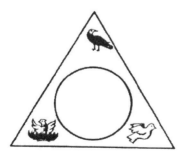

The eagle (also called the Bird of Jove)[52] is frequently identified with the phoenix.[53] As is well known, the eagle is used extensively in Masonry. In a Masonic Bible was the question: "What is the symbolism of the Eagle in

Freemasonry?" The answer given was: "The eagle has been a symbol among the different peoples of the world from time immemorial. In Egypt, Greece, and Persia **it was sacred to the sun;** among **pagans** it was the **emblem of Jupiter;** among the **Druids** it was the **symbol of their supreme god.**"[54]

This Masonic Bible also asked what an emblem was. The answer was: "An emblem is an **OCCULT** representation of an idea, principle, or truth which cannot be seen with the natural eye, but may be perceived by the mind and heart."[55]

The 15° in Masonry is called Knight of the Eagle and the 30° is called the Knight of the White and Black Eagle.[56] The white and black on the eagle symbolize the yin/yang.

An ad for a belt buckle said this: "The eagle is also one of the most ancient symbols of the **supernatural and the occult.** In Egypt and Greece it was sacred to the Sun; it was also the venerated bird of Zeus. For the learned Druids it was transcendent, their foremost divinity. The Roman Legions adopted it as a consecrated mascot."[57] By the way, the word mascot comes from a French word meaning witch!

The eagle was worshipped by the Greeks as the god of lightning.[58] "They nailed eagles to the peaks of temples to serve as magic lightning rods; these were the precursors of today's weathercocks seen atop many buildings."[59] In mysticism, the eagle represents initiation.[60] Masonic author, Rex Hutchens, relates: "Since the eagle also represented the great Egyptian Sun god Amun Ra, it is a symbol of the infinite Supreme Reason of Intelligence."[61]

Albert Pike reveals that the *"Eagle* was the living Symbol of Egyptian God *Mendes...*and the representative of the Sun...."[62] Remember the Satanic God of Mendes? Well, the eagle is **his** emblem. Hall remarks:

> "The eagle was also the Hermetic symbol of sulphur, and signified the mysterious fire of Scorpio—the most profoundly significant sign of the zodiac and the *Gate of the Great Mystery.* Being one of the three symbols of Scorpio, the **eagle, like the Goat of Mendes, was an emblem of the theurgic art [magic]** and the secret processes by which the infernal fire of the scorpion was transmuted into the spiritual *light-fire* of the gods."[63] [Italics in the original; Boldface added]

The eagle was Jupiter's bird.[64] Horus was an eagle.[65] "In Sarmatian art, the eagle is the emblem of the thunderbolt and of warlike endeavour."[66]

In the chapter on "Winged Symbols" we look at the symbolism of Saturn, an old man dying (the old year ending) and a baby bringing in the new year. This is related to the oroboros[67] (which will be covered soon) and in *The Mysteries of Osiris* we find that this symbolism is also connected to the eagle:

> "When they [the heathen] desired to express the renewal, or *beginning,* of the year, they represented it in the form of a door-keeper.

> "It could easily be distinguished by the attributes of a *key;* a procedure that was copied, without credit, in another *new age* or a new *year of an age,* in the symbolism of Peter and his 'key.' At times they gave it two heads back to back, the one an old man, which marked the expiring year, and the other a young man, which denoted the new. In time, this became the double-headed Eagle of Symbolic Masonry...."[68] [Emphasis in the original]

"Thus arises the two-headed eagle (related to the Janus symbol) which is usually depicted in two colours of great mystical significance: red and white."[69] *A Bridge to Light* adds: "The double headed Eagle is symbolic of the past and future for in this Apartment the candidate sacrifices his own personal ambitions and desires on the altar of Truth."[70]

In *Freemasonry: Ancient Egypt and the Islamic Destiny* we are told:

"It is also believed that the **double-headed eagle alludes to the nature of man.** The head that looks to the East is symbolic of man's spiritual vision, and the looking towards the West refers to his material vision.

"The **Masonic order attempts to initiate** or teach man the material or human science and the spiritual sciences **in imitation of the Ancient Egyptian Mystery Systems** that taught man the 'lesser' and 'greater' mysteries."[71]

James 1:8 says: "A **double minded man** is unstable in all his ways."

The July 1998 issue of *The Scottish Rite Journal* states that the eagle was also a symbol of regeneration and rebirth.[72] Another Masonic and occultic symbol of regeneration is the serpent.[73] *A Dictionary of Symbols* explains more about the snake:

"Snakes are guardians of the springs of life and of immortality, and also of those superior riches of the spirit that are symbolized by hidden treasure....

"...the serpent is the life-force which determines birth and rebirth and hence it is connected with the Wheel of Life...."

"The snake was an important symbol for the Gnostics....Hippolytus...asserted that the snake was said to live in all objects and in all beings. This brings us to the Yoga concept of the Kundalini or the snake as an image of inner strength. Kundalini is represented symbolically as a snake coiled up upon itself in the form of a ring *(kundala),* in that subtle part of the organism corresponding to the lower extremity of the spinal column; this, at any rate, is the case with the ordinary man. But, as a result of exercises directed towards his spiritualization—Hatha Yoga, for instance—the snake uncoils and stretches up through wheels *(chakras)* corresponding to the various plexuses of the body until it reaches the area of the forehead corresponding to the third eye of Shiva. It is then, according to Hindu belief, that man recovers his sense of the eternal."[74] [Emphasis in the original]

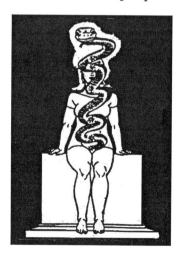

The word "chakras" was just mentioned.

"In the Hindu/yoga world of 'reality,' they believe, as do much of the occult and New Age meditators, that the body contains seven basic energy centers, known as chakras. When these centers are properly aligned by practicing **yoga and meditation,** there will then occur a 'merging' of the spinal chakra (the serpent of Kundalini) together with Shiva, located in the frontal chakra **(psychic third eye)** and this 'spiritual union' is believed to **increase extrasensory and psychic powers."**[75]

Representation of the seven chakras

In *The Gods of India* we are told:

"Siva carries a snake around his neck. Snakes always surround his image, and a snake is coiled around his phallus (*linga*)....

"But the main meaning attached to the serpent is to represent the basic dormant energy, akin to the sexual power, which is coiled at the base of the spinal cord and which is the support of the yogi in his attempt to conquer the higher worlds during his inward journey. The energy, source of all spiritual conquests, is called Kundalini (the coiled), the serpent power."[76]

The Seeker's Handbook mentions that the serpent is also a symbol of infinity.[77] The symbol for infinity is the lazy eight which is covered elsewhere in this book.

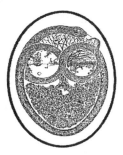

"The Druids had a high veneration for the Serpent. Their great god Hu was typified by that reptile; and he is represented by the Bards as 'the wonderful chief *Dragon, the sovereign of heaven.*"[78]

Like the eagle, the snake is also a symbol of the sun.[79] Additionally, it denoted fertility.[80] "The tree of life with the serpent entwined around it is also seen, and this symbol also represents the solar and generative processes."[81]

"In representing the ancient Babylonian Nergal, Lord of the Underworld, the phallus and the serpent were identical. In New Guinea, where tradition connects woman and the serpent sexually, the female idols are invaginated by serpent-like creatures."[82]

"The union of the female with the male triad, was designated by the sacred mystic number 4, often symbolized by a serpent with its tail in its mouth; two fishes bent to form a circle [yin/yang], and many other figures."[83]

A snake with its tail in its mouth is called an oroboros (also spelled uroboros). Another form of the oroboros is a dragon with its tail in its mouth.

"In alchemy a dragon, or more often a serpent, eating its own tail is known as the uroboros. The dragon was a symbol of the god Mercury and the circle a powerful symbol of the eternal cycle of nature. Because the uroboros recreates itself by feeding on its own body, it is a symbol of transforming matter, i.e. alchemy itself."[84]

URÓBOROS

In this form the snake represents "the endless succession of incarnations which form the wheel of life."[85] In other words, the oroboros is an emblem of reincarnation. It is also a symbol of eternity.[86] In fact, we are told that the oroboros *actually signifies the beginning and the end of life; the Alpha and Omega.* [87] [Emphasis in the original] Of course, this is blasphemous. The Bible clearly tells us that Jesus Christ is the Alpha and Omega. Revelation 22:13 states: "I am Alpha and Omega, the beginning and the end, the first and the last." (See also Revelation 1:8, 11; and 21:6.)

The Alpha and Omega is used in Masonry, but now we can see that it is in reference to the snake, and not Jesus Christ, when these symbols are used.

As Masonic author, George Oliver, states: "The Serpent is universally esteemed a legitimate symbol of Freemasonry."[88] Occultist and Mason, Manly Palmer Hall, brags that "the **serpent is the symbol and prototype of the Universal Savior,** *who redeems the worlds by giving creation the knowledge of itself and the realization of good and evil.* "[89]

Masonic apron

Do you realize what Hall just admitted? When God placed Adam and Eve in the garden, He said: "Of every tree of the garden thou mayest freely eat: **But of the tree of the knowledge of good and evil, thou shalt not eat of it:** for in the day that thou eatest thereof thou shalt surely die" (Genesis 2:16-17). Of course, **SATAN** came along and asked: "Yea, hath God said, Ye shall not eat of every tree of the garden?" (Genesis 3:1) Eve responded that they could eat of every tree **except** the tree of the knowledge of good and evil because they would die if they did so. Satan (the **serpent**) brazenly remarked: "Ye shall not surely die: For God doth know that in the day ye eat thereof, then your eyes shall be opened, and ye shall be as gods, **knowing good and evil**" (Genesis 3:4-5). Satan, THROUGH ENTICEMENT AND LIES, had just deceived the first man and woman by promising them godhood! He told Eve that she would know both good and evil. Satan's offer to know BOTH good and evil presented an option that was previously unknown to her. She had never known evil and, therefore, the lure of learning about something new and different must have intrigued her. Up to this point she had only known good, truth, perfection, health, and beauty. Now, because of the attraction of the unknown offered through Satan's deception, she would learn of evil, death, sorrow, defilement, pain, and separation from God. The very moment Adam and Eve partook of the forbidden fruit they died spiritually and were driven from the beautiful garden of Eden. That very day they experienced death to innocence, death to perfection, death to the joys they had known, and eventually they experienced a physical death even passing this physical death on to **ALL** humankind for "in Adam all die" (I Corinthians 15:22).

Yet, Hall tells us that the one who gave the realization of good and evil (who was Satan) is the **"Universal Savior!"** According to Masonic writer, Lynn Perkins, the fall of mankind was something **GOOD.** It was not a "fall" but a betterment of our situation.[90] He boldly declares that man "**rose** to Divine Status by partaking of the **'fruit of the tree of knowledge of good and evil.'**"[91] [Emphasis in the original] He adds that the advice the serpent gave to Eve was "wiser than the recorded command of God that would have, if obeyed, confined Adam and Eve and their descendants to the status of animals forever...."[92]

Albert Pike, another occultist and Mason, brags that the oroboros *"is the body of the **Holy Spirit**, the universal Agent, the Serpent devouring his own tail...."* [93] [Italics in the original; Boldface added] What blasphemy!

The oroboros is also representative of the androgyne.

> "The serpent's head and neck is distinctly a masculine symbol, but the serpent is sometimes symbolized with its tail in it mouth, the body forming a circle which is feminine. Also, the mouth is feminine, while the tail, which is in the mouth, is masculine. Thus for two good reasons the serpent with its tail in its mouth represents both sexes."[94]

As stated earlier, the androgyne (meaning male and female in one body) was considered to be "the image of **human perfection and wholeness.**"[95]

Another creature with some snake-like features is a basilisk. It is a:

> "fabulous animal with a snake's body, pointed head and a three-pointed crest. In mediaeval descriptions it was said to be born of a yolkless egg laid by a cock and hatched by a toad on a bed of dung, and to have a three-pointed tail, glittering eyes and a crown on its head. Its glance was believed to be lethal, so that it could only be destroyed while its assailant was watching it in a mirror. This belief is related to the myth of the Gorgon's head. In the East, its body was supposed to be a mixture of cock, snake and toad. According to Diel, this projected image of the human psyche is clearly **infernal in character,** as is shown by its threefold attributes (its three-pointed crest and trifurcated tail) since they are an **inversion of the qualities of the Trinity;** and also by the

predominance of **evil components,** such as the toad and the snake. It is one of the many 'keepers of treasure' mentioned in legend."[96]

Another Masonic symbol is the bee and beehive. One source reveals:

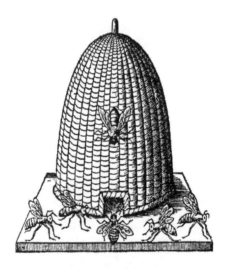

"The **bee is sacred to the goddess Venus** and is considered a sacred feminine symbol. According to mystics wheat, bananas, and bees are forms of life which came to the earth from the planet Venus millions of years ago....

"In Greece the bee was considered a priestly creature. The priestesses of Eleusis and Ephesus were called Melissae or 'bees,' probably with reference to the virginity of worker bees. They served at the greatest Greek festival in honor of **Demeter, the Queen Bee,** celebrating the return of Persephone from Hades for two-thirds of each year at which time the earth would bloom profusely with flowers—associating **bees with rebirth.** And because of their importance in pollenizing flowers, **bees are an accepted symbol of generative power.**

"The bee is also considered a symbol of the soul influenced by the Sun and possessing immortality and spiritual **telepathy."**[97]

One Masonic bulletin admits:

"The Egyptians always excellent and Antient Free-Masons **paid Divine Worship to a Bee under the outward Shape of a Bull, the better to** *conceal the mystery;* which Bull, by them called Apis, is the Latin word for a Bee; the Enigma of presenting the Bee by a Bull consisteth in this, that according to the doctrine of the Pythagorean Lodge of Freemasons, the souls of all the Cow-King transmigrate into Bees...."[98]

The Royal Masonic Cyclopaedia adds that the beehive is an:

"emblem of industry; appropriate to the third degree. This virtue is ever **held in high esteem in the Craft,** for the Old Charges tell us that 'all Masons shall work honestly on working days, that they may live creditably on holidays.' The **esoteric** meaning of the beehive was that of **regeneration**; and a hive was a type of the ark. 'Hence,' says Faber (*Orig. of Pag. Idol.*, vol. ii, p. 133), 'both the diluvian priestesses and the regenerated souls were called bees; hence bees were feigned to be produced from the carcase (sic) of a cow, which also symbolized the ark and, hence, as the **great father was esteemed an INFERNAL god**, honey was much used both in funeral rites and in the mysteries.'...Bees and lilies have many **esoteric** significations."[99]

In *The Masonic Report* the question is asked: "In what way does the bee figure into the **phallic** philosophy of Freemasonry?" The answer given is:

"In the fertilization of the queen bee, the drone is deprived of his organs of generation, and thus mutilated, is left to perish on the ground. The description applies with striking exactness to the death of Osiris who lost his generative power and to Hiram Abiff who supposedly lost the Master's word, which is actually a veiled symbol of his generative power. Thus we conclude that the emphasis laid upon the bee hive in the lecture is to be understood in the phallic sense."[100]

"'In India,' writes Manly P. Hall, 'the God Prana—the personification of the universal life force—is sometimes shown surrounded by a *circle* of bees. Because of its importance in pollinating flowers, the bee is the accepted symbol of the generating power.'"[101]

Masonic author, H. L. Haywood, informs us that "the Bee was made the emblem of heaven, as may be seen in certain old Hindoo (sic) pictures of the god Krishna wherein Bees hover over the deity's head...."[102] He adds: "Both the Persians and the Egyptians sometimes embalmed their dead in honey because they believed it to possess antiseptic properties; out of this custom, we may believe, arose the latter habit of using the Bee as a symbol of immortality."[103]

Rosicrucianism (which is closely related to Masonry) also used the symbol of the bee and the rose. In the picture on page 137, the "bees around the rose represent believers receiving divine nourishment."[104] (For more information on Rosicrucian symbolism, including the rose, see the chapter entitled "Organizational Logos.")

Psalms 119:103-104 tells us that the word of God surpasses honey: "How sweet are Thy words unto my taste! yea, **sweeter than honey** to my mouth! Through Thy precepts I get understanding: therefore **I hate every false way.**" Also, Psalms 19:9-10 says: "The fear of the Lord is clean, enduring for ever: the judgments of the Lord are true and righteous altogether. More to be desired are they than gold, yea, than much fine gold: **sweeter also than honey and the honeycomb.**"

Nimrod was represented as a lion with a bee in its mouth.[105] Nimrod, I'm sure you will recall, was Noah's great-grandson (Genesis 10:8-9) and was called "a mighty hunter before the Lord." The word "before" in the Hebrew has several meanings, but one meaning is "against." By reading the entire context, you will notice that this is the correct explanation for this word. You see, it was **NIMROD** who **BUILT THE TOWER OF BABEL IN DEFIANCE AND REBELLION AGAINST GOD** (Genesis 10:10; 11:2). Masons, however, are proud of this building for Arthur Edward Waite

brags: "As regards Masonry, **BABEL** of course **REPRESENTED A MASONIC ENTERPRISE....**"[106] John Yarker, another Masonic author, boasts: "It is well known that the **TOWER OF BABEL WAS ONE OF THE MOST ANCIENT TRADITIONS OF MASONRY....**"[107]

In the *Masonic Quiz Book,* the question is asked "Who was **NIMROD?**" The answer is: "He was the son of Cush. In the Old Constitutions referred to as **ONE OF THE FOUNDERS OF MASONRY,** and in the Scriptures as the architect of many cities."[108] In the York manuscript we find: "At the making of the Tower of Babel there was Masonry first much esteemed of, and...**NIMROD WAS A MASON** himself and loved well Masons."[109]

Interestingly, Masonic author, Kenneth R. H. MacKenzie, tells us that Hermes was also one of the founders of Masonry.[110] Remember occultist, New Ager, and Theosophist, Helena Petrovna Blavatsky, links Hermes and Satan together when she writes:

"**...Hermes,** the god of wisdom, called also Thoth, Tat, Seth, Set and *Sat-an;* and that he was, furthermore, when viewed under his bad aspect, Typhon, **the Egyptian Satan,** who was also *Set.* "[111] [Italics in the original; Boldface added]

Another representation of Thoth

The bee is also a regal symbol.[112] The Merovingians' main symbol was that of the bee.[113] The Mormon church also uses the bee as a symbol.[114] (For a thorough study of Mormonism, see my book *Mormonism, Masonry, and Godhood* [ISBN: 1-891117-01-7], which can be ordered through Sharing or any bookstore.)

A Masonic bulletin, *The Bee Hive* states that the Kings of France (who were Masons):

> "carried three Bees for their Arms, but to avoid the Imputation of the Egyptian Idolatry of **worshipping a Bee,** Clodovaeus, their first Christian King, **called them Lilies,** or Flower-de-Luces, in which, notwithstanding the small **Change made for Disguise Sake,** there is still the exact Figure of a Bee....You have perhaps read of a great Number of Golden Bees found in the Coffin of a Pagan King of France...which he had ordered should be buryed (sic) with him, in Token of his having been a Mason."[115]

Pope Urban VIII also had a seal that included bees. We are told:

> "This seal was used for **magical purposes** by Pope Urban VIII, a seventeenth century leader of the Catholic Church who wickedly became involved in **astrology and occult rituals.** The bee has long been the symbol of the harlot of Mystery Babylon, the religious system of the Antichrist to come (Rev. 17). A triangle of three bees represents the pagan unholy trinity (Lucifer, his queen and their son, the Antichrist)."[116]

Pope Urban's magical seal

The scarab is yet another sacred insect. Since the "scarab was thought to be able to renew itself...it became a symbol of **past and future lives.**"[117] This means that the scarab symbolizes

reincarnation. The Bible clearly teaches that there is no such thing as reincarnation. Hebrews 9:27 states: "It is appointed unto men **once to die,** but after this the judgment."

> "The scarab was, from very ancient times, and still is, sacred in Egypt; it was thought to be neither male nor female, but, instead, to contain within itself the power to create. It symbolized Khebera, the god of creation and resurrection, who was self-begotten."[118]

Another name for Khepri (also Khebera or Khepera) was Atum.[119] *Egyptian Mythology* explains more about this aspect:

> "Atum was 'He who created himself.' His next act was to create further gods. As he was alone in the world, he had to produce offspring without a mate. His means was union with his shadow, or masturbation....**Atum** seems often in the texts to be regarded as a **bisexual god** and was sometimes called the 'Great He-She.'"[120]

> "Thus, Khepri symbolized the resurrection of the body and rebirth [reincarnation] of the soul through transformation and renewal. It is for this reason that the Egyptian custom of wearing scarabs, as well as that of placing scarabs within the tombs and on the bodies of the dead, became so popular."[121]

"**Khepri** (or **Khepera**) signifies at the same time 'scarab' and 'he who becomes.' For the Heliopolitans he represented the rising sun which, like the scarab, emerges from its own substance and is reborn of itself. Khepri was the god of the transformations which life, for ever renewing itself, manifests. He is represented as a scarab-faced man or as a man whose head is surmounted by this insect. Sometimes he appears simply as a scarab."[122] [Emphasis in the original]

Anton LaVey, the founder of the Church of Satan, states:

"The Phoenicians worshipped a fly god, Baal, from which comes the devil, Beelzebub. **Both Baal and Beelzebub are identical to the dung beetle or scarabaeus** of the Egyptians which appeared to resurrect itself, much as the mythical bird, the phoenix, rose from its own ashes."[123]

Matthew 12:24 says that Beelzebub is the prince of the devils, so this is what the scarab is actually representing! (See also Luke 11:15 and Mark 3:22.)

The scarab is also a symbol of fertility and "one of the most ancient symbols of deity...."[124] Additionally, scarabs were used as powerful amulets for healing and magic.[125] In fact, one of the tools of the magician is listed as the scarab.[126]

Since Masonry is based mainly on Egyptian mythology, it is no surprise to find that the scarab is featured on the 25° Masonic apron along with the serpent with his tail in his mouth (the oroboros).[127]

We've already covered the goat somewhat in the chapter "The Pentagram." As mentioned, the goat is a representation of the devil.[128] Occultist Manly P. Hall declares: "The goat is both a **phallic symbol** and also an **emblem of courage or aspiration** because of its surefootedness and ability to scale the loftiest peaks. To the alchemists the goat's head was the symbol of sulphur."[129]

In Matthew 25 we find that Christ will separate the sheep from the goats:

"When the Son of man shall come in His glory, and all the holy angels with Him, then shall He sit upon the throne of His glory: And before Him shall be gathered all nations: and He shall separate them one from another, as a shepherd divideth his sheep from the goats: And He shall set the **sheep on His right hand, but the goats on the left.** Then shall the King say unto them on **His right hand, Come, ye blessed of My Father, inherit the kingdom prepared for you** from the foundation of the world....Then shall He say also unto them on the **left hand, Depart from Me, ye cursed, into everlasting fire, prepared for the devil and his angels:**...And these shall go away into everlasting punishment: but the righteous into life eternal" (Matthew 25:31-34, 41, 46).

Seeing that the occult world believes that the goat represents Satan, it is fascinating to see what the occultist, Alice Bailey, teaches about this passage of Scripture. She discloses:

"I would like to point out that the distinction between the 'sheep and the goats' is mainly hierarchical. The term **'goats' is esoterically applied to initiated disciples** and to those who have climbed the mountain of initiation. The term **'sheep' is applied to those who are following blindly** the inner urge of their souls and who are groping their way (in relatively large numbers) toward the Hierarchy. For them still has to come the great revelation that the 'kingdom of God is within you'. Such is the word for them at this stage in humanity's history."[130]

She also states (through her demonic spirit guide, Djwhal Khul):

"It has been thought that the sheep went to heaven and the goats went to hell. **It is the other way around.** The goat in Capricorn is the initiate and from a certain **esoteric** angle the **goats do go to heaven because they function in the spiritual kingdom....The sheep remain on earth...until they become goats....**"[131]

It's easy to see how the occult has turned everything around and distorted the truth of God's Word.

Below is a symbol for four stylized goats. The goats are symbols of Ea-Oannes who is Lord of the Waters.[132]

The unicorn is a mythological creature. In astrology, the unicorn represents the Moon and is also a symbol of rebirth (or reincarnation).[133]

The unicorn is yet another androgyne symbol. In China the unicorn is known as the k'i lin which means male-female.[134]

Al Dager explains:

"The androgynous unicorn has been merely a foreshadowing of the uni-sex mentality exhibited in modern art and music, as well as in the general acceptance of the homosexual and lesbian lifestyles.

"But more than this, the unicorn is considered by New Agers as the symbol of innocence and gentleness personified in the conquering child Horus. This Egyptian solar hero is said to conquer through gentility.

"According to New Age teaching, the world is about to enter into the second Golden Age, which should begin about the year 2000. The Golden Age—or New Age—is also known as the Age of Aquarius and the Eon of Horus, an era of peace and brotherly love.

"Thus we see that the unicorn is, in reality, the symbol of a future conqueror who will bring peace to the earth. Who is this but the anti-Christ (the little horn that rises in the midst of the ten horns in Daniels (sic) vision [Daniel 7:8- A.J.D.]) for whom the world waits, unaware of his true nature?...

"How many Christians will yield to the unicorn's beauty when it rears its head to pierce the last vestiges of God's order?"[135]

This is a good question, especially since we are told:

"In China, the Unicorn or Ki-Lin is said to appear intermittently on Earth and **his appearance signifies the dawning of a new age** of harmony and enlightenment. One appeared, it is said, at the birth of Confucius in 551 BC."[136]

"In both European and Oriental traditions, the **Unicorn is identified with a Messiah** who comes when the world is in danger, and **who heralds the coming of a new and better age.** As the alchemical symbol for the element Earth, he represents Earth consciousness and a reawakening of natural values."[137]

Symbol for Earth

Anyone who knows Bible prophecy can readily recognize that this "Messiah" is none other than the Antichrist.

The horn growing out of the unicorn's head represents the third eye or the all-seeing eye, which is covered elsewhere in this book.[138]

In *The Seeker's Handbook,* under "Unicorn," we find:

"In Celtic mythology and European folklore, a fabulous beast in the form of a horse, with a single spiraling horn growing from the center of its brow. In alchemy, a symbol of the complete mastery of **phallic sexuality** by ritual (nonorgasmic) intercourse, and its conversion into the forces of pure VISUALIZATION."[139]

In *The Lore of the Unicorn* we are told that the **unicorn was used as a talisman or a charm.**[140]

Several pagan and witchcraft groups have taken the name "Unicorn" for their organization or newsletter. Some of these names are: Unicorn Astrological Services,[141] The Unicorn Coven,[142] *The Unicorn Speaks, The Unicorn Newsletter,*[143] *The Quill and Unicorn,*[144] *Magical Unicorn Messenger,* and *The Littlest Unicorn.*[145]

It is also interesting to note that the Rothschilds have a unicorn on their coat-of-arms.[146]

12. WINGED SYMBOLS

The idea of wings is very important in mythology. In *A Dictionary of Symbols* we find:

"Wings In the more general sense, wings symbolize spirituality, imagination, thought. The Greeks portrayed love and victory as winged figures, and some deities, such as Athena, Artemis and Aphrodite were at first—though not later—also depicted with wings....In alchemy, wings are always associated with the higher, active, male principle; animals without wings are related to the passive female principle."[1]

Mercury is one god who has a number of wings on his being. He has the caduceus (with winged snakes) and his hat and sandals also have wings.[2] The winged hat (called a petasus) and winged sandals symbolize Hermes' swiftness.[3] In fact, he is called the "flying man."[4]

In Roman mythology Mercury:

"was the god of commerce and travel, and the patron of thieves, gamblers, and ambassadors. The Greeks called him Hermes or Cyllenius, because he was born on Mount Cyllene, in Arcadia. He was the son of Jupiter (Zeus) and Maia, a daughter of Atlas. Pan, the god of shepherds, was the son of Mercury."[5]

Apollo gave him:

"a magic wand called the *caduceus*. Mercury used this to guide the souls of the dead to the Lower World. He also could control the living and the dead with it, or turn anything to gold."[6] [Emphasis in the original]

In one book on mythology, you will find Mercury "seated naked on a rock...."[7] A book on witchcraft informs us that **Mercury was the "inventor of incantation**s [and] was wont to be **invoked in the rites of magicians...."**[8] Mercury was also one of the names of gods invoked in Roman **Necromancy.**[9] Necromancy is sorcery or communication with the dead. Other books mention that Mercury was "the conductor of the dead to Hades [hell]."[10] Masonic author, Albert Pike, of course, claims that Mercury is the "Guardian and Guide of Souls."[11] Do you want a god that is conjured up by magicians and is the conductor of the dead to hell to be the "Guardian and Guide" of **YOUR** soul?

This god is portrayed in Masonry and the Eastern Star—but in a different guise. In the Eastern Star, the "Star in the East," the inverted/Satanic pentagram, is a depiction of Mercury. In Masonry, the Orator is a representation of Mercury. Albert Pike states:

"Of HERMES, the Mercury of the Greeks, the Thoth of the Egyptians, and the Taaut of the Phoenicians, we have therefore spoken sufficiently at length. He was the inventor of letters and of Oratory, the winged messenger of the Gods, bearing the Caduceus wreathed with serpents; and **IN OUR COUNCIL HE IS REPRESENTED BY THE ORATOR.**"[12]

Are you beginning to get a picture of the god that is being portrayed in Masonry and the Eastern Star? Their god has magical powers. He is the god of the underworld (hell) and the patron of thieves and gamblers. Note also that Mercury's son is Pan.[13]

The caduceus (or magic wand) that Mercury carries "consists of three elements: a rod, a pair of wings and two intertwined serpents. The rod is emblematic of power and authority. In the hands of primitive man, the largest club and the power to wield it were mighty persuaders as to just who was the leader of the tribe."[14] The caduceus "was reported to have the power of producing sleep. Milton refers to it as the opiate rod."[15]

In *A Dictionary of Symbols* we find:

"For the Romans, the caduceus served as a symbol of moral equilibrium and of good conduct. The wand represents power; the two snakes wisdom; the wings diligence; and the helmet is the emblem of lofty thoughts....According to esoteric Buddhism, the wand of the caduceus corresponds to the axis of the world and the serpents refer to the force called **Kundalini,** which, in Tantrist teaching, sleeps coiled up at the base of the backbone—a symbol of the evolutive power of pure energy. Schneider maintains that the two S-shapes of the serpents correspond to illness and convalescence. In reality, what defines the essence of the caduceus is the nature and meaning not so much of its individual elements as of the composite whole. The precisely symmetrical and bilateral arrangement, as in the balance of Libra, or in the tri-unity of heraldry (a shield between two supporters), is always expressive of the same idea of active equilibrium, of opposing forces balancing one another in such a way as to create a higher, static form. In the caduceus, this balanced duality is twice stated: in the serpents and in the wings, thereby emphasizing that supreme state of strength and self-control (and consequently of health) which can be achieved both on the lower plane of the instincts (symbolized by the serpents) and on the higher level of the spirit (represented by the wings)."[16]

Pike explains the caduceus like this:

"It was originally a simple Cross, symbolizing the equator and equincoctial Colure, and the **FOUR ELEMENTS** proceeding from a common centre. This Cross, surmounted by a circle, and that by a crescent, became an emblem of the Supreme Deity—or of the active power of **GENERATION** and the passive power of **PRODUCTION** conjoined,—and was appropriated to Thoth or Mercury. It then assumed an improved form, the arms of the Cross being changed into wings, and the circle and crescent being formed by two snakes, springing from the wand, forming a circle by crossing each other, and their heads making the horns of the crescent; in which form it is seen in the hands of Anubis."[17]

The caduceus, says Pike, additionally symbolizes the four elements. Of course, the four elements figure prominently in witchcraft. One witch writes:

"In casting a magic circle we first purify the space we will use with the four elements of earth, air, fire, and water. We walk around the area that will become the magic circle carrying a bowl of salt and water (for earth and water) and an incense burner (for fire and air). As we walk the path of the circle we say, 'By water and earth, by fire and air, by Spirit, be this circle bound and purified as we desire. So mote it be.'"[18]

Four Elements Symbol

Did you notice that the caduceus "became an emblem of the Supreme Deity" and that it represented "the active power of generation and the passive power of production conjoined"? In other words, this emblem is a veiled symbol for the sex act and it is this symbol that represents the Supreme Deity of the Masons (and, by extension, the Eastern Stars as well)! Eliphas Levi, the **OCCULTIST** whom Albert Pike plagiarized in *Morals and Dogma*[19] (which we are told by Masonic author Lucien V. Rule "is the greatest single work on Masonic philosophy ever given to the world"[20]), also mentions that the god Mercury was assigned "to the parts of **GENERATION.**"[21]

Blavatsky remarks:

"That the Serpents were ever the emblems of wisdom and prudence is again shown by the caduceus of Mercury....The two serpents, entwined around the rod, are **phallic** symbols of Jupiter and other gods who transformed themselves into snakes for purposes of **seducing** goddesses....The **serpent has ever been the symbol of the adept,** and of his powers of immortality and divine knowledge....It shows the dual power of the Secret Wisdom: the **BLACK AND THE WHITE MAGIC.**"[22]

Of course, one Masonic symbol after another has this sexual connotation, but in spite of the sexual innuendoes, Past Master Albert L. Woody, Grand Lecturer in Illinois, tells us:

"As late as 1812, in Pennsylvania, the Deacons in procession carried columns—the **SAME** columns which now rest on the Wardens' pedestals. Deacons first carried blue rods tipped with gold, symbolizing friendship and benevolence; later these were tipped with a **PINE CONE** in **IMITATION OF THE CADUCEUS** of Mercury, the messenger of the gods."[23]

One Masonic book, after explaining about the caduceus, brags: "The rod of the Master of Ceremonies is an analogue [equivalent or parallel]."[24] Another Masonic book claims that "Mercurius Caducifer [Mercury], the bearer of the herald's staff, finds his analogue in a Mason's Lodge, in the Senior Deacon, who accompanies the initiate throughout the ceremonies, and assists at his restoration, although himself unable to restore life."[25]

The caduceus is also a symbol for immortality.[26] Of course, Mercury is not the only god who carries a caduceus. Pike indicates that it was also borne "by Cybele, Minerva, Anubis, Hercules Ogmius the God of the Celts, and the personified Constellation Virgo, was a winged wand, entwined by two serpents."[27]

Virgo

The Migration of Symbols reveals that the caduceus "has alternately been considered to be **an equivalent** of the Thunderbolt, a form of the Sacred Tree, a contraction of the Scarab, a combination of the solar Globe and the Crescent of the moon, and so forth."[28]

Another symbol using wings is the called the winged globe (or solar globe). Helena Petrovna Blavatsky, an occultist and New Ager, says the **"'winged globe' is but another form of the egg, and has the same significance as the scarabaeus [scarab]**...which relates to the rebirth of man, as well as to his spiritual generation."[29] The Egyptians used this symbol to represent their creator and this symbol was so prevalent in Egypt that it was known as "the land of the winged globe."[30] Pike relates: "In Egypt, a Sun supported by two asps was the emblem of *Horhat* the good genius; and the serpent with the winged globe was placed over the doors and windows of the Temples as a tutelary God."[31] [Emphasis in the original] *The New Age Magazine,* a Masonic journal, notes: "The winged globe and serpent symbolized their [the Egyptians'] triune deity."[32]

George Oliver, in his Masonic book, *Signs and Symbols,* says:

"Egypt was the great conservator of ancient idolatry....Cneph was the Serpent-god of this people; he was the second person of the sacred Triad, and said to be the Creator of the world. He was usually represented by a hooded snake, sometimes called Basiliscus, or the Royal Serpent....Did he [the worshipper] meditate on the mysterious Tri-Une deity, Eicton-Cneph-Phtha, he was presented to the worshipper's recollection by the figure of a Globe and a Winged Serpent; the Globe symbolized the Supreme and eternal God; the Serpent, the animating principle; and the Wings, the hovering Spirit of God, which moved on the face of the waters at the creation of the world."[33]

Pike remarks:

"Serpents encircling rings and globes, and issuing from globes, are common in the Persian, Egyptian, Chinese, and Indian monuments. Vishnu is represented reposing on a coiled serpent, whose folds form a canopy over him. Mahadeva is represented with a snake around his neck, one around his hair, and armlets of serpents on both arms. Bhairava sits on the coils of a serpent, whose head rises above his own. Parvati has snakes around her neck and waist. Vishnu is the Preserving Spirit, Mahadeva is Siva, the Evil

Masonic columns

Principle, Bhairava is his son, and Parvati his consort. The King of Evil Demons was called in Hindu Mythology, *Naga,* the King of Serpents, in which name we trace the Hebrew *Nachash,* serpent."[34] [Emphasis in the original]

The winged globe, says H. G. Wells, is "to become the symbol of the New World Order when it overtly rules the world."[35]

The Rosicrucians also lay claim to this symbol. R. Swinburne Clymer said that "the Winged Globe is primarily a Rosicrucian symbol." He adds: "The Winged Globe is the symbol of the perfected soul making its flight back to the source of its creation in the Elysian fields beyond."[36]

Another name for the winged globe is Lynx. This is the "living winged globe of Chaldean magic tradition, symbolizing the universal spirit."[37]

The rock music group, Journey, also used the winged globe in at least three of their album designs.[38] Eric Barger notes that the winged globe "signifies a **DEMON DEITY** and the omnipresence of the sun god Ra."[39]

Winged Ra

One symbol that incorporates the winged globe into its symbolism is the figure of Azoth. In *Ancient Operative Masonry* we are told that "Azoth" is **OCCULT** language for the fifth element.[40] Pike explains this symbol:

"Upon it you see a Triangle upon a Square, both of these contained in a circle; and above this, standing upon a dragon, a human body, with two arms only, but two heads, one male and the other female. By the side of the male head is the Sun, and by that of the female head, the Moon, the crescent within the circle of the full moon. And the hand on the *male* side holds a *Compass,* and that on the *female* side, a *Square....*

"The Hermaphroditic figure is the Symbol of the double nature anciently assigned to the Deity, as Generator and Producer, as BRAHM and MAYA among the Aryans, Osiris and Isis among the Egyptians. As the Sun was male, so the Moon was female; and Isis was both sister and the wife of Osiris. The Compass, therefore, is the Hermetic Symbol of the Creative Deity, and the Square of the productive Earth or Universe....

"The COMPASS, therefore, as the Symbol of the *Heavens,* represents the spiritual, intellectual, and moral portion of this double nature of Humanity; and the SQUARE, as the Symbol of the *Earth,* its material, sensual, and baser portion."[41] [Emphasis in the original]

Masonic writer, John Yarker, adds: "The symbolism here clearly alludes to the dual sexual nature of all metals."[42] Yet another Mason, John Sebastian Marlow Ward, relates:

"The figure with the two heads probably represents Man natural and Man regenerate, surrounded by the seven planets and trampling with his left foot on the dragon which crouches over the winged globe. The fact that the figure bears in its hands the square and compasses, suggests some inter-relationship between these philosophers and the Masonic Guilds, while the emphatic way in which the left foot is planted first proves that to them this mantric sign had a very definite inner meaning. Possibly the dragon who is thus being attacked symbolises exoteric religion and the popular **ideas of right and wrong,** which the alchemists thought **should be overthrown** so that the light of the sun and of the planets could once more shine on the world shrouded in darkness."[43]

It's no surprise, then, to discover that the winged globe, a symbol of immortality,[44] is also used in one of the Masonic degrees. Here's what takes place in the 31st Degree pageantry according to Masonic author, Rex R. Hutchens:

"The Hall of Justice. The Egyptians believed that aspects of a man's *ka,* or double, could be seen in the material world. Such was the explanation given for a man's shadow or his reflection in a mirror. These physical manifestations of the *ka* were, to them, evidence of its existence. They believed that the *ka* accompanied the body to the Abode of the Dead to be there judged and to answer for both virtues and vices of life.

"In the land of Chemi, there lived an architect whose name was Cheres, the character assumed by the candidate. When he passed away, his *ka* descended with his body to the Abode of the Dead for judgment. We now follow him on his journey and enter the Court of the Dead to see what this man's end will be.

"In the East is a transparency of a winged globe with two serpents. In the center of the Hall is a large balance. In one pan is a vase, heart shaped, and in the other is a figure of *Ma,* goddess of truth and justice. The heart shaped vase represents the deeds of the soul when it dwelt within the body. West of the balance is a funeral bier with a representation of a corpse upon it, swathed like a mummy with a skull cap and the seed vessel of a lotus plant near the head. Near each corner of the Hall is a small table upon which is a censer for burning perfume. For the Egyptians this was the Hall of Two Truths, the meaning of which will soon be explained.

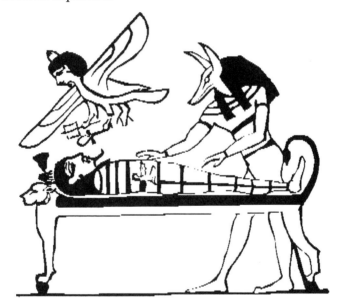

"The Egyptian deities present in the hall are:

1. Osiris: the Lord and Judge of the dead;

2. Atum: called the 'Father of Souls';

3. Ma: goddess of Truth and Justice whose image weighs upon one side of the balance;

4. Thoth: Scribe of the gods;

5. Anubis: Conductor of Souls; son of Osiris by his sister Nephthys;

6. Horus: son of Osiris, who presents the deceased to his father;

7. Isis: wife and sister of Osiris, mother of Horus;

8. Nephthys: sister of Isis and Osiris, mother of Anubis by Osiris;

9. Four sons of Horus—Kebhsenuf, Tau-mutef, Hapi and Amset.

"The candidate is brought into the Court of the Dead to be judged for actions while living and to determine if he deserves to dwell among the gods. His escort is Horus. Isis, Horus' mother, speaks first, inquiring whose *ka* has come to be judged."[45] [Emphasis in the original]

Inspector Inquisitor, Thirty-first Degree

Once again you can observe the paganism that is so prevalent in Masonry. You can also see that the Mason is being taught that if his good deeds outweigh his bad deeds, he will "dwell among the gods." This is a teaching that is contrary to God's Word, for we can never be saved by works. II Timothy 1:9 mentions that God "hath saved us, and called us with an holy calling, **NOT ACCORDING TO OUR WORKS,** but according to His own purpose and grace, which was given us in Christ Jesus before the world began." In Titus we are told: "**NOT BY WORKS OF RIGHTEOUSNESS** which we have done, but according to His mercy He saved us, by the washing of regeneration, and renewing of the Holy Ghost" (Titus 3:5). Of course, just a few verses later we find "that they which have believed in God might be careful to maintain good works" (Titus 3:8). We also know that many profess "that they know God; but in works they deny Him, being abominable, and disobedient, and unto every good work reprobate" (Titus 1:16), but good works alone will not get us to heaven. As Paul wrote: "For **BY GRACE ARE YE SAVED THROUGH FAITH;** and that not of yourselves: it is the gift of God: Not of works, lest any man should boast" (Ephesians 2:8-9). However, once we are saved, we will want to obey God's commands and work for Him out of love for God, but our works cannot save us. "Even so faith, if it hath not works, is dead, being alone" (James 2:17).

Another winged symbol is the winged disk or winged solar disk. It is a symbol of the sky god[46] and was "originally used for magic."[47]

"This symbol originated in ancient Egypt, where it was the quintessential symbol representing Horus, the sun god. The winged disk was used throughout the centuries to represent the supreme god of other pagan cults and societies. It was the symbol for the baal god during Jezebel's reign, as well as the god of the Zoroastrian cult, founded by Zoroaster, the Persian religious prophet...."[48]

A Dictionary of Symbols further informs us:

"**Disk** An emblem of the sun and also of the heavens. In China, the 'sacred disk' is a symbol of celestial perfection, and the disk that actually represents the sky (the jade disk called *Pi*) has a hole in the centre. The 'winged disk' is one of the most widespread of ancient symbols, which is still in use today in signs and emblems; in the profoundest sense, it represents matter in a state of sublimation and transfiguration. The two small serpents which are often to be seen next to the disk are those of the caduceus, alluding to the equipoise of opposing forces. But in a more esoteric sense, the winged disk signifies the disk in movement—in flight; it is therefore correctly used today in emblems created by an age which has learnt how to dominate the air and space."[49] [Emphasis in the original]

Different gods are represented by a winged solar disk. For example, the Egyptian god Behdety usually appears in the form of a winged solar disk. "He often appears in battle scenes hovering above the Pharaoh like a great falcon with outspread wings...."[50] Horus also is represented by a winged solar disk.[51] In *Egyptian Mythology,* we are told:

> "The sun, most important of the Egyptian deities, had many names, and the interpretations given to his functions were extremely varied. As a sun-disk he was called Aten; as the rising sun his name was Khepri, a great scarab beetle rolling before him the globe of the sun, just as on earth the scarab rolls before it a ball of dung in which it has laid its eggs and from which will burst forth life; as the sun climbed to its zenith he was called Ra, supreme god of Heliopolis; and as he set as an old man he was called Atum. He was also called Horus, and when this aspect was combined with that of Ra as Ra-Harakhte he was seen as the youthful sun of the horizon, a winged sun-disk."[52]

The Assyrian sun god, Shamash, was also represented by the winged sun-disk,[53] as was Asshur, an Assyrian war god.[54]

Isis

The winged solar disk also was used by Charles Taze Russell, the founder of the Jehovah Witnesses. He wanted the winged disk put on all his covers (which were later removed from the books by Joseph Rutherford).[55] Of course, this is not surprising that Russell used a 33° Masonic symbol since he himself was a Mason.[56]

There are also numerous creatures that are winged. Isis, an Egyptian goddess, is often portrayed with wings.

Then there's the winged serpent (or uraeus), a symbol of royalty.[57] Quetzalcoatl, an Indian god, was portrayed as a plumed, feathered, or winged serpent. "The serpent was a wisdom symbol, and when plumed it meant that wisdom had been given wings and had become spirit-wisdom, or illumination."[58]

Uazit, an Egyptian goddess, is also represented by the winged serpent.[59] Another Egyptian goddess, Buto, was symbolized by a winged cobra. She was the protector of Pharaoh.[60] The *New Larousse Encyclopedia of Mythology* explains:

> "Buto was a snake-goddess, frequently represented in the form of a cobra, sometimes winged and sometimes crowned. She also often has the features of a woman wearing, either directly on her head or on a head-dress in the form of a vulture, the red crown of the North, of which she was the official protectress as Nekhebet was of the white crown of the South."[61]

Closely related to the winged serpent is the winged dragon.

> "The dragon has symbolic importance to many people, however each person gives a different meaning to the dragon.

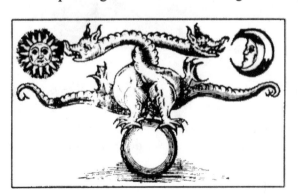

To some it stands for great wisdom and immortality. To others, it is a symbol of good fortune. Still others know the dragon as a powerful, benevolent friend."[62]

A catalog from Dancing Dragon Designs offered a "Golden Dragon Poster." The advertisement said: "A golden winged dragon rises from the roiling sea." Actually, the serpent and the dragon are really symbols for Satan.[63]

In connection with the dragon is the wyvern. It is a creature that is usually "represented as a 2-legged winged creature resembling a dragon."

The pegasus is another winged animal that is quite popular today. It is depicted as a flying horse or a horse with wings. Phil Phillips states: "The unicorn and the winged horse (Pegasus) are common neopagan symbols. They are derived from Greek and Roman mythology, where they were generally ridden by gods and goddesses."[64]

> "In fact, *Pegasus,* owned by *Bellerophon,* was a winged steed, unwearying of flight, which swept through the air as swift as a gale of wind. It was believed by the Greeks that *Pegasus sprang from Gorgon's blood after Perseus, another mythological character, killed her. Pegasus* received its powers to fly when fitted with a golden bridle. After the death of his master, which *Pegasus* deliberately caused, *Pegasus* went to live in *Zeus's,* god of thunder and lightning, stables. It was *Pegasus's* job to bring the lightning bolts and thunder to *Zeus* whenever he needed them."[65] [Emphasis in the original]

One researcher explains:

"The *pegasus,* or winged horse, originated in Greek
mythology as the symbol of the Pegae, a water-priestess.
The pegasus was said to be the son of the Moon Goddess
Medusa. His hoof was shaped like a *crescent moon,* which
today is yet another New Age and occult symbol. The
pegasus is depicted today in the kids' cartoon series 'She-
Ra,' and crystal pegasus horses are common as amulets and
decorative pieces in the homes of New Agers."[66]

For clarification, one account mentions Gorgon and the other
report refers to Medusa. There is no contradiction here. There were
three Gorgons who were sisters, one of whom was Medusa.[67]
Poseidon seduced Medusa in the temple of Athene. She became
angry over this and "turned Medusa's hair into snakes. When
Perseus decapitated Medusa, the blood which escaped from the
wound gave birth to Chrysaor and the horse Pegasus."[68]

Cronus is another god that is sometimes represented as winged.
Cronus, Horus, and Saturn are all considered to be a "god of time."[69]
Cronus (also spelled Kronus, Chronus, Chronos, Cronos, and
Kronos), from which we get our word "chronology,"[70] was the
Greek name and Saturn was the Roman name of the same god.[71]
Masonic writer, J. S. M. Ward, in his book *Freemasonry and the
Ancient Gods,* tells us that Saturn "is the Satan, the *Tempter,* or
rather Tester."[72] [Emphasis in the original] Eliphas Levi claims:

"Works of malediction and death" were "under the care of Saturn."[73] It's no wonder, then, that Saturn is called the "Lord of Death."[74] In fact, human sacrifices were even offered to him.[75]

Masonic writer, Robert Macoy, reveals that some men believed:

"that Baal was the Saturn of Greece and Rome; and there was a great conformity between the rites and sacrifices offered to Saturn and what the Scriptures relate of the sacrifices offered to Baal."[76]

Blavatsky also confirms that **SATURN IS BEL OR BAAL.**[77] The Bible condemned Baal worship on numerous occasions. Whenever the Israelites forsook the true God, they turned their worship to false gods, usually Baal. They went so far as to even burn their children as sacrifices to Baal: "They have built also the high places of Baal, to burn their sons with fire for burnt offerings unto Baal, which I commanded not, nor spake it, neither came it into My mind" (Jeremiah 19:5). Some other verses that deal with the abomination of Baal worship are: Judges 2:11, 13; 3:7; 8:33; 10:6, 10; I Samuel 7:4; 12:10; I Kings 18:18; 22:53; II Kings 17:16; 21:2-3; II Chronicles 17:3; 24:7; 28:2; 33:3; Jeremiah 11:13, 17; 23:13; 32:29, and 35.

Additionally, **SATURN WAS** known as the god **SET.**[78] Remember Set, the "Egyptian god of evil,"[79] which we covered earlier?

In ancient mythology a festival was held in honor of Saturn which was called the Saturnalia.[80] "[T]emple **PROSTITUTION AND SEXUAL LICENSE**...was most prolific during the Roman Saturnalia."[81] This festival was also to celebrate the winter solstice,[82] which is still commemorated in witchcraft and Masonry today.[83]

Saturn "is represented as an old man bent with age, carrying a scythe in his right hand."[84] We find that "the scythe is also symbolic of the harvest—of renewed hopes for rebirth"[85] or **REINCARNATION**. The scythe is also a symbol of time.[86]

"Time is [r]epresented by winged old man, with scythe and hourglass, disentangling ringlets of weeping virgin."[87] Sometimes the hourglass is even drawn with wings.

You have probably encountered Cronus on the TV and elsewhere without even realizing what was being depicted. Cronus (or Saturn) is most likely to be encountered at the end of a year or at the beginning of the new year. Cronus is the old man that is leaving the old year behind and the baby crawling (or bringing in the new year) is the rebirth of the god.

Incidentally, Saturn is also represented by a goat's head![88] Does that remind you of the Goat of Mendes in the inverted pentagram which we covered earlier? It should!

Another holiday that uses a winged god as a symbol is Valentine's Day. In a *Short Dictionary of Mythology* we find:

> **"Cupido [Cupid],** god of love, son of Jupiter and Venus, is depicted as a **NAKED,** winged infant, armed with bow and arrows. On ornaments he is generally represented amusing himself in some childish diversion. He could, in common with the rest of the gods, assume different forms. In the Aeneid he is represented as putting on the form of Ascanius, at the request of his mother, and going to Dido's court where he inspired the queen with love."[89]

Another name for Cupid is Eros.

"Eros was the youngest of the gods; he was a winged child, gracious though rebellious, whose pranks and caprices caused much suffering among men and gods. He was armed with a bow and arrows whose prick stirred the fires of passion in all hearts. In his malice he respected not even his own mother, and Aphrodite sometimes had to punish him by taking away his wings and quiver. Normally, however, he was her zealous servant. He helped with her toilet and accompanied her abroad."[90]

"Cupid is often portrayed shooting arrows into the hearts of hapless victims. Usually naked, winged and armed with a bow and arrow, cupids are still portrayed in modern times on Valentine cards, in theater decor and the like."[91]

As just mentioned, Cupid (Eros) was the son of Venus (Aphrodite). From Eros we get the word "erotic" and Venus was also considered to be the Roman goddess of erotic love. In fact, the word "venereal disease" was derived from the name "Venus."[92] Also, the bow and arrow that Cupid carries has a sexual connotation. In *A Dictionary of Symbols* we are told that the bow and arrow "stand for the sun's energy, its rays and its **fertilizing** and purifying powers. The symbolism of the crossbow is similar, but more complex, including, as it does, the **'conjunction'** of the bow and its stock."[93]

Cupid is not some adorable, little, mischievous god who makes couples fall in love. He is a god (really a demon) of vulgarity and indecency—but he is presented in a cute way with such an innocent-looking disguise. Our society is so inundated and saturated with paganism. It has become so commonplace that we don't even notice it any more. We just accept it as part of life not realizing how we must be offending God by using and propagating pagan symbolism and idolizing debauched, perverted, and evil pagan gods and goddesses.

"But the wisdom that is from above is first pure, then peaceable, gentle, and easy to be intreated, full of mercy and good fruits, without partiality, and without hypocrisy" (James 3:17).

Two mythological creatures that are winged are the sphinx and the griffin.

Below are some more winged items that appear in Masonry, the occult, etc. Notice the snake biting its tail on two of these pictures.

13. ORGANIZATIONAL LOGOS

Many organizations use occultic symbols in their logos. Some of these symbols may be used innocently by some groups but many other groups know the exact meaning behind the symbols they have chosen. In fact, certain organizations even proudly tell you about the logo they've chosen. For instance, the Rosicrucian group called the Ancient and Mystical Order of the Rosae Crucis (AMORC) gives a very detailed explanation about the Hermetic Rose Cross. They state (in part):

"The intricate symbol above is called the alchemical and hermetic Rose Cross, and is a very old **MYSTICAL** symbol. It is composed of two Rosy crosses united into one: the small Rosy cross at the center—representative of man, the microcosm—is in turn, the center point of a larger rose residing at the heart of the large cross—symbolic of the macrocosm. Upon the four ends of the large cross are inscribed the three **ALCHEMICAL** symbols: mercury, sulphur, and salt. At the top of the cross, mercury is placed in the center, sulphur on the left, and salt on the right. Upon the other ends of the cross the symbols have been inscribed in such an order as to conform to the **ESOTERIC** tradition.

"Also upon each arm, adjacent to the alchemical symbols, is the symbol of the **PENTAGRAM.** This five-pointed figure is a symbolic representation of the Rosy Cross itself: the victory of the quintessence over the four alchemical elements. The wheel at the top of each pentagram represents the quintessence....

"On the lower arm of the figure, below the large rose is a **HEXAGRAM**—symbol of the macrocosm—composed of two interlaced triangles. At its points are inscribed the six planets, according to the ancient **ASTROLOGICAL** tradition: at the bottom is the moon, at its right is Venus, followed in turn by Jupiter, Saturn, Mars, and Mercury. At the center of the hexagram is the **SUN.** The order of arrangement of these symbols conforms to certain **CABALISTIC RITUALS.**

"The lower end of the longest arm is divided into four sections by two diagonal lines. These sections are colored according to the four colors of Malkuth of the Cabalistic 'Tree of Life.' The four sets of three rays which extend outward from the center of the large cross symbolize the Divine light. The letters inscribed upon each large center-ray combine into INRI, which combination, according to the Rosicrucian historian Fr. Wittemans, represents a Latin motto meaning 'Nature is renewed by fire.' The letters upon the smaller rays represent **INVOCATIVE** names of Latin, Egyptian, and Greek origin.

"The petals of the large rose on the cross are twenty-two in number, and stand for the twenty-two letters of the Hebrew Cabalistic alphabet. The outer circle of twelve petals represents the twelve single letters of this alphabet, and in particular the twelve signs of the **Zodiac.** The next circle of seven petals symbolizes the seven double letters—in particular the seven **ASTROLOGICAL** planets. The innermost circle of three petals represents the three Mother-letters—air, fire, and water.

"At the center of the large rose is the microcosmic rose cross, an unfolded **CUBE** with a five-petaled rose at its center. Four barbs emerge from behind this cross, pointing into the four directions in space.

"The complete symbol or 'Encyclopedic' Rose Cross symbolizes all the majesty, power, beauty, and protection of the Rosicrucian Order."[1]

The above description is just filled with **OCCULTIC** connotations. It is far too extensive to mention here but I want to point out three things. First of all, the word "alchemy" was mentioned. According to the book, *Power of the Witch,* written by a witch, Laurie Cabot, we discover:

"**Witches** are called many things—shamans, sages, medicine people, **ALCHEMISTS,** mystics, psychics. But no matter what the appellation, these **magical** people share a common bond: a unique relationship with nature, with divinity, and with human society."[2]

Cabot states elsewhere:

"The Science Tradition [Witchcraft] is based on the Hermetic principles that parallel the principles of the new physics. They have their origins in the teachings of Hermes, known to the Egyptians as Thoth, and to the Romans as Mercury....Actually **HERMES** seems to have been a universal Indo-European god who **TAUGHT ASTROLOGY, ALCHEMY, AND THE MANY MAGICAL PRACTICES THAT ARE AT THE HEART OF WITCHCRAFT.** He seems to have taught the universal truths everywhere, for he even pops up among Native Americans as the trickster gods Raven, Coyote, and Hare."[3]

We can easily see that **witchcraft uses alchemy.** Of course, alchemy is also important in Masonry. For example, in the 21st degree of Masonry, the initiates are told the following:

> "The Hermetic philosophers may also be called speculative alchemists. The name 'Hermetic' comes from a tradition that the founder of alchemy was an Egyptian (Thoth) whom the Greeks called Hermes Trismegistus or Hermes the Thrice Great, identifying him with their Hermes, the Roman Mercury.

> "The tradition of alchemy is best understood by separating its practitioners into two groups: the first group, who we may term 'operative alchemists,' truly believed the transmutation of metals was possible. Their goal was to transform base metals, such as lead or copper, into silver or gold thereby creating wealth. The second group, the 'speculative alchemists,' were mystics who declared that alchemy was not the science of making gold but a **SPIRITUAL SCIENCE OF REGENERATION AND A SACRED ART DEVOTED TO INTERPRETING THE MYSTERIES OF GOD** and life. When we speak of **alchemy in Masonry** our reference is to the second group."[4]

Remember Hermes, Mercury, and Thoth which we covered earlier? These are synonyms for Satan says occultist Helena Petrovna Blavatsky.[5]

The Masonic book, *A Bridge to Light,* declares: "The 28th Degree is purely philosophical and the most mystical of all. The tenets of **NUMEROLOGY, ASTROLOGY AND ALCHEMY ARE EXPLAINED."**

Mysteries of Mind, Space and Time states:

> "It was natural to suppose that, if a **MAN COULD MAKE HIMSELF TRULY GOD-LIKE,** he would gain the power to transform baser metals into gold, by exactly

the same processes that they underwent in the Earth. This belief was expressed on the Emerald Tablet, a record said to have been inscribed by the god Thoth, who was supposed to have taught the ancient Egyptians the sciences and the art of writing. (The Greeks identified Thoth with one form of their god Hermes—Hermes Trismegistos, the 'thrice-great.' Hence the term 'hermetic art' for alchemy.)

"All these various strands came together: the primitive belief that the search for a way to transmute base metals into gold involved a succession of god-like actions developed into the belief that an **IMPORTANT PART OF ALCHEMY WAS THE ATTEMPT TO BECOME LIKE GOD**—'as above, so below.' From this, no doubt, stems the conviction that the **FINAL RESULT OF THE ALCHEMICAL QUEST WAS TO ACHIEVE ETERNAL LIFE....**

"At the lower levels of Taoist practice, the mixing of *yin* and *yang* could be achieved by controlled sexual intercourse; the more advanced mystics practised various meditative procedures, designed to bring about a kind of 'distillation' of *yang* within the body. These practices were commonly known as 'sexual alchemy.'"[6] [Italics in the original; Caps and boldface added]

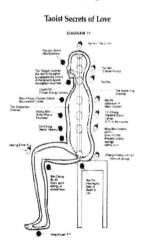

Taoist Secrets of Love

In *Dictionary of Mysticism* it is explained that "Hermetic" is now "used to mean **OCCULT** or **esoteric** in general....Used also as a noun meaning a student or practitioner of **alchemy** or **OCCULTISM** or **esoteric** science."[7]

Yet another book, *A Pictorial History of Magic and the Supernatural* remarks: "The Greeks believed Hermes Trismegistus to be the initiator of **OCCULT PHILOSOPHY, OF MAGIC.** In fact, this was really a composite personage, half Hermes, half the Egyptian god Thoth."[8]

Occultist and psychologist, Carl Jung, adds: "Alchemy, on the other hand, exalted the most heinous transgression of the law, namely incest, into a symbol of the union of opposites, hoping in this way to bring back the golden age."[9]

I think it is quite interesting that in *The Occult* we find: "It is worth bearing in mind that the psychologist Jung, who considered "the discovery of alchemy as one of the greatest intellectual adventures of his life,"[10] regarded **ALCHEMY AS THE PREDE-CESSOR OF MODERN *PSYCHOLOGY....* "**[11] [Italics in the original; Caps and boldface added]

Other names for alchemy (besides hermetic art) are spagyric art[12] and wai tan.[13]

Let's return to the explanation of the AMORC's logo for the second point. Notice that "quintessence" was mentioned twice. Mason, occultist, and the artist of the Baphomet drawing, Eliphas Levi, comments: "The guiding star is that same blazing star which is a symbol in all initiations. For alchemists it is the sign of the **QUINTESSENCE,** for magicians the great arcanum, for Kabbalists the sacred **PENTAGRAM.**"[14]

Third, the Cabala was mentioned. Briefly, the Cabala:

> "assumes the magical power of words, signs, and numbers, and the possibility through the knowledge of this power to foresee and influence future events. It recognized the power of **amulets, magic formulae, conjurations of spirits** and other supernatural agencies."[15]

In an article entitled "Jung and the Qabalah," we are told:

> "The Qabalah is one of the most ancient Western philosophical systems. **IT FORMS MUCH OF THE INNER FOUNDATIONS UPON WHICH ASTROLOGY, TAROT, ALCHEMY, NUMEROLOGY, MYTHOLOGY AND CEREMONIAL MAGIC ARE BASED.**"[16]

The book, *Magical Arts,* claims: "Like most of the occult systems within the European tradition of high magic, the **CABALA INCLUDED SPELLS** designed to induce an unseen population of spirits to carry out the magician's wishes."[17]

In fact, in the *Dictionary of Mysticism,* we are told that the **CABALA "IS AN ESSENTIAL ELEMENT IN MOST SCHOOLS OF OCCULTISM."**[18]

So, now you should have a little better idea about the extensive occultism represented in the Rosicrucian logo. We can see that the person who designed that logo knew exactly what he was doing. We can also see that the Rosicrucians were anticipating a one world order and a one world religion. Listen to what appeared in *The Rosicrucian Digest* in June 1941:

> *"We predict a mystical-pantheism as the religion of tomorrow....There will not be churches, but a church....Since the earth is a habitat of humanity, it is also the common property of all men....The World State will provide and maintain community hospitals, sanitariums, and clinics....Physicians will be paid by the state and their entire professional services will be absorbed by the state....Every citizen will enjoy these health benefits and guarantees....Quotas will be placed upon all professions, in each of the zones of the World-State."*[19] [Emphasis in the original]

A few other Rosicrucian symbols appear below.

The Occult Emporium, which sells human bones, has an oil lamp as their logo. They explain:

"Our logo is a drawing of a fine bronze oil lamp. Nine were made for Aleister Crowley's Order of the Golden Dawn (OTO). It is pictured in the book 'WITCHES AND SOR-CERERS' by Arkon Daraul, page 226. One resides in our personal collection of magical art objects."[20]

They add that this "magic lamp" "represents earth, fire, air, water. Sign of the Heathen occultist, the solitary wanderer wise in the ways of the cosmos....See, 'The Magic Circle; Its Successful Organization & Leadership,' by Rev. Yaj Nomolos, for more information."[21] Nomolos is with the Church of Satan.[22]

The Council for a Parliament of World Religions (CPWR) also describes the logo they use. The November 1993 issue of *CPWR Journal* proclaims:

"Five years ago, when Hyde Parker Larry Janiak designed the symbol of unity for the Parliament of the World's Religions, he believed that someday the people of Chicago might get to see his creation. He had no idea that his symbol would become known to people all around the world. 'I'm very happy and I hope it helps to unify the world's religions,' said the 55-year-old Janiak....

"After researching traditional religious symbols, within two weeks Janiak developed his symbol of unity. The symbol is a circular shape called the **mandala.** The mandala symbolizes completeness and unity, Janiak said.

"The design is 'the sun in the form of the radiating shape of the iris of the eye of God,' according to Janiak. The symbol is based on ancient poetic spiritual concepts: the all seeing eye of God; fire, flame and the sun as the source of all life on earth; the sun as the sustenance and source of life on earth; and a single candle flame, as the proverb, 'Light one candle instead of cursing the darkness.'

"Nine individual flames surround the core, representing the different paths of the **WORLD'S RELIGIONS, WHICH ALL COME FROM THE SAME SPIRITUAL SOURCE,** according to Janiak."[23]

Once again we can see that the designer of this logo knew exactly what he was doing. He even said that the symbol is a **MANDALA.** However, to fully understand what Janiak had in mind, we need to find out what a mandala is. In the book, *The Tantric Mysticism of Tibet,* we are told that the **yin/yang concept forms the mandala's basis.**[24] This is interesting since we've already seen the occultic yin/yang symbolism.

One magazine tells us: "The word *mandala* can be translated from Sanskrit as **MAGIC CIRCLE.** When we fill the circle with color, forms and symbols, it can be a **MAGICAL** experience."[25] [Italics in the original; Caps and boldface added]

A New Age organization, describing one of their workshops, states:

"Techniques of visualization, meditation and color breathing will be practiced....All these factors will be put to use as each person makes their *own* mandala....

"The Sanskrit word mandala, usually a circle, is a **MYSTICAL** diagram. In Eastern Philosophy it is used as a point of focus. It is considered to be an 'engine of power,' believed by many to have talesmanic (sic) properties, radiating a power that projects qualities associated with it for which it was constructed, i.e. tranquility, healing, protection, etc."[26] [Italics in the original; Caps and boldface added]

A catalog from the Theosophical Society says:

"The word <u>mandala</u> originates from Sanskrit, meaning holy or magical circle. Three principles of order determine structure of a mandala: the center, the radiation that emanates from the center, and a periphery of the circle. The center represents the **MYSTERIOUS SPIRITUAL FORCE,** birthplace of all existence within space and time. The emanation streams from the center toward the circle's periphery, uniting the inner and outer. Our road to self-realization may lead to the center of being. There, too, we may discover a peaceful centeredness and healing energy of color therapy."[27] [Emphasis in the original]

In *A Color Guide to Yoga* we are told that the every detail in a mandala has a **SPIRITUAL** significance.[28] This book adds: "A *mandala* is a design in which the whole pattern leads you to the center. Gazing steadily at a mandala helps to center your thoughts and to bring you to the required state of single-minded concentration."[29] [Emphasis in the original]

Laurie Cabot proudly declares:

"On many pages [of my Book of Shadows] I have drawn small pentacles, as I do when I sign my name on letters and documents. I believe the pentacle to be one of the oldest geometric symbols known to humans. It consists of a **FIVE-POINTED STAR INSIDE A CIRCLE. IT IS THE KEY SYMBOL OF THE CRAFT. IT IS THE WITCH'S *MANDALA,*** a geometric diagram of all existence, that encompasses both creatrix and creation."[30]

Another book explains:

"The *Mandala* is known as a 'power diagram,' having its origins in Tantric Buddhism, which is designed to alter consciousness and awaken the Kundalini energy in an individual, thereby leading to 'enlightenment' or the realisation of personal divinity."[31] [Emphasis in the original]

So we can see that Janiak knew exactly what he was doing when he designed the logo for the Council for the Parliament of the World's Religions.

The next logo we'll look at is from *The Beacon* magazine. There is an accompanying article explaining this symbol entitled "A New Age Symbol" followed by an asterisk. The note reads: "This deeply **ESOTERIC** symbol now appears on the cover of *The Beacon.*" The article was written by Foster Bailey, a 32° Mason[32] and husband of Alice Bailey (founder of the Lucifer Publishing Company[33] now called Lucis Trust, which was an offshoot of the Theosophical Society[34]). Bailey elaborates:

"The symbol is set in a limitless field of blue, which signifies the sphere of life expression of our solar Logos, who is said to be a deep blue, second-ray Logos. The potency and quality of his pervading life maintains and conditions all within the solar system including the life and destiny of our planetary Logos, Sanat Kumara. It is the most powerful factor which we are able to touch mentally.

"The golden disc, against which the triangle and the star appear, symbolises the all inclusive background of our life on this planet. Sanat Kumara may look through it....It is spoken of in that most ancient of all mantrams, the Gayatri: 'Unveil to us the face of the true spiritual Sun, hidden by a disc of golden light, that we may know the truth.'

"Behind the entire symbol, extending beyond the disc of golden light, emerges the cosmic cross, which is found in the consciousness of the great ones on that distant Sun, Sirius....

"Some of these forces are partially available in the council chamber of Shamballa....Our symbol touches only a few of these new potencies and includes a blend of both the old age and the new....

"The triangle superimposed upon the disc is yellow, because that is the colour of buddhi. The Hierarchy functions on the buddhic plane, so-called, and the potencies of this triangle make their entry into our planetary life there. This triangle is formed by the three great extraplanetary entities [demons!] now aiding the Plan for the planet....

"One of these three great beings is known to us as the Lord Buddha....He is the closest of the three to the Christ.

He stands at the right hand of the Christ, depicted, therefore, at the lower right hand point of the triangle.

"At the lower left hand point stands the great Entity who carries the potency of solar equilibrium, now newly available to Sanat Kumara. He is referred to by the Master Djwhal Khul as the 'spirit of equilibrium' and also as the 'spirit of peace,' the peace that passeth all understanding.'...

"At the top point of this new and unique triangle stands that Avatar of Synthesis....His permeating influence hastens the realisation by humanity that, in fact, we live in one world as one humanity with a common destiny....

"Superimposed upon the triangle of new age forces is the five pointed star of the Christ....The **old and the new MUST merge.** The problem is not to fight to kill out the old, but a wise and rightly timed **INFILTRATION** of the new into the boiling cauldron of our times.

"Our symbol, therefore, blends the two eras and rightly pictures the work of the Christ today and the forces He must wield. The point in the centre is the place where the Christ stands. It is the centre of the star, the centre of the triangle, and the centre of the disc of golden light.

"From that centre He works, and as He works the cross of the new era emerges. This is the equal-armed cross, reflecting its cosmic archetype, which will in its own right become the cross of humanity in the days to come. It symbolises the balanced life of right relation to God through aspiration, and right relation to man through service and sharing. Eventually we shall know and live by the fact that nothing actually belongs to any individual man."[35]

The above description is filled with occultic terminology which could take a book in itself to explain. However, a few items need to be addressed briefly. One thing that must be pointed out is that when Bailey refers to "the Christ" he is not referring to Jesus Christ of the Bible. The New Agers teach that everyone is a Christ. They also believe that Lucifer was Christ. For instance, on the magazine from the Theosophical Society called *Lucifer* (edited by Helena Petrovna Blavatsky and Annie Besant) is the following: *"'I Jesus....am the bright, the Morning Star,' (...Lucifer)."* They add: "The **Light-bearer is the Morning Star or Lucifer;** and 'Lucifer is no profane or Satanic title. It is the Latin *Luciferus,* the Light-bringer, the Morning Star....'"[36]

Besides this, Sirius was mentioned in the explanation of the logo just given. "Throughout the centuries Sirius has been recognized by most occultists and esoteric teachers as the location where **LUCIFER** and his hierarchy dwell. In Christian terminology, Sirius is simply a secretive codeword for 'hell.'"[37] In the book, *Sirius,* we find:

> "The Euphrateans, Persians, Phoenicians, and the peoples of Vedic India called Sirius The Leader, while the **Romans knew Sirius as** Janitor Lethaeus, or **Keeper of Hell,** both of which titles are perhaps reminiscent of Anubis, the Egyptian god who led the deceased through the underworld. The Egyptian (sic) themselves reverenced Sirius under several other names as well, including Sothis, Sothi, Sept, Sepet, Sopdet, Sot, and Sed."[38]

One form of Anubis

It is interesting to note that Venus also "became the goddess of the Dog Star, Sirius...."[39] Venus, by the way, is another name for Lucifer![40] Sirius is so important to the occultists that a New Age organization even named their society the Sirius Community and their newsletter is called the *Sirius Journal*.[41] This group was started by former members of the Findhorn Community located in Scotland. Their logo appears below.

One former member and co-director of the Findhorn Community was David Spangler.[42] Spangler seems to be quite enthralled with Lucifer. Some of his quotes about Lucifer were given earlier in this book. Here are two more of his quotes:

"Lucifer prepares man in all ways for the experience of Christhood and the Christ prepares man for the experience of God....But the light that reveals to us the presence of the Christ, the light that reveals to us the path to the Christ comes from Lucifer. He is the light giver. He is aptly named the Morning Star because it is his light that heralds for man the dawn of a greater consciousness. He is present when that dawn is realized. He stands no longer as the tester or the tempter but as the great initiator, the one who hands the soul over to the Christ and from the Christ on into ever greater realms."

"Christ is the same force as Lucifer but moving in seemingly the opposite direction."

Of course, quotes like this aren't really surprising since Masons themselves (and others) tell us that Lucifer (or Venus) is the Light-bearer and the Morning Star.[43] Blavatsky writes about the Druids, Magi, Zoroastrians, etc., greeting "the Morning Star—the beautiful Venus-Lucifer."[44]

Symbol representing Venus

As already mentioned, Lucis Trust was an offshoot of the Theosophical Society, founded by Helena Petrovna Blavatsky, an occultist,[45] Luciferian, magician,[46] and Mason.[47] She remarked: "...Lucifer or Luciferius is the name. Lucifer is divine and terrestrial Light, 'the Holy Ghost' and 'Satan' at one and the same time."[48] In other words, Blavatsky claims that Lucifer is the Holy Ghost **AND** Satan, but she is not the only one who has called Lucifer the Holy Ghost. Masonic author, Albert Pike, insulted and blasphemed the Holy Ghost when he recorded that "the body of the Holy Spirit, the universal Agent, [is] the Serpent devouring its own tail."[49] In fact, in the 28th degree of the Masonic lecture, the Masons being initiated are told the **IDENTICAL** thing![50]

Notice the hexagram and the snake biting his tail

As also mentioned, the Theosophical Society's newsletter was called *Lucifer*. One person who had material printed in this magazine was Eliphas Levi, the individual who drew Baphomet. He stated: "The intellectual **LUCIFER IS THE SPIRIT OF INTELLI-GENCE AND LOVE;** it is the paraclete, it is the Holy Spirit...."[51] The word "paraclete" means "advocate" or an "intercessor." St.

John penned: "If any man sin, we have an advocate [paraclete] with the Father, Jesus Christ the righteous" (I John 2:1). Christ is our mediator: "For there is one God, and one mediator between God and men, the man Christ Jesus" (I Timothy 2:5). The occult tries to steal the title of Jesus Christ and apply it to Lucifer (Satan), but this is no surprise for Lucifer has boasted:

> **"I WILL** ascend into heaven, **I WILL** exalt my throne above the stars of God: **I WILL** sit also upon the mount of the congregation, in the sides of the north: **I WILL** ascend above the heights of the clouds; **I WILL BE LIKE THE MOST HIGH"** (Isaiah 14:13-14).

Satan's boast, however, rings hollow since God reveals: "[T]hou shalt be brought down to hell, to the sides of the pit" (Isaiah 14:15).

The "light" (or "the Christ") that the occultists refer to is actually the **LIGHT OF LUCIFER.** As Eliphas Levi and Albert Pike have written: "LUCIFER, the *Light-Bearer!*...Lucifer, the Son of the Morning!"[52] [Emphasis in the original] Blavatsky boasts "that Satan, or the Red *Fiery* Dragon...and *Lucifer,* or 'Light-bearer' is in us: it is our *Mind*—our tempter and Redeemer, our intelligent liberator and Saviour from pure animalism."[53] [Emphasis in the original]

In Blavatsky's book we also find:

> "Holy is the Sabbath of god: *blessed and sanctified is the name of the Angel of Hades*—SATAN.

> "For, 'The glory of Satan is the shadow of the Lord': God in the manifested world; 'the throne of Satan is the footstool of Adonai'—that footstool being the whole KOSMOS."[54] [Emphasis in the original]

A little later in her book she adds that the name "adversary" does not belong to Satan but to Jehovah (the Christian's God), whom she refers to as "the first and cruelest *adversary of all the other gods'....* "[55] [Emphasis in the original] She said that the serpent (Satan) "spoke only words of sympathy and wisdom...."[56]

Manly Palmer Hall, also a **MASON AND OCCULTIST, BELIEVES THAT THE MESSIAH IS "THE PLANET VENUS, OTHERWISE CALLED *LUCIFER....*"**[57] In Hall's book, *Initiates of the Flame,* we find an astounding statement. He says:

> "There are two parts, or divisions, of humanity whose history is closely related to that of the Wisdom Teachings. They embody the doctrines of fire and water, the two opposites of nature. Those who follow the path of faith (or the heart) use water and are known as the Sons of Seth, while those who follow the path of the mind and action are the Sons of Cain, who was the son of **SAMAEL, the Spirit of Fire.** Today **we find the latter among the alchemists, the Hermetic philosophers, the Rosicrucians, and the Freemasons.**"[58]

What is so amazing to me is that Blavatsky explains just who Samael is. She notes that "in the Kabala **SAMAEL...IS SATAN....**"[59] (See picture on page 53.) So, according to Hall, the Masons, alchemists, and Rosicrucians are sons of Satan!!

Also notice that in the writings of Lynn Perkins, a Mason, he claims: "The **PATH TO HEAVEN SEEMS TO BE BY THE WAY OF HELL** and intended that way by the Creation."[60] There's one problem with this view, however, and that is **THERE IS NO ESCAPE FROM HELL** (see Luke 16:26).

Let's observe another logo. Target stores use the point within a circle for their symbol. As mentioned earlier, this sign is a representation of the phallus. The obelisk (e.g. the Washington Monument) is another phallic symbol. With this in mind, it is quite interesting that the Target stores are helping to restore the Washington Monument. They also have a punch out paper where you can build your own obelisk.[61] Just "coincidental"?

Another logo comes from the Satchidananda Ashram—Yogaville. Notice the mandala-like center with the point within a circle, a hexagram, triangle, yin/yang, crescent and moon, etc. This logo is obviously a representation of the uniting of all religions into one. Of course, this is exactly what the New Age has been desiring to do. They want to bring all religions together. "Fabian Socialist H. G. Wells wrote that *'the coming World-State...will be based upon a common World Religion, very much simplified and universalized and better understood.'*"[62] [Emphasis in the original] Robert Muller, former Assistant Secretary General of the United Nations, said: "We must move as quickly as possible to a one-world government; **A ONE-WORLD RELIGION;** under a one-world leader."[63]

Muller has also stated: "My great personal dream is to get a tremendous **ALLIANCE BETWEEN ALL MAJOR RELIGIONS AND THE UN.**"[64]

Muller refers to himself as a humanist[65] and is one of the editorial advisors for the New Ager's Marilyn Ferguson's *Brain/ Mind Bulletin.* He is also on the advisory boards of The Center for Attitudinal Healing,[66] another New Age organization, the Institute for Educational Studies, and The Temple of Understanding,[67] where he is listed as one of the "Founding Friends." He is on the Board of Trustees of the Global Education Associates.[68] Muller also is on the Board of Directors of Planetary Citizens[69] and was one of the co-founders of this group, as well as a board member of the Planetary Initiative for the World We Choose,[70] another New Age group. Furthermore, "Muller has encouraged the work of Benjamin Creme, of the Tara Center, which has placed ads in leading newspapers of the world proclaiming: 'THE CHRIST IS NOW HERE.'"

Since he founded the School of Ancient Wisdom in Fort Worth, Texas, he is considered the Father of global education[71] and his World Core Curriculum is used in schools around the world.[72] In fact, Muller, who is an ardent follower of the occultist/New Ager, Alice Bailey,[73] claims that this World Core Curriculum was given to him by his spirit guide (which is actually a demon) by the name of Djwhal Khul, also known as the Tibetan![74] This is the same spirit guide that directed Bailey to write many of her own occultic books. Muller is quite proud of this fact for the literature received from the Robert Muller School clearly admits that the philosophy underlying this curriculum "is based on the teachings set forth in the books of Alice A. Bailey by the Tibetan teacher Djwhal Khul and the teachings of M. Morya."[75]

Muller spoke at the Conference in Search of the True Meaning of Peace which was held in Costa Rica on June 25-30, 1989. He urged them to work towards a one world religion. Here is part of his speech:

"We need a *World* or *cosmic spirituality*...religious leaders will get together to define before the end of this century the cosmic laws which are *common to all their faiths*....They should tell the politicians what the cosmic laws are, what *God,* or the *gods,* or the *cosmos* are expecting from humans.

"We must hope also that the Pope will come before the year 2000 to the United Nations, speak for all the religions and spiritualities on this planet and give the world the religious view of how the third millennium should be a spiritual millennium, a millennium which will see the integration and harmony of humanity...."[76] [Emphasis in the original]

Muller also claims:

"The world's major religions must speed up dramatically their ecumenical movement and recognize the unity of their objectives in the diversity of their cults. Religions must actively cooperate to bring to unprecedented heights a better understanding of the mysteries of life and of our place in the universe. 'My religion, right or wrong,' and 'My nation, right or wrong' must be abandoned forever in the planetary age."[77]

Along with the idea of a one world religion comes the idea of one humanity and one world. Global Forum of Spiritual and Parliamentary Leaders on Human Survival has a logo that gives the idea of humanity uniting together to form one world as does the Quartus Foundation and the Planetary Commission for Global Healing.

Global Forum

The Center for the Dances of Universal Peace has a circle-of-hearts logo which doesn't seem to suggest a one world order, but below their logo was this phrase: "Through music and dance, **TOWARD ONE WORLD,** within and without."[78] This group also explains their logo. They state:

> "Actually, the heart-circle is original art, produced by graphic artist Marc Takaha, who **RECEIVED THE DESIGN IN VISION** specifically as the logo for the Dances of Universal Peace. The **VISION CAME UNBIDDEN,** and Marc graciously donated the art to the Center. We wish to respect the intention of **THIS GIFT FROM THE COSMOS....**"[79]

Did you notice that this logo came through a vision? In other words, this logo was evidently given by spirit (demonic) intervention! They also brag that these:

"Dances have spread around the world and are used in a variety of settings, including peace studies, transpersonal counseling, holistic health education, ecumenical conferences and cross-cultural arts celebrations. These have included the United Nations Day Celebrations, Association of Humanistic Psychology National Conference, San Francisco Folk Music Festival, Interfaith Peace Celebrations, Association for the Study of Cross-Cultural Consciousness Studies Conference, American Macrobiotic Society Conference, Whole Life Expos and others."[80]

By the way, the "Dances were originally the creation of the **SUFI** Murshid (teacher) Samuel L. Lewis and inspired by his teacher Hazrat Inayat Khan, as well as American dance pioneer Ruth St. Denis."[81]

A Sufi logo

The viewpoint of one humanity and one world is also expressed in the logo which appeared in a pamphlet from the Spiritual Unity of Nations (SUN). The front cover states: "DEDICATED TO THE SPIRITUAL UNITY OF RELIGIONS, NATIONS AND PEO-PLES."[82] [Emphasis in the original]

One author informs us:

"In May 1968 the S-U-N [Spiritual Unity of Nations] held an international conference of Spiritual and **ESOTERIC** Organizations in Hove, Sussex, England. 1650 delegates attended, some coming from behind the Iron curtain and even as far afield as Iceland. There is a S-U-N Centre in detroit (sic), and groups in Chicago, Atlanta, Costa Mesa [California], Bulawayo [Rhodesia], New Zealand; and many in South Africa. The Americans sponsored a large S-U-N conference in November 1968 to formulate 'A New Age World Religion' to complement the New World Order of the Aquarian Age."[83]

The illustration above appeared in one of SUN's pamplets. SUN also has an interesting logo on their stationery. Note the point inside the triangle, the circle, the seven-pointed star, and the twelve pointed star—all enclosed by a circle.

Another group working to bring all cultures and religions together is the Unity-and-Diversity World Council (UDC). Previous names for this same group are International Cooperation Council and Unity-and-Diversity Council.[84] The *"Unity-in-Diversity Council is a powerful New Age promotional network...which* [in 1982—D.L.C.] *linked arms with the international network of* ***'Mind, Body, and Spirit Festivals.'*** *This formed a vast army dedicated to the merger of all religions into one, under a world leader."*[85] They have produced a *Directory for a New World.*[86] Their purpose is "to foster the emergence of a new person and civilization based on the dynamic integration of diversity among all peoples and all life."[87] Their website states: "The methods we use are based upon our search for universal moral and **SPIRITUAL** principles. We welcome the **COMING TOGETHER OF ALL** races, cultures and **RELIGIONS** into a unity-and-diversity type of community both locally and around the world."[88] Their activities include Interfaith Celebrations.

> "Since September 1995 this World Interfaith Network has been meeting at religious and spiritual centers around Los Angeles such as the Vedanta Society, the Islamic Center, the World Peace Prayer Society, and the Mormon Temple....Celebrations include meditation...and messages from the different faith groups."[89]

Unity-and-Diversity World Council

Leland P. Stewart was the founder of Unity-and-Diversity World Council. On May 10, 1998 he spoke at the Taurus Wesak Festival (sponsored by the Los Angeles InterGroup). Before mentioning some of Stewart's remarks, I think it is necessary to explain what the Wesak Festival is. The Group for Creative Meditation tells us:

> "Held in the solar month of Taurus at the full moon of May, this Festival **HONORS THE BUDDHA, THE LORD OF LIGHT,** Messenger of the East. It is this great living Avatar Who brings the 'Light of Illumination' from 'the centre where the Will of God is known' closer to humanity. During Wesak we are reminded that it is the Will of God to awaken humanity and reveal its true purpose on earth.

> "Year after year, the Forces of Light make an effort at Wesak to increase the flow of enlightenment into the world and to throw the light of wisdom and understanding 'into the minds of men.' If the demand from humanity is strong

enough, mentally powerful and adequately focussed, the Forces of Enlightenment can be invoked and brought forth into human affairs."[90]

Symbol for Enlightenment

This festival is referred to as "the supreme moment of the year."[91] Tom Carney says that Wesak "is a wonderful time to talk about the rising sun, for that is what the Festival is all about. It is about the eye being single and the whole body being full of light. It is about the impact of will upon the dedicated server, a single eye, a single will."[92]

A symbol representing the "Three Linked Meditation Festivals of Spring" (one of which is the Festival of Wesak) appears below.

It was at this festival in honor of Buddha, where Stewart commented:

"In preparing for my remarks today, I took the trouble to locate all of our Alice Bailey books and to look them over, especially the one entitled *The Externalisation of the Hierarchy.* What I discovered was a number of areas of COMMON GROUND with the work of the Unity-and-Diversity World Council. I'd like to mention a few of those areas now.

"I discovered that Synthesis is a very important term in the Alice Bailey teachings....In these teachings, the Buddha represents **light,** the Buddha being 'the illumined one.'...The central goal of these teachings is to help give birth to a **new world religion.** All of these dimensions resonate with our work.

"The meaning of **unity-and-diversity** in this arena is to serve both the synthesis, which we call the **unity,** and also to pay close attention to the **diversity,** which each aspect of the unity represents....

"Let me just comment on the Wesak Festival itself in that regard. Wesak in Buddhism symbolizes the birth, life, and death of the Buddha....

"In addition to Buddhism and Christianity, we need to pay close attention to Judaism, Islam, Taoism, Confucianism, and a host of modern spiritual movements such as Baha'i, Vendanta (sic), and the like. All of them are making their contribution to the religious life....

"The NEW WORLD RELIGION is also a focus of common ground. We have been working on a *World Scripture* since the 1950's as a document which people can use to learn to live in harmony with our universal heritage....Certainly we should include some of the most pertinent esoteric teachings....

"May our spiritual work together be an increasingly powerful force in the awakening of individuals and groups throughout the planet to the <u>NEW WORLD RELIGION</u> and the new world at large!"[93] [Boldface and italics in the original; Caps and underline added]

Leland Stewart is not the only person looking for a new world with unity and diversity. The Sufi Order, founded by Hazrat Inayat Khan, is an interfaith group whose purpose is:

"to spread the message of unity, and promote the awakening of humanity to the divinity in all; to provide a program of spiritual training that brings about a deep personal transformation, culminating in a balanced, harmonious and creative life; to find ways to apply the spiritual ideals of love, harmony, and beauty to the challenges of everyday life; to promote understanding and acceptance among adherents of various faiths, and encourage the unfoldment of universal loving kinship."[94]

Notice that their logo uses wings as well as the moon and crescent.

Thomas Ehrenzeller has been associated with the World Federalist Association and the Association to Unite the Democracies.[95] Both of these organizations are working for world government. Ehrenzeller remarks:

"The era in which the people of the world finally cast off the bonds of nationalistic self-deception, freeing themselves to join together in one free community, will be a true Solar Age. As solar citizens, we will be part of one mighty race....We could build a world society...and so we will....Human society must finally become one single society,

UNITED IN ITS DIVERSITY....The New Era is coming, whether the guardians of the old are ready or not....There can be a New World Order....We will save the world by making of it a bright New Age. "[96] [Italics in the original; Caps and boldface added]

Mikhail Gorbachev also calls for unity in diversity. Addressing the United Nations (U.N.) on December 7, 1988, Gorbachev:

"praised the *'tremendous impetus to mankind's progress'* that came from the French and Russian revolutions, and he called for a new role for the U.N., saying: *'World progress is only possible through a search for universal human consensus as we move forward to a **new world order**....What we are talking about...is **unity in diversity.'*** (The *Newsweek* article regarding this on December 19, 1988, was titled, 'Brave New World.')"[97] [Italics in the original; Boldface added]

Gorbachev, who was president of Russia, is now the President of the Green Cross International. Their logo appears below. (Notice the yin/yang in the logo.)

The Gorbachev Foundation USA is based at the Presidio in San Francisco, California. Below is the Presidio Alliance's logo. They have the same logo as the United Religions Initiative which was seeking to set up their headquarters at Presidio.[98]

It is also interesting to note that Russia has now changed their symbol of the hammer and sickle to that of the two-headed eagle.[99] (The eagle symbolism is covered elsewhere in this book.)

Gorbachev mentioned that we need a new world order. Plans have been and are being laid for this new world order. There is even a flag called the "One World Flag." They explain their symbol like this:

> "Representing sky above and earth below, the circular icon grabs the eye and pulls our attention to *center.* Like the familiar 'yin-yang' symbol and other mandalas, it encompasses all, with everything in balance. Placed within a framework of colors representing the four directions—as generally agreed upon by native americans (sic) and many of the world's indigenous peoples—we are called to continually think and act from a larger perspective. And with the overlapping of these stripes, we are inspired to move forward—into a future we have always imagined as possible."[100]

THE ONE WORLD FLAG tm

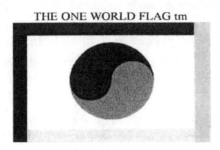

They add: "The steps of our paths may be diverse, but we will all arrive at the same destination!"[101] There's that **unity in diversity** theme again. Incidentally, this website has won the "Pagan Best of the Web" award and the "Mystic's Award."[102]

Global Education Associates is also working for world order. They describe their logo like this:

> "The sphere is each of us and it is all of us together and it is the earth as a whole in the system/mystery that is the universe.

> "The tree is life—our life—becoming what it can be within and dependent on the larger sphere of life.

> "The contrasting fluid fields of dark and light are the ancient elements: earth and water (dark), air and fire (light).

> *"The dark and light are also the yin and yang of life. They are the opposites which cannot exist apart, and which together are an integrated whole. They are the inner and outer dimensions of our humanization—of our shared present and future."*[103] [Emphasis in the original]

The Council on Foreign Relations (CFR) is also pushing for a one world order. The CFR publishes a magazine called *Foreign Affairs* as well as printing "position papers." One of these papers was published on November 25, 1959, and was entitled *Study No. 7*.[104] This document called for the "building (of) a new international order (which) may be responsible to world aspirations for peace (and) for social and economic change...An international order——...including labelling themselves as Socialist (Communist)."[105]

They have an interesting logo. It is a naked man astride a white steed. His hand looks like he could possibly be making the sign of the horned devil.

The Bible tells us in Psalms 9:17 that "the wicked shall be turned into hell, and all the nations that forget God."

A fascinating bit of information concerning the letters "CFR" is found in the *Encyclopaedia Britannica*. The Moslems believe that an Antichrist is to appear who will have "one eye."

"Nor is Antichrist unknown to Mohammedan theology in which he is called Masth (sic) *al Dajjal, the false or lying Christ...He is to be one-eyed and marked on the forehead with the letters C.F.R., i.e. Cafir or infidel."*[106]

The Trilateral Commission, another group working for world government, has a logo that is a variation of the triskelion and 666. Notice also that the arrows form a triangle, the center of which yields a broken cross.

Americans United for Separation of Church and State (AU) is yet another organization whose logo forms a triangle. Notice that flame at the top of this logo. The torch is covered elsewhere in this book. I also mention that a Masonic publisher is called The Torch Press. It should be noted that "about eighty percent of the funding for the predecessor of Americans United for Separation of Church and State came from Masons."[107] Their address is the very same address as that of the Masonic Service Association. In fact, a former Executive Director, Dr. Glenn L. Archer, and a former Associate Director, Dr. C. Stanley Lowell, were both 33° Masons.[108]

AU is against creation being taught in the classroom and they are for abortions, contraceptives, and sex education. A letter received from Barry Lynn, the Executive Director of AU, declares:

"Now I'm asking you to join with Americans United as we prepare for a massive clash with the Religious Right.

"I don't know about you, but personally I have seen enough, heard enough and read enough about the powerful new political influence of the revamped Religious Right. There's no point in mincing words: they must be stopped! And the sooner the better.

"If the Religious Right prevails, they will destroy our wondrous American mosaic. They'll thumb their noses at pluralism and stifle diversity. They'll inject their own moral code into our personal lives. We cannot—must not—let them do that!

"That's why I'm writing today to ask you—to urge you, really—to join Americans United and play a personal role in our battle against the Religious Right."[109] [Emphasis in the original]

The Trismegistus Press printed a Masonic book (which was full of veiled occultism) by W. L. Wilmshurst. You can see that their logo also uses the torch along with the circle and triangle. By the way, remember that the god Hermes was called Hermes **TRISMEGISTUS** or Hermes the Thrice Great.[110] It was Hermes Trismegistus who was the initiator of **OCCULT PHILOSOPHY and MAGIC.**[111] Is this what the Trismegistus Press represents?

Alcoholics Anonymous (AA) also uses the circle and triangle in their logo. Bill Wilson, a co-founder of AA, explained their logo. He said: "The circle stands for the whole world of A.A., and the triangle stands for A.A.'s Three Legacies: Recovery, Unity, and Service."[112] That doesn't sound bad but then he added: "It is perhaps no accident that priests and seers of antiquity regarded this symbol as a means of warding off spirits of evil."[113]

What this symbol (with the triangle pointing upward, called a **MAGIC TRIANGLE**) actually represents is interesting. It is a "symbol of importance to **WITCHES**,"[114] and "represents the protection of the 'circle' and the power of the triangle. It is also associated with the **OCCULT** and used to procure the services of **DEMONS** in various rituals."[115]

Al-Anon, a group based on the principles of AA, also uses a circle and triangle as their logo.

The California Institute of Integral Studies' logo has numerous triangles incorporated into it. A pamphlet from this group states:

> "The Integral Counseling Center offers the San Francisco community growth counseling based on an integral perspective which recognizes the individual as a body-mind-spirit continuum. Counselors have a wide variety of backgrounds in both Eastern and Western philosophy and **psychology:** psycho-dynamic, cognitive, **psychosynthesis, yoga, meditation, Gestalt, Jungian psychology,** Rankian therapy and **dreamwork.**"[116]

The logo for Apple Computers is an apple with a bite out of it.

"To many occult insiders, this signifies that the eating of the forbidden fruit (symbolically, the apple) by Adam and Eve in the Garden of Eden was *a good* thing. Occultists and New Agers teach that taking a bite out of the apple gave the first two humans knowledge, or *gnosis,* putting them on the path to self-divinity and godhood."[117] [Emphasis in the original]

Interestingly, the price tag on the first personal computer from Apple was $666.[118]

An unusual logo is that of the Raelists. One author points out:

"Last year [1991] they met in Canada; this year the sunny beaches of France hosted the 600 naked worshippers. They call themselves *Raelists* and their leader and prophet is *Rael,* a Frenchman who used to be a sports reporter but now proclaims, 'I am the Messiah!'

"The name 'Rael' comes from combining the word *RA,* one of the names of the ancient Egyptian sun god, and *EL,* a Hebrew title for deity. The 45 year-old Rael says that in 1973 he was whisked to the 'planet of the Elohim' by a flying saucer. There, two, tiny, oval-eyed aliens briefed him on his earthly mission as the messenger and savior of mankind.

"Rael explains that the spacemen also gave him a symbol for the new faith—a swastika inside the Jewish Star of David. This, he indicates, means peace, love, and harmony and has nothing to do with Hitler or Nazism.

"The primary method of worship by the Raelists is sacred sex, engaged in open, outside spaces as their messiah sits lotus-legged playing a wind instrument. The fast-growing UFO cult now has devotee's (sic) from 38 countries, including the USA, Japan, Belgium, Switzerland, Italy, and Canada."[119] [Emphasis in the original]

The Brookridge Institute had previously used a hexagon symbol but they are now using a different logo. The editors relate:

"Our energy model hexagon served us well but this **ancient Celtic symbol,** the *triscele*, speaks more eloquently about the consciousness approach....The *triscele* represents the three cycles of life, and we likewise are moving our publication frequency to three times a year."[120] [Italics in the original; Boldface added]

In an accompanying article called "The Triscele," we are informed:

"The **Triscele, the Celtic version of the YIN-YANG** symbol, represents the wholeness of life. It is a circle enclosing three spiral figures that appear to move in the same direction from a single central point. Triplicity symbolizes the stages of Life: Birth, Death and Re-Birth. The **CELTIC GODDESSES** typically showed three faces....

Triple Goddess

"Brookridge Institute has adopted this symbol as its logo because the Institute has two of nature's four elements in its name (Brook and Ridge) and we also espouse wholeness and the cyclic, regenerative quality of life."[121]

Many other groups use the triskele (or triscele) as their logo. Remember that this is a variation of the yin/yang symbol but it is also a representation of 666!

Institute of Transpersonal Psychology

World Future Society

New Ager, Richard (Dick) Sutphen, defines the logo he uses for his Reincarnationist organization.

> "It incorporates a variation of the pentacle, combined with the dove holding an olive branch. The pentacle, the five-pointed star with the **point up,** represents the highest power of spirituality on earth and is a seal against evil and negativity. It is often called the 'Star of Man', and the top point represents the Higher Self dominating the four lower points—the elements of fire, water, air and earth—symbolic of man controlling and creating his own reality."[122] [Emphasis in the original]

Sutphen also received a symbol during **meditation** on the night that his son, Hunter Shane, was born (June 2, 1986). He bragged: "He is a Gemini with Scorpio rising and moon in Aries. **Astrologically,** that adds up to a very determined young man who knows exactly what he wants."[123] This symbol appears on page 213. The caption that was under this picture proclaimed:

> **"Hunter's birth announcement included a symbol of Hunter, received by Richard in meditation on the night of Hunter's birth. It was a young man on horseback in Crusader's attire, holding a grail, and behind it, a glowing golden pentagram."**[124] [Emphasis in the original]

Hunter's birth announcement included a symbol of Hunter, received by Richard in meditation on the night of Hunter's birth. It was of a young man on horseback in Crusader's attire, holding a grail, and behind it, a glowing golden pentagram.

It is interesting to note that "at least 20 or 30 **psychics** around the country predicted that Tara (Dick Sutphen's wife) would have a girl. Only two predicted a boy, one of whom was the Sutphens' close friend, author Jess Stearn."[125] That should show how inaccurate psychic predictions are—and they even had a 50/50 chance of being correct and that many still missed it!

One issue of Sutphen's paper mentioned the words "New Age," or "New Ager(s)," at least 169 times in 26 pages.[126] His magazines are full of advertisements for books, videos, and cassettes on handwriting analysis, automatic handwriting, past life experiences, the Tarot, how to contact spirit guides, hypnosis, etc. He also held psychic seminars.

Cagliostro was an occultist and Mason who used a symbol with a snake. His symbol can be explained as thus:

"Because of his knowledge of alchemical mysteries, his familiarity with Hermetism and his skill in transmutation, Cagliostro was accorded new honors. It was at this time that a scholar of Nuremberg turned over to him a symbol which he was to adopt as his emblem and engrave on his seal in recognition of the powers that had been conferred on him. The symbol represented a serpent reared on its tail, swallowing an apple as an arrow pierced him through and through while blood gushed from the wound. The arrow was pointed downward, the serpent stretching its jaws upward—the symbol and hallmark of the Rosicrucians. The serpent is thus seen eating the fruit of knowledge, but then dying of it. Cagliostro informs us that he found the esoteric tracing of this symbol in the great manuscript of the 'Unknown Superiors' of Germany. He also relates that a dignitary of Freemasonry who saw it on his seal, bowed before him reverently. In Nuremberg, another Master, noticing this mark of respect, offered him in homage a ring set with a beautiful diamond."[127]

Another logo that utilizes the snake is the Himalayan Institute. Notice that the circle is actually a snake biting its tail.

The American Medical Association's symbol is the caduceus. This is not surprising when you read the oath that doctors take. The Hippocratic Oath states: "I swear by **Apollo,** the physician, and **Aesculapius** and health and all-heal and **all the gods and goddesses** that, according to my ability and judgment I will keep this oath and stipulation...."

The chiropractic emblem is often the caduceus with just one snake. The International Chiropractors Association uses a logo that seems to be a variation of the yin/yang. Below (in the center) is yet another chiropractic representation.

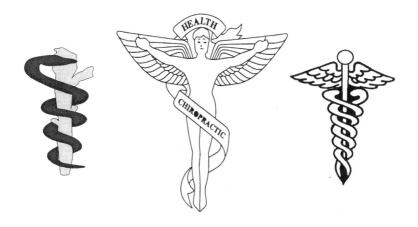

The Theosophical Society is another society that incorporates the snake into its logo. Observe that there are a number of symbols besides the snake in this drawing. There's an ankh, a white and black triangle making a hexagram, a swastika, and an Om. Masonic writer, J. D. Buck, reveals:

"The perfect equilibrium of spirit and matter is symbolized by the six-pointed star, which is again only another form of the Square and Compass, each now having a base-line from which to form a triangle. Inclose (sic) the star in a circle, which symbolizes Infinity, and you symbolize the harmony, or at-one-ment of the Spirit that descended, and the body, now purified, with Divinity, or the Over-Soul. Place within the Star thus inclosed (sic) the Egyptian emblem of Life [the ankh], and we symbolize *Immortality,* as the result of regeneration. Transform the circle into a serpent and it now symbolizes Wisdom, as the crown or result of equilibrium; and is also a double glyph of the return of matter to its source in spirit. Separate the tongue and tail of the serpent by a *Thor's Hammer,* or Svastica [swastika], inclosed (sic) within a circle, and it symbolizes regeneration through conquest of animal sense, precisely as taught in the Lodge, under the spiritual meaning of the symbol of the Compass."[128]

Notice the center of the large picture above. It's the same as the small picture. Below is another logo for the Theosophical Society.

THE THEOSOPHICAL SOCIETY IN AMERICA

DASO has a catalog that offers all kinds of occultic paraphernalia including statues of gods and goddesses. Their logo also has a snake in it. DASO explains:

"Our latest offering is rich in mystic symbolism. Notice the person in the picture. He has both winds and roots, symbolizing freedom while being grounded. His head is bent in surrender.

"Surrounding him is a serpent, symbolizing the **KUNDALINI** force. Notice the serpent's head: the shape is in a heart, between the eyes, the brow is in the shape of the Aries symbol [astrology], symbolising (sic) renewal and rebirth. The serpent has roses as a scale pattern, representing the enjoyment of life and it's (sic) corresponding disappointments.

"The combining of the serpent and the man has produced an oasis in the desert, where a lotus blooms and two dragonflies play. Behind them you see the sun rising over the pyramids, a new day dawning for an ancient knowledge....

"The activation of the Kundalini is a dangerous step, but once activated the vital life force is flowing through the student. When that happens, the **INITIATE** becomes an overflowing river of love, affecting those who come in contact.

"The pyramids symbolize the revival of knowledge once held sacred in Ancient Egyptian times. The secret processes of awakening your soul!

"DASO selected this picture for its logo because of the meaning behind it. We are now making the complete picture available as a **MEDITATION** Tool. We hope you will meditate on this picture and find the **HIDDEN MEANINGS** held within."[129]

Former President, George Bush, belongs to a secret society called the Skull & Bones. "The initiation ritual of Skull & Bones is bizarre and grotesque. New members must pass through a harrowing ordeal. At one point, the initiate, lying naked in a coffin in a darkened room, must reveal the most intimate details about his sexual history and experiences."[130] The logo for this association is a skull and bones with the mysterious number 322 below it.

Mountain Luminary is a New Age paper. Their logo uses the all-seeing eye.

The logo for the Ordo Templi Orientis also utilizes the all-seeing eye.

"Around the turn of the century, Karl Keller, a German, founded the Ordo Templi Orientis (OTO), a ritual magick group which taught sex magick. Crowley joined the OTO and was made the head of its British affiliate. To the heterosexual ninth degree he added a homosexual eleventh degree. OTO sexual magick seems to have been derived from Oriental sources as well as from P. B. Randolph of the American-based Fraternitas Rosae Crucis. It was perfected by Crowley during three years (1920-23) at the Abbey of Thelema in Sicily. Crowley also succeeded Theodor Reuss in 1922 as outer head of the OTO."

"Upon Crowley's death in 1947, Karl Johannes Germer succeeded to the outer headship of the order. Germer had been with Crowley in England, but returned to his native Germany in the 1930's."[131]

The American Psychotherapy Association has pentagrams in their emblem.

Shree Gurudev Ashram utilizes the "Om" for their symbol.

Below are a number of organizations (many of them government associations) that use various occultic symbolism. I am not saying that these groups **intentionally** used any particular symbol with occult connections in mind, but it is important to remember that many of our government officials do belong to secret societies such as Freemasonry or the Skull & Bones. In the book, *Sirius,* we are reminded:

> "Many of the founding fathers of the United States of America were Masons and they used its rituals in the consecration of their inspired work, including the erection of important government buildings. Study will reveal that there is more to Masonry than meets the modern eye, for there reside important aspects of the Mysteries within it, as we are told by the Tibetan."[131]

The Tibtean is a spirit guide (actually a demon) that many New Agers such as Alice Bailey, Robert Muller, M. Temple Richmond, etc., have received guidance from.

National Sheriffs Association   University of Seven Rays

Lucent Technologies

Eternal State of Buddha—
Isn't this somewhat similar
to Lucent's logo?

14. HAND SIGNALS

Proverbs 6:12 tells us: "A naughty person, a wicked man, walketh with a froward mouth. He winketh with his eyes, he speaketh with his feet, he teacheth with his fingers." It sounds as though this verse could be applied to Masons, occultists, gang members, and many other groups of people because they often use their hands and their feet to give messages to one another. For example, the Masons have their secret hand grips. They also position their feet in a particular manner to form a Tau cross. This type of position can be helpful if a Mason is called into court. With this stance, the judge (if he is also a Mason) can readily see that the person before his bench is a fellow member of his society.

You see, the Mason, taking the oath of the 3°, **PROMISES TO CONCEAL ALL CRIMES COMMITTED BY A FELLOW MASON** except those of treason and murder.[1] By the 7° of Masonry, the candidate has to promise that he "will assist a Companion Royal Arch Mason when I see him engaged in any difficulty, and will espouse his cause so far as to extricate him from the same, **WHETHER HE BE RIGHT OR WRONG.**"[2]

In the 13° the oath is taken to the effect that **ALL CRIMES ARE TO BE CONCEALED, INCLUDING MURDER AND TREASON.**[3]

This, of course, means that if a Mason has committed murder and the judge is also a Mason, the judge is **obligated** by his Masonic oath to set the murderer free, even if it results in placing the blame on an innocent person! In fact, this command is given in one handbook:

> **"YOU MUST CONCEAL ALL THE CRIMES OF YOUR BROTHER MASONS...AND SHOULD YOU BE SUMMONED AS A WITNESS AGAINST A BROTHER MASON BE ALWAYS SURE TO SHIELD HIM....IT MAY BE PERJURY TO DO THIS, IT IS TRUE, BUT YOU'RE KEEPING YOUR OBLIGATIONS."[4]**

Witches tell us that hand signals are very important. In *Wicca: A Guide for the Solitary Practitioner* we find:

"Gestures are silent counterparts to words. Gestures can enhance Wiccan rituals when performed in conjunction with invocations or dance, or can be used alone for their real power....

"My introduction to Wicca happened to include some of these old gestures. In 1971 I saw some photographs of **MAGICAL** protective **GESTURES** such as the *mano figo* (a hand clenched into a fist, the thumb jutting out between the first and middle fingers) and the *mano cornuta,* a 'v' formed by the first and little fingers and held upside down....the latter is **USED IN WICCA,** with points up to represent the God in his Horned aspect....

"Gestures in Wiccan ritual can easily became second nature. When invoking the Goddess and God, the hands can be held uplifted with the fingers spread to receive their power. The Goddess can be individually invoked with the left hand, the thumb and first finger held up and curled into a half-circle, while the rest of the fingers are tucked against the palm. This represents the crescent Moon. **The God is invoked** with the first and middle fingers of the right hand raised, or **with the first and fourth fingers up, the thumb holding down the others against the palm, to represent horns.**

"The elements can be invoked with individual gestures when approaching the four directions: a flat hand held parallel with the ground to invoke Earth at the North; an upraised hand, fingers spread wide apart to invoke Air at the East; an upraised fist for the South to invite Fire, and a cupped hand to the West to invoke Water....

"GESTURES ARE ALSO USED IN MAGIC. Each of the fingers relates to a specific planet as well as an ancient deity. Since **pointing is a magical act and is a part of many spells,** the finger can be chosen by its symbolism.

"The thumb relates to Venus and to the planet Earth. Jupiter (both the planet and the god) rules the forefinger. The middle finger is ruled by the god and planet Saturn, the fourth finger the Sun and Apollo, and the little finger by the planet Mercury as well as the god after which it is named....

"Gestures are magical tools as potent as any other, ones we can always take with us, to be used when needed."[5] [Italics in the original; Caps and boldface added]

The "mano figo," also called "fica gesture" (mentioned above), "has been regarded as a defense against the evil eye, a crude insult, and a sexual symbol as well."[6]

The "mano cornuta" was also mentioned. This is known by a number of other names such as: the devil's triad, il cornuto, cornuto, the horn, horned devil, twin-horned salute, horned hand, devil salute, and devil horn salute.

The Devil's triad is a recognition sign among Satanists and witches. Remember that Satan (or Pan) is called "The Horned God," so the hand signal is formed so as to resemble horns. Many people in heavy metal music or rock music also use this sign. Even some within the so-called "Christian" rock world (there is no such thing as Christian rock!) use this signal. Some of the rock groups who use this are: Gene Simmons (from KISS), Heart, Cheap Trick, Utopia,[7] and so-called "Christian" rock group Petra.[8] The Beatles were the first rock band to use the devil's triad on a record album cover.[9]

Another rocker who frequently uses the devil salute is Ronnie James Padovana who calls himself "Dio" (which is Latin for "God"). He admits that he knows about the occult[10] and he at one time "led thousands in 'altar calls' to Satan at concerts...."[11]

His album covers also feature this sign. In addition, it is interesting to note his name on the cover. When his name is turned upside down, the word changes from "Dio" to "Devil"!

The Devil's triad "is a Silician sign of the Devil used to cast spells and to ward off the 'Evil Eye,'"[12] as well as a sign for hexing and charming (casting spells), which is explicitly forbidden by Deuteronomy 18:10-12a: "There shall not be found among you any one that maketh his son or his daughter to pass through the fire, or that useth divination, or an observer of times, or an enchanter, or a witch, Or a **CHARMER,** or a consulter with familiar spirits, or a wizard, or a necromancer. For all that do these things are an abomination unto the Lord."

This sign is "also used by the Mafia for signaling death."[13]

It is also intriguing to note that the god Shiva (Siva), which is a synonym for Satan (according to *The Satanic Bible*[14]), also is seen making the Devil's triad in some pictures. One Mason, J. S. M. Ward, brags: "Shiva, who carries in His second right hand the cabletow of death...is the Lord of Death, and therefore of rebirth [reincarnation], it is **particularly significant** that He should be represented as making the sign He is."[15]

In *The Gods of India,* we find:

"I bow to Siva as Isana, the Ruler, who has five faces. Followed by the She-Goat...he holds in his hands the Vedas, an elephant hook, a noose, a hatchet, a skull, a drum, a rosary, a trident, and he shows the **gestures** of removing fear and granting boons."[16]

Below is the "moon sign." It is used by witches to salute the rising moon.

A hand signal can also be seen in the Tarot deck:

"*The Magician* (also called the Magus or the Juggler). A young man holding up a wand in his right hand, and pointing to the earth with his left. On a table before him are the four elemental symbols, and above his head is the sign of eternity or infinity....He is the Magus, the Adept, the human being integrated on all planes, the will liberated through understanding. His **GESTURE** refers to the basic **OCCULT** principle 'That which is above is as that which is below, but after another manner.'"[17]

Notice that the artist of Baphomet, Eliphas Levi (who was a Mason and occultist), drew Baphomet making the same **OCCULT** gestures!

S. R. Parchment boasts:

> "Those who received initiation into the mysteries were given certain keys pertaining to both **white and black magic** which were portrayed by the **right hand of Baphomet pointing upward** to the bright disc of the waxing moon while the **left pointed downward** to Luna in darkness. That **MANY OF** the leading lights of **MASONRY WERE IN QUEST OF THE MAGICAL SECRETS NO STUDENT OF OCCULT SCIENCE WILL DENY....**"[18]

Another hand gesture is called a mudra. *The Seeker's Handbook* explains that a mudra is:

> "A ritual gesture of the hand or body, often seen in Oriental art and sculpture, as in figures showing the Buddha with one hand raised in the gesture of granting peace and dismissing fear. Also, trancelike motions, or convulsive-ecstatic poses and hand gestures, often performed in a convulsive manner by someone receiving a direct transmission of spiritual power from a master (shaktipat)."[19]

A *Dictionary of Mysticism* notes that the mudra is a "'mystic seal' of Oriental **occultism; a series of occult signs** made with the fingers, and considered to have **magical** effects."[20]

In *The Gods of India* we find:

> "In addition to *mantras* and *yantras,* the third way of representing deities is through gestures *(mudra).* There is a large number of symbolic gestures used in ritual and believed to evoke supranatural beings. Many of the *mudras* through which a deity can be evoked are also used in the sacred dance."[21] [Emphasis in the original]

Notice how the fingers of both figures on page 231 are formed into circles. This is called a mudra.

Another hand gesture is that of benediction. The **shadow "represents Satan.** That shadow, according to Satanists, is the symbol of malediction. A modernized use of this sign appeared in the *Daily World* of October 18, 1969, as the insignia...of the **Communist** GIs & Vets for Peace."[22] The Pope makes this sign frequently, especially when giving blessings.[23]

A former witch, Mason, and Satanist explains:

"However, the two-fingers TOGETHER *mudra* symbolizes:

"1) the Masonic/Gnostic Law of opposites. The need for both dark and light, good and evil, pain and pleasure which is exemplified in such Masonic icons as the 'Master's Carpet,' which is intended to be a black and white checkerboard. This is rooted in Persian dualism (the doctrine that there is a god of good and a god of evil; and that both gods are equal in power and are necessary to the equilibrium of the cosmos), and is totally un-Biblical....

"b) These also symbolize the 'Abba' or 'Father Current' of Magic and the 'Aima' or 'Mother Current' of Magic. These currents or 'lines of power' come down to us through the centuries from Babylon and Nimrod....

"In Satanism, that gesture is known as the sign of 'The Bowman.' It is a symbol of the anti-Christ. This Bowman/anti-Christ association IN THE OCCULT...is because of the connection between the Horned God of witchcraft and the hunt. A popular name for the Horned God in England is, in fact, Herne the Hunter."[24] [Emphasis in the original]

The *Complete Book of Witchcraft* reveals:

"There was a deeply seated belief in the fascination or enchantment of shadows; so that the witch, or magician, could use them to either produce sickness and death or to inspire love....the shadow of the priest's fingers raised in blessing was considered [*by Satanists—American Opinion*] to have evil significance....A remarkable thing connected with the hand so lifted, is that its shadow resembles the head and horns of the Goat of Baphomet...the symbol of black magic. The use of the 'shadow of blessing' was regarded as the legitimate prerogative of the Pope, and was most terribly exercised during the Dark Ages and at the times of the Inquisition."[25] [Emphasis in the original]

A related hand signal is the "peace sign" or "v sign." The signal "actually began as a symbol of Satanic benediction during the rituals."[26] This sign has been used by Yasser Arafat, Richard Nixon, Winston Churchill, and Stewart Meacham, Co-Chairman of Reds' New Mobilization Committee."[27] Churchill said that the sign stood for victory but remember that Churchill was one of the insider "elite" and a Mason. He most likely knew the evil significance of this symbol but tried to give it a facelift.

The "v sign" has a colorful history. "V" is the Roman sign for the number five and Adam Weishaupt used it in the Illuminati to symbolize the "Law of Fives,"[28] but there's more. In the Cabala:

> "the meaning for the Hebrew letter for V (Vau) is 'Nail.' Now, 'The Nail' is one of the secret titles of Satan within the Brotherhood of Satanism. Satan is letting us know that this is one of his favorite signs. Why else does he like the PENTA-gram (Penta = five!) and the FIVE-fold salute used in Masonry and Witchcraft?"[29] [Emphasis in the original]

Furthermore:

> "The Leftists, radicals, and Satanists who have popularized that sign...know its ancient significance very well. In fact, that 'V' sign is now used **extensively** by such **Communist** organizations as the Young Socialist Alliance, Vets for Peace in Vietnam, and the Students for a Democratic Society."[30]

Although not a hand sign, the peace symbol itself needs to be examined.

> "Known as the 'peace sign' throughout the 1960's and into the present day, this symbol is the **Teutonic rune of death.** 1950's peace advocate Gerald Holtom may have been commissioned by **communist sympathizer Bertrand Russell to design a symbol to unite leftist peace marchers in 1958.** It is clear that either Holtom or Russell deemed the Teutonic (Neronic) cross as the appropriate symbol for their cause.

"Throughout the last 2,000 years this symbol has designated hatred of Christians. Nero, who despised Christians, crucified the Apostle Peter on a cross head downward. This hideous event resembled the Teutonic cross and became a popular **pagan insignia** of the day. Thereafter, this sign became known as the 'Neronic cross.'

"The symbol's origin in history proves it to be the visual mystic character for 'Aum' (the split 'Y'). This is the sacred word to the Hindu. Chanting 'Aum' is supposed to help awaken 'the serpent power of Brahma' at the base of the human spine. Occultist Albert Pike also identifies this symbol as mystical in his book on Freemasonry *Morals and Dogma.* "[31]

The peace symbol (also called the "broken cross," "crow's foot," "witch's foot," "Nero Cross," "sign of the 'broken Jew,'" and the "symbol of the 'anti-Christ'"[32]) is actually a cross with the arms broken. It also signifies the "gesture of despair," and the "death of man."[33]

"The Germanic tribes who used it attributed strange and **mystical** properties to the sign. Such a 'rune' is said to have been **used by 'black magicians' in pagan incantations and condemnations....**To this very day the inverted broken cross—identical to the socialists' 'peace' symbol—is known in Germany as a *'todersrune,'* or death rune. Not only was it ordered by Hitler's National Socialists that it must appear on German death notices, but it was part of the official inscription prescribed for the gravestones of Nazi officers of the dread SS. The symbol suited Nazi emphasis on **pagan** mysticism."[34] [Italics in the original; Boldface added]

With the arms of the cross raised in an upright position, it is "a Pythagorean emblem of the course of life, in the form of a rising path with fork roads to Good and Evil."[35] It also signifies fertility, but with the arms pointing downward, it denotes evil and death.[36]

"In fact, the inverted 'Man-rune'—the figure encircled in the common sign which the Communists tell us means 'peace'—has for centuries been a favorite sign of Satanists."[37]

Anton LaVey, the founder of the Church of Satan, used the peace symbol as the backdrop for his altar.[38]

One former witch makes the following comment about the peace symbol:

"It is an ancient and powerful symbol of Antichrist. During the dark ages it was used in Druid Witchcraft and by Satanists of all sorts during the initiation of a new member to their order. They would draw the magic circle and give the initiate a cross. The initiate would then lift the cross and turn it upside down. He would then renounce Christianity in all three dimentions (sic) of time (past, present and future) and break the horizontal pieces downward forming the design of the 'Raven's Foot.' This ugly symbol is nothing short of blasphemy against the Holy Ghost. For one to wear or display this symbol is to announce either knowingly or unknowingly that you have rejected Christ. Remember, symbolism is a picture language, and a picture is worth a thousand words."[39]

Below are a few examples of how the peace symbol is being used.

ECOLOGY **NOW!**

This symbol is used nationwide by revolutionary Marxists

Another hand signal is the Vulcan peace sign. It is supposed to mean "Live Long and Prosper," and can be seen in *Star Trek.*

Vulcan was a sun deity who was associated with fire, thunderbolts, and light.[40] The festival in honor of him was called the Vulcania in which **human sacrifices** were offered.[41] "According to Diel, he bears a family relationship to the Christian **devil.**"[42] It is fascinating to know that he married Venus,[43] another name for Lucifer or the devil. What is even more interesting is that Vulcan is adored in Masonry under the name of Tubal Cain.[44] In the *Masonic Quiz Book* the question is asked: "Who was Tubal Cain?" The answer is: "He is the **Vulcan** of the **pagans.**"[45]

In Masonry, Tubal Cain is the name of the password for the Master Mason (or third) degree.[46]

Listen to what occultist and Mason, Manly Palmer Hall, has to say:

> "When the Mason learns that the key to the warrior on the block is the proper application of the dynamo of living power, he has learned the mastery of his Craft. The **seething energies of Lucifer** are in his hands and before he may step onward and upward, he must prove his ability to properly apply energy. **He must follow in the footsteps of his forefather, Tubal-Cain,** who with the mighty strength of the war god hammered his sword into a plowshare."[47]

There is also a sexual connotation associated with Vulcan and Tubal Cain. Former Mason, Bill Schnoebelen, explains:

> "For Masons who wish to conceal their membership from non-Masons, but still advertise it to their Lodge brothers, there is a special pin (or tie tack) they can wear. It looks like an upside down golf club with two balls near the top....Many people assume the person is a golfing enthusiast, but it is actually a visual Masonic pun.

> "This is called the 'Two Ball Cane,' and is a pun on the secret password of a Master Mason, 'Tubalcain (sic).'...It is also an all-too-obvious pun on the 'god' of Masonry, the male reproductive organ. Nice, eh?...especially when many men wear these wretched things to church on Sunday!"[48]

While we are on the subject of Masonry, there is another Masonic symbol called the clasped hands. Of course, the Masons aren't the only ones who use this symbol.

"It is now used by the...A.F.L.-C.I.O., and is frequently reproduced in the Communist *Daily World* to indicate union between Comrades. This insignia is the official symbol of the Communist-controlled Student 'Nonviolent' Coordinating Committee, and serves as the logo for the Trotskyite Communists' *Workers World.*"[49]

This emblem was also a Pythagorean symbol.[50] (Pythagoras was a **MAGICIAN.**) Many Masonic sources reveal that the clasped hands are a "symbol of fidelity,"[51] but they don't stop with that explanation. For example, Albert G. Mackey, 33° Mason, confesses:

> "The *right hand* has in all ages been deemed an emblem of fidelity, and our ancient brethren worshiped **DEITY UNDER THE NAME OF FIDES** or Fidelity, which was sometimes represented by **TWO RIGHT HANDS JOINED,** and sometimes by two human figures, holding each other by the right hands....

> "Numa was the first who erected an altar to **FIDES,** under which name the **GODDESS OF OATHS** and honesty was worshiped. Obligations taken in her name were considered as more inviolable than any others."[52] [Italics in the original; Boldface and caps added]

Oh, so here again the Masonic symbol represents a **PAGAN GOD**—this time it is Fides.

In fact, the very first degree of the Masonic ritual contains the following question and answer:

> "*Q.* Why were you caused to rest your right hand on the Holy Bible, square, and compasses?

"*A*. Because the right hand was supposed by our ancient brethren to be the seat of fidelity, and so they worshipped Deity under the name of *Fides,* which was supposed to be represented by the right hands joined, and by two human figures holding each other by the right hand; the right hand, therefore, we masonically use to signify in the strongest manner possible the sincerity of our intentions in the business in which we are engaged."[53] [Emphasis in the original]

How can a Christian worship Fides and at the same time worship the God who commanded: "Thou shalt have **NO** other gods before Me" (Exodus 20:3)? Another of God's precepts is: "Make **NO MENTION** of the name of other gods, neither let it be heard out of thy mouth" (Exodus 23:13).

15. A MEDLEY OF SYMBOLS

As mentioned earlier, the triskele (or triskelion) is one symbol that appears in many logos today. Although many people would probably not recognize the name "triskele," they certainly would recognize a picture of this symbol. "The **triskelion** (Greek for three legs) **is a symbol of the sun** intended to express motion. A similar device, with four legs, called a tetraskelion, is a modification of the swastika."[1] Like the swastika, it is considered to be a good luck symbol.[2]

An occult organization sells a triskelion and serpent pendant. They brag: "Double **magic!** Designs on both side (sic) of this unusually attractive pendant. One side bears the three-legged triskeles symbolizing rising, zenith, setting. On the other [side the] serpent portrays strength, divine power, infinite wisdom, eternity."[3] Another catalog tells us that the "'legs' represent birth, death, and **rebirth.**"[4] Of course, this is a reference to **REINCARNATION.**

We must remember that since the triskele is "a Celtic version of the Yin-Yang symbol of life,"[5] and a modification of the swastika,[6] that what has been said previously about the yin/yang and the swastika (to be covered later) applies to this symbol as well.

A New Age organization sells a Celtic Goddess Pin. It is described like this:

> "Symbols of the triskele (the sea, good luck) and cauldron (abundance, inspiration) celebrate *Cerridwen:*

Celtic goddess of transformation, who offers guidance and spiritual renewal at crucial junctures in the lives of her devotees. In Welsh mythology, she guarded the cauldron of inspiration and was the muse of the bards."[7] [Emphasis in the original]

Cerridwen is the goddess of wisdom[8] and **witchcraft.**[9] A former witch reveals: "Cerridwen is the traditional name of the Crone. I learned that in ancient legend, she is the keeper of the Black Cauldron of Immortality. This is the Cauldron from which one sip could bring incredible insights, wisdom and supernatural powers."[10]

Cerridwen is also another name for Venus (also known as Lucifer), Isis,[11] and Hecate.[12] In *Mythology* we find that "Hecate was the Goddess of the Dark of the Moon, the black nights when the moon is hidden. She was associated with the deeds of darkness, the Goddess of the Crossways, which were held to be ghostly places of evil magic."[13]

Laurie Cabot, a witch, states: "At death Hecate was said to meet the departed souls and lead them to the Underworld....And so Hecate became known as the Queen of the Witches...."[14] It's no wonder that Hecate is called the "Queen of the Witches" since she taught **SORCERY** and **WITCHCRAFT.**[15]

Marilyn Ferguson, a New Ager, used the symbol of the triquetra (another name for the triskele) on her book *The Aquarian Conspiracy.* This is a variation for the number 666.[16] Other books and materials have a similar design printed on them, such as books from David

Spangler, the person who lauds Lucifer,[17] and *The Witch's Grimoire.* As most people know, the number 666 is the number of the beast (see Revelation 13:18) and is evil, yet the occultists and New Agers love this number and consider it to be a sacred number.[18]

As stated earlier, many organizations, such as the World Future Society and the Trilateral Commission, incorporate this symbol into their logo. I think it is quite interesting to see that this same symbol appears on the cover of the *New King James Bible* as well!

The symbol below is used to exorcise evil spirits. Isn't there a striking similiarity to the logo on the *New King James Bible?!*

A few more variations of the triskele appear on the next page.

I think it is interesting to note that Paul (David) Yonggi Cho, a former Buddhist who is now supposedly a Christian, is pastor of the world's largest church with about 800,000 members. His church in Seoul, Korea, the Yoido Full Gospel Church, belongs to the Assemblies of God conference. The logo he uses is the triskele (see below). As a former Buddhist, I'm fairly sure he would be quite aware of the symbol he is using.

Satanists love to use 666 but sometimes it is disguised as "FFF," since "F" is the 6th letter of the alphabet. Sometimes they will use 999 since 9 is an upside down 6. Also used in Satanism is 3 circles connected at the center which is another symbol representing the mark of the beast.

Another symbol used in Satanism is the anarchy sign. It is a large A surrounded by a circle and it "represents the abolition of

all law. Initially, those into 'punk' music used this symbol, but it is now widely used by Heavy Metal followers."[19] [Emphasis in the original]

This symbol is really an emblem of rebellion. I Samuel 15:23 tells us that "rebellion is as the sin of witchcraft." It isn't hard to see how rebellion can result in witchcraft. King Saul was rebellious and he eventually sought out a witch. Satan rebelled against God and now his followers obviously are following in his footsteps.

Below are two symbols that are used in Satanism. The first one is a "blood ritual symbol [that] represents human and animal sacrifices"[20] and the second is a "sexual ritual symbol often...painted on objects near the side of the road to show the Satanists' use of the location."[21]

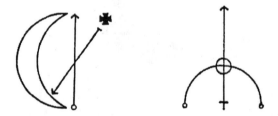

Satanists also reverse the double-headed axe to represent "anti-justice to Satanists."[22]

Of course, the doubled-headed axe (or labrys) in the upright position isn't a good symbol, either. One witchcraft magazine states:

"A Labrys is a double-headed ax that some say dates back to matriarchal times. Women involved in Dianic **Witchcraft** and related paths of **Feminist Spirituality** wear **Labrys amulets** for protection, strength, and empowerment. For some, the Labrys also is the emblem of the Amazon."[23]

In fact, the labrys is one of the symbols in witchcraft used to honor the Goddess.[24] Another book on witchcraft states: "The labrys is symbolic of the phases of the Moon and of the Goddess. It was extensively used in Crete."[25]

A gay and lesbian organization proudly uses the labrys. They brag:

"The Labyris (sic) comes from the time when women lived equal and free. It symbolized power and strength, transformation and the Goddess. Labyris (sic) takes its name from labia and gives its name to **labyrinth, place of**

initiation. Lesbians are self-initiated women who have transformed and empowered ourselves. The **double-axe is our symbol,** wear it with pride!"[26]

Marduk, a pagan god, was known as the Lord of the double-headed axe[27] and a Masonic book tells us that the double-headed axe was the chief symbol of Sandan and that it was also "associated with the Syrian god of fertility...."[28] *A Dictionary of Symbols* gives some revealing information about the axe:

"A symbol of the **power of light**....But much more important and complex is the significance of the **twin-bladed axe, related to the sign *tau*.**...According to Luc Benoist, this twin-bladed axe is the same as the Hindu *vajra* and Jove's **thunderbolt,** becoming, therefore, a **symbol of celestial illumination.** Nowadays, the **double-bladed axe** (the *labrys*) is **associated with the labyrinth,** both being symbols in the Cretan cult."[29] [Italics in the original; Boldface added]

The tau is a Masonic symbol. The Mason makes the tau cross with his feet during his initiation ceremony and the triple tau appears on the Masonic apron. J. S. M. Ward, a Mason, reveals that the tau cross is "placed on the apron of the Master of the Lodge, though placed [upside down], so as to give also the symbol of the square, and also to emphasise its **phallic** meaning."[30] He adds: "The *tau cross* is also a symbol of the male or creative side of the deity, and is really a conventionalised form of the phallus."[31] [Emphasis in the original] *The Sign Language of the Mysteries* states somewhat the same thing: "The tau cross is a very ancient symbol, representing the phallus and hence it often stands for our animal passions."[32]

Upside down Tau

The book *Anacalypsis* reveals:

"The Tau, T, is the emblem of Mercury, of Hermes. It is the *crux ansata,* and the *crux Hermis*....the **crux Tau was also the emblem of the generative power,** of eternal transmigrating life, and thus was used indiscriminately with the Phallus. It was, in fact, *the phallus.* The Tau is the Thoth, the Teut, the Teutates of the Druids; and Teutates was Mercury...."[33] [Italics in the original; Boldface added]

A former Mason mentions that the tau cross "is actually the symbol of the pagan slain and risen god, Tammuz (Ezekiel 8:13-14). It is a symbol for just another counterfeit Masonic 'Christ.'"[34]

The Phoenicians used the tau cross as a **magic** symbol.[35]

As just mentioned, the tau and the double-headed axe are the same as the thunderbolt. Thor, Set, Zeus, and Jupiter (as well as other gods) were considered to be the gods of thunder and lightning.[36] It's interesting to note that Thor (who is covered more thoroughly in the chapter on "Masonic and Eastern Star Symbols") is another name for Satan. Remember that Satanists love to use the lightning or thunderbolt (also called the Satanic S).

A Satanic rock group called KISS ("the name stands for 'Knights in Satan's Service'"[37]) uses the Satanic S for the last two letters in their name. They also have a song on one of their albums entitled "God of Thunder."[38] Some other rock groups that use the Satanic S are *"Black Sabbath, AC-DC, Raven, Metallica, Krokus, Judas Priest, Keel, [and] Bowie...."*[39] [Emphasis in the original]

A little history of where the Satanic S came from should prove fascinating. We're told:

> "In the early stages of the total Nazification of Germany, Gestapo chief Heinrich Himmler, one of the most feared and hated men in the entire nation, undertook archeological excavations in various parts of Europe, digging for clues to the 'magnificent' past of the Aryan 'super-race.' At a site in Bavaria, ancient **runic** inscriptions were uncovered. **Runes** were part of a centuries-old Germanic alphabet which **possessed mystical significance** to the Teutonic tribesmen of that time. One of the tokens unearthed was the **lightning bolt 'S.' Himmler incorporated the sign into the Gestapo, making it the infamous 'SS' (for Schutzstaffel). Several other runes were also used in secret SS rituals.**

"The two letters of *KISS'* logo are identical to those of Himmler's SS...."[40]

"These jagged symbols were also used by the Nazi **S.S.** as their **sign of Satanic terror. The sign represents the power of Lucifer falling to earth from Grace as a lightning bolt.** (Luke 10:18)."[41] [Italics in the original; Boldface added]

A Dictionary of Symbols claims:

"The **thunderbolt** is held to be an emblem of sovereignty. The winged thunderbolt expresses the ideas of power and speed. Jupiter's three thunderbolts symbolize chance, destiny and providence—the forces that mould the future....The *vajra*, the Tibetan symbol for both 'thunderbolt' and 'diamond', is also connected with the world-axis....It **is also related to the glance from the third eye of Shiva** (or Siva), the destroyer of all material forms."[42] [Italics in the original; Boldface added]

The thunderbolt, in the form of the dordj, "is used by the lamas and bonzes to bless the faithful, and to exorcise demons."[43] As just noted, it is also related to the third eye of Shiva. The third eye is covered in the chapter on the "All-Seeing Eye," but it should be noted, according to *The Satanic Bible,* that Shiva is another name for Satan.[44]

Shiva carries the **trisula**[45] (or trident, which is referred to as the **Caduceus of India**[46]) and Jupiter's thunderbolt was three-forked.[47]

The number three is very important in Masonry and the occult. A Masonic author, John T. Lawrence, reminds us:

"Thus we [the Masons] have **three** degrees, **three** great lights, **three** lesser lights, **three** principal officers, **three** assistant officers, **three** sets of **three** working tools, **three** steps, **three** pillars, **three** ornaments, **three** articles of furniture, **three** movable jewels and **three** immovable jewels, **three** grand principles, **three** assassins, **three** searching lodges, **three** who rule a lodge, **three** Grand Masters, and **three** orders of architecture. In fact, the respect paid by Freemasons to this number goes far to suggest that our mysteries have affinities not only with the Egyptian rites and ceremonies, but with those of a good many other nations. In the **mythologies** of Greece and Rome **the thunderbolt of Jupiter was three-forked; the sceptre of Neptune was a trident.** There were **three** Fates and **three** Furies. Both the sun and moon had **three** names—Apollo, Sol, and Liber, and Diana, Luna, and Hecate respectively. Cerberus was **three-headed.** In Hindu mythology **the worshipper of Vishnu has his forehead decorated with a trident.**"[48]

A Dictionary of Symbols explains that the **trident "is an attribute of the god** of the unconscious and **of sin—Neptune,** whose realm is the haunt of monsters and base forms of life. The triple character of the **trident is an 'INFERNAL replica of the Trinity....'"**[49] Neptune, the god of the sea, is also known as Poseidon, Hades (hell), and Shiva.[50]

Neptune

Mythologist Joseph Campbell reminds us that the "trefoil or trident, [is] the symbol of Shiva, Poseidon, Satan."[51] The Lord of the Abyss is pictured with a hammer which "is symbolic, also, of the **lightning bolt of *illumination....* "**[52] The trident "is also a fire symbol...."[53] Remember, that Lucifer (Satan) is called the **Light-bearer** and the Bible tells us that Satan comes as "an angel of light" (II Corinthians 11:14).

The trident or lightning bolt is used in many ways. It's the symbol used for psychology and Neptune, the emblem on the flag for Barbados, as well as The United States Naval War College.

Psychology   Astrological symbols for Neptune

Another Satanic symbol is the **lazy eight** or the **infinity sign.** *The Seeker's Handbook* states that this sign is the "Western counterpart to the **YIN/YANG.**"[54] [Emphasis in the original]

Helena Petrovna Blavatsky comments that it "is symbolized in its turn by the **Caduceus.**"[55] One witchcraft book asserts that it is the symbol for immortality.[56] To occultists, it represents Lucifer's eternal victory.[57] It also symbolizes reincarnation and karma.[58]

This symbol can be seen on certain Tarot cards such as "The Magician"[59] (for picture, see the chapter on "Hand Signals") and "Strength."

The infinity symbol sometimes encircles a globe in which case it means that Satan has put the earth under his control.

The rock group, Duran Duran, also incorporates the lazy 8 and the globe in their album cover.

There is yet another meaning according to Starhawk, a witch. She maintains:

"In the Faery tradition of Witchcraft, the unconscious mind is called the Younger Self; the conscious mind is called Talking Self....

"In the Faery tradition, a third 'self' is recognized: the Deep Self or God Self....The **Deep Self is the Divine within**....and is conceived of as both male and female....It is often **symbolized as** two linked spirals, or as **the infinity sign,** the 8 on its side. In the Faery tradition, it is called Dian Y Glas, the Blue God. Blue symbolizes spirit; the Deep Self was said to appear blue when psychically 'seen.'...'Dian' is related to both Diana and Tana, the Faery name of the Goddess; also to Janicot, the Basque name of the Horned God....

"In modern occultism, the Deep Self often appears as the 'Spirit Guide....'"[60]

As a Christian knows, a spirit guide is really a demon. The Bible warns "that in the latter times some shall depart from the faith, giving heed to seducing spirits, and doctrines of devils" (I Timothy 4:1). We can see that this is happening frequently today. Our society is quickly heading back to paganism.

The infinity sign also represents "the adept's hourglass from which flows infinite time."[61] Once again we find that the hourglass is a Masonic symbol.[62] It is also used in the Odd Fellows organization, which is known as "poor man's Masonry."[63]

We've seen in the chapter on "Winged Symbols" that Cronus (or Saturn) is depicted as an old man with a scythe and an hourglass.[64] The hourglass is also the symbol for Shiva's drum (the Damaru).[65]

As mentioned before, Shiva is another name for Satan. His drum is an hourglass which is the representation of the infinity sign. With this in mind, it was fascinating to learn that the sign for brimstone incorporates the infinity figure in its symbol. It was also interesting to see that the brimstone symbol appears at the top of the Church of Satan's "Nine Satanic Statements."

THE
NINE
SATANIC
STATEMENTS

1   Satan represents indulgence, instead of abstinence!

2   Satan represents vital existence, instead of spiritual pipe dreams!

3   Satan represents undefiled wisdom, instead of hypocritical self-deceit!

4   Satan represents kindness to those who deserve it, instead of love wasted on ingrates!

5   Satan represents vengeance, instead of turning the other cheek!

6   Satan represents responsibility to the responsible, instead of concern for psychic vampires!

7   Satan represents man as just another animal, sometimes better, more often worse than those that walk on all-fours, who, because of his "divine spiritual and intellectual development," has become the most vicious animal of all!

8   Satan represents all of the so-called sins, as they all lead to physical, mental, or emotional gratification!

9   Satan has been the best friend the church has ever had, as he has kept it in business all these years!

Brimstone

Satan (Baphomet, Lucifer) is proclaimed by the New Agers, occultists, and Satanists as the light-bearer. In the drawing of Baphomet (the Goat of Mendes) by Eliphas Levi, a Mason and occultist, we see that he has a **flaming torch** between his horns. The goat is used in Hermetic **MAGIC** where it represents **FIRE** and is also the symbol of generation.[66]

The torch, therefore, is another symbol that needs to be examined but first we'll look at one of the witchcraft holidays called Imbolc (held on February 2nd). This festival:

> "marks the recovery of the Goddess after giving birth to the God. The lengthening periods of light awaken Her. The God is a young, lusty boy, but His power is felt in the longer days. The warmth fertilizes the Earth (the Goddess), causes seed to germinate and sprout. And so the earliest beginnings of spring occur.

> "This is a Sabbat of purification after the shut-in life of winter, through the renewing power of the Sun. **It is also a festival of light and of fertility,** once marked in Europe with **huge blazes, torches and fire in every form. Fire here represents our own illumination and inspiration** as much as light and warmth.

"**Imbolc is also known as Feast of Torches,** Oimelc, Lupercalia, **Feast of Pan,** Snowdrop Festival, Feast of the Waxing Light, Brigid's day (sic), and probably by many other names. Some female Wiccans follow the old Scandinavian custom of wearing crowns of lit candles, but many more carry tapers during their invocations."[67]

Notice that the Feast of Torches is also called the Feast of Pan.

"The god **Pan** is a symbol of nature, and **is usually represented with horns** (expressive of the sun's rays and of the aggressive force of Aries) and with legs covered with hair (denoting the vitality of base forces, earth, shrubs and the instincts). In astrology, Pan is one aspect of Saturn, **and is also equated with Satan** and with life in its involutive, and, in particular, its base, aspects."[68]

"**PAN WAS THE PATRON SAINT OF SEXUAL PASTIMES**....He often tried to capture women, and because of his lustfulness, they lived in such fear of him that his name is still associated with fear, in the adjective 'panicky' and the noun 'panic.'"[69]

In *The Satanic Bible* Pan is called the "Greek god of lust" who was "later relegated to devildom."[70] Since Pan is represented with horns it is no wonder that he is called the "Horned God" by the witches.[71]

Returning to the Feast of Pan or Brigid's Day, did you notice that some witches (wiccans) have the custom of wearing crowns of lit candles on **February 2nd?** Starhawk, a witch, reveals:

> "Brigid is the Irish Goddess of smithcraft, poetry, and healing—the **fire Goddess** who is also worshiped at holy wells. Her festival, on the eve of **February 2,** is a festival of the waxing light, celebrated when the sun begins to grow stronger and the days begin to grow longer. **Also called Candlemas,** it is a time of purification and strengthening, and seemed an appropriate time for our ritual."[72]

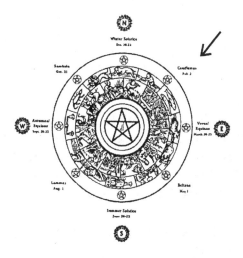

Candlemas is "[o]ne of the eight religious festivals of Witches."[73] What is interesting is that this **VERY SAME FESTIVAL (including the candles)** under the same name, **CANDLEMAS,** is celebrated in the Catholic Church. Stewart Farrar, a witch, comments about Candlemas:

> "This is the classical Lupercalia or **Feast of Pan.** More anciently still, it is the **celebration of the Goddess's recovery from giving birth to the new year's Sun God,** coming as it does six weeks after the winter solstice. The **same concept** has survived **undisguised** in the Christian festival of the **Purification of the Blessed Virgin Mary....**"[74]

A Christian author notes:

"Another day adopted from paganism, supposedly to honor Mary, is called 'Candlemas' or the 'Purification of the Blessed Virgin' and is celebrated on February 2....In pagan Rome, this festival was observed by the carrying of torches and *candles* in honor of Februa, for whom our month February is named! The Greeks held the feast in honor of the goddess Ceres, the mother of Proserpina, who with *candle*-bearing celebrants searched for her in the underworld. Thus we can see how adopting February 2 to honor the purification of Mary was influenced by pagan customs involving candles, even to calling it 'Candlemas' day. On this day all of the candles to be used during the year in Catholic rituals are blessed....Says *The Catholic Encyclopedia*, 'We need not shrink from admitting that candles, like incense and lustral water, were commonly employed in *pagan* worship and in rites paid to the dead.'"[75] [Emphasis in the original]

Candlemas, the Festival of Torches, is just one of the pagan uses of the flame. Many of the gods and goddesses of mythology carried torches. Some of these are: Hecate (the "Queen of the Witches"),[76] Comus,[77] Eros,[78] Hymenaeus (or Hymen),[79] Apollo,[80] Ilithyia,[81] Eos (or Aurora),[82] Iakchos,[83] and Phosphorus[84] (who is also called Lucifer[85]).

Listen to what occultist Edouard Schure says about Lucifer and his flaming torch:

> "**Lucifer,** having regained his star and his diadem, will assemble his legions for new works of creation. Attracted by his **flaming torch,** celestial spirits will descend...and he will send these messengers from unknown spheres to earth. Then the **torch of Lucifer** will signal 'From Heaven to Earth!'—and the ...(New Age) Christ will answer 'From Earth to Heaven!'"[86]

Light (as signified by the torch) is a very important Masonic term. Masonic writer, Arthur H. Ward, in *Masonic Symbolism and the Mystic Way,* notes: "When later he [the Mason] is given **LIGHT,** it means really that he is taught the principles of **OCCULTISM....**"[87] Occultist and Mason, Manly Palmer Hall, states that "the **torches represent the OCCULT arts** and sciences, the doctrines and dogmas by the light of which Truth is made visible."[88]

A magical tool--Notice the flames, hexagram, triangle, circle, and moon.

In fact, a book publisher that prints Masonic and Eastern Star books is called The Torch Press. The torch is also prevalent in the Olympics. We mentioned the Olympics briefly in the chapter "Humanist Symbols," but let's look at this topic a little more. In the New Age *Rainbow Bridge Newsletter,* we find some interesting information.

"**The torch has been a symbol for ages of the light** of God as it flames in the spirit of man. As it has been lighted at Olympics past and sent on its way to other nations, it has carried that symbology of the flame of spirit being extended from one nation to another. This time, it came to a land at whose doorstep stands a lady with another lighted lamp, significantly lighting the way for those seeking freedom. Our national motto is 'I light the way.'...

"So, the Olympic torch came to a land prepared for its arrival....The torch reached the 'City of the Angels,' the heart **chakra** of our country, and was held proudly aloft by *one* of us for *all* of us....

"John Sinclair, speaking earlier at Meditation Mount about the Games said, **'The Olympic Games are the heritage of the early forms of which the Yoga of Synthesis is the new yoga to come. It is the yoga of union, effort, enterprise, all of which is enshrined in the Games.** The ages of man are represented and the future of man is expressed in the effort and excellence which they represent. The Avatar of Synthesis is the inspirer of the Yoga of Synthesis which **man has now to evolve.**

"The symbol of the **five-pointed star** was presented over and over. It is the symbol of the New Group of World Servers, the symbol of perfected man, the **star of initiation.** As an energy it is expansion, progress, freedom dominion over the material plane, and a purificatory energy on all planes."[89] [Italics in the original; Boldface added]

Torch races have a pagan origin. The Hephestia was an "Athenian festival in honour of Hephaistos, the Greek Vulcan, in which races were run with lighted torches, handed from one to another."[90] Also the Prometheia was a "festival held at Athens in honour of Prometheus, in which a torch race was run, from the belief that Prometheus stole fire from heaven, and hence was called the torch-bearer."[91]

"Torch races date back to the ancient Greeks. A sanctuary in Olympia dedicated to the goddess Hes ia, sister of Zeus, 'housed the glowing embers which, every four years, would be fanned into flame by the winning athletes. To preserve the purity and power of the fire, it had to be moved with speed. Soon competitions developed to see which individual or group—a relay—could move the torch the fastest. The winner won the honor of lighting the fire in the name of the patron deity of the city.'"[92]

As just mentioned, the Statue of Liberty also holds a torch in her hand. It's no surprise to learn that the Masons gave us this "goddess."

"Towering above the shimmering but polluted waters, she holds in her **outreached arm and hand** a **torch of fire and light. A gift of the Masonic Order,** the modern inheritors of the Illuminati heritage, the Statue of Liberty was sculptured by Frederic Bartholdi, a member of the

Masonic Lodge of Alsace-Lorraine in Paris, France. The statue is significant to the secret societies plotting the New World Order."[93]

The Migration of Symbols reveals: "The **hand uplifted towards the sky** is...figured on native houses...to **ward off evil spirits** from the dwellers therein."[94]

Another popular symbol with the New Agers and occultists is the rainbow. God gave the rainbow as a promise to mankind that He would never send a worldwide flood again to destroy man (Genesis 9:13-16).

The New Agers have taken this symbol and made it into something that it was never meant to be. Masonic author, George Oliver, remarks:

"It is remarkable that in all the ancient systems of **MYTHOLOGY,** the Great Father, or the **MALE GENERATIVE PRINCIPLE** was uniformly symbolized by a **POINT WITHIN A CIRCLE.** This emblem was placed by the Scandinavian priests and poets on the central summit of a **RAINBOW,** which was fabled to be a bridge leading from earth to heaven."[95]

Another author reveals:

"In the practice of voodoo black magic in Haiti and Africa today, the **RAINBOW IS DEPICTED AS AN EVENT CELEBRATING THE MARRIAGE OF A 'RAINBOW GOD' TO THE 'SERPENT GOD.'**

"In the ancient Jewish **KABBALA**—now being revived by New Age teachers of today—mystical rabbis taught that the **RAINBOW SYMBOLIZED A SEXUAL RITE.** The bow of the rainbow was supposedly the phallus of the male god which descended into the kingdom of the womb, the queen or goddess. The union was said to create immense divine powers."[96]

Notice the astrological symbols under the rainbow

In Scandinavian mythology, there was a rainbow bridge called Bifrost.[97] This bridge was "also known as the 'devil's bridge'"[98] and was equated with the river Styx of the Egyptians,[99] which was the river that they believed flowed through hell.

"In Greek mythology, the rainbow is the embodiment of the messenger of the goddess, Iris...."[100] The Chinese rainbow differs somewhat in that it only has five colors (instead of the typical seven), "their synthesis symbolizing the union of YIN AND YANG."[101] [Emphasis in the original] In Babylonian literature the rainbow was "a sign of wrath, of terror, and of ill, and as an attribute of the goddess Tir-an-na, bringer of misfortune."[102]

In Masonic symbolism, we find that the Rainbow appears as the representation of Lucifer, the Light Bearer.[103]

The rainbow bridge (also called the antahkarana) is referred to frequently by the New Age movement and is found repeatedly in occult literature.[104] One Christian author explains: "In the occult, the rainbow is a hypnotic device supposedly forming a bridge between the individual and the over-soul or Great Universal Mind. This 'Mind' is not God."[105]

Lynn F. Perkins, a Mason and author of *Masonry in the New Age,* reveals the following about the **antahkarana:**

"Masons, as 'Builders of a Spiritual Fabric,' should become familiar with this old **Hindu** term. It refers to the 'Bridge' or 'Pathway' that every human being is consciously or unconsciously building between his 'lower self' and his 'High-Self,' between his imperfect self and his perfect self. The process of the 'Builder' never ceases **FROM LIFE TO LIFE EITHER IN OR OUT OF A PHYSICAL BODY.** The 'rough stone' ultimately becomes the 'Perfect Ashlar.'"[106]

In passing, notice that Perkins is also promoting **REINCAR-NATION** by his remark about "life to life"!

In the teachings of Tibetan Buddhism:

> "the **RAINBOW SYMBOLIZES MAN'S** ultimate perfect state—**DIVINITY,** when he has achieved an inner unity of good and evil, shadow and light, and becomes one with the Great One.

> "In other words, **THE NEW AGE TEACHES THAT MAN'S PATH TO GODHOOD IS SYMBOLIZED BY THE 'RAINBOW BRIDGE,'** which man crosses over by achieving higher consciousness. The reward at the other end of the rainbow: self-empowerment, immortality, divinity."[107]

With this in mind, it's no surprise to see the following notice in a witchcraft magazine. It states:

> "CARRY A BEAUTIFUL SYMBOL OF THE **NEW AGE** SPREAD THE WORD—**JOIN THE LEGIONS OF LIGHT....**

> "Ashtar and the 'Space Brothers' have repeatedly said that it is time we New Agers show our belief in the existence of more advanced life in space. As a special memento to coincide with the release of this important volume we are offering for a limited time only a beautiful medallion depicting the **symbol of the New World Order—a rainbow with a flying saucer** flying over it...."[108]

A New Age book, *The Light Shall Set You Free,* states:

> "Since the seven major **chakras** comprise the seven colors of the **RAINBOW**...and since the **seven colors of the RAINBOW form WHITE LIGHT,** we must keep these chakras vibrating at their maximum strength within us at all times. This is done through the power of the mind and

through **VISUALIZATION.** The process is also enhanced through **MEDITATION....**

"When each chakra is fully activated, vibrating with its purest color, the seven colors combine within and create an auric field of **WHITE LIGHT.** This forms a protective shield of energy around us and gives off a glow of energy that is often called **ILLUMINATION.**"[109]

The **white light** is an important symbol in the New Age. A former witch wrote: "In the upper three levels of witchcraft **LUCIFER IS REPRESENTED BY A WHITE LIGHT.**"[110] The Tara Center, a well-known New Age organization who is promoting the "New Age Christ," called Maitreya, explains:

"Triangles work is easy. Mentally link up with the two other members; visualize a **TRIANGLE OF WHITE LIGHT** circulating above your heads; then say The Great Invocation aloud (whenever possible). See your **TRIANGLE** linked with all other triangles, transmission and meditation groups on the planet. See the **WHITE LIGHT** circulating among this network of focal points and pouring out to envelop the world, thus helping to form a channel for the downpouring of Light and Love into the body of humanity.

"When you say: 'From the centre where the Will of God is known,' which is **Shamballa,** visualise a great sphere of **WHITE LIGHT.**"[111]

Shamballa, by the way, is the mythological place where the "Lord of the World," Sanat Kumara or Shiva (who is actually Satan), is supposed to live![112]

Dennis Carpenter, a witch, advises: "Connect with the Divine as you know it. Imagine yourself surrounded with **WHITE LIGHT,** a protective sphere of light that will keep you safe throughout this meditation."[113] Lazaris, a spirit guide (actually a demon), "suggests that he be visualized, simply, as a sphere of **WHITE LIGHT.**"[114]

Kundalini is the name of the **serpent** that is supposed to lie coiled at the base of the spine but which is raised during yoga. New Ager, Elizabeth Clare Prophet, calls Kundalini the **white light.**[115]

Prophet, as well as other occultists, refer to the Great White Brotherhood. New Agers, Shirley McCune and Norma Milanovich, explain:

"The Great White Brotherhood (white meaning **WHITE LIGHT)** is composed of many of the beings in the Cosmic Hierarchy. This organization includes seventy Orders/Brotherhoods of the universe....

"Beings of Light can hold membership simultaneously in the Order of Melchizedek and in the Great White Brotherhood. In fact, most, if not all, do belong to both."[116]

Both Masonry and Mormonism refer to the Melchizedek Priesthood. In fact, for one to become a god, according to Mormon doctrine, one must belong to the Melchizedek Priesthood. In Scottish Rite Masonry, the 19th degree is called "Grand Pontiff." It is during this ceremony that the "Candidate is anointed with oil, is made and proclaimed a priest for ever according to the Order of Melchizedek." Hebrews 5:5, 9 tells us, however, that "Christ glorified not Himself to be made an high priest" but was "called **OF GOD** an high priest after the order of Melchizedek," but occultists, Mormons, and Masons glorify **THEMSELVES** and take **ON THEMSELVES** the honor of priesthood that was given to Christ **ALONE.**

The Bible goes on to reveal that Christ "because He continueth ever, hath an unchangeable priesthood" (Hebrews 7:24). The word "unchangeable" is "aparabatos" in the Greek and means **"UNTRANSFERABLE."** In other words, this priesthood cannot be passed on from one person to another. Christ is the one and only one who can hold this priesthood.

Example after example could be given of such quotations about the **"white light."**[117] It is also interesting to note that *The White Light* is the name of a publication of the **OCCULT** organization the Temple of Truth.[118] It is billed as "The Magazine of Ceremonial Magick."[119] The name of their bookstore is The Magick Circle.[120]

For much more information on the rainbow and the white light, see my book *Hidden Secrets of the Eastern Star.*

Another symbol that is frequently seen today is the lotus flower. Blavatsky says that the lotus:

> "is the flower sacred to nature and her Gods....With the Hindus, the lotus is the emblem of the productive power of nature, through the agency of fire and water (spirit and matter)....The lotus, in India, is the symbol of prolific earth....The lotus is the two-fold type of the Divine and human **hermaphrodite,** being of dual sex, so to say....

> "The lotus flower, represented as growing out of Vishnu's navel—that God resting on the waters of space and his Serpent of Infinity—is the most graphic allegory ever made: the Universe evolving from the central Sun, the POINT, the ever-concealed germ."[121] [Caps in the original; Boldface added]

Hall, writes:

"You will sometimes see strange little Chinese gods or Oriental Buddhas sitting on the blossom of a Lotus. In fact, if you look carefully you will find nearly all the Oriental gods are so depicted. This means that they have opened within themselves that Spiritual Consciousness which they call the **KUNDALINI.**"[122]

One of the emblems of Isis is the lotus, which is a symbol of the resurrection.[123] Of course, in Egyptian mythology, the idea of resurrection means rebirth or **REINCARNATION.** The lotus was also associated with sun gods.[124]

"One Egyptian legend tells that before creation there was nothing but a stagnant ocean upon which floated a lotus. When the beautiful flower opened, all of creation, including the Gods, spilled forth from it. Another tale tells how a great lotus opened to reveal a scarab which became the sun, and each day as mighty Ra opens His eye (the lotus), the sun appears. The lotus flower opens and closes each day as the sun rises and sets so the connection between the flower and the sun is very clear."[125]

Hall explains:

"In the Western World the **Lotus has been changed to the Rose.** *The Roses of the Rosicrucians, the Roses of the Masonic degrees, and also those of the Order of the Garter in England* **ALL stand for the SAME THING: the awakening of spiritual consciousness** and unfolding into full bloom the soul qualities of man. When man opens this bud within himself, he finds, like the golden pollen in the flower, this wonderful spiritual city, **SHAMBALLA,** in the heart of the thousand-petalled Lotus of the brain."[126]

Pike says that the *"Rose* was anciently sacred to Aurora and the Sun."[127] In another book Hall declares:

"Of all symbolic flowers the lotus blossom of India and Egypt and the rose of the Rosicrucians are the most important. In their symbolism these two flowers are considered identical. The esoteric doctrines for which the Eastern lotus stands have been perpetuated in modern Europe under the form of the rose. The rose and the lotus are **yonic** emblems, signifying primarily the maternal creative mystery...."[128]

Hall just said that the lotus and the rose are symbols of the female generative parts. An expanded definition is given in *A Dictionary of Symbols.* Another author writes:

"For example, the *lotus* symbolizes the female vulva of the Mother Goddess, the *diamond* the male organ of the ancient Father God of paganism. Thus, when a New Ager speaks mysteriously of the 'diamond entering the lotus' during religious initiation ceremonies, he literally is referring to sexual intercourse as a New Age holy ritual."[129] [Emphasis in the original]

"There is a certain parallel between the symbolism of the lotus and that of the rose in Western culture. In Egypt, the lotus symbolizes nascent life, or first appearance. Saunier regards it as a natural **symbol for all forms of evolution**....As an artistic creation it is **related to the mandala,** its significance varying according to the number of its petals: the eight-petalled lotus is considered in India as the **Centre where Brahma dwells** and as the visible manifestation of his **occult** activity....The 'thousand-petalled' lotus symbolizes the final revelation....From the remotest days of antiquity, the lotus was unanimous choice of the Chinese, the Japanese, the Hindus, the Egyptians and the Aryans. The lotus flower growing out of the navel of Vishnu, symbolizes the universe growing out of the central sun—the central point or the 'unmoved mover'. It is the attribute of many deities."[130]

The mandala, mentioned in the previous paragraph, is:

"a Hindu term for a circle. It is a kind of *yantra* (instrument, means or emblem), in the form of a ritual geometric diagram, sometimes corresponding to a specific, divine attribute or to some **form of enchantment** *(mantra)* which is thus given visual expression....They are to be found all over the Orient, and always as a means towards contemplation and concentration—as an aid in inducing certain mental states and in encouraging the spirit to move forward along its path of evolution from the biological to the geometric, from the realm of corporeal forms to the spiritual."[131] [Italics in the original; Boldface added]

One item that is used in Buddhism is the prayer wheel. "In Buddhist countries the wheel or chakra is twirled for **divination** and as a means of gaining inspiration."[132] The Tibetans put a prayer inside the wheel and then spin it over and over again. They feel that every time they spin it, the prayer is being sent forth. This is a repetitious form of prayer. In *Numerology: The Magic of Numbers* we find:

"We are all aware today that with the new interest in Indian **occultism** the modern gurus or teachers are fond of giving a 'word' to their disciples which they use as a prayer form and which has vibrations which build up in the body of the person using them by repetition. The word, such as *ohm*, must always be a specific one given to the individual, and it is the work of the guru to find out which word will indeed vibrate harmoniously with the vibrations of the individual receiving it. The **'magic' appears to be in the constant use of the word** rather **like the Tibetan prayer wheel** churning out its monotonous prayers."[133] [Italics in the original; Boldface added]

The Bible address this issue. In Matthew 6:5-8 we are told:

"And when thou prayest, thou shalt not be as the hypocrites are: for they love to pray standing in the synagogues and in the corners of the streets, that they may be seen of men. Verily I say unto you, They have their reward. But thou, when thou prayest, enter into thy closet, and when thou hast shut thy door, pray to thy Father which is in secret; and thy Father which seeth in secret shall reward thee openly. But **when ye pray, use not vain repetitions, as the heathen do:** for they think that they shall be heard for their much speaking. **Be not ye therefore like unto them:** for your Father knoweth what things ye have need of, before ye ask Him."

16. ZODIAC SIGNS

Astrology (a form of **divination**) is a practice in which a person consults the sun, moon, stars, and planets to **foretell future events.** One occult magazine relates:

> "Anxious to know the future, they believed that by watching the stars they could deduce ahead of time the actions of their gods and goddesses who controlled every facet of their lives. Astrology can be traced back to ancient Babylon where the Zodiac was established."[1]

AQUARIUS   SAGITTARIUS   ARIES

CAPRICORN   LIBRA   PISCES

TAURUS   VIRGO   LEO

GEMINI   SCORPIO   CANCER

The astrologers claim that the position of the heavenly bodies at the exact time of one's birth will influence this person's entire life including his personality, romance, and career. Given the exact time and location of one's birth, astrologers (those who study astrology) can then determine which days will be "lucky" and which days will be "bad". These good and bad days differ from person to person. If August 18th has been determined as a good day for you, you would then be encouraged to make a large business deal, apply for that special job opening that you always wanted, or take that long-awaited trip to Europe on **THAT** day. However, if August 18th is one of your bad days, you should not make any major decision until one of your "good" days, thus avoiding the possibility of having things turn sour.

The World Book Encyclopedia recounts: "During ancient times there was wide belief in **OCCULT** sciences. The best-known of the old **OCCULT subjects included ASTROLOGY,** alchemy, necromancy, and magic."[2] Under "ASTROLOGY" we find: "Judicial astrology is the astrology of today. It was and still is closely related to other **pseudo** sciences and superstitions such as palmistry, numerology, and the use of charms and magic."[3] Related articles under **"Magic"** include: **ASTROLOGY,** clairvoyance, divination, evil eye, exorcism, hypnotism, necromancy, shaman (witch doctor), telepathy, trance, voodoo and witchcraft![4]

Nat Freedland, in *The Occult Explosion,* writes that **"astrology is clearly the MOST IMPORTANT part of the OCCULT explosion."**[5] He also says: "The greatest common denominator of **OCCULTISM** in the United States is the **astrology** column."[6]

The *Treasury of Witchcraft* states: "Stemming from the **Black Arts,** and involving **goetic** premises, assuming the techniques and conditions of **occult practices** are alchemy, divination, **astrology,** and levitation."[7] **Goetic magic,** by the way, **is black magic or sorcery.**[8] Mason Kenneth MacKenzie says that goetia is the "term for black magic, in contradistinction to Theurgia, or white magic. The powers of darkness were invoked in this system with horrible rites."[9]

One book explains the **Goetic Circle of Pacts** (see picture on page 277) like this:

> *"Symbols play a vital role in infernal conjuration....the Goetic Circle of Pacts, drawn by Eliphas Levi in the 19th century, is supposed to be used when the sorcerer is to make a pact with the Descending Hierarchy. The three circles in the center are the standing positions of the sorcerer and his apprentices. The skull must be from a parricide, the horns from a goat, the bat must have been drowned in blood, and the black cat, whose head is place opposite the skull, must have been fed on human flesh."* [Emphasis in the original]

Once again we can find Masonry **PROMOTING** an **OC-CULT** practice. One Masonic author, Mr. Castells, brags: "The Zodiac is still with us in the Royal Arch, although...like so many other symbols of Freemasonry, its real import and significance has been obscured."[10] He adds: "In 1775, when the Freemasons' Hall was erected, the **ZODIAC WAS ACKNOWLEDGED TO BE A MASONIC SYMBOL** by placing it over the main entrance of that edifice."[11]

In *Masonry and Its Symbols in the Light of "Thinking and Destiny,"* we find: "The Zodiac is the best symbol of the circle with the twelve points on the circumference which give a value to geometrical symbols....**Masonry has its symbols from the Zodiac.**"[12]

Notice the astrological symbolism on the Masonic globe

Another Mason claims: "According to **Occult** teaching, each **reincarnation** is under the adjoining sign of the zodiac, hence a sign, thirty degrees, is a **symbol of rebirth,** and the moving over (the advancement) of thirty degrees is emblematic of rebirth."[13]

The **zodiac** is based on astrology which is and **ALWAYS HAS BEEN associated with the OCCULT and WITCHCRAFT.** In spite of this, however, some "evangelical" people (such as D. James Kennedy of Coral Ridge Ministries) promote the zodiac and refer to "Biblical astrology." An ad in *Charisma and Christian Life* announced:

"Startling discoveries made by eminent theologian Dr. D. James Kennedy prove that God created the Zodiac! God intended the stars to foretell the future of the world. Discover what Dr. Kennedy calls **BIBLICAL ASTROLOGY** or the Gospel in the stars. Order, 'The Real Meaning of the Zodiac' book on cassette...."[14]

Let's look at some of what Kennedy teaches. He claims:

"Fourthly, in the signs of the zodiac, is Sagittarius, the Archer. Sagittarius is a CENTAUR WITH THE BODY OF A HORSE AND THE TORSO OF A MAN. He is a man with a drawn bow and arrow. The Bible speaks of one in Revelation 6:2, **'And I saw, and behold a white horse, and he that sat on him had a bow...and he went forth conquering, and to conquer.'** THIS IS A PICTURE OF ONE WHO HAS TWO NATURES: OF CHRIST WHO IS

THE GOD-MAN (the *theanthropos,* both man and God) who is going forth conquering and to conquer."[15] [Italics and boldface in the original; Caps added]

SAGITTARIUS

Personally, I feel that this is blasphemy. The centaur is a **MYTHOLOGICAL** animal, so does this make Christ a mythological being? In Revelation 6 we see **TWO DISTINCT** beings—a horse **AND** a man, not a horse-man. Supposedly this represents the two natures of Christ, but does the horse represent the man aspect of Christ or the divine aspect? Or, does the man represent the man aspect or the divine aspect? We cannot make either the horse or man DIVINE. Romans 1:22-23, 25 warns:

> "Professing themselves to be wise, they became fools, And *changed* **the glory of the uncorruptible** *God into an image made like to corruptible man,* **and to birds,** *and fourfooted beasts,* **and creeping things....**Who **changed the truth of God into a lie,** and worshipped and served the creature more than the Creator, who is blessed for ever. Amen."

Kennedy admits:

> "Remarkably, the stars in the heaven which represent those twelve signs bear **absolutely no resemblance to the pictures or the signs themselves.** For example, what we call the Big Dipper has been called Ursa Major (Great Bear). One thing it does not look like is a great bear! Neither do

any of the other signs look like what they are supposed to represent."[16]

This is some admission! Kennedy claims that "God intended the stars to foretell the future of the world,"[17] but if the signs do not "look like what they are supposed to represent," then how can the Gospel be clearly proclaimed by the constellations? The Bible tells us: "Have **NO** fellowship with the unfruitful works of **DARKNESS,** but rather **REPROVE** them" (Ephesians 5:11). We are not to try to "Christianize" the occult.

There are many explicit warnings AGAINST ASTROLOGY in the Bible. We covered Deuteronomy 18:10, 12 before but it's well worth repeating:

> "There shall not be found among you ANY ONE that maketh his son or his daughter to pass through the fire, or that useth **DIVINATION [ASTROLOGY!]**, or an **OBSERVER OF TIMES [ASTROLOGER]**, or an enchanter, or a witch....For **ALL** that do these things are an **ABOMINATION** unto the Lord."

Jeremiah 10:2 warns: "Learn not the way of the heathen, and be not dismayed at the SIGNS OF HEAVEN; for the heathen are dismayed at them. For the CUSTOMS of the people are VAIN...." Speaking about the doom of Babylon, Isaiah prophesied:

> "For thou hast trusted in thy WICKEDNESS....Therefore shall evil come upon thee....Stand now with thy enchantments, and with the multitude of thy sorceries....Let now the ASTROLOGERS, the STARGAZERS, the MONTHLY PROGNOSTICATORS, stand

up and save thee from these things that shall come upon thee....**NONE** shall save thee" (Isaiah 47:10-15, in part).

A former witch cautions us that astrology, occult jewelry, face painting, tarot cards, playing cards, incense, drugs, nakedness, and occult games are definitely part of **witchcraft.** Let's do what I Thessalonians 5:22 tells us to do: "Abstain from **ALL** appearance of evil."

Connected to astrology is another symbol that is quite popular nowadays. It is called the enneagram. One Christian researcher explains:

"A currently popular variation of the triangle is the *enneagram,* a symbol that has several triangles arranged so that nine points touch an outer circle. Sir John Sinclair, in his commentary on the legacy of Alice Bailey, founder of Lucis Trust, remarks that the **enneagram originated in ancient Egypt.** He suggests that the nine points on the enneagram represent nine different groups of **New Age** workers: financiers and economists, psychologists, telepathic communicators, workers in the field of religion, educators of the New Age, trained observers, scientific servers, political organizers, and magnetic healers.

"Djwhal Khul, the spirit guide who revealed this diagram and its meaning to Alice Bailey, confided to her that once these nine groups come together, a 'tenth group'—which he failed to identify—will come forth to bring in a One World Order.

"The enneagram also is a Hindu symbol. Sri Aurobindo, an Indian Hindu guru whose writings and teachings hold a strange fascination for American and European New Agers, **connect the enneagram not only to the Mother Goddess of the Hindus but also to the goddess myths of Greece and Rome."**[18] [Italics in the original; Boldface added]

"Also tying the Enneagram in with occult astrology, Aurobindo maintained that the secrets of the Enneagram are so important that he who unravels its secrets 'will enjoy riches and wealth and be sexually fertile.'

"Regrettably, the Enneagram is also in vogue and gaining popularity amongst a number of Christian groups, with both Protestant and Catholic, whose leaders evidently are ever on the lookout for something new to give their audiences. It is especially popular in Catholic circles, with both priests and nuns promoting the use of the Enneagram to determine basic personality types, compulsions, and obsessions. One Catholic priest has even attempted to relate each of the nine points of the Enneagram with nine personality traits of Jesus! But it is not only used in the Catholic Church. Though its ancient occultic origins are undebatable, I have also received reports that the teaching of the Enneagram is being popularized at Southern Baptist retreats and in Methodist, Episcopal, and Charismatic circles."[19]

An ad in *Yoga International* stated the following:

"**CREDENCE CASSETTES** features audio and video cassettes by authors who are free-spirited Catholics, many of whom are at home with and drink from the wells of Jung, Native American Spirituality, New Age music, guided imagery, and the Enneagram. Not your mother's church, but probably your children's!"[20] [Emphasis in the original]

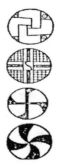

Some Native American symbols—Note the swastikas

It was an occultist, George Gurdjieff, who introduced the enneagram to Europe.

> "[He] claims it originated about 2500 years ago in a Babylonian wisdom school....This may implicate the enneagram with Babylonian astrology, since those characteristics would be signified by a point on the enneagram. Gurdjieff's use of the enneagram also parallels the esoteric cabala's 'Tree of Life' of Jewish mysticism."[21]

It doesn't matter what type of personality a person has, God can use him or her **IF** he or she is wholly committed to the Lord. God can take a hardened, drunken, wicked sinner and change that person into a kind, considerate, caring person. The Lord can take a shy person and make him or her into a bold individual who is willing to die, if need be, for the sake of the Gospel. Peter, as well as the other disciples, forsook Christ when it came time for Him to be crucified, yet just fifty-some days later these same disciples were bold enough to testify of Christ's resurrection (Acts 2:1-47). When they were imprisoned and admonished not to speak about Christ, they boldly replied: "We ought to obey God rather than men" (Acts 5:29).

Let's forget all the man-made (and demonic) devices and personality testing, and let us also "obey God rather than men." "[Y]our faith should not stand in the wisdom of men, but in the power of God" (I Corinthians 2:5).

17. TALISMANS

Webster tells us a talisman is "an object bearing a sign or character engraved under **astrological** influences and thought to act as a **charm** to avert evil and bring good fortune."

In *Amulets and Superstitions* we are told:

> "The object of the talisman is quite different from that of the amulet. The amulet is supposed to exercise its protective powers on behalf of the individual or thing continually, whereas the talisman is only intended to perform one specific task. Thus a talisman may be placed in the ground with money or treasure, which it is expected to protect and to do nothing else. But the line which divides the amulet from the talisman has rarely been observed by any people who regard such things as parts of the machinery of magic, and in modern times the use and meanings of the two objects are generally confounded, even by educated folk who are superstitious. And the experts are not agreed on the subject."[1]

One occult catalog that sells talismans and amulets states:

> "The word **TALISMAN** is believed to come from Arabic as there are great similarities in that language. One of the root words means 'to make marks as would a magician. The word **AMULET** is derived from the Latin *Amuletum,* and is a **magical** object.

> "At one time there was a difference between an amulet and a talisman in that a talisman was made for a specific task, and an amulet had broader uses. With time, down through the centuries, this difference disappeared, and today, an amulet or talisman is considered one and the same as far as having magical powers is concerned.

"There are uncounted forms of amulets and talismans. They can be in the form of a seal, pentacle, charm, circle, Voodoo veve, table (name given certain engraved tablets), signets, gemstones, roots, bones, miniature statues of gods and goddesses, and any other item that represents a magical force that benefits its owner....

"There are also amulets and talismans that are connected with ceremonial **magic** rituals. These are seals, signets, tablets, and other forms that are used in summoning supernatural powers, and causing them to give help and aid in any endeavor. Such supernatural beings have varying powers, and the proper ritual and required items must be used in accordance with whom is being invoked."[2]

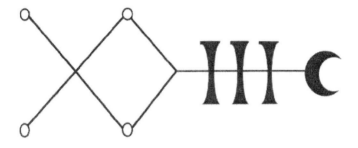

Magical seal of Sirius

Arthur Edward Waite, a Mason and occultist, reveals:

"Talismans may be made either of the seven kabbalistic metals—gold, silver, iron, copper, fixed mercury, brass, and lead—or of precious stones, such as carbuncles, crystals, diamonds, emeralds, agates, sapphires, and onyxes."[3]

One talisman is called "Satan's Seal." It shows "Lucifer depicted as king, wielding a prong with which he catches sinners, and with hands of claws like those of a beast of prey. Inscription around edges reads, 'Master of the abyss of Hell.'"[4]

An amulet in one catalog is described like this: "Let this strange little Japanese SPIRIT DEMON insure your safety and security. Many people claim that wearing this amulet brings serenity and peace of mind."[5]

One talisman sold by The Pyramid Collection is a Japanese Water Charm. It is described like this:

> "In Japan, the ideographic symbol for 'water' can also represent that element's properties of life, cleansing, and the emotions. Pendants similar to that shown...(its design is taken from an ancient crest) were commonly worn as **charms** against fire. A strong, graphic **talisman** for men and women."[6]

Water charm—This is the same symbol that is used for "Tao."

Other talismans they sell are Rune Jewelry. The catalog explains:

"The **Runes are secret, occult symbols** used by Norse runemasters until the 17th century. Modern runemasters consult the runes to communicate with the subconscious self. The six brass Runes, with raised sterling-silver symbols, are **talismans** that promote inner growth."[7]

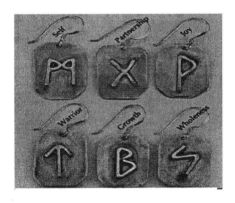

Notice that runes are **OCCULT symbols.** What then, is so-called "Christian" Michael Smith doing with runic characters on his record? Several of the letters (M, E, and T) in his name are exact representations of the runes. When I wrote to Smith about this, his manager responded. He denied that the record contained runic characters, but he did tell me that if I wanted to know more about runes that I should check out my library for more information! He may not be fully endorsing the runes, but he certainly didn't try to warn me that runes were occultic symbols. Incidentally, the flip side of this album has Smith's name written backwards.

Figure 22. "The Big Picture" (1986)

"Writing reversal is a SATANIC principle. Master satanist Aleister Crowley taught his disciples to walk backwards, talk backwards, think backwards, speak backwards, write backwards and even listen to phonograph records backwards to gain insight into the future."[8] [Emphasis in the original]

It is also interesting to note that in this "Christian" album the name of Jesus is only mentioned **ONE** time![9]

Returning to the runes, we find the word rune means "secret."[10] "The runes were associated with secrecy or mystery because only a few persons knew them. Heathen priests probably first used the characters in their **charms and magic spells.**"[11] The runes are considered to be comparable to the I Ching and the Tarot[12] and are a form of **DIVINATION.**[13]

Magical Arts states:

> "More than 2,000 years ago in the cold, rugged lands of Scandinavia, **shamans** seized evanescent, **magical** ideas and gave them form in symbols they called runes. These stick-like character, scratched onto pebbles and bits of wood, functioned as **talismans** and implements for **divination,** protection and guiding those who sought their wisdom....

> "The original runic symbols developed into the letters of the earliest Germanic alphabet, known as the Elder Futhark. Even when put to this practical use, **the markings retained their old occult meanings....**and runes were ubiquitous during the Viking era as tokens of **magical** power. People covered their home with the symbols to ward off evil; warriors engraved them on the hilts of their swords, hoping for strength in battle; midwives scratched them on the palms of women in childbirth to ensure safe delivery; and **shamans used them to commune with the dead, to cast spells,** and even, reportedly, to fly."[14]

The runes "were so connected with **witchcraft,** the early Christian missionaries in Europe refused to use them. They replaced this **satanic sign language** with the Latin alphabet instead."[15]

Let's look at a talisman sold by Papa Jim. It is a 666 variation which is supposed to defeat witchcraft or voodoo!

Notice the three sixes

Isn't it strange how Satan has blinded people's eyes to think that by wearing an occult piece of jewelry, the occultic forces can be restrained? This would be like Satan casting out Satan. Jesus said:

> "How can Satan cast out Satan? And if a kingdom be divided against itself, that kingdom cannot stand. And if a house be divided against itself, that house cannot stand. And if Satan rise up against himself, and be divided, he cannot stand, but hath an end" (Mark 3:23-26).

The Satanic Cross, adopted by Satanists and devil worshippers,[16] is another talisman. It is the Christian Cross which is inverted or turned upside down. Satanists reverse many things such as "praying" the Lord's prayer backwards.

Satanists also turn a question mark upside down. We're told: "The upside down question mark asks mockingly, 'Did Jesus really die for our sins?'"[17]

Below are some talismans for different purposes. One is called the "Clairvoyance Talisman" which is supposed to allow one to read another person's thought. One talisman is alleged to destroy the evil of Black Magic. Another one is to "discover the most hidden secrets, enabling its possessor to penetrate everywhere unseen." One talisman is for exorcism. Yet another one claims: "Will make the most taciturn man unbosom himself to its possessor, to confess his machinations."[18] As can be seen, these talismans certainly have nothing to do with godliness and Christianity!

We do not need to have talismans to protect us or to "destroy the evil of Black Magic." Our hope and confidence is in the Lord and He will keep us safe from harm if we trust in Him. "I will both lay me down in peace, and sleep for Thou, Lord, only makest me dwell in safety" (Psalm 4:8). "For the Lord shall be thy confidence, and shall keep thy foot from being taken" (Proverbs 3:26). "The angel of the Lord encampeth round about them that fear Him, and delivereth them" (Psalm 34:7). "It is better to trust in the Lord than to put confidence in man" (Psalm 118:8) or in occultic talismans and amulets.

18. JEWELRY

Many Christians, I believe, are aware of some occultic jewelry such as a ring with a pentagram on it. However, there is far more to jewelry than just some occultic symbol engraved on it. A witch, Scott Cunningham, explains:

> **"Jewelry's origins lie in magic.** That should come as no surprise to us, for as I've said, nearly all human customs and the technologies which result from those customs stem from ancient magical practices and beliefs.

> "In earliest times, jewelry was probably worn to avert negativity, then envisioned as 'evil spirits.' Jewelry was also often placed in tombs with other grave goods to guard the dead.

> "As perception of the energies within objects sharpened, certain stones and metals were associated with various organs and regions of the body and were worn to guard the health. Later, stones, metals, horn, feathers, bone and many other materials were donned for their power to attract love, health, money and other necessities of life....

> "When materialism has ruled over naturalism, jewelry has survived purely as ornamentation or, at times, as a statement of class definition. Yes, jewelry still has a few ceremonial roles, such as engagement and wedding bands, but even these have lost their **original magical** messages....

> "Until the nineteenth century in much of the Western world, **the history of jewelry was a history of magic....**"[1]

Laurie Cabot, another witch, comments:

"Many Witches wear crystals as jewelry, along with other gemstones that have magical powers. **Jewelry is a way to have magic on your body** without anyone knowing it but you and others who are wise in the ways of the Craft. In general, Witch jewelry is worn because it directs energies to various parts of the body."[2]

In the *Freemasons' Book of the Royal Arch,* we find that "the finger-ring, the bracelet, the anklet, and the necklace, all of which came to be worn as ornaments, were originally regarded as means of protection from evil."[3]

Another well known witch, Sybil Leek, also brags about the protective properties of jewelry. She states:

"Jewelry and metals have their own vibrations and corresponding numbers, and again there is a link with the vibrations and colors of the planets. A favorite piece of jewelry will take on the vibrations of the person wearing it, especially over a long period, which gives the vibrations time to build up and become forceful. **Charms, amulets and talismans have been worn** throughout the ages not as a form of decoration but as **a focal point that can be charged with the appropriate vibrations.** We are not free from the use of such things even today, for there is an increasing business in the sale of charms, even though now they be only part of a dangling bracelet. It seems that the **amulet and talisman are gaining a new lease on life WHETHER OR NOT THE BUYERS AND WEARERS ARE AWARE OF THEIR SIGNIFICANCE."[4]**

"In the early days, mystical, magical properties were assigned to the star polygons, but their influence is still felt today even if the forms are used only in cheap charm-type jewelry. Pythagoreans regarded the star polygon, derived from the pentagon, as the symbol of health."[5]

Many people find particular designs appealing but they have no idea what is being represented. For instance, in the 1993 issue of *Light Speed* we discover: "For several years the Cosmo Tech clothing and jewelry have had an amazing effect in their support of **beings accessing their Divinity** and living their True reality. All of the exquisite clothing and jewelry are **channeled** through Rahztar and Astara."[6] New Ager, Dick Sutphen, sells jewelry that is called a "Circle of Unity Symbol." This is a:

> "symbol of the unity of mankind. In **regressive hypnosis,** Dick Sutphen **channeled** this symbol from a highly advanced period in Atlantis. This was a time when all people were connected psychically—enabling everyone to **communicate telepathically.** The symbol is made up of three people with their arms raised and connected by the circle of oneness. The three also represent God, man and spirit."[7]

When you pick up some jewelry, you may well be choosing an item that has been channeled through demons! Prisma catalog reveals: "The **amulets** of ancient times **have become the popular jewelry of today.** There is a resurgence of interest in the metaphysical attributes of gems and symbols."[8] As explained earlier, an amulet is "a charm...often inscribed with a magic incantation or symbol to protect the wearer against evil or to aid him." *The Occult Sciences* explains that "the word amulet came to mean a small bag hung round the neck and containing roots, seeds and other articles which had an efficacious **OCCULT** power, or a metal disc engraved with Kabbalistic signs."[9]

We've all heard of a **"charm** bracelet." People wear it without giving a thought as to what the word "charm" means.

Many people carry a rabbit's foot or a four leaf clover for luck or put a horseshoe on their home to bring luck. All of these items are charms. You will even hear the phrase "it works like a charm," in reference to some product that produced good results.

GOOD LUCK

Just a few days ago I was looking through a "Christian" book catalog from Christian Book Distributors. I was surprised and disappointed to see a "Nativity **Charm** Bracelet" advertised. The descriptions reads: "Fashioned of gold-plated metal, these seven **CHARMS** include two wise men, two angels, a shepherd, a nativity scene, and Jesus carrying the cross."[10] We cannot "Christianize" pagan practices—even if we include a "Jesus" **CHARM.** Remember, **a charmer is also called an enchanter or a magician!**

Deuteronomy 18:10-12 warns:

> "There shall not be found among you any one that maketh his son or his daughter to pass through the fire, or that useth divination, or an observer of times, or an **enchanter,** or a witch, Or a **charmer,** or a consulter with familiar spirits, or a wizard, or a necromancer. For **all that do these things are an abomination unto the Lord."**

In *Wicca: A Guide for the Solitary Practitioner* a witch remarks:

> "Selecting and donning ritual jewelry naturally follows dressing. Many Wiccans have collections of exotic pieces with religious or magical designs. Then too amulets and talismans (devices made to ward off or to attract forces)

often double as ritual jewelry. Such wonders as necklaces of amber and jet, silver or gold bands worn on the wrists, crowns of silver set with crescent moons, rings of emeralds and pearls, even ritual garters set with tiny silver buckles are often part of Wiccan regalia."[11]

A Christian author comments:

"Personal jewelry is also very important to those in witchcraft, since they receive it during ritual ceremonies, having had it 'blessed' (cursed) with clinging demons. Since such things are worn close to the body, the witch or warlock always has his or her familiar spirits 'on call.' The symbols on the jewelry are very important; they are never accidental or harmless. The crescent or crescent and star are two of the most common symbols representing the Queen of Heaven and the 'bright morning star'—Lucifer."[12]

As should be evident by now, it's not just the design or symbol on the jewelry, but the jewelry itself that has a magical meaning. Many people wear a ring or a necklace with their birthstone. However, these different gemstones are used for magical purposes and are based on **ASTROLOGY.**

Tanya Turner, a Christian, informs us:

"Birthstones were created during the Classical Period by the Romans, with each holding an **astrological** significance. In astrology, there are 12 signs of the zodiac each showing specific signs of weaknesses and/or strengths. A specific gem, possessing the necessary properties was assigned to each zodiac time frame in order to strengthen weaknesses and build on strengths supposedly possessed by persons born in that month or period of the zodiac. An article in *The Gatson Gazette,* March 22, 1990, made the following analysis: 'The concept of birthstones assigns a specific crystal thought especially beneficial to each astrological sign chosen specifically to counteract or protect from weaknesses and to enhance strengths inherent in each house of zodiac.'"[13]

"In earlier cultures, shamans, witch doctors and medicine men utilized gems, believing them to have mystical healing powers. Certain stones were also used for protection against supposed mental and physical evils. They have been used to adorn Egyptian pharaohs' death masks and sarcophagi, European crowns, and the fingers, wrists, and necks of innumerous women in love. With the coming of the New Age we are seeing a revival of the use of stones and gems for these same purposes."[14]

Prisma catalog advertises jewelry. It says that ruby "increases vigor and renews vital life forces."[15] "This beautiful stone," claims Scott Cunningham, "was considered the most perfect offering to Buddha in China and Krishna in India....In 13th-century magic, rubies were well established as wealth-increasing stones. They were especially effective if engraved with the image of a dragon or snake before using."[16]

Opal is supposed to heighten "the emotions and restores dim vision. Known as 'The Gem of the Gods,' it is believe to open the Third Eye."[17] Another book proclaims: "Opals are worn during astral projection for protection as well as to facilitate the process."[18] Opals are also used to help recall one's past lives,[19] which is the false teaching of reincarnation. Witch Cunningham continues:

"The stone is favored by many to develop psychic powers and is often worn in jewelry for this purpose. Earrings are ideal....

"*Black opals* are prized by magicians and Wiccans as power stones. They are often worn in ritual jewelry designed to increase the amount of power aroused and released from the body during magic."[20]

Moonstone "symbolizes the Third Eye, sharpens spiritual awareness, and assists in the astral realms."[21] Psychic ability is improved by wearing azurite, this catalog claims. So, the gemstones have an occult meaning behind them.

"In some contemporary Wiccan coven women—usually High Priestesses—wear necklaces consisting of alternative amber and jet beads. Though reasons for the use of these materials vary, it is said that **these two stones represent the Goddess and God, the feminine and masculine principles,** the projective and receptive forces of nature. They **also heighten magical effects....**

"Witches, Wise Women, and shamans wear amber beads to strengthen their spells, whether cast in caves, deserted valleys or at lonely seashores, or within magically created spheres of power in urban bedrooms. A large piece of amber placed on that altar increases the effectiveness of your magic."[22]

"BANGLE BRACELETS were worn in India to ward off negative astral forces. Hand-made bangles of copper, silver, and gold are said to exert an electromagnetic influence on the cells of the body."[23] [Emphasis in the original]

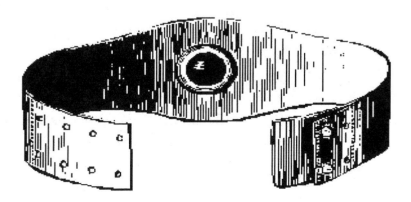

Let's look at the ring for a few minutes.

"The **ring is** a circle, **symbolic of eternity, unity, reincarnation** and the universe. In earlier times the **ring was associated with the Sun and Moon. It was** an object of protection, **a magical guard** that warded off negativity through its continuity....

"All rings were once magical or sacred. Even goddesses and gods wore rings; Babylonian mythology is replete with stories of the rings of Shamash and Marduk. **Rings have also been linked to the zodiac, the yin/yang and the 'magic circle' of magicians and Wiccans.** Their **magical** history is complex and fascinating.

"In a magical sense, **wearing a ring 'binds' you with power, with energy.** The materials of which the ring is constructed, plus your **visualization,** determine the nature of this energy....

"The appearance or attractiveness of a ring, and certainly its material value, are of little importance in magic. The ring's design, the metals and stones used are the only factors involved in selecting rings for magic....

"The finger on which a ring is worn has magical significance. The index or 'ring' finger was once thought to be especially powerful. Herbal medicines were applied to the body with the ring finger to strengthen the effectiveness of the cure. Thus, rings containing stones which speed the body's healing are best worn on this finger....

"Once, rings were usually worn on the third finger, because it was thought to contain a nerve that went directly to the heart. *Betrothal rings are still traditionally worn on this finger."*[24]

Another book reiterates:

"In **astrology**, the THUMB is correlated with Venus, the index finger with Jupiter, the middle finger with Saturn, the ring finger with the sun, and the small finger with Mercury.—In popular parlance, the ring finger used to be called the 'heart finger' because people believed that it was directly connected to the heart by a special vein or nerve; the symbolism of love and fidelity of the ring finger, particularly of the left hand (the side of the heart), also has to do with this."[25] [Caps in the original; Boldface added]

Our Phallic Heritage says this about the ring:

"The **Wedding Ring,** customarily put on during the marriage ceremony and worn continuously thereafter, **had a phallic origin.** In the **Buddhistic hand sign** of blessing, the thumb and index fingers are joined at the tips, forming a circle, symbolizing the **yoni**, while the other three fingers (the middle, ring, and little fingers) are extended, symboliz-ing...the male [genital] triad. When the ring is placed on the ring finger (the penis symbolized), it symbolizes the union of the male and female; hence, through this symbolism, the wedding ring means marriage or union."[26]

Occultist and Mason, Manly Palmer Hall, asserts:

> "The wedding ring originally was intended to imply that in the nature of the one who wore it the state of equilibrium and completion had been attained. This plain band of gold therefore bore witness of the union of the Higher Self (God) with the lower self (Nature) and the ceremony consummating this indissoluble **blending of Divinity and humanity in the one nature** of the initiated **mystic** constituted the *hermetic marriage* of the Mysteries."[27] [Italics in the original; Boldface added]

More about the wedding ring can be found in *The Occult Sciences*. There we find:

> "It may be pointed out that **wedding rings are a remnant of the magic rings.** They are worn on the ring finger, because in **chiromancy** that finger corresponds to the heart. The husband will be master in the home, if, on placing it on his wife's finger, he is careful to push it right down."[28]

According to *A Pictorial History of Magic and the Supernatural,* "**Chiromancy** is based on the cabbala...."[29]

Also, chiromancy is another name for **PALMISTRY!**[30] This is a form of **DIVINATION.**[31] For instance, *Dictionary of Mysticism* states: "**Chiromancy:** The art of **DIVINATION** from the shape of the hand and fingers and the lines and other markings which appear on them."[32] *The World Book Encyclopedia* indicates under "palmistry": "It is sometimes called *chiromancy.* It is a combination of **astrology** and handreading....See also **FORTUNETELLING.**"[33]

Of course, divination and astrology are strictly forbidden by the Scriptures in Deuteronomy 18:10-12. See also II Kings 17:17 and Acts 16:16.

Now, let's turn our attention to the necklace. Cunningham discloses:

> "The necklace is simply a large ring worn around the neck. Its powers and uses are much the same as those of rings. Because necklaces are often worn near the heart, they can be used to work on the emotions, or to attract or strengthen love.

> "In contemporary Wicca, **women often wear necklaces of stones to represent reincarnation and the Goddess.**

> "Wearing a necklace of stones increases their energies because you are surrounding yourself (**binding** yourself) with their powers. Thus, **the necklace is much more powerful than any one stone used separately.**"[34]

Another book relates:

> "Broadly speaking, the threaded bead-necklace stands for the **unifying of diversity....**Regarded as a string, the necklace becomes a cosmic and social symbol of ties and bonds. Because it is usually worn on the neck or breast, it acquires a symbolic relation with those parts of the body

and with the **signs of the Zodiac** pertaining to them. Since **the neck has an astrological association with sex, the necklace also betokens an erotic link.**"[35]

One item that is often found on the end of a necklace is the **Italian Horn** or the leprechaun staff. This was "introduced by the lord druids of Scotland and Ireland"[36] and was "used as the instrument of the druids for castrating animals and humans. It has been hexed and is used for luck and fortune. **Satanist priests wear this emblem for prosperity,** as a **charm** around their neck."[37]

"The **Italian horn,** also known as the Unicorn Horn, **is an occult symbol for the devil to bless one's finances.** It is believed that this **charm** is an offshoot from the word 'malucka' where the word 'luck' is derived."[38] A former witch says that "the word 'luck' is derived from the word 'Lucifer.'"[39] He adds that the cornucopia (which is covered in the chapter entitled "Masonic and Eastern Star Symbols") "is derived from the word 'uni-corn.'"

Another item worn as a necklace is the squash blossom. The "pendant is shaped to look like the moon in its first or last quarter;

it is a fertility symbol."[40] A former witch writes the following about the squash blossom:

> **"This symbol represents the Crescent star.** The person making it is offering it for a sacrifice to the goddess of fertility. The forming (budding) of the blossom on the squash represents youth. The wearer is usually unaware of the evil intent behind the making. The curse is being worked out and the wearer is acting as a catalyst because demons need bodies to carry their messages. **The wearer becomes a messenger of Satan."**[41]

According to *Magical Arts* evil spirits were thought to be able to enter the body through any of its openings and take control. "The first earrings were probably worn to bar the way to these spirits and so was the first lipstick."[42]

"Earrings are rings that are worn in the ears. Piercing the lobes to allow the wearing of earrings is an ancient practice.

"Most parts of the body have been pierced for various magical and religious reasons throughout the ages. Ears may have been among the first, along with the nose which is still pierced in India for protective, as well as cosmetic reasons.

"Folklore still surrounds this practice. Pierced earrings in general are often recommended to strengthen weak eyes—if set with emeralds, they are particularly effective. Gold earrings are often worn by those wishing to cure headaches, though some say to wear one gold earring and one silver for this purpose."[43]

In Genesis, when God told Jacob to go the Bethel, Jacob:

"said unto his household, and to all that were with him, Put away the strange gods that are among you, and be clean, and change your garments: And let us arise, and go up to Bethel; and I will make there an altar unto God, who answered me in the day of my distress, and was with me in the way which I went. And they **gave unto Jacob all the strange gods which were in their hand, and all their earrings** which were in their ears; and **Jacob hid them under the oak** which was by Shechem" (Genesis 35:2-4).

When Jacob's household was ready to seek God, they got rid of all their earrings and idols. What some people don't realize is that Satan is a liar and a deceiver. Instead of these items protecting an individual **FROM** the evil spirits, they are actually **ATTRACTING** evil spirits.

Hosea 2:13 says that Israel "decked herself with her earrings and her jewels, and she went after her lovers, and forgat Me, saith the Lord."

I Timothy 2:9-10 advises: "In like manner also, that women adorn themselves in modest apparel, with shamefacedness and sobriety; not with broided hair, or gold, or pearls, or costly array; But (which becometh women professing godliness) with good works."

Concerning pierced ears, a former witch, David Meyer, reports:

"I think it is interesting to note at this point that Hillary Clinton said that she did not allow Chelsea to have her ears pierced until she was 13. There is, of course, a very good reason for that. It is a known fact **among occultists** that when a girl is 13, she is taken into what is called the 'outer court' of a coven, and the **token of this child becoming a neophyte witch is the piercing of the ears.**"[44]

Earrings were also a symbol of slavery.[45]

With our culture returning to many pagan practices, it isn't surprising to see an increase in body piercing. Some are doing this "just for the fun of it," or because it is a fad, or because their favorite rock star had it done. Whether innocently or not, our children are nonetheless opening themselves to demonic influences and doctrines of devils by taking part in such activity. Tattooing parts of the body is also quite prevalent at the present time. The Bible warns: **"Ye shall not** make any cuttings in your flesh for the dead, nor **print any marks upon you:** I am the Lord" (Leviticus 19:28). Laurie Cabot, a witch, comments:

"The origins of **tattooing come from ancient magical practices** of painting designs and **talismans** on the skin either for temporary ceremonial purposes or permanently....

"Pay particular attention to how you adorn your forehead where the **Third Eye** is located. East Indians wear a red dot over this chakra point, ancient **Druids** wore crowns with a band of jewels in the center of the forehead; the African Berbers use black **makeup to tattoo** their faces with stars, moons, and other **magical** symbols. A quartz crystal worn across the **Third Eye** can be particularly powerful."[46]

Could the piercing of the body, along with the acceptance of tattoos, be preparing the way for the mark of the beast where a chip may be placed in the right hand or forehead?

Body painting is also a magical practice.

> "Both men and women use some type of **makeup as a form of magic in Witchcraft.**...Native Americans, Polynesians, the ancient Egyptians, the Chinese and Japanese, and African tribal peoples have also **used makeup and body paint for magical purposes.** The use of color affects our behavior and emotional dispositions."[47]

Cabot elaborates:

> **"Outlining the eye emulates the Goddess,** who is often portrayed with large, distinctive eyes, capable of seeing through space and time as well as into our innermost hearts. Ishtarte, the Goddess of Light, was known in the ancient Middle East as the Eye Goddess because the light she brings from heaven to earth illuminates the world. The Egyptian Goddess Maat originally possessed the All-Seeing Eye, which later was transferred to Horus. In Syria the Goddess Mari had large, strong eyes that could see deep into the human soul. The Goddess's ability to see and know all things became a terrifying concept in patriarchal times, and her **mystical eye** was turned into the **'evil eye,'** associated during the time of the Inquisition with Witches....

> "But the tradition of **outlining the eye to honor the Goddess of Love** and to make one's own eyes more radiant and mysterious is a time-honored custom. Green, rose, or

copper eyeshadow or eyeliner draw in energy from Venus, the planet of love and romance. Pink eyeshadow, blush, or lipstick will strengthen self-esteem. Glitter refracts and reflects light and will send out light to others. **Affixing jewelry to your body or face is also powerful.** Remember to charge your makeup and jewelry and body paint before you use them, catalyzing them with the specific intention of your spell."[48]

Another magazine states:

"The use of makeup is also said to stem from witchcraft where the painting of one's face was believed to ward off evil. **Makeup was used extensively by American**

Indian witch doctors and European witches. Mascara was particularly a charm inasmuch as it is made of antimony, an old witch metal."[49]

On three occasions the Bible refers to face painting. Jeremiah 4:30 and Ezekiel 23:40-44 refer to wicked women who tried to lure men into the sins of immorality. II Kings 9:30 mentions that Jezebel painted her face. Of course, Jezebel was a pagan woman who practiced witchcraft (II Kings 9:22) and worshipped Baal. King Ahab married her and he also started to worship Baal (I King 16:31-32). Since the pagans painted their face, it is no surprise to see Jezebel doing the same thing. In fact, wicked and immoral women today are often called a "Jezebel."

"In this connection, I should like to share an incident. About 25 years ago, a returned missionary from China spoke at our church and related the following. He had been in China for seven years, and upon return to this country for furlough he immediately noticed something different about the American women. In the seven years that he had been gone, many of the women had adopted the popular fad of painting their faces [makeup]. In China, **the prostitutes were the only women who painted their faces, wore ear rings, and had long painted fingernails.** This was their means of identifying themselves to their men-partners in sin. The shocking thing to the missionary was that the **American women had taken on the custom of the heathen harlot."**[50]

The Bible says: "Abstain from all appearance of evil" (I Thessalonians 5:22) and "have no fellowship with the unfruitful works of darkness, but rather reprove them" (Ephesians 5:11).

19. MASONIC AND EASTERN STAR SYMBOLS

Masons use many symbols which have already been covered such as the point within the circle, the pentagram, the circle, the triangle, the clasped hands, etc. We'll briefly look at a few other symbols that the Masons use.

The "G" is quite prominent in Masonry. In the lower degrees, the Mason is told that the "G" stands for "Geometry" or "God." The occultist Eliphas Levi, however, informs us that the "G" stands for Venus and that Venus' symbol is a lingam (a symbol of the male private part)![1] Remember, Venus is another name for Lucifer.[2]

Levi also states that the:

"G which Freemasons place in the centre of the Burning Star signifies GNOSIS and GENERATION, the two sacred words of the ancient Kabbalah. It also signifies GRAND ARCHITECT, for the Pentagram, from whatever side it may be looked at, always represents an A. By placing it in such a manner that two of its points are above and only one below, we may see the horns, ears, and beard of the hieratic god of Mendes [Baphomet], when it becomes the sign of infernal evocations."[3] [Emphasis in the original]

Osiris, by the way, "was represented by the Ram of Mendes, sporting the horns natural to the ram."[4]

Many other Masonic authors reveal that the "G" really means generation or carries a sexual connotation. Albert Pike claims that he "generative principle" is "represented by the letter G...."[5]

"A Masonic symbol seen less frequently is the 33° cross because it appertains only to the highest degrees. It is more commonly called the Crusader's Cross or the Jerusalem Cross....It was supposedly worn by the first Grand Master of the Knights Templar, Godfrey de Bouillon, after he liberated Jerusalem from the Muslims.

"This symbol is on the hat of the Sovereign Grand Commander of all 33° Masons in a very slightly modified form. **It is part of the magical signature of Aleister Crowley, the supreme satanist of this century!** It is also found as the **logo of the new Catholic Bible, the Jerusalem Bible!**"[6]

The broken column is used in both Masonry and the Eastern Star. The initiates are told that the broken column signifies an early death[7] and the symbolism of the column can be traced back to ancient Egypt.[8] We learn, however, that **columns represented gods.**[9]

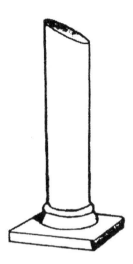

In a *Short Talk Bulletin,* entitled "The Broken Column," published by the Masonic Service Association for use in the Masonic Lodge, we find that: "In **EGYPTIAN MYTHOLOGY, ISIS IS SOMETIMES PICTURED WEEPING OVER THE BROKEN COLUMN** which conceals the body of her husband Osiris, while behind her stands Horus or Time pouring ambrosia on her hair."[10] (See "Winged Symbols" for a picture of Isis weeping over the broken column.) A former Satanist and Mason explains:

> "Isis was both virgin and mother, so the 'beautiful virgin' is Isis weeping. The broken column is the missing member of Osiris [the phallus], the acacia, an allusion to the eternal life preached by the Egyptians as well as the fertility cults' emphasis on vegetation. The urn is an evocation of the canopic jars used in Egyptian funerals to store the vital organs of mummies.

> "Finally, we have 'Time,' the god Saturn, a later form of the mysterious and evil god, Set. In astrology, Saturn is called the 'greater malefic,' or greater evil."[11]

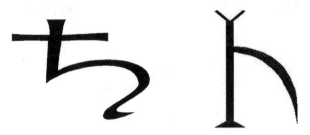

Astrological representations of Saturn

Another name for Osiris is Saturn.[12] Masonic writer, J. S. M. Ward explains that Saturn is really Satan.[13] *A Dictionary of Symbols* mentions that Saturn "is related to the Ouroboros (or the serpent which bites it own tail)."[14]

Saturn's symbol is a scythe.[15] The scythe is really symbolic of renewed hopes for rebirth or reincarnation.[16] This is quite fitting since the symbolism of the broken column represents Isis and Osiris. Osiris had a "rebirth" due to **SPELLS** performed by Isis.[17]

Isis was known as a powerful **SORCERESS**,[18] "the **GREAT ENCHANTRESS, the MISTRESS OF MAGIC, the SPEAKER OF SPELLS.**"[19] Not only was Isis a sorceress but she "has always been seen as the guiding light of the profession of **PROSTITUTION....**"[20] Incidentally, Isis' name among the Syrians was Achot, meaning "**SISTER.**"[21] Isn't it interesting to learn that the degree of Martha is known as the "**SISTER**" degree in the Eastern Star?

Saturn is symbolized by the goat's head![22] Remember that the pentagram used in the Eastern Star also represents the goat's head. Is this just another "coincidence"?

Saturn is also another name for Nimrod[23] who is considered by some Masons to be one of the founders of Masonry. According to the Bible, Nimrod built the Tower of Babel which displeased God, but Masonic writer John Yarker boasts that: "It is well known that the **TOWER OF BABEL WAS ONE OF THE MOST ANCIENT TRADITIONS OF MASONRY....**"[24]

Additionally, the acacia of Masonry and the fern or pine branch of the Eastern Star, which is used for Martha, symbolizes eternal life or immortality.[25] The acacia, which is actually dedicated to the powers of darkness,[26] is placed on the Mason's grave, but going back to Egyptian mythology we find that the acacia protected the grave of Osiris.[27]

Yet another name for Osiris and Saturn is Baal.[28] Of course, the Bible condemns Baal worship, but this is the god who is being represented in Masonry and the Eastern Star under the symbolism of the broken column, but there is an even deeper meaning.

Baal

The broken column actually represented the phallus of Osiris. Albert Mackey, a 33° Mason, specifies that "the **PHALLUS** was an imitation of the male generative organ. It was represented usually by a **COLUMN,** which was surrounded by a circle at its base, intended for the *cteis,* or female generative organ."[29] [Italics in the original; Boldface and caps added]

The square is used in both Masonry and the Eastern Star. Eastern Star writer, Mary Ann Slipper, states:

> "When turning square corners in floor work it is well to remember that this is acknowledging in action the great truth of being. The square not only means the acknowledgement of that Power but also our belief in the finished work of the Master Builder, who some day will summon each one into that Great Temple not made with hands, eternal in the heavens."[30]

In other words, the square used in the Eastern Star floor work represents passing from earth to heaven. Also of interest is that both J. D. Buck and Harold Waldwin Percival mention that the Masonic Square and Compass is just another form of the six pointed star, which we have already covered.[31]

The Masons use a square and compass combined in their degrees.

"The square represents the female (passive) generative principle, the earth, and the baser, sensual nature; and the Compass represents the male (active) generative principle, the sun/heavens, and the higher, spiritual nature."[32]

The two symbols displayed together once again represent sexual union. In fact, in witchcraft, the square is actually the symbol of the lingam or the male reproduction organ and the compass represents the female organs.[33] Combining the two symbols gives an obvious and vulgar meaning.

Another meaning of the square is that it represents a god or gods. Just which god is it? We don't have to wonder for long, for a number of Masons have already revealed some of these gods to us. For instance, in *The Symbolism of Freemasonry* by Albert G. Mackey, 33° Mason, we see that the "Thebans worshipped Bacchus under the form of a rude, **SQUARE** stone."[34] He also explains that "Mercury, or Hermes, was always represented by a cubical stone, because he was the type of truth...."[35] In a footnote, he says: "In the most primitive times, all the gods appear to have been represented by cubical blocks of stone; and Pausanias says that he saw thirty of these stones in the city of Pharae, which represented as many deities."[36]

Masonic author, Albert Churchward writes: "The Square is also very clearly depicted, symbolically, in the Egyptian *Ritual* and is plainly **SHOWN IN 'THE BOOK OF THE DEAD,'**...This Square you find depicted in many of the ancient temples and in the Great Pyramid, as two seats, one for Osiris and one for Maat—**IT IS THE MASONIC SQUARE."**[37]

Tibetan Book of the Dead—Notice the triskele (666) on the cover

Joseph Fort Newton, also a Mason, claims that "Mercury, Apollo, Neptune, and Hercules were worshiped under the form of a **SQUARE** stone, while a large black stone was the emblem of Buddha among the Hindoos (sic), of Manah Theus-Ceres in Arabia, and of Odin in Scandinavia."[38]

The labyrinth is used in the Eastern Star. We are told that the **LABYRINTH** "was made to conform to the idea of a **FIVE POINTED STAR, WITHIN A COMPLETE CIRCLE."**[39] A witch, Laurie Cabot, explains that the **"CIRCLE AROUND THE PENTAGRAM** represents the totality of all intelligence. It is the

SIGN FOR THE GOD AND GODDESS, the fullness of cosmic intelligence."[40]

Albert Pike mentions that a **LABYRINTH "WAS BUILT IN HONOR OF THE SUN...."**[41] We also learn that some labyrinths were designed with the purpose of luring devils into them so that they might never escape.[42]

The labyrinth is also one of the symbols of the goddess,[43] which is interesting knowing that the original names of the five Eastern Star women were actually names of goddesses. How appropriate, then, to use one of the goddess' symbols!

Was the labyrinth chosen intentionally or was it just a coincidence? In *The Symbolism of the Eastern Star* we read: "The meaning of the word Labyrinth is a series of winding passages, a maze of intricate windings; **copied from the structure made in Crete by Dadalus** (sic)."[44] *The Seeker's Handbook* explains more about this:

"By a second derivation, labyrinth comes from the ancient Greek word *labrys,* 'the double-headed axe.' In **Cretan myth, the maze of Daedalus,** where Theseus found and slew the Minotaur, was known as the place of the double-headed axe—this being, apparently, the weapon of slaughter or sacrifice that the hero used. But deep research into Mediterranean culture of five to seven thousand years B.C. (reported by Marija Gimbutas) turns up the curious notion that the doubled-headed axes may have been a visual pun: At the earliest stage it appears to have been more common as the image of a butterfly! Now the butterfly itself—in Greek, *psyche*—is the earliest symbol that we have for the immortal human soul. It was also **an emblem held sacred to the Great Goddess or Mother Earth.** Somehow **the butterfly is deeply connected with the labyrinth,** as much as the double-headed axe. These two images, one so masculine and the other so feminine, appear to spring from an ancient unity of some kind."[45]

Minotaur

This book adds that the word labyrinth is:

"From the Latin *labor* + *intus,* 'into': the place of entering into labor, birth, or **rebirth.** At sacred sites, such as Chartres, Glastonbury, and Knossos in Crete, a maze constructed of earth-walls, ruts, tiles, or underground windings, believed to have been used in **initiations** as a place of ordeal and initiation through the **PSYCHO-DRAMA....**They are also closely related to **SACRED DANCE,** for which they may have provided a sort of ground plan."[46] [Italics and caps in the original; Boldface added]

The Labyrinth Walk is becoming popular in the United States.

"This is a mystical medieval practice of walking a 42' wide maze-like design (a sign of wholeness appearing also in Tibetan mandelas (sic) and Hopi Indian medicine wheels) which becomes a 'walking meditation.' People walk and 'contemplate,' walking to the 'center of their spirituality.' In San Francisco, new ager, Jean Houston (Mrs. Clinton's guru) introduced the Labyrinth to Episcopal Priest(ess), Rev. Lauren Arness, who now travels the U.S. with a mobile model to introduce it to others.

"The Unitarian Church made one and loaned it to the Washington National Cathedral in DC. St. Luke's Episcopal church in Stuart, FL has one and here, locally, the Pilgrim Congregational Church (Blue Roof Church) on Montclair Road has made one, as well. The Pilgrim Church regularly celebrates **WITCHCRAFT** and other new age events there."[47]

Mimi Lobell "designed a 'Goddess Temple' with a labyrinth and ring of fire (upper level) symbolic of the conscious, and a lower level symbolic of the unconscious."[48] Her husband, John Lobell, gave a speech at the World Service Forum which was distributed by the Lucis Trust.[49]

The balance scales appear in Masonic and Egyptian symbolism. In Egypt, it was "Anubis' duty to attend to the ritual preparation of bodies, to weigh the heart of every man on the **scale of justice,** and to judge a man's good and bad deeds on earth."[50] "In many traditions, The **Law of Karma has been symbolized by the Scales of Justice.** The Scale or Balance is also the symbol for the astrological sign of Libra."[51]

Not surprisingly, Anubis is one of the gods adored in **witchcraft.** One witchcraft magazine tells how to make an Anubis protection amulet. After the instructions are given, the writer of the article then adds: "Anubis can be anyone's best friend, (He's definitely mine!) even if He is considered by many to be the **most ominous God of the Underworld [hell]."**[52] Personally, I don't need (or want) the protection of the "God of the Underworld"! Do you?

Albert Pike tells us: "Isis was also aided in her search [for Osiris] by **Anubis,** in the shape of a dog. **HE WAS SIRIUS OR THE DOG-STAR....**"[53] It was Anubis who supposedly guarded "the gates of death"[54] and he "was associated with magic and divination."[55]

Another representation of Anubis

The description of Anubis given above clearly signifies to us that this god cannot possibly be the God of the Christians. For one thing, the Bible definitely states that "God is not the God of the dead, but of the living" (Matthew 22:31-32, Mark 12:26-27, and Luke 20:37-38). Notice also that Anubis is depicted in the shape of a dog (or a jackal).[56] Many of the gods are presented in animal (or part-animal) forms. Thoth was illustrated as an ibis-headed man, a baboon, or sometimes as a "dog-headed ape" or a "dog-headed baboon."[57] Set was "represented by the head of a strange-looking animal that may have been a cross between a donkey and a pig"[58] and was also worshipped under the crocodile and hippopotamus forms.[59] Horus was symbolized as a hawk or falcon[60] and Pan was portrayed as "half-goat, half-man."[61]

Horus

Hapi

Kebeh

Hathor

Ra (or Re)

Anubis

Sebek

Ra (or Re)

Garuda

You see, the "gods were originally believed to be animals or birds—and in later years were anthropomorphized and pictured with human bodies with the head of the animal or bird."[62] Of course, the Bible speaks about such a situation. Romans 1:21-23 and 25 state that:

> "when they knew God, they glorified Him not as God, neither were thankful; but became vain in their imaginations, and their foolish heart was darkened. Professing themselves to be wise, they became fools, And **changed the glory of the uncorruptible God into an image made like to corruptible man, and to birds, and fourfooted beasts, and creeping things....**Who changed the truth of God into a lie, and worshipped and served the creature more than the Creator, who is blessed for ever."

This passage continues:

> "For this cause God gave them up unto vile affections: for even their women did change the natural use into that which is against nature:...And even as they did not like to retain God in their knowledge, God gave them over to a reprobate mind, to do those things which are not convenient; Being filled with all unrighteousness, fornication, wickedness, covetousness, maliciousness; full of envy, murder, debate, deceit, malignity; whisperers, Backbiters, haters of God, despiteful, proud, boasters, inventors of evil things, disobedient to parents, Without understanding, covenantbreakers, without natural affection, implacable, unmerciful..." (Romans 1:26, 28-31).

It's no wonder, then, that all kinds of unrighteousness follow such a worship of pagan gods for the gods that are being revered are themselves portrayed as doing evil acts. Just a quick glance at mythology will show the gods lying, cheating, committing fornication, incest, adultery, murder, and such like. This is certainly a completely different lifestyle from the righteous life Christ lived (see Hebrews 7:26). Peter also admonishes us: "But as He which hath called you is holy, so be ye holy in all manner of conversation; Because it is written, Be ye holy; for I am holy" (I Peter 1:15-16).

Also presented in the description of Anubis is the idea that if good deeds outweigh bad ones, the person is rewarded and vice versa. A book printed by the Masonic Publishing and Manufacturing Company reveals:

"A painting of the Funeral Ritual represents the judgment of a soul; it advances toward the goddess *Thme,* who wears an ostrich feather on her head; beside this divinity of justice and truth, appears the **scale** in which *Anubis* and *Horus* weigh the actions of the deceased—they place in one side the ostrich feather, and in the other the vase containing the heart; if the weight of the heart is greater than that of the ostrich feather, the scale descends, and the soul is received in the celestial courts; above this scene appear the forty-two judges of the souls seated, and having the head ornamented with the ostrich feather."[63] [Italics in the original; Boldface added]

What is interesting about this explanation is that **THIS "EGYPTIAN WITCHCRAFT" SCENE**[64] **IS ACTUALLY PORTRAYED IN THE MASONIC LODGE** in the 31st degree[65] where the candidate's actions are weighed on a **balance scale.** In this Masonic degree the "candidate is brought into the Court of the Dead to be judged for actions while living and to determine if he deserves to dwell among the gods."[66] (For picture, see chapter entitled "Winged Symbols.") This is a teaching that is contrary to God's Word, for we can never be saved by works. II Timothy 1:9 mentions that God "hath saved us, and called us with an holy calling, **NOT ACCORDING TO OUR WORKS,** but according to His own purpose and grace, which was given us in Christ Jesus before the world began." In Titus we are told: "**NOT BY WORKS OF RIGHTEOUSNESS** which we have done, but according to His mercy He saved us, by the washing of regeneration, and renewing of the Holy Ghost" (Titus 3:5).

The gavel is an important Masonic and Eastern Star symbol. Sarah Terry, in her Eastern Star book, *The Second Mile,* tells us that "in ancient times the **GAVEL** referred to the **HAMMER OF THE GOD THOR.**"[67] Thor is another **PAGAN** god—a god of fertility.[68] He is part of the Scandinavian Trinity.[69] What is interesting is that **THOR IS ANOTHER NAME FOR SIRIUS—THE BLAZING STAR OR THE PENTAGRAM!**[70]

Albert Pike gives us some additional names for Thor. He explains: **"THOR WAS THE SUN, THE EGYPTIAN OSIRIS** and Kneph, the Phoenician **BEL OR BAAL."**[71] **BAAL IS ALSO A SYNONYM FOR THE DEVIL.**[72] This god Baal, under the name of Thor, is called "the Prince of the Power of the Air."[73] Baal worship is condemned by the Bible (I Kings 16:30-33, 22:53; II Kings 17:16, etc.), and in Ephesians 2:2 we find that Satan is called the "prince of the power of the air." Not only does Satan have the same title as is given to the god Thor, but we should notice that the word "Thor" means "thunder."[74] Thor "was the god of lightning and thunder in Norse mythology."[75] This is a significant statement for Satanists use the symbol called a "Satanic S," which resembles a lightning bolt. In Luke 10:18 Jesus says: "I beheld Satan as lightning fall from heaven."

Is it any wonder that the Bible further informs us that this "prince of the power of the air" is "the spirit that now worketh in the children of **DISOBEDIENCE"** (Ephesians 2:2)?

Additionally, the gavel, like so many of the other symbols, also has a sexual connotation. Masonic author, J. S. M. Ward, remarks: "Thus we see that the **HAMMER, OR GAVEL,** and the **TAU** were originally the same, and this is a natural evolution of symbols, for the **TAU CROSS IS EVOLVED FROM THE PHALLUS,** and that is the **SYMBOL OF GOD** the Creator...."[76]

This reference shows us that the gavel, the hammer, and the tau cross were all the same and, therefore, the meanings would be the same.

Ward continues:

"But this is not the only place where the tau cross occurs. The gabels, or gavels, are all T crosses and combine in one symbol the hammer, the sign of rule, and the T cross, the symbol of the male or creative side of the Deity; and, lest there should be any mistake, the T is placed on the apron of the Master of the Lodge, though placed [upside down], so as to give also the symbol of the square, and also to emphasise its **PHALLIC** meaning."[77]

"The Tau, T, is the emblem of Mercury, of Hermes. It is the *crux ansata,* and the *crux Hermis.* It was the last letter of the ancient alphabets, the end of boundary, whence it came to be used as a terminus to districts; but the crux Tau was also the emblem of the generative power, of eternal transmigrating life [reincarnation], and thus was used indiscriminately with the Phallus. It was, in fact, *the phallus. "*[78] [Emphasis in the original]

The ankh (or crux ansata) is a symbol of life.[79] A *Dictionary of Mysticism* explains the ankh as the "Egyptian cross, shaped like a capital T with an oval loop on the top, symbol of life in **occult** tradition."[80] It was "used by the gods as an instrument for awakening the dead to a new life."[81]

One Masonic book relates: "The Crux Ansata, so frequently observed in the hands of the statues of the old kings and gods of

Isis and Amon each holding an ankh

Egypt, was evidently both solar and **Phallic** in signification, and represented a combination of the male and female principles in nature."[82]

In *The Origins, Practices, and Traditions of Halloween,* we find that the ankh is an "ancient symbol for immortality, fertility; a cross with a ring at the top worn and used in Satanic rites."[83] A former witch reveals that the ankh is:

"An embelm (sic) to identify the wearer as a worshipper of the sun god Ra, a seeker of the Satanist beliefs, and one who practices the worship to the unknown gods of the supernatural. The wearer acknowledges the sun god Ra, works the voodoo of the unseen world through this **hex.**"[84]

Ankh variations

It is interesting to discover that, according to a Masonic book, that the "**caduceus is a variant of** the earliest form of the Cross, the *Crux Ansata* of the ancient Egyptians."[85] [Italics in the original; Boldface added] (The caduceus is covered in more detail in "Winged Symbols.")

A related item to the ankh, the hammer of Thor, the tau cross, and the gavel, is the swastika. Occultist Helena Petrovna Blavatsky remarks: "Few world-symbols are more pregnant with real **OCCULT** meaning than the Svastika."[86] In *The Royal Masonic Cyclopaedia of History, Rites, Symbolism, and Biography* we find that the **swastika:**

"**was the hammer of Thor,** celebrated in the mythology of the Norse nations, and the tradition ran that when Thor threw this golden cross, it struck, and, like the boomerang, returned again to his hand....**In Masonry,** however, **we find this hammer of Thor exceedingly important,** and of very ancient usage among the Goths, and **in the Masonic fraternity it has survived in the form of the mallet.**"[87]

In *Amulets and Superstitions* we are told that it has been suggested that the four arms of the swastika "represent the four quarters of the heavens or earth, and also that the whole sign is an emblem of INDRA, or DYAUS, or ZEUS, or JUPITER, or THOR."[88] [Emphasis in the original]

In fact, Thor used the hammer for his weapon and the swastika as his emblem.[89]

Rudyard Kipling, a Mason, used the swastika as his symbol.[90] What most Masons today probably do not realize is that the swastika itself was also a **MASONIC** symbol.[91] It is an older form of the Tau Cross (the ankh).[92]

I have read quite a number of old Masonic books from the 19th and early 20th century. Many of these books will mention the swastika. For instance, one of the most popular Masonic books ever written is *The Builders* by Joseph Fort Newton.[93] In this book he refers the reader to an essay by Thomas Carr "in which he shows that the **Swastika is the symbol of the Supreme Architect of the Universe among Operative Masons today....**"[94]

Hinduism Today gives a little history on this symbol.

"When Buddhism fomented its birth out of India's spiritual wellspring, it inherited the right-angled emblem. On the backs of monks, the little double-jointed **good luck** design journeyed north over the Himalayas into China—often carved into Buddha's feet—and splayed into a spectrum of decorative 'meandering' swastikas, the classical, geometric oriental motif. Nineteenth century Americans picked up the symbol from the American Indians. Boy Scouts tightened their britches with brassy swastika buckles and a US World's Fair minted flashy swastika commemorative

Buddha's footprint—Notice the swastikas on the toes

coins. Deformed into a mark of demonic racism by Hitler, the ancient symbol soon disappeared except in India where it still retains its auspicious identity and aura of blessings."[95]

Women's Mysteries relates:

"Among the Hindus the right-handed swastika represents the male principle—light, life, and glory; it is the sun in its daily course from east to west. The left-handed swastika is, on the contrary, the emblem of the goddess Kali; it is the female principle—darkness, death, and destruction. These are four-armed swastikas, based on the equilateral cross; in addition three-armed, or three-legged, swastikas called triskeles also occur, for example, in Sicily and the Celtic countries....A three-legged swastika is the official emblem or arms of the Isle of Man, where the Celtic Moon Goddess, under the title of Anu or Aniis, was formerly worshipped."[96]

In *Dictionary of Mysticism* we find that the swastika is a "very ancient and widespread symbol, one of the most **sacred** and **mystic** diagrams in **OCCULTISM**....In general it is regarded as the **symbol of the sun;** in India, especially, it is used as a symbol of good luck."[97]

As is well known, Hitler used the swastika to represent his Nazi party. Hitler belonged to the occult Thule Society which also used the swastika.[98] Additionally, Hitler was a disciple of the occultist Helena Petrovna Blavatsky.[99]

"By 1914 her Aryan doctrine had spread through Germany and Austria. It was a member of the inner circle of the Thule Society, Dietrich Eckart, who first introduced Hitler to the teachings of Madame Blavatsky. Reportedly, Hitler kept a copy of her book, *The Secret Doctrine,* by his bedside, and it was from her writings that he learned the meaning of the Aryan swastika. (The swastika is the symbol of the seventh ray of initiation, and Hitler was a sixth ray initiate.)"[100]

Blavatsky says that the swastika is "purely phallic."[101] She also states: "The *Svastika,* the most sacred and mystic symbol in India, the 'Jaina-Cross' as it is now called by the Masons....It is the 'devil's sign,' we are told by the Indian missionaries."[102] [Emphasis in the original] "The Nazi symbol has become popular with Satanists to represent nature out of harmony."[103]

A few more representations of the swastika appear below.

The Druids also used the swastika,[104] but this is no surprise since Masonic author, William Hutchinson, acknowledges that "our mode of teaching the principles of our profession **[MASONRY] IS DERIVED FROM THE DRUIDS**...[and] our chief emblems originally [came] from Egypt...."[105] Albert Churchward, another Mason, also writes about Masons as **"OUR PRESENT DRUIDS"!**[106]

In *The Masks of God* we discover that the Lord of the Abyss has a "hammer in his right hand and on his left arm a **cornucopia....**"[107]

The cornucopia (or horn of plenty) is likewise a Masonic symbol. It can be seen on the jewel worn by the Steward.[108] We're told that the cornucopia "was introduced by the early American **WITCHES** that came over from Scotland."[109]

Many Masonic authorities give us the meaning of this particular emblem. The Grand Lodge A.F. & A.M. of Canada admits:

> "The emblem has allusion to the ancient **Greek legend** of Amalthea, a she-goat who nursed the god Zeus when he was a baby. Her horns were miraculous; from one of them flowed nectar, and from the other ambrosia. On one occasion she broke her horn off on a tree. Some one picked it up, filled it with fruit, and brought it to the baby god. According to some versions of the story it continued to replenish itself miraculously. The **cornucopia is appropriated to the Steward as his emblem** because of his function in ministering to the brethren at the hours of refreshment."[110]

Another Masonic writer, Carl Claudy, comments:

> "A curious derivation of a **Masonic symbol** from the heavens is that universally associated with the Stewards, the **cornucopia.**

> "According to the **mythology of the Greeks** which goes back to the very dawn of civilization, the **god Zeus** was nourished in infancy from the milk of the goat,

Amalthea. In gratitude the god placed Amalthea forever in the heavens as a constellation, but first he gave one of Amalthea's horns to his nurses with the assurance that it would forever pour for them whatever they desired.

"The horn of plenty, or the **cornucopia, is thus a symbol of abundance.** The goat from which it came may be found by the curious among the constellations under the name of **Capricorn.** The Tropic of Capricorn of our school days is the southern limit of the swing of the sun on the path which marks the ecliptic, on which the earth dips first its north, then its south pole toward our luminary. Hence there is a connection, not the less direct for being tenuous, between our Stewards, their symbol, the lights in the lodge, the place of darkness, and Solomon's Temple."[111]

Astrological representation of Capricorn

The cornucopia is another example of an androgynous symbol. "The horn was masculine and the inside was feminine. The fruit inside symbolized productiveness of the female."[112] *A Dictionary of Symbols* gives more information about this under the entry "cornucopia":

"In mythology, it was the goat Amalthea who fed the infant Jupiter with milk. Given that the general symbolism of the horn is strength, and that the goat has maternal implications, and in addition that the shape of the horn (phallic outside and hollow inside) endows it with a complex symbolism (including that of the *lingam*, or symbol of generation), it is easy to understand its allegorical use as the horn of abundance. Piobb points out also that the cornucopia is an expression of prosperity deriving from its association with the zodiacal sign of Capricorn."[113] [Emphasis in the original]

In spite of this interpretation of the cornucopia, the Masons are proud to use this symbol. In fact, the logo for the Job's Daughters (a Masonically-affiliated organization) is a double triangle with the letters "IYOB FILIAE" between the two triangles and inside the inner triangle are three girls wearing crowns. One girl is holding the horn of plenty (cornucopia), another girl is holding a dove, and the third girl is holding an incense burner.[114]

Another Masonic symbol that stands for plenty is the pomegranate.[115] A Masonic book, *The Perfect Ashlar,* states: "The pomegranates, being a fruit remarkable for the number of their seeds, are **symbolic of fertility,** and the wreaths, or network, spread over the surface, indicate the courses of the heavenly bodies around the earth."[116]

Another Masonic book, *The Lodge and the Craft,* gives an expanded (and more vulgar) definition about the meaning of the pomegranate in Masonry. The author claims:

"To illustrate some of the lines of thought which pass among the present philosophers of the Craft, we will describe a late theory that a certain brother, than whom *there is none brighter among our acquaintance.* Said he, 'The lodge is a representation of King Solomon's Temple and the Temple was calculated to symbolize the maternal human body, wherein the candidate must enter to be born again. The uterus and vagina represent the porch of the Temple, the pillars of the porch represent the fallopian tubes, the network, the broad ligament with its accompanying blood vessels, the lily-work, the ampulla or fimbriated extremity of the tube, and the **pomegranate,** the ovary and its exuberant seeds, the ova cells. The winding stairway is represented by the three divisions of the intestine. The three steps are represented by the ascending, transverse and descending colon, the five steps by the coils of the ilium and the seven steps by the coils of the jejunum. The veil of the Temple represents the diaphragm, the shechinah and the altar represent the heart, which is the source of life, the first to live and the last to die. This is overshadowed by the wings of the cherubim, in the shape of the lungs. The seven-branched candlestick is represented by the arch of the aorta, the great artery of the chest, which is itself the sanctum sanctorum, while the abdomen was the holy place or Middle Chamber. The brain represents the Deity, which governs all things, and is the analogue of the Holy Royal Arch, whose ark contains the Ineffable Name of God.' There are many other analogues which might be mentioned, which suggest themselves to the trained anatomist."[117]

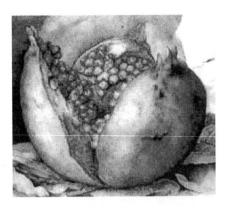

Knowing the meaning behind the pomegranate, isn't it interesting to learn that Milenko Matanovic, a friend of David

Spangler (who praises Lucifer), started an organization called the Pomegranate Foundation?[118] Matanovic and Spangler worked on a musical play. Spangler explains:

> "One of my very close associates and friends whom I met here at Findhorn, a Yugoslavian named Milenko Matanovic who was largely responsible for creating the New Troubadours and much of the music which we sang, worked with me on a three-act musical play....In this play we tried to look, in a comic and a musical way, at the course of human evolution. In the first act of the play, four great beings have gathered together evaluating the situation here on Earth. Three of the beings are actually present and the fourth being is suggested as a being who is trying to be present. The three who are present were: **Pan, representing the overlord of nature** and all the principles of nature; **Lucifer,** representing the principle of self and of selfhood and of all that is involved in learning to be separate from the universe in order that you can reunite with the universe; the **Logos,** who represented the power of that reunion through love. The **fourth suggested entity was the one who would appear when these three elements of Pan, Lucifer and the Christ were all blended into a wholeness."[119]

Matanovic also wrote a song entitled "Festival of Light," which was sung at the Cathedral of St. John the Divine in New York City.[120] This is a very ungodly place where they took Christ off the cross and put a **FEMALE** "Christ" (called Christa) in His place on the cross.[121]

Returning to the symbolism of the pomegranate, a Masonic book, *The Historical Landmarks and Other Evidences of Freemasonry, Explained,* declares: "The names of the **pillars** signified potency and perpetuity; the **pomegranates** on their capitals **were symbols of generation.** Hence **they were esteemed to be of Phallic reference."**[122] He adds:

> "'The **two pillars,**' says Fellows...'represent two imaginary columns, supposed to be placed at the equinoces (sic)

to support the heavens....The one on the left is called Boaz, and **indicates Osiris, or the sun,** the one on the right is called Jachin, **and designates Isis,** the symbol both of the earth and its productions, and of the moon.'"[123]

Another name for a four-sided pillar is the obelisk.[124] Pillars have always been worshipped as gods.[125] In Egypt, the obelisk stood for the sun god.[126] *The New Age Magazine* had an article by 33° Mason, Henry Ridgely Evans, in which he said that Osiris, the god of the underworld, was also depicted in the form of a pillar.[127]

In fact, in *Numbers: Their Occult Power and Mystic Virtues,* we find that the lingam (the male sex organ) was an upright pillar.[128]

H. L. Haywood, another Mason, states:

"In some cases these crude rock **pillars were thought to be the abodes of gods or demons;** in others, homes of the ghosts; and often as **symbols of sex.** Of the last-named usage one writer has said that 'pillars of stone, when associated with worship, have been from time immemorial regarded as symbols of the active and passive, the generative and fecundating principles.' In Egypt, Horus and Sut [Set] were regarded as two living pillars, twin builders and supporters of the heavens...."[129]

Masonic author, Rollin Blackmer, elaborates:

"The symbolism regarding solar worship indicated by the point within the circle has many variations, but one of the most primitive and natural was that the Sun was to be regarded as the male generative power of nature. To the ancient philosopher the origin and creation of life led to the contemplation of only one process, the generative act. The Sun God was certainly the generator of life, light and heat, the male principle, and this was symbolically represented by the Phallus or Lingam, which was some picture, more or less veiled, of the human male generative organ. The most frequent illustration was of a **pillar** set up in the center of a circle. The circle just as distinctively represented the earth or female principle. The Sun was the Great Father. Under his benign influence all nature germinated, and the earth was the Universal Mother, in whose ample womb all these germs grew to maturity."[130]

In *Our Phallic Heritage* we are told that "All pillars or columns originally had a phallic significance, and were therefore considered sacred."[131] Pan, the goat god and god of sensuality, was often represented as an obelisk.[132]

A former witch gives some interesting information about the obelisk. He writes:

"The obelisk is a long pointed four-sided shaft, the uppermost portion of which forms a pyramid. The word **'obelisk' literally means 'Baal's Shaft'** or Baal's organ of reproduction. This should be especially shocking when we realize that we have a gigantic obelisk in our nation's capital known as the Washington Monument."[133]

Of course, the Masons and Egyptians aren't the only ones who had high regard for the obelisk. In front of the Vatican stands the very same obelisk that once stood in Egypt![134] Ralph Woodrow explains:

"The very same obelisk that once stood at the ancient temple which was the center of Egyptian paganism, now stands before the mother church of Romanism! This seems like more than a mere coincidence.

"The red granite obelisk of the Vatican is itself 83 feet high (132 feet high with its foundation) and weighs 320 tons. In 1586, in order to center it in front of the church in St. Peter's square, it was moved to its present location by order of Pope Sixtus V. Of course moving this heavy obelisk— especially in those days—was a very difficult task. Many movers refused to attempt the feat, especially since the pope had attached the *death penalty* if the obelisk was dropped and broken!

"Finally a man by the name of Domenico Fontana accepted the responsibility. With 45 winches, 160 horses, and a crew of 800 workmen, the task of moving began. The date was September 10, 1586. Multitudes crowded the extensive square. While the obelisk was being moved, the crowd, upon penalty of death, was required to remain silent. But after the obelisk was successfully erected, there was the sound of hundreds of bells ringing, the roar of cannons, and the loud cheers of the multitude."[135] [Emphasis in the original]

When the children of Israel would forsake God, they turned to worshipping idols. One of the idols they worshipped was the obelisk. God had specifically forbidden them to do so. Leviticus 26:1 warns: "Ye shall make you no idols nor graven image, neither rear you up a **standing image**, neither shall ye set up any image of stone in your land, to bow down unto it: for I am the Lord your God." They were also told that when they went into pagan nations, they "shall overthrow their altars, and **break their pillars,** and burn their groves with fire; and ye shall hew down the graven images of their gods, and destroy the names of them out of that place. Ye shall not do so unto the Lord your God" (Deuteronomy 12:3-4). Many other such warnings are also in the Bible. The following references use the same Hebrew word for "pillar" but it is translated as "images." See: Exodus 23:24, 34:13; Deuteronomy 7:5, 16:22; I Kings 14:23; II Kings 10:26, 27, 17:10, 18:4, 23:14; II Chronicles 14:3, 31:1; Jeremiah 43:13; Hosea 10:1-2; and Micah 5:13.

How can anyone who truly loves the Lord belong to Masonry, the Eastern Star, or any other Masonically-affiliated organization when they so blatantly promote paganism? The Bible clearly states: "Come out from among them, and be ye separate, saith the Lord, and touch not the unclean thing; and I will receive you" (II Corinthians 6:17).

Leviticus 18:3, 30 warns:

"After the doings of the land of Egypt, wherein ye dwelt, shall ye not do: and after the doings of the land of Canaan, whither I bring you, shall ye not do: neither shall ye walk in their ordinances....Therefore shall ye keep mine ordinance, that ye commit not any one of these abominable customs, which were committed before you, and that ye defile not yourselves therein: I am the Lord your God."

One other phallic symbol, although not a Masonic symbol, is the maypole. A New Age magazine, *Utne Reader* gives a little explanation about the maypole and May Day.

"In preindustrial Europe, the first of May was widely celebrated as the beginning of warm weather and natural fruition. The Romans held games in honor of the goddess of flowers around this date, and the Druids lit new fires in honor of the god Bel. In the Middle Ages, most European communities celebrated May by decorating their homes with new flowers (the custom of carrying in baskets of flowers was known as 'bringing in the May'), choosing a Queen of the May, and erecting and dancing around a maypole. **It was the maypole, with its phallic and pagan connotations,** that brought May Day into disrepute among the 17th-century Puritans. In both Old and New England the custom of dancing the maypole was outlawed by the religious authorities."[136]

Another author notes:

"The May pole was formerly a huge phallus decked with flowers and brightly colored ribbons and set upright in an open area, around which the young people joyously danced at the return of the mating season. This typified the rejoicing of the return of spring, with its fructifying powers, after the earth had awakened from its long winter's sleep."[137]

Witch Laurie Cabot tells us that May Day is a witchcraft holiday called Beltane in which:

"fires are lit and the great fertility ritual of the God and Goddess is celebrated with Maypoles, music, and considerable frolicking in the greening countryside. May is a lusty month. The fifth month in the year expresses all the sexual and sensual meanings in the number five....Nature celebrates the great fecundity of the earth in rituals of sex, birth, and new life....

"The sexual forces of springtime abound everywhere, and as the folk songs say, 'We go a-Maying.' Symbolically we celebrate the forces of the season by erecting Maypoles, around which young men and women dance, entwining multicolored ribbons, weaving themselves together as they wrap the pole in festive colors."[138]

Feminist Naomi Goldenberg adds:

"The God's mother is the Goddess herself. As the year waxes into spring, her son becomes her lover [incest] and their union makes the whole world bloom with sexual energy. The first of May, **May Day,** is the time for this celebration— probably the **most joyous holiday of the witch's year.** The famous **Maypole** represents the God's erect phallus and is used as the rallying point for dancing and playing games."[139]

Many other authors (such as Masons and witches) reveal that the Maypole is a phallic symbol. With information like this, it was disappointing to see the May 1995 issue of *Clubhouse Jr.* This is a magazine for children distributed by Dr. James Dobson's Focus on the Family. On the back cover they mentioned May Day and the maypole and showed a maypole with adults and children dancing around the pole. The children were supposed to find hidden flowers in this drawing.[140]

Those who profess to be Christians should not be promoting such a festivity which is actually held in honor of the god Belenos.[141]

Not only is May 1st a prominent **WITCHCRAFT** and **SATANIST** holiday, it is also celebrated as a Communist holiday. Additionally, **it is the day that the Illuminati was founded and the day that appears on the back of our dollar bills** (which was orchestrated by Masonry).

James Walker, 32° Mason, mentions the **Masonic symbolism in the dollar bill.** Here is what he says:

"13 leaves in the olive branches

13 bars and stripes in the shield

13 feathers in the tail

13 arrows

13 letters in the 'E Pluribus Unum' on the ribbon

13 stars in the green crest above

32 long feathers representing the 32° in Masonry

13 granite stones in the Pyramid with the Masonic 'All-seeing Eye' completing it.

13 letters in Annuit Coeptis, 'God has prospered.'

"On the front of the dollar bill is the seal of the United States made up of a key, square, and the Scales of Justice, as well as a compass which, of course, is an important symbol in Masonry."[142]

A former Mason and witch, Bill Schnoebelen, gives a little more detail about the Masonic symbolism in a dollar bill.

"On the front of the Seal is an eagle. Amazingly, the eagle *happens* to have 32 feathers in its right wing—32 being the number of ordinary degrees of the Scottish rite. The left wing of the bird has 33 feathers, which corresponds to the 33°. The tail-feathers number 9, the number of degrees in the York rite. The eagle itself is a prominent icon of Masonry, being used extensively in the Scottish rite.

"To magicians, the eagle is often a stand-in for the Phoenix....

"In a bit of historical irony, the Scottish rite had its beginning in France, and the York rite had its greatest success in America. Thus, this eagle can be thought of as a symbol of Franco-American unity. This theme is carried further when one realizes that the total number of feathers in the two wings is 65. This is the Cabalistic number of the Hebrew, *'Yam Echad,'* meaning 'to dwell in unity.'...

"Over the eagle's head is a cloud with 13 pentagrams in the shape of a hexagram—or greater Seal of Solomon. To the sorcerer, the hexagram is a powerful tool to invoke Satan, and is a sign of anti-christ. (6 points, 6 angles, 6 planes—**666**) The **5** pointed pentagrams multiplied by the **13** stars equals 65, the same cabalistic number above! This makes one wonder with *whom or what,* we are to dwell in unity?

"Though there is an obvious rationale for the 13 stars (13 colonies) there is also a more subtle reason—13 is a key number of Satan."[143] [Emphasis in the original]

One Masonic symbol that **appears** to be Christian is the cross and the crown emblem. However, this **is not** the case. Masonic author, Ray Denslow, reveals:

KNIGHTS TEMPLAR

"The Cross and Crown may be said to be confined almost exclusively to the historical degrees in Masonry as exemplified in the various orders of knighthood of York and Scottish rites. In Gaul we find the *cross to have been a solar symbol* when it had equal arms and angles; to the Phoenicians it was *an instrument of sacrifice* to their God, Baal; and to the Egyptians, the *crux ansata was his symbol of eternal life.*"[144] [Emphasis in the original]

In *The Masonic Report* we find more about this emblem:

"Question: What does Masonry's emblem of the 'Cross and Crown' actually symbolize?

"Answer: The 'Cross' of Freemasonry is a philosophical cross, according to Albert Pike, 'Morals and Dogma,' p. 771. It is philosophical in the sense that it represents the generating fecundating principle by the perpendicular shaft, and the matrix or womb of nature, the female producing principle, by the horizontal shaft. The philosophy of the Masonic cross is totally phallic.

"The 'Crown' of this Masonic emblems is also phallic, it being the first emanation of the Cabalistic Sephiroth...."[145]

A former Mason also explains:

"The other York Rite jewelry you may see is the Templar symbol....It is a large Maltese cross with a circle in the center. Inside the circle is a red Latin cross within a crown. Around the arms of the cross is the Commandery motto, 'In Hoc Signo Vinces.' (In this sign, conquer!)

"Although this may seem harmless enough, the motto is originally attributed to the emperor Constantine, who used it in conjunction with a supposedly heavenly vision to begin the subversion and politicization of Biblical Christianity into the false, apostate Alexandrian cult....

"A similar shell game is played with the word 'sign.'...The sign Constantine referred to was NOT a Christian cross, but a kind of 'X' which had both Christian and pagan associations. In modern magic, it is the sign of the slain and risen Egyptian god, Osiris (another version of the 'slain and risen' Hiram Abif).

"Again Masonry has downgraded Jesus and replaced Him with its own 'christ.'"[146] [Emphasis in the original]

Two other groups (both with Masonic connections) use the cross and crown. Charles Taze Russell was a Mason who started the Jehovah Witnesses.[147] He used the red cross and other distinctive features of the Knights Templar logo.[148]

He also used the Masonic symbol of the winged sun-disk with snakes and he is "buried in a pyramid with masonic symbols on its capstone."[149]

The other group that uses the cross and crown emblem is Christian Science. This group was founded by Mary Baker Eddy in Massachusetts but Mason Henry Steele Olcott, who was co-founder of the Theosophical Society with Helena Petrovna Blavatsky,[150] was an associate of Mary Baker Eddy.[151] Some Eddy Brothers held seances and it was at these seances that Blavatsky met Col. Henry Steele Olcott.[152] Mary Baker Eddy herself had married a Mason and this was the only secret society which she allowed other Christian Science members to join.[153] She even had some of her material published in the *Freemason's Monthly Magazine.*[154] Several people connected with Christian Science such as directors and board members and a number of the editors of *The Christian Science Monitor* were Masons.[155] Even the presidents of the Mother Church in 1922-23 and 1923-24 were Masons.[156]

Below are some more Masonic symbols as well as some logos for different Masonic organizations.

TYRE

SHRINE

SHRINE

DEMOLAY

SOJOURN

Most of the symbols covered in this chapter (plus some others as well) are covered in greater detail in my book *Hidden Secrets of the Eastern Star.* You can obtain a copy of this 512 page book (with Index) for $17.50 by writing to Sharing, 212-Y East Seventh Street, Mt. Carmel, PA 17851-2211.

20. THE ALL-SEEING EYE

One of the most prominent symbols in Masonry is the all-seeing eye. A single eye appears almost everywhere you look today.

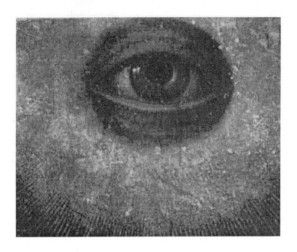

Ralph Anderson, a 32° Mason, gave a speech in 1985. He said:

"A brief word about the future. The Tibetan [a demonic spirit guide] tells us: 'The **three main channels through which the preparation for the New Age is** going on might be regarded as **the church, the Masonic fraternity and the educational field.** All of them are as yet failing to meet the need and to respond to the inner pressure. But in all of these three movements, disciples of the Great Ones are to be found and they are steadily gathering momentum and will before long enter upon their designated task.'

"He tells us further, 'The **Masonic Movement** when it can be divorced from politics and social ends and from its present paralysing condition of inertia, will meet the need of those who can, and should, wield power. It is the custodian of the law; it is the home of the Mysteries and the seat of initiation. It holds in its symbolism the ritual of Deity, and the way of salvation is pictorially preserved in its work. The methods of Deity are demonstrated in its Temples, and **under the All-seeing Eye the work can go forward.** It is **a far more occult organisation than can now be realised,** and is intended to be the training school for the coming advanced **occultists.** In its ceremonials lies hid the wielding of the forces connected with the growth and life of the kingdoms of nature and the unfoldment of the divine aspects in man. In the comprehension of its symbolism will come the power to cooperate with the divine plan. It meets the needs of those who work on the first Ray of Will or Power.'"[1]

The eye used in Masonry is a representation of **OSIRIS.**[2] Pike clearly reveals that **the all-seeing eye is "the emblem of Osiris, the Creator."**[3] He also maintains that Osiris' "power was symbolized by an Eye over a Sceptre. The Sun was termed by the Greeks the Eye of Jupiter, and the Eye of the World; and **HIS [OSIRIS']** is the All-Seeing Eye in our Lodges."[4] Masonic author, Carl Claudy, writes: "This is one of the oldest and most widespread symbols denoting God. We find it in Egypt, in India....The **Open Eye of Egypt represented Osiris. In India Siva** is represented by an eye."[5]

Albert Mackey, 33° Mason, agrees. He states:

"A symbol of the omniscient and watchful providence of God. It is a very ancient symbol, and is supposed by some to be a **relic of the primitive sun-worship.** Volney says (*Les Ruines,* p. 186) that in most of the ancient languages of Asia, the *eye* and the *sun* are expressed by the same word.

Among the Egyptians the eye was the symbol of their supreme god, Osiris, or the sun."[6] [Emphasis in the original]

"To the ancient Egyptians, the right eye symbolized the sun and the left eye the moon."[7]

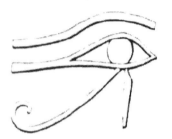 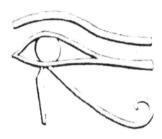

"Legend recounts how an Eye of Ra which had fled from Egypt was brought back from Nubia by Anhur, and how this divine Eye became enraged upon seeing that another Eye had taken its place. Ra then set it on his forehead where it became the Uraeus which protected the god against his enemies."[8]

"The Eye, or *uraeus,* was to become the effective rule of the world, and as such was to be worn by the pharaohs as a symbol of their majesty and their descent from the sun god."[9] [Emphasis in the original]

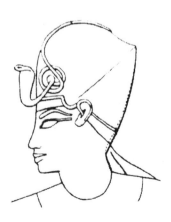

Since the all-seeing eye represents Osiris, let's look at who Osiris is. He committed incest with his sister, Isis, which resulted in the birth of Horus.[10] Pike says: "Osiris was the image of generative power."[11] He is also the Egyptian **god of the dead** as well as a **SUN GOD.** Remember that the Bible reminds us that the Christians' "God is not the God of the dead, but of the living" (Matthew 22:31-32, Mark 12:26-27, and Luke 20:37-38).

Osiris is known by many other names in other countries. In Thrace and Greece he is known as Dionysus, the god of pleasures and of partying and wine. A contrast between this pagan god and the true Christ once again becomes obvious when we look at the Bible. When Jesus was on earth He was called a "man of sorrows," not a "god of pleasures." Isaiah 53:3 prophesied of Jesus that "He is despised and rejected of men; a man of sorrows, and acquainted with grief: and we hid as it were our faces from Him; He was despised, and we esteemed Him not."

Festivals held in Dionysus' honor often resulted in **HUMAN SACRIFICES AND ORGIASTIC** (sexual) rites. In Rome Osiris is called Liber or Bacchus. The Lydians named him Bassareus and in Persia he is identified as Mithras, where **ASTROLOGY** is practiced by his followers. He is Zagreus to the Cretans and "became an **underworld divinity** who welcomed the souls of the dead to Hades [hell] and helped with their purification."[12] The Phrygians know Osiris as Sabazius where he is honored as a solar deity (a sun god) who was represented by **horns** and his emblem was a **SERPENT.**[13] In other places he went by yet other names such as Deouis, The Boy Jupiter, The Centaur, Orion, Saturn, The Boy Plutus, Iswara, The Winged One, **NIMROD,** Adoni, Hermes, Prometheus, Poseidon, Butes, Dardanus, Himeros, Imbors, Iasius, Zeus, Iacchus, Hu, Thor, Bel, Serapis, Ormuzd, Apollo, Thammuz, Atus, Hercules, **SHIVA, MOLOCH,** and, believe it or not, **BAAL!**

The Bible condemned Baal worship. In Jeremiah 32:35 we find that the Israelites "built the high places of Baal, which are in the valley of the son of Hinnom, to cause their sons and their daughters to pass through the fire unto Molech; which **I commanded them not, neither came it into My mind,** that they should do this abomination, to cause Judah to sin." Jeremiah 19:5 mentions that the Israelites burnt their children with fire as burnt offerings for Baal. So, now we have a little better idea of who Osiris is and what the all-seeing eye represents.

The symbolic sign for Osiris and the sun is the point within the circle.[14] This symbol was covered in the chapter "The Circle," but as a brief reminder, the point within the circle is a phallic symbol.[15] This symbol also stands for the sun and for air.

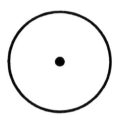

Mason and occultist Albert Pike contends:

"These two Divinities [Isis and Osiris], the Active and Passive Principles of the Universe, were commonly **symbolized by the generative parts of man and woman**....The Indian lingam was the union of both, as were the boat and mast and the **point within a circle:** all of which expressed the same philosophical idea as to the Union of the two great Causes of Nature, which concur, one actively and the other passively, in the generation of all beings...."[16]

In *Signs and Symbols of Primordial Man* we find that the point within a circle "**is an equivalent for the Eye,** and the two are co-types. Therefore it may be inferred that, as the fixed star at the centre, it was the Primordial All-Seeing Eye in the Astral Mythology."[17] The all-seeing eye, then, has the same phallic meaning as the point within the circle. In spite of this, *The Short Talk Bulletin,* a Masonic pamphlet, has an article entitled "The All-Seeing Eye." It states: "The All-seeing Eye is to Freemasons the **cherished symbol....**Therefore the thinking **Freemason has reverence for this symbol.**"[18]

Robert Hieronimus, an occultist, wrote: "The single eye, alone or in a triangle, was used extensively by Freemasons and other secret societies."[19]

Alice Bailey, whose husband, Foster Bailey, was a 32° Mason, also talked about the eye. She said:

> "I would first have you note the emphasis upon the *'eye'* in this formula. It is a keynote and appears in various guises. Behind all the ideas lies the concept of seeing, of a Seeing One, looking on at the created Whole. This same concept is to be found in the fundamental Masonic symbol of the Eye of God which dominates everything within the Temple."[20] [Emphasis in the original.]

Bailey then goes on to mention that the "Eye of God" is Shiva (or Siva), the Destroyer.[21] Remember, Shiva is the Indian god who is equivalent to Osiris.[22] Shiva is also a synonym for Satan.

Shiva

Charles Vail, a Mason, writes:

> "This is the symbol of the higher **clairvoyance.** The Master always possessed this sight. **In India this All Seeing Eye was called the Eye of Siva.** The **Egyptians represented Osiris by the symbol of an open eye,** and placed this hieroglyphic of him in all their temples. In the Lodge the All Seeing Eye represents the Omniscence (sic) of God,—The Eye that never sleeps. It may also represent, as in the Ancient Mysteries, the higher vision."[23]

Masonic author, J. D. Buck, agrees:

> "The EYE of SIVA is, in fact, an All-Seeing Eye; for it practically annuls Space and Time as concepts on the physical plane....A real Master, then, has the Eye of SIVA; the pineal gland, dormant in others, is active in him; and the vibrations of his brain correspond to the synthesis of sound and light."[24] [Emphasis in the original]

Hieronimus remarks: "The single eye also has been identified with the **third or spiritual eye** and therefore with **clairvoyance.** The **esoteric** tradition relates the single eye to the inner light, intuitive power, illumination, and the philosopher's stone...."[25]

Many authors recognize that clairvoyance is gained through use of the third eye. For instance, a book entitled *The Third Eye* describes how T. Lobsang Rampa "entered Chakpori Lamasery, the Temple of Tibetan Medicine where he learned **clairvoyance, levitation and astral projection** by learning to **open the third eye.**"[26]

In *Yoga Made Easy* we find that the sixth chakra "is said to be the seat of the mystical 'third eye' which accounts for the **clairvoyance** claimed by some Yogis."[27] In fact, yoga and visualization are two methods used to open the third eye.

"For centuries, the secrets of **Kundalini yoga** have been guarded by the yogis of India. Known to the ancients as 'the **sixth sense**,' this extraordinary life-force which makes it possible to open 'the **third eye**' is located at the base of the spine, and can provide an inexhaustible reserve of energy and knowledge!"[28]

Alice Bailey, an occultist, declared: "Through the practice of the power of visualization the third eye is developed."[29] Bailey also wrote:

"No man is a magician or worker in white magic until the third eye is opened, or in process of opening, for it is by means of that eye that the thought form is energised, directed and controlled, and the lesser builders are swept into any particular line of activity....

"The *'Eye of Shiva'* in the human being has its position...in the centre of the forehead, between the two physical eyes."[30] [Emphasis in the original]

Mother Goddess with third eye

Laurie Cabot, a witch, remarks:

"Furthermore, the term 'Third Eye' is not just a fanciful metaphor conjured up by Witches and psychics to sound mysterious. Anatomists believe that the gland is indeed a remnant of a third eye that never developed in the course of **evolution.** From the oldest times, sages, **magicians, and Witches have spoken of the Third Eye as the doorway to all knowledge.** Ancient peoples have intuitively understood the importance of this power spot and honored it in various ways. In the Orient it is one of the seven chakras. Egyptian monarchs wore a cobra-headed ornament at the center of the forehead. In India a red dot is placed over the Third Eye. Celtic priestesses painted the area blue. Cultures that use ritual face makeup often single out this area in front of the pineal gland for special attention."[31]

"Pay particular attention to how you adorn your forehead where the Third Eye is located. East Indians wear a red dot over this chakra point, ancient Druids wore crowns with a band of jewels in the center of the forehead; the African Berbers use black makeup to tattoo their faces with stars, moons, and other magical symbols. A quartz crystal worn across the Third Eye can be particularly powerful."[32]

A Masonic book states:

"These considerations lead us to an interesting topic, the Eye of Mind or the Eye of Horus, a subject elaborated in the Chapter on 'Horus' and conveying the idea of the 'All seeing Eye.' The end set before the Egyptian neophyte was **illumination,** that is to be **'brought to light.'** The Religion of Egypt was the Religion of Light."[33]

A former witch and Mason comments:

"To 'open' the eye a little bit is to experience psychic powers. To open the eye completely is to have your brain flooded with the 'pure' consciousness of Lucifer himself. This is why one of the Masonic symbols is the 'All-Seeing Eye.' It is a symbol of Illumination.

"This is Satan's counterfeit for being Born Again. In it, you acquire a 'personal relationship' with Lucifer. You begin to think his thoughts and see with his eyes. You begin to look at humans the way he does. It is not a pretty experience!"[34]

There is some very revealing information found in *The Power of Karma* (written in 1937 by Alexander Cannon). The author says that "much of that which is prophesied in the book of Revelation is to come to fruition."[35] He goes on to mention that those who have the mark of wisdom have nothing to fear.[36] He then notes that "this mark of wisdom needs explanation."[37] He indicates that those who have had superior past lives (meaning reincarnation) have been singled out for leadership. It results in seership, in **clairvoyant** gifts, in a type of intellect that perceives the hearts of men, their innermost ambitions, without the necessity for physical speech."[38] He finally explains:

> "YOU HAVE A LITERAL SIGN UPON YOUR FOREHEADS, PLACED BETWEEN YOUR EYEBROWS! DOUBT IT NOT! WE SPEAK WHEREOF WE KNOW!

> "NOW, THAT SIGN UPON THE FOREHEAD IS EVER THE MARK OF THE SOUL IN CHRIST. It is ever the mark of those aligned with the great truth of Light. It is the Mark of those who have incarnated to render unto God the things that are God's, and found a **new order** in the current generation....

> "The time has come to tell you that as you minister, so shall you be saved! As you join the ranks of those who presently walk with the **Sign on their foreheads,** so are your wants supplied by those who recompense you for the services performed to them and their children."[39] [Caps in the original; Boldface added]

If you read Revelation 13 you will find some astonishing information. The mark that is put upon the foreheads is not the "mark of the soul in Christ," but is rather the mark of the beast or the antichrist. Once again we can see how the occultists and New Agers twist the Scriptures and make the good evil and the evil good. The Bible warns: "Woe unto them that call evil good, and good evil; that put darkness for light, and light for darkness; that put bitter for sweet, and sweet for bitter! Woe unto them that are wise in their own eyes, and prudent in their own sight!" (Isaiah 5:20-21).

Also notice that Cannon said that those who have this mark will have their wants supplied. Again turning to Revelation 13 we find that only those who have the mark can buy or sell:

> "And he causeth all, both small and great, rich and poor, free and bond, to receive a mark in their right hand, or

in their foreheads: And that no man might buy or sell, save he that had the mark, or the name of the beast, or the number of his name" (Revelation 13:16-17).

We need to point out, however, that those who take this mark will end up in hell. Receiving the mark of the all-seeing eye or the third eye is not something glorious like the New Agers would have you think. Revelation 14:9-11 points out:

> "And the third angel followed them, saying with a loud voice, If any man worship the beast and his image, and **receive his mark in his forehead, or in his hand,** The same shall drink of the wine of the wrath of God, which is poured out without mixture into the cup of his indignation; and **he shall be tormented with fire and brimstone** in the presence of the holy angels, and in the presence of the Lamb: And the **smoke of their torment ascendeth up for ever and ever: and they have no rest day nor night, who worship the beast and his image, and whosoever receiveth the mark of his name."**

The all-seeing eye is also related to the Blazing Star. Pike tells us:

> "...the **Blazing Star has been regarded as** an emblem of Omniscience, or **the All-seeing Eye,** which to the Egyptian Initiates was the emblem of Osiris, the Creator. With the YOD in the centre, it has the kabalistic meaning of the Divine Energy, manifested as Light, creating the Universe."[40] [Caps in the original; Boldface added]

> "The **Blazing Star in our Lodges,** we have already said, **represents Sirius, Anubis, or Mercury,** Guardian and Guide of Souls. Our Ancient English brethren also considered it an emblem of the Sun....accordingly the Blazing Star has been regarded as an emblem of Omniscience, or the All-Seeing Eye, which to the Ancients was the Sun."[41]

We've already covered some of these pagan gods (like Anubis and Mercury) earlier in this book. Riane Eisler, a feminist, mentions that the eye is one of the symbols of the goddess.[42] One goddess that was represented by an all-seeing eye was Maat.

> "The Egyptian priesthood taught first that Maat, the Goddess of truth and judgment, possessed a **third eye.** Later the central text of the Egyptian Mystery Religion was revised and a male god, Horus, son of the Goddess, was given the **all-seeing eye.**"[43]

Laurie Cabot agrees that the "Egyptian Goddess Maat originally possessed the All-Seeing Eye, which later was transferred to Horus."[44] She adds:

> "Outlining the eye emulates the Goddess, who is often portrayed with large, distinctive eyes, capable of seeing through space and time as well as into our innermost hearts. Ishtarte, the Goddess of Light, was known in the ancient Middle East as the Eye Goddess because the light she brings from heaven to earth illuminates the world."[45]

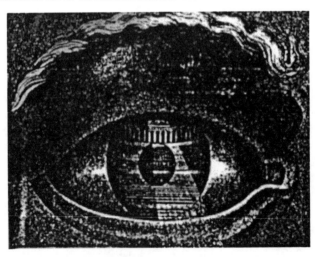

She continues: "The Goddess's ability to see and know all things became a terrifying concept in patriarchal times, and her mystical eye was turned into the **'evil eye.'**..."[46] The "evil eye" is defined in *The Complete Book of Witchcraft and Demonology* as the "power of the glance to harm others."[47] In *Witches* we are told: "No one would want a witch as an enemy. Some witches used 'the evil eye' on their victims. One glance from a bad witch could mean real trouble."[48]

People became afraid of the evil eye and therefore they sought ways to "protect" themselves from it. Different charms and amulets were used.[49] For instance, in *Amulets and Superstitions,* we find:

> "The amulet used against the Evil Eye...was called BASKANION or PROBASKANION, and FASCINUM, and it was usually in the form of the PHALLUS. As children were specially liable to be attacked by the Evil Eye, models of the phallus were hung around their necks....Other names of the phallus amulet were *mutonium, scaevola,* and *Satyrica signa....* "[50] [Emphasis in the original]

Another object used as protection was the "horned hand" or the "devil salute." Budge writes that "a closed hand with the first and fourth fingers outstretched represents the 'horns of the Devil.'

Nevertheless models of such a hand were worn as amulets. A closed hand with the first finger alone outstretched was in some countries regarded as a sure protection against the Evil Eye."[51]

Cabot remarks:

> "Many customs and terms continue to reflect the importance that horns once held in local folklore. The word *scorn* comes from the Italian word that means 'without horns,' for to be without horns was a sign of disgrace, shame, or contempt. Holding up the index and little fingers in the form of horns was a gesture to ward off the **evil eye**....And since it was the male animal that had horns, the horn easily became a phallic symbol."[52] [Italics in the original; Boldface added]

In fact, Shiva (a synonym for Satan) can sometimes be seen making this gesture.

> "In India, where the **occult** sciences are still followed, figures of Shiva, the Destroyer...is not only placing his right hand over his solar plexus, but has folded his fingers so as to form the **sign of the horns,** thereby combining the sign which drives away the **evil eye** with that of Destruction, of which he himself is the embodiment....although he is the Lord of Death and Destruction, he is also Lord of Birth, through whose hands the dead man's soul passes once more into **reincarnation."**[53]

We must remember that the devil salute (which is covered in the chapter entitled "Hand Signals") "is a Sicilian **sign of the Devil** used to cast spells...."[54] This certainly is not any sign that a Christian would want to make. When one makes this gesture, one is actually calling on the devil to "protect" him from evil. Satan must laugh when someone "innocently" uses this signal to ward off the evil eye.

Hex signs are also used to fend off the evil eye.[55] To hex means to place a curse on someone or something to bring bad luck.[56] A witch remarks: "Many people say that the Hex signs were painted on barns to protect livestock from harmful spells, negative influences, and the Evil Eye, and to bring luck and prosperity."[57] She then gives extensive instructions on how to make your own **hex sign talisman.** She starts by saying: "On the night of a **Full Moon,** cast a **Magic Circle** in your customary manner and consecrate your Hex sign with tools of the Elements. Sprinkle salt on the Hex sign for Earth,"[58] etc.

Again, many people are attracted to the Pennsylvania Dutch hex signs not knowing the **occult** connection behind them. J. Gordon Melton asserts:

> "Among the Pennsylvania Dutch there is the survival of what seems to be genuine **'witchcraft-life'** practice, locally termed **powwowing.** One must call it witchcraft-life because, while it involves magick and the psychic, it is theologically a Christian derivative with Kabbalistic elements....The most obvious manifestations of the powwow power are the many colorful **hex signs** on the farmhouses in Eastern Pennsylvania. Each sign is a circle; within the circle are birds, hexagonal stars, etc.

> "Powwowers are, in essence, Christianized **witches** working in the agricultural society of the Pennsylvania Dutch. They have a **grimoire** (a book of **spells** and **magical** procedures)...and they are as feared for the ability to **hex** as they are liked and sought after for their ability to heal."[59]

Grimoire is a "name applied to any book on **black magic** which pretends to teach the practice of black magic, especially the art of the **evocation of evil spirits** and making an alliance with them."[60] Another resource states that the grimoire is "a book containing formulas for **calling up and controlling demonic beings.** A manual of ceremonial magic."[61]

Of course, there is no such thing as **"Christianized** witches" for the Bible clearly states that no one who practices witchcraft will go to heaven.

> "Now the works of the flesh are manifest, which are these; Adultery, fornication, uncleanness, lasciviousness, Idolatry, **witchcraft,** hatred, variance, emulations, wrath, strife, seditions, heresies, Envyings, murders, drunkenness, revellings, and such like: of the which I tell you before, as I have also told you in time past, that they which do such things **shall not inherit the kingdom of God"** (Galatians 5:19-21).

> "But the fearful, and unbelieving, and the abominable, and murderers, and whoremongers, and **sorcerers,** and idolaters, and all liars, shall have their part in the lake which burneth with fire and brimstone: which is the second death" (Revelation 21:8).

Many other amulets and talismans are used to supposedly protect an individual from the evil eye.[62]

Earlier we mentioned that the **Blazing Star** was connected to the all-seeing eye. Well, in a Masonic bulletin on the Blazing Star we are told that it is a **"hex sign."**[63] Interesting!

One author reports:

> "One of the oldest, and most important symbols of Masonry is the Egyptian hieroglyph of the eye—or the 'evil eye.' It represents their god Osiris. It dominates the top of most Masonic documents, and now dominates the back of the Great Seal of the United States...its presence on the Great Seal suggests that secret societies were instrumental in creating the new nation of America, and still have an important influence in the present day."[64]

Not only does the Great Seal of the United States sport an all-seeing eye but so does our dollar bill. We've already covered some of the Masonic symbolism in the dollar bill in the last chapter.

What does the United Nations Meditation Room, the Egyptian Pyramids, The Temple of Understanding, and the Prayer Room in the United States Capitol have in common with the Great Seal of the United States?[65] The all-seeing eye, of course!

Since this all-seeing eye represents the third eye of occultists and New Agers, as well as Masons, it's no wonder that we see an increase in the widespread use of single eye designs. One author wrote:

> "Perhaps not coincidental is the recent commercial for an 'Eos' (meaning 'dawn' in Greek) camera which zooms in close on only one of the sports figure's eyes. There are also recent television ads (e.g., by Glidden Paint) that focus on one eye (the left eye) for a long time."[66]

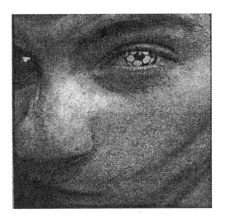

> "Concerning the New Age, one will increasingly see figures showing or emphasizing only one of their eyes on television ads, or on magazine covers, etc. In esoteric or occult terms, the right eye represents Osiris (the male) and the left eye represents Isis (the female). A single eye, indistinguishable as left or right, represents the All-Seeing Eye (Horus Hawk from Egypt). In the last few months, covering just over a year, Time magazine has had 10 covers with single eyes prominent. Secretary of Education Lamar Alexander on the 9/16/91, Ted Turner 1/6/92, Susan Faludi 3/9/92, Ross Perot 6/29/92, Kevin Buchberger with a caption 'come out of the darkness' 7/6/92, Bill Clinton 1/4/93, Zoe

Baird 2/1/93, Cyberpunk 2/8/93, Boris Yeltsin 3/29/93, and 'The Info Highway' 4/12/93. Also see Ross Perot on Newsweek's cover 4/27/92.

"It is noteworthy that Ted Turner (1990 Humanist of the Year) is on one of the covers with only one eye showing, because June 14, 1986 when addressing about 1000 'futurists' at John Denver's Windstar Institute, Turner said at Snowmass Village, Colorado, that 'America must elect a "new age" president if it wants to survive through the year 2000' (according to 'Broadcaster Ties Survival to "New Age" President,' The Denver Post, June 15, 1986)."[67] [Emphasis in the original]

Other magazine covers with single eyes (or an emphasis on one eye) are: *Science Digest* (March 1981), *Time* (April 26, 1993, May 17, 1993, and June 14, 1993), and *Discover.* There are also books such as *The Illuminatus! Trilogy, The Unschooled Mind,* and *Multiple Intelligences* that have a single eye on the cover.

It is interesting to note that Time Warner's logo is an all-seeing eye. It was Time Warner who made a seven year, $80 million deal with Madonna in 1992.[68] They also published her filthy, pornographic book.[69]

A report put out in 1995 said that in 1994 there were 14,313 sex incidents, 8,333 violence incidents and 23,556 profanity incidents on primetime TV. One of the top twelve sponsors for this trash was none other than Time Warner.[70] They also fund the Council on Foreign Relations, a one world order organization.[71] Time Warner gave $1 million (or more) to the New American Schools Development Corporation.[72] Additionally, they gave $100,000 or more to the Points of Light Foundation.[73]

"The Points of Light Foundation was begun with a $5 million grant from the U.S. Congress and the President. Its first chairman was J. Richard Munro, formerly the chairman of Time Warner, Inc....

"Not surprisingly, the logo for the Points of Light Foundation is also of an occultic nature. It depicts the golden sun disk with what at first glance appears to be a torch of light within. But wait, is it not the concealed image of two entities, a male and a female, facing each other? Occultic philosophers can easily recognize these two as the Sun God and his Goddess."[74]

Of course, the interest in the eye goes back many centuries. Dr. Dennis Cuddy writes:

"Both King Henry VII and his granddaughter, Queen Elizabeth I (Queen of England, 1558-1603), used the 'phoenix' as one of their badges. Queen Elizabeth I (to whom President Bush is related) was also fascinated by men's eyes....Favored servants of the queen signed their letters to her with symbolic eyes...and John Dee (who headed the British espionage network) signed himself '007.' Dee, an acquaintance of the queen's husband (the Earl of Leicester), was an alchemist, astrologer, psychic, and spy. According to *Mind Wars* (1984) by Ron McRae (former associate of columnist Jack Anderson), the basis for his '007' signature was: *'Each zero representing an eye and the seven being the sum of two eyes, four other senses, and last, mystical knowledge from "the nine" spirits (muses) who spoke through Dee's crystal ball, the "shew stone." Dee credited the nine and his shew stone with uncovering a Spanish plot to burn the forests that provided wood for English shipbuilding. Whatever the source, the plot was real. Had it succeeded, the Spanish Armada might have sailed unopposed in 1588.'*[75] [Emphasis in the original]

In *The Eye* Queen Elizabeth's garment is described in detail. We are told: "The sumptuous robe of Elizabeth I is embroidered with a remarkable **SERPENT** upon the sleeve, and a deft scattering of **EYES** and ears elsewhere, no doubt to signify that nothing escaped the attention of the Virgin Queen, our English Diana."[76]

In Masonry, the symbol of the all-seeing eye can be disguised by the use of other symbols. *Ancient Operative Masonry* reveals: **"Instead of the ever-watching eye,** you at times behold the **square and compass** and the **letter 'G'** floating in a spiritual light which words cannot describe. These visions are but glimpses of the human Ego which is veiled from the eyes of the profane."[77] We've covered these symbols elsewhere in this book, but when these symbols are seen, remember that a Satanic all-seeing eye stands behind them!

G

Below are a few more illustrations which use the all-seeing or single eye.

21. SYMBOLS IN BRIEF

Many people think that the Ouija Board is just a "game" to be played. However, this is not the case. It is used by spirit mediums and others to contact the spirit world. Using this board can bring people in contact with demons. The planchette is controlled by demonic entities to spell out messages from the spirit world. The idea of the ouija board is not new. Some boards were in use six centuries before Christ.[1]

A werewolf is a man who can change himself temporarily into a wolf.[2]

The mermaid is a mythological creature that is half-female and half fish. You encounter mermaids in fairy tales and elsewhere. The movie *Splash* popularized the mermaid.[3]

"The pa kua is made up of eight combinations of solid and broken lines, the solid line representing symbolically the yang or male principle, and the broken line the yin or female principle. To each pair a third is added, representing the result of union, that is, offspring. The eight figures are arranged about a t'ai chi, or aboriginal One, forming the first of the 24 circles on the divining board...."[4] [Emphasis in the original]

"PENTACLE OF THE GODDESS. With its five points—spirit, air, fire, water, and earth—the pentacle is the embodiment of power and perfection. Like the endless circle, it binds negative elements and denotes good luck,"[5] [Emphasis in the original] claims a catalog which sells this pentacle.

A. PENTACLE OF THE GODDESS. With its five points—spirit, air, fire, water, and earth—the pentacle is the embodiment of power and perfection. Like the endless circle, it binds negative elements and denotes good luck. Our intricate, double-sided pendant is crafted of polished pewter and hangs gracefully from a 30" black nylon cord.

A spiral is an ancient goddess emblem symbolizing the universal pattern of growth in Nature.

An occult catalog advertises one of their products like this:

"The Eleven-Pointed Star symbolizes the Divine Will expressing itself through humanity. This magically-correct design fuses elementary and planetary forces, enabling you to alchemically accomplish the Great Work."[6] [Emphasis in the original]

A similar-looking design is called the unicursal hexagram which is also called the Aquarian Star. It "is used to channel psychic energy. It's (sic) function is to connect earth-plane consciousness to the infinite universal mind."[7] It was designed by Satanist and 33° Mason, Aleister Crowley, and was the symbol of his Order of the Silver Star (Astrum Argentum or AA).

The "magic hand amulet" is supposed to protect the wearer's destiny and is considered to be "the ultimate goodluck (sic) **charm.**"[8]

The hand was important in occultism. For instance, the hand of glory was "a hand cut off from a criminal, who had been hanged on a gibbet. In the Middle Ages, such a hand, dried and steeped in various salts, was used in **spells.**"[9]

One occult catalog states:

"The hand is a universal symbol of healing, giving, blessing—and good luck because it wards off the 'evil eye.'...Wear the Palm Chakra Hand to stimulate higher consciousness; wear the Heart Hand to increase love flowing from and to you."[10]

"When the eyes are situated in the hand, for example, by association with the symbolism of the hand they come to denote **clairvoyant** action. An excessive number of eyes has an ambivalent significance which it is important to note."[11]

Below is another hand that was "connected with the old Rites of the *Mater Deorum.* "[12] [Emphasis in the original] The pine cone "was an important symbol in the Mysteries of Ceres, as also in those of Bacchus. It has descended thence to the Secret Orders of modern times."[13]

Earlier we discussed May Day and the Maypole. There are also peace poles. *Meditation* newsletter states:

"Peace Poles are obelisks inscribed with the message 'May Peace Prevail on Earth.' They have been dedicated the world over as an international symbol of peace. Their purpose is to spread the message of peace and act as a constant reminder of the necessity to wish and pray for peace at all times."[14]

Remember, obelisks are phallic symbols, but this is the object that's been chosen to help promote peace.

The Tree of Life is used in magic and the Cabala. It is:

"A design consisting of ten points (SEPHIRA) linked by twenty-two lines, taken as a model of the creative emanations from the Godhead. Used for elaborate metaphysical speculations, psychological exercises, and ceremonial magic."[15]

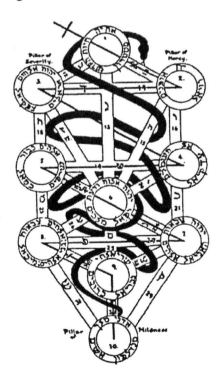

The Celtic Knot's "loops symbolize **Infinity, good luck,** and the harmony between peoples of the world."[16]

The hypno-disc is used for hypnosis. "Achieve the hypnotic state in shortest possible time,"[17] says the ad.

The symbol below is called a veve and is used in Voudoun (or Voodoo) rites to summon the loa (demonic spirits that possess voodoo worshippers). This particular veve is for Baron Samedi, the Lord of the Graveyards and Death.

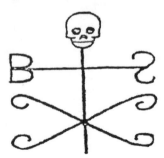

"The ecology symbol is seen almost everywhere since it has been foisted on the unsuspecting people of America just after the demonic revolution days of the 1960's which served as the springboard for the 'Age of Aquarius' or the last generation. The symbol is a circle with a diagonal line through it and means 'God Sleeps.'...The 'God Sleeps' concept is the primary doctrine of 'Deism,' a religion that was embraced by such famous men as Benjamin Franklin and Thomas Jefferson. Their doctrine states that, 'God, the Supreme Architect of the Universe created all things,' but then isolated Himself from the entire creation and lets it operate on its own.' This is the very essence of the teachings of Freemasonry. Most people never look beyond the surface of anything. That is why we have this blasphemous Masonic symbol on our roadways, in our parks, in public buildings and even in churches."[18]

The skull necklace shown below was advertised with these words:

"An interesting symbol, the skull...it is an emblem of the mortality of man, yet it is in truth that which survives of the living being once its body has been destroyed. It is prominent in **WITCHCRAFT and DEMON WORSHIP** as a celebration of death. Our skull has a movable jaw, on a triangle...and makes a fascinating, macabre ornament for those who dare to be different."[19]

Another necklace is the Baphomet necklace.

"Called the God of the Witches, he is said to possess the wisdom of God. This is a most popular symbol, sometimes called the Goat of Nedes or the Sabbatic Goat. It is a **sacred witchcraft** sysmbol (sic), and no witch, warlock, or unique amulet collector should be with[out] this...."[20]

The man in the moon necklace below is labeled as "Jewelry of the Occult!"[21]

The Islamic religion uses the crescent star and moon for their symbol. This emblem can be seen on many of the Islamic nations' flags.

The Islamic God is called Allah. He was the moon god, who married the sun goddess. "Together they produced three goddesses who were called 'the daughters of Allah.' These three goddesses were called Al-Lat, Al-Uzza, and Manat."[22] The *Encyclopedia of Religion* mentions that "'Allah' is a pre-Islamic name...corresponding to the Babylonian Bel."[23] The symbol for Allah appears below.

The Islamic holy book is called the Koran (or Quran). This symbol looks like this:

Om (or Aum) is often used as a mantra for meditation. It signifies the Hindu pagan trinity of Brahma, Vishnu and Shiva. The Om symbols below are also used for Brahman, the impersonal god of the Hindus.

The goddess Isis sometimes wears a crown with a solar disk and at other times she wears horns. The symbol below shows the disk and the horns combined.

God's Eye (or Ojo de Dios) is an emblem used for enchantment and the worship of pagan deities. "With the work of the forces of the spirit world, the worshipper of the dieties (sic) calls (chants) to the supernatural, and the demon spirits bring into being whatever the chanter is seeking."[24]

Another symbol associated with the eye is the Rx sign. In *Healing Without Medicine* we find:

> "In one aspect of modern medicine Egyptian magic continues to be practiced to the present day. When the 20th-century doctor writes out a prescription he prefaces it with the sign Rx. He may think this is an abbreviation of the Latin word *recipe,* but he will be wrong. It is a simplified form of the **Egyptian hieroglyph for the Eye of Horus**—a symbol familiar as a jewel among the treasures of Tutanka-mun.

> "This symbol derives its power from the myth of death and resurrection of the god Osiris. The myth says that after Osiris had been treacherously murdered, his son Horus set out to avenge his death. In the course of the long struggle one of his eyes was plucked out. This was eventually restored by Thoth, the god of wisdom, and came to be linked with the art of healing. Roman physicians introduced Egyptian symbols into their prescriptions to impress their patients, and the eye of Horus was one....Over the centuries the outline was modified until it became the simpler symbol we know today. **Unwittingly,** then, even the most orthodox of **today's doctors make use of a magic sign."**[25]

The "triple sceptre of the Nile" can be seen in several of the Egyptian gods' hands. The triple sceptre comprises the flail (or whip), the shepherd's crook, and the Anubis-headed staff. This triple sceptre represented the powers which an Initiate had mastered.

> "With the Whip he had subjugated his physical body; with the Shepherd's Crook he was the guardian and keeper of his emotional body; with the Anubis-headed Staff he was master of his mind and worthy to wield the powers of

government over others because, first of all, he obeyed the laws himself."[26]

Ptah   Osiris

Below are several more representations of gods and goddesses (some in picture form and some only identified by a symbol).

Two forms of Buddha   *Hotei*

Athene   Ceres   Aton   Hermes   Juno

Brahman

Kama

Anhert

Kukulcan

Quetzacoatl

Quetzacoatl

Isis

Ea

Vishnu

Athena

Venus/female

Pluto

Jupiter/
fortunetelling

Mercury

Sun goddess

Uranus

Uranus

Mars/male

Vesta

Below are a number of other symbols to watch out for.

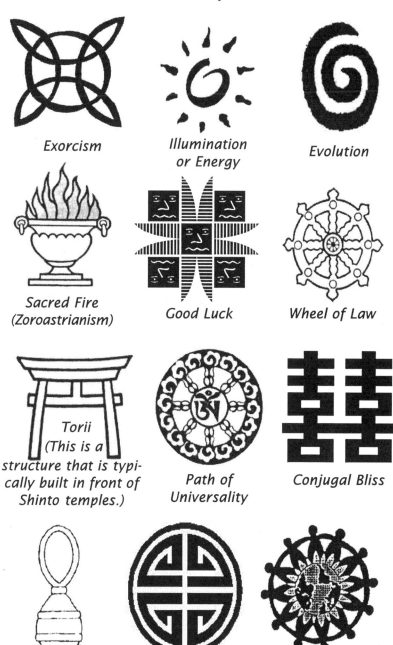

Exorcism

Illumination
or Energy

Evolution

Sacred Fire
(Zoroastrianism)

Good Luck

Wheel of Law

Torii
(This is a
structure that is typi-
cally built in front of
Shinto temples.)

Path of
Universality

Conjugal Bliss

Energy

Good Fortune

Community

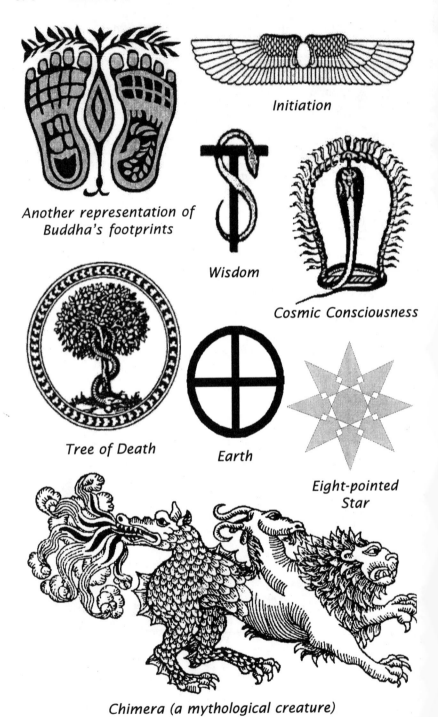

Another representation of Buddha's footprints

Initiation

Wisdom

Cosmic Consciousness

Tree of Death

Earth

Eight-pointed Star

Chimera (a mythological creature)

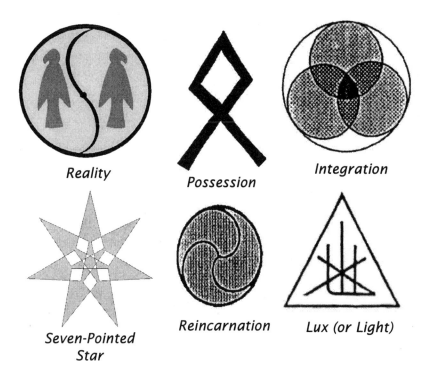

Reality

Possession

Integration

Seven-Pointed
Star

Reincarnation

Lux (or Light)

As stated at the beginning of this book, there are many other symbols that could have been added but those shown and explained here will give you a good idea about many symbols that have not been included. How many of these symbols have **YOU** been using unknowingly?

Christ has a bride, the church, which is supposed to be **holy.** Paul refers to this bride in Ephesians 5:25-27: "Christ also loved the church, and gave Himself for it; That He might sanctify and cleanse it with the washing of water by the word, That He might present it to Himself a glorious church, not having spot, or wrinkle, or any such thing; but that it should be holy and without blemish." The Antichrist, too, will have a bride, but instead of being pure and spotless, she will be a whore (Revelation 17:1, 15, 16).

Are you waiting for Christ or the Antichrist? Which person are you following? Are you professing to be a Christian while using the paraphernalia, amulets, talismans, jewelry, runes, etc., of Satan? Who are you depending on for your protection? Do you think you need Satan's devices to supposedly keep evil away from you and your family or are you resting securely in Christ? "The angel of the Lord encampeth round about them that fear him, and delivereth them" (Psalm 34:7). "I sought the Lord, and He heard me, and delivered me from all my fears" (Psalm 34:4). "Every word of God is pure: He is a shield unto them that put their trust in Him" (Proverbs 30:5).

If you claim you are following Christ, does your life match your profession? We are admonished by Peter: "But as He which hath called you is holy, so be ye holy in all manner of conversation" (I Peter 1:15). "The fruit of the Spirit is love, joy, peace, longsuffering, gentleness, goodness, faith, Meekness, temperance" (Galatians 5:22-23). On the other hand, the fruits of the flesh are:

> "Adultery, fornication, uncleanness, lasciviousness, Idolatry, witchcraft, hatred, variance, emulations, wrath, strife, seditions, heresies, Envyings, murders, drunkenness, revellings, and such like: of the which I tell you before, as I have also told you in time past, that they which do such things shall not inherit the kingdom of God" (Galatians 5:19b-21).

> "In this the children of God are manifest, and the children of the devil: **whosoever doeth not righteousness is not of God,** neither he that loveth not his brother" (1 John 3:10). "They that are Christ's have crucified the flesh with the affections and lusts" (Galatians 5:24). Does your life reflect the fruits of the Spirit?

Regardless of what man may say, the Bible is our final authority. No church can save you. Only Jesus Christ can do that. Even though you may be a moral and honest person, if you have never invited Christ into your heart as your own **PERSONAL** Savior, you, too, need to repent. Maybe you are not committing a blatant sin, but the Bible tells us that **"ALL** have sinned and come short of the glory of God" (Romans 3:23). The **"ALL"** includes both you and me, and "the wages of sin is [eternal] death; but the gift of God is eternal life through Jesus Christ our Lord" (Romans 6:23). God's gift to us is eternal life, but we must accept this gift to make the transaction valid. If I had a gift to give to you and you refused to accept it, that gift would do you no good. You must **RECEIVE** this gift for it to become effective.

Even though **ALL** of us are born in sin, the good news is that "Christ Jesus came into the world to save sinners" (I Timothy 1:15). If you have never accepted Christ as your **PERSONAL** Savior and would like to do so, the first step is to be born again. John 3:3 emphasizes: "**EXCEPT** a man be born **AGAIN, he CANNOT** see the kingdom of God." How can one be born **AGAIN?** We all know that we were born once, our physical birth, but can we enter into our mother's womb and be born the second time (see John 3:1-17)? No. The second birth comes by being born into the family of God. John 3:16: "For God so **LOVED** the world [that includes **YOU!**] that He **GAVE** His only Begotten Son, that **WHOSOEVER** [that includes **YOU**] **BELIEVETH** [trusts, clings to, relies on] Him [God's Son, Jesus] should not perish [in hell], but have everlasting life."

All you need to do is sincerely believe with all your heart that Jesus is the Son of God and to be willing to turn from your sins, whatever they are—big or small. Ask Jesus to come into your heart and help you to live for Him, and He **WILL** do it. "He that covereth his sins shall not prosper: but whoso **CONFESSETH AND FORSAKETH** them shall have mercy" (Proverbs 28:13). John 6:37 promises: "Him that cometh to Me I will **IN NO WISE** cast out." Romans 10:9 states: "If thou shalt **CONFESS** with thy mouth the Lord Jesus, and shalt **BELIEVE** in thine heart that God hath raised Him from the dead, thou **SHALT** be saved [born again]."

If you would like to be born again, pray your own prayer or sincerely pray the following: *Dear Jesus, I realize that I am a sinner. I believe that You died for my sins. Please forgive me of my past sins and come into my heart. Save me for Your sake, and help me to live for You. I ask this in Your name. Amen.*

If you sincerely prayed and asked Jesus to forgive you of your sins, you will have the assurance that you are now a child of God. John 1:12 reveals: "But **AS MANY AS RECEIVED HIM,** to them gave He power to become the sons of God, even to them that **BELIEVE** on His name." Read your Bible **EVERY** day (start with the book of John), and find a Bible-believing church where you can worship God with other born again believers.

"Therefore being justified by faith, we have peace with God through our Lord Jesus Christ" (Romans 5:1), "and the peace of God, which passeth all understanding, shall keep your hearts and minds through Christ Jesus" (Philippians 4:7). "If the Son [Jesus Christ] therefore shall make you free, ye shall be free indeed" (John 8:36).

APPENDIX

Below are other names (and spellings) for some of the symbols covered in this book.

All-Seeing Eye
All Seeing Eye of Deity
All Seeing Eye of God
Divine Eye
Egyptian Eye
Eye of Divine Providence
Eye of Divinity
Eye of Fire
Eye of God
Eye of Higher Perception
Eye of Horus
Eye of Jupiter
Eye of Mind
Eye of Providence
Eye of Ra
Eye of Reason
Eye of Siva
Eye of the Hawk
Eye of the World
Eye of Thundera
Eye of Vision
Eye of Zarnoth
Eye That Knows
Great Eye

Illuminated Eye
Lunar Eye
Mystical Eye
Open Eye of Egypt
Oudja Eye
Sacred Eye
Single Eye
Spiritual Eye
Strong Eye
Third Eye
Third Eye of Clairvoyance
Travelling Eye
Udjat
Uraeus

Ankh
Ansated Cross
Cross of Life

Crux Ansata
Crux Hermis
Crux Tau
Handled Cross
Hydrometer
Key of Life
Key of the Nile
Long Life Seal
Looped Tau Cross
Satanic Cross
Universal Cross

Judas Goat
Sabbatic Goat
Scapegoat
Star of Mendes

Caduceus
Caduceus of Mercury
Esculapius Rod
Opiate Rod
Rod of Life
Staff of Life
Staff of Shiva
Wand of Hermes

Aquarian Star
Unicursal Hexagram
Unicursive Hexagram

Cornucopia
Horn of Plenty

Baphomet
Black Goat
Goat of a Thousand Young
Goat of Nedes
Goat's Head Star
God of the Witches

Crusader's Cross
Jerusalem Cross

Devil's Triad
Cornuto
Devil Horn Salute
Devil Salute
Horned Devil
Horned Hand
Il Cornuto
Mano Cornuta
Nish Kati
The Horn
Twin-horned Salute

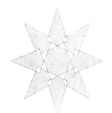

Eight-pointed Star
Star of Baptism
Star of Regeneration

Evil Eye
Dark Eye
Hypnotic Eye
Jettatura
Nazar
Overlooking

Double-headed Axe
Double-bladed Axe
Twin-bladed Axe
Labrys

Eagle
Lightning Bird
Thunderbird

Fig gesture
Fica Gesture
Mano Figo

Five-pointed Star
Blazing Star
Bright Morning Star
Dog Star
Druid's Foot
Druttenfuss
Fuga Daemonorum
Goblin's Cross
Horned Star
L'Etoile Flamboyante
Morning Star
Nile Star
Pantacle
Pentacle
Pentagram
Pentalpha
Pentangle
Pentagon
Signum Solomonis
Sirius
Solar Federational Star
Solomon's Seal
Star in the East
Star of Hathor
Star of Horus
Star of Isis
Star of Isis-Sothis
Star of Knowledge
Star of Man
Star of Nuit
Star of Saturn

Star of Set
Star of the Annunciation
Star of the White Spirits

Infinity
Blue God
Dian Y Glas
Horizontal Eight
Lazy Eight
Lemniscate
Sign of Eternity
Sign of the Holy Spirit

Inverted Five-pointed Star
Baphomet
Devil's Sign
Footprint of the Devil
Goat of Mendes
Goat of Nedes
Goblin's Cross
Satanic Pentagram
Sign of the Cloven Hoof
Solomon's Seal
Witch's Foot
Wizard's Star

Italian horn
Fairy Wand
Horn
Leprechaun's Staff
Unicorn Horn

Neroic Cross
Raven's Foot
Sign of the "Broken Jew"
Symbol of the "Anti-Christ"
Teutonic Cross
Todersrune
Witch's Foot

Oroboros
Kundala
Ringed Serpent
Serpent Circle
Uroboros

Phoenix
Fire Bird

Rainbow Bridge
Antahkarana

Peace Symbol
Druid's Foot
Druxtenfuss
Nero Cross

Seven-pointed Star
Mystic Star
Pole Star

Sirius
AEsculapius
Astron
Anubis
Blazing Star
Canicula
Canis
Canis Major
Canis Majoris
Dog of Orion
Dog Star
Greater Dog
Hannobech
Hept
Horus
Janitor Lethaeus
Keeper of Hell
Lucifer
Mercury
Morning Star
Nile Star
Rubeola
Sed
Seirios
Seitois
Sepet
Sept
Septet
Set

Sihor
Sopdet
Sot
Sothi
Sothis
Sothos
Star in the East
Star of Bethlehem
Star of Hathor
Star of Horus
Star of Isis
Star of Isis-Sothis
Star of Nuit
Star of Set
Star of the Annunciation
Star of the Dog
Star of the White Spirits
Taaut
Tahaut
Thaaut
Thayuat
The Leader
Thor
Thot
Thotes
Thoth

Six-pointed Star
Crest of Solomon
Double Triangle

Hexagram
Hexagram of Solomon
Hexalpha
Hexangular Seal of Solomon
Magen David
Mogen David
Seal of Solomon
Shield of David
Solomon's Seal
Star of Creation
Star of David
Star of the Microcosm
Talisman of Saturn

Fylfot Cross
Gamma Cross
Gammadion
Hammer of Creation
Hammer of Thor
Hermetic Cross
Jain Cross
Jaina Cross
Lei-Wen
Miolnir
Sauvastika
Storm-hammer
Svastika
Swavastika
Tetragammaton
Tetrascele
Thor's Hammer
Thunder-Scroll

St. Andrew's Cross
Crux Decussata

Tau Cross
Crux Commissa
Egyptian Cross
St. Anthony's Cross

Swastika
Cross Pattee
Croix Pattee
Cross Dissimulata
Crux Gammata
Filfot
Fylfot

Third Eye
All-seeing Eye
Ajna Center

Deva-Eye
Divya Chakshu
Eye of Intuition
Eye of Siva
Eye of the Soul
Frontal Eye
Inner Eye
Magic Eye
Odd Eye
Primeval Eye
Spiritual Eye
Tirsa Til
Urna

Triangle
Delta

Triskele
Trinacria
Triquetra
Triquetrum
Triscele
Triskelion

Thunderbolt
Dordj
Dordje
Dorje
Hitler S
Lightning Bolt
Lightning Staff
Satanic S
Shaft of Light
Shaft of Lightning
Thunderweapon
Trident
Trisula
Vajra
Wand of Energy and Inspiration

Trisula
Caduceus of India
Vardhamana

Upside Down Cross
Satanic Cross
Southern Cross

Yin/Yang
Tai-gi-tu

Winged Disk
Winged Solar Disk

Winged Globe
Solar Globe
Winged Circle

World Egg
Orphic Egg

ENDNOTES

Chapter 1: What Is a Symbol?

[1] George H. Steinmetz, *Freemasonry: Its Hidden Meaning* (New York: Macoy Publishing and Masonic Supply Company, 1948), p.43-44; See also: Charles H. Vail, *The Ancient Mysteries and Modern Masonry* (New York: Macoy Publishing and Masonic Supply Company, 1909), p.182; "Symbolism," *Short Talk Bulletin* (March 1925; Vol. 3, No. 3; Reprinted May 1982), p.6, 9.

[2] Mary Ann Slipper, *The Symbolism of the Order of the Eastern Star* (no other information available), p.7; See also: Sarah H. Terry, *The Second Mile* (Corpus Christi, Texas: Christian Triumph Press, 1935), p.5.

[3] Edmond Ronayne quoting Albert Mackey, *The Master's Carpet (Mah-Hah-Bone)* (n.p., 1879), p.132.

[4] Shirley Plessner, *Symbolism of the Eastern Star* (Cleveland, Ohio: Gilbert Publishing Company, 1956), p.195; See also: *What? When? Where? Why? Who? in Freemasonry* (Silver Spring, Maryland: Masonic Service Association of the United States, 1956), p.73; "Veiled in Allegory and Illustrated by Symbols," *Short Talk Bulletin* (November 1974; Vol. 52, No. 11), p.3.

[5] Slipper, *op. cit.,* p.6.

[6] "Symbolism," *Short Talk Bulletin* (March 1925; Vol. 3, No. 3; Reprinted May 1982), p.15.

[7] Charles G. Berger, *Our Phallic Heritage* (New York, New York: Greenwich Book Publishers, Inc., 1966), p.48.

[8] Count Goblet D'Alviella, *The Migration of Symbols* (Westminster: Archibald Constable and Company, 1894), p.3.

Chapter 2: Yin/Yang Symbol

[1] Philip G. Zimbardo and Floyd L. Ruch, Editors, *Psychology and Life* (Glenview, Illinois: Scott, Foresman and Company, 1977, Ninth Edition), p.317; See also: Elizabeth Seeger, *Eastern Religions* (New York: Thomas Y. Cromwell Company, 1973), p.106; Geoffrey Parrinder, Editor, *World Religions: From Ancient History to the Present* (New York, New York: Facts on File Publications, 1971, 1983), p.334; Texe Marrs, *Mystery Mark of the New Age: Satan's Design for World Domination* (Westchester, Illinois: Crossway Books, 1988), p.117; Albert James Dager, *Acupuncture: Magic or Medical Science* (Redmond, Washington: Media Spotlight, 1985).

[2] Paul E. Desautels, *The Gem Kingdom* (New York: Random House, n.d.), p.237.

[3] Claire Chambers, *The SIECUS Circle: A Humanist Revolution* (Belmont, Massachusetts: Western Islands, 1977), p.v.

[4] Gary Jennings, *Black Magic, White Magic* (Eau Claire, Wisconsin: The Dial Press, Inc., 1964), p.50.

[5] Sybil Leek, *Reincarnation: The Second Chance* (Briarcliff Manor, New York: Stein and Day, 1974), p.190.

[6] *Ibid.*

[7] William J. Petersen, *Those Curious New Cults* (New Canaan, Connecticut: Keat Publishing, Inc., 1973), p.44; See also: Stephan Palos, *The Chinese Art of Healing* (New York, New York: Herder and Herder, Inc., 1971), p.31-32; *The Divine Principle* (New York, New York: Holy Spirit Association for the Unification of World Christianity), p.26-27; *Personal Energy Patterns: How They Affect Your Personality, Health and Relationships* (Albany, California: Taoist Healing Centre, n.d.), unnumbered page; Frank Gaynor, Editor, *Dictionary of Mysticism* (New York: Philosophical Library, 1953), p.168, 202; David Eisenberg, "Encounters with Qi: A Harvard Doctor Explores the Ancient Chinese Concept of 'Vital Energy,'" *The New Age Journal* (January/February 1987, Vol. 3, Issue 1), p.35-36; Leek, *op. cit.,* p.190; Elizabeth Seeger, *Eastern Religions* (New York: Thomas Y. Cromwell Company, 1973), p.118; Geoffrey Parrinder, Editor, *World Religions: From Ancient History to the Present* (New York, New York: Facts on File Publications, 1971, 1983), p.334.

[8] Desautels, *op. cit.,* p.235-237.

[9] Frank Gaynor, Editor, *Dictionary of Mysticism* (New York: Philosophical Library, 1953), p.168.

[10] Dennis Chernin and Gregory Manteuffel, *Health: A Holistic Approach* (Wheaton, Illinois: Theosophical Publishing Houses), p.33.

[11] Catalog from Wayfarer Publications (n.p., n.d.), p.20.

[12] Jeffrey S. Stamps, *Holonomy: A Human Systems Theory* (Intersystems Publications), p.208.

[13] Albert Pike, *Morals and Dogma of the Ancient and Accepted Scottish Rite of Freemasonry Prepared for the Supreme Council of the Thirty-Third Degree, for the Southern Jurisdiction of the United States, and Published by Its Authority* (Richmond, Virginia: L. H. Jenkins, Inc., 1871, Reprinted 1944), p.14; See also: "Mosaic Pavement and Blazing Star," *Short Talk Bulletin* (April 1951, Vol. 29, No. 4, Reprinted April 1990), p.5.

[14] "The Significant Numbers," *Short Talk Bulletin* (September 1956; Vol. 34; No. 9), p.5; See also: Wes Cook, Editor, *Did You Know? Vignettes in Masonry from the Royal Arch Mason Magazine* (Missouri Lodge of Research, 1965), p.34.

[15] Charles G. Berger, *Our Phallic Heritage* (New York, New York: Greenwich Book Publishers, Inc., 1966), p.36, 26; See also: John Blofeld, *The Tantric Mysticism of Tibet* (Boston, Massachusetts: Shambhala Publications, Inc., 1970), p.118.

[16] George Oliver, *The Historical Landmarks and Other Evidences of Freemasonry, Explained* (New York: John W. Leonard and Company, 1855), p.186.

[17] Heinrich Zimmer with Joseph Campbell as Editor, *Myths and Symbols in Indian Art and Civilization* (Harper & Row, 1962), p.127-128.

[18] Catalog from JBL, p.12.

[19] Berger, *op. cit.,* p.37

[20] John Lash, *The Seeker's Handbook: The Complete Guide to Spiritual Pathfinding* (New York: Harmony Books, 1990), p.224.

[21] Catalog from JBL, p.12.

[22] "Letters," *Whole Life Times* (Mid-November/December 1984), p.9.

[23] Texe Marrs, *America Shattered* (Austin, Texas: Living Truth Publishers, 1991), p.80; See also: Texe Marrs, *Mystery Mark of the New Age: Satan's Design for World Domination* (Westchester, Illinois: Crossway Books, 1988), p.117.

[24] Albert James Dager, *The Unicorn: Fabled Beast of Myth and Magic* (Costa Mesa, California: Media Spotlight, n.d.).

[25] Berger, *op. cit.,* p.60.

[26] *Ibid.,* p.62.

[27] Chambers, *op. cit.*

[28] Dennis Cuddy, *Chronology of Education with Quotable Quotes* (Highland City, Florida: Pro Family Forum, Inc., 1994, Updated, Bound Volume), p.37.

[29] Gary H. Kah, *The Demonic Roots of Globalism* (Lafayette, Louisiana: Huntington House Publishers, 1995), p.153; See also: Dennis Cuddy, *Now Is the Dawning of the New Age New World Order* (Oklahoma City, Oklahoma, 1991), p.192.

[30] Geoffrey Parrinder, Editor, *World Religions: From Ancient History to the Present* (New York, New York: Facts on File Publications, 1971, 1983), p.334; See also: Lash, *op. cit.,* p.293.

[31] William Spear, "Ancient Chinese Philosophy, Astrology and the I Ching," *Rowe Conference Center* (Spring 1989), p.4.

[32] *Ibid.;* See also: Whalen W. Lai, "Before the Yin-Yang Circle Was Created: Individuation in a Soto Zen Circle Series," *Anima* (Spring Equinox 1984, Vol. 10, No. 2), p.136-137; *Personal Energy Patterns: How They Affect Your Personality, Health and Relationships* (Albany, California: Taoist Healing Centre, n.d.), unnumbered page; MoonStar, "Casting the Stalks for Understanding and Guidance," *Circle Network News* (Spring 1985, Vol. 7, No. 1), p.14.

[33] Ad entitled "Diane Stein Balances Yin and Yang in an I Ching for the New Age," *New Times* (March/April 1986), p.32.

[34] MoonStar, "Casting the Stalks for Understanding and Guidance" *Circle Network News* (Spring 1985, Vol. 7, No. 1), p.14.

[35] Stamps, *op. cit.*

[36] Michael Tierra, *The Way of Herbs* (New York, New York: Washington Square Press, 1980), p.50.

[37] *Ibid.,* p.51.

[38] *Ibid.*

[39] *Ibid.*

[40] *Ibid.,* p.53.

[41] O. J. Graham, *The Six-Pointed Star* (New Puritan Library, 1988 Edition), p.34.

Chapter 3: The Circle

[1] Albert G. Mackey, *The Symbolism of Freemasonry* (New York: Clark and Maynard, 1869), p.109, 111, 115, 353; "Point Within a Circle," *Short Talk Bulletin* (August 1931; Vol. 9, No. 8; Reprinted

July 1990), p.4; Albert G. Mackey, *A Manual of the Lodge* (New York: Charles E. Merrill Company, 1870), p.57; "Blazing Star" (Part 1), *Short Talk Bulletin* (March 1965; Vol. 43, No. 3), p.7; F. De P. Castells, *Genuine Secrets in Freemasonry Prior to A.D. 1717* (London: A. Lewis, 1930), p.261; George Oliver, *Symbol of Glory Shewing the Object and End of Freemasonry* (New York: John W. Leonard and Company, American Masonic Agency, 1855), p.152; R. Swinburne Clymer, *The Mysticism of Masonry* (Quakertown, Pennsylvania: The Philosophical Publishing Company, 1924), p.167; George H. Steinmetz, *Freemasonry: Its Hidden Meaning* (New York: Macoy Publishing and Masonic Supply Company, 1948), p.92; See also: J. E. Cirlot (Translated by Jack Sage), *A Dictionary of Symbols* (New York: Dorset Press, 1991 Edition), p.46.

[2] Sarah H. Terry, *The Second Mile* (Corpus Christi, Texas: Christian Triumph Press, 1935), p.71.

[3] J. S. M. Ward, *Freemasonry and the Ancient Gods* (London: Simpkin, Marshall, Hamilton, Kent and Company, Ltd., 1921), p.30; See also: George Oliver, *Symbol of Glory Shewing the Object and End of Freemasonry* (New York: John W. Leonard and Company, American Masonic Agency, 1855), p.162; Charles Scott, *The Analogy of Ancient Craft Masonry to Natural and Revealed Religion* (Philadelphia, Pennsylvania: E. H. Butler and Company, 1857), p.93.

[4] Harry E. Wedeck, *Treasury of Witchcraft* (New York: Philosophical Library, 1961), p.50.

[5] Harold Waldwin Percival, *Masonry and Its Symbols in the Light of "Thinking and Destiny"* (New York, New York: The Word Foundation, Inc., 1952), p.21.

[6] William O. Peterson, Editor, *Masonic Quiz Book: "Ask Me Another, Brother"* (Chicago, Illinois: Charles T. Powner Company, 1950), p.163; See also: George H. Steinmetz, *Freemasonry: Its Hidden Meaning* (New York: Macoy Publishing and Masonic Supply Company, 1948), p.92; Herbert F. Inman, *Masonic Problems and Queries* (London, England: A. Lewis Ltd., 1978), p.172.

[7] Albert G. Mackey, *A Manual of the Lodge* (New York: Charles E. Merrill Company, 1870), p.56; See also: Edmond Ronayne quoting Albert Mackey, *The Master's Carpet (Mah-Hah-Bone)* (n.p., 1879), p.324-326.

[8] "Albert Gallatin Mackey," *Short Talk Bulletin* (February 1936; Vol. 14, No. 2; Reprinted July 1980), p.7.

[9] Albert Churchward, *Signs and Symbols of Primordial Man* (London: George Allen and Company, Ltd., 1913, Second Edition), p.325; See also: Ward, *op. cit.,* p.36; F. De P. Castells, *Genuine Secrets in Freemasonry Prior to A.D. 1717* (London: A. Lewis, 1930), p.256.

[10] Ward, *op. cit.,* p.15.

[11] Arthur Edward Waite, *Emblematic Freemasonry and the Evolution of Its Deeper Issues* (London: William Rider and Son, Ltd., 1925), p.185.

[12] George H. Steinmetz, *Freemasonry: Its Hidden Meaning* (New York: Macoy Publishing and Masonic Supply Company, 1948), p.92; See also: Peterson, *op. cit.,* p.52.

[13] A. T. C. Pierson, *The Traditions, Origin and Early History of Freemasonry* (New York: Masonic Publishing Company, 1865), p.84; See also: R. Swinburne Clymer, *The Mysticism of Masonry* (Quakertown, Pennsylvania: The Philosophical Publishing Company, 1924), p.164.

[14] "Point Within a Circle," *Short Talk Bulletin* (August 1931; Vol. 9, No. 8; Reprinted July 1990), p.4.

[15] Albert Pike, *Morals and Dogma of the Ancient and Accepted Scottish Rite of Freemasonry* (Richmond, Virginia: L. H. Jenkins, Inc., 1871), p.401.

[16] Wes Cook, Editor, *Did You Know? Vignettes in Masonry from the Royal Arch Mason Magazine* (Missouri Lodge of Research, 1965), p.173.

[17] William T. Still, *New World Order: The Ancient Plan of Secret Societies* (Lafayette, Louisiana: Huntington House, Inc., 1990), p.73.

[18] J. Edward Decker, Jr., *The Question of Freemasonry* (Issaquah, Washington: Free the Masons Ministries, n.d.), p.39-40.

[19] Laurie Cabot with Tom Cowan, *Power of the Witch: The Earth, the Moon, and the Magical Path to Enlightenment* (New York, New York: Delacorte Press, 1989), p.95-96.

[20] Texe Marrs, *Mystery Mark of the New Age: Satan's Design for World Domination* (Westchester, Illinois: Crossway Books, 1988), p.109.

Chapter 4: The Triangle

[1] *The Authorized Standard Ritual of the Order of the Eastern Star of New York* (New York, Press of Andrew H. Kellogg Company, 1876; Twentieth Edition, 1916), p.224; Robert Macoy (Arranged by), *Adoptive Rite Ritual* (Virginia: Macoy Publishing and Masonic Supply Company, 1897), p.237.

[2] Shirley Plessner, *Symbolism of the Eastern Star* (Cleveland, Ohio: Gilbert Publishing Company, 1956), p.18; Mary Ann Slipper, *The Symbolism of the Eastern Star* (n.p., 1927), p.5, 92; Mary Ann Slipper, *The Symbolism of the Order of the Eastern Star* (no other information available), p.26; Robert Macoy (Arranged by), *Adoptive Rite Ritual* (Virginia: Macoy Publishing and Masonic Supply Company, 1897), p.237.

[3] Mary Ann Slipper, *The Symbolism of the Order of the Eastern Star* (no other information available), p.19; William O. Peterson, Editor, *Masonic Quiz Book: "Ask Me Another, Brother"* (Chicago, Illinois: Charles T. Powner Company, 1950), p.272.

[4] Plessner, *op. cit.,* p.49; Alice A. Bailey, *A Treatise on White Magic (or The Way of the Disciple)* (New York: Lucis Publishing Company, 1951), p.553; Sarah H. Terry, *The Second Mile* (Corpus Christi, Texas: Christian Triumph Press, 1935), p.70; Mary Ann Slipper, *The Symbolism of the Eastern Star* (n.p., 1927), p.29, 30; See also: R. Swinburne Clymer, *The Mysticism of Masonry* (Quakertown, Pennsylvania: The Philosophical Publishing Company, 1924), p.157; *Pocket Encyclopedia of Masonic Symbols* (Silver Spring, Maryland: The Masonic Service Association of the United States, 1953), p.36, 56; George Oliver, *Signs and Symbols* (New York: Macoy Publishing and Masonic Supply Company, 1906), p.92-93; Paul Foster Case, *The Masonic Letter G* (Los Angeles, California: Builders of the Adytum, Ltd., 1981), p.50; Thomas Albert Stafford, *Christian Symbolism in the Evangelical Churches* (Nashville, Tennessee: Abingdon Press, 1942), p.35; Charles H. Vail, *The Ancient Mysteries and Modern Masonry* (New York: Macoy Publishing and Masonic Supply Company, 1909), p.190; Rex R. Hutchens, *A Bridge to Light* (Washington, D.C.: Supreme Council, 33° Ancient and Accepted Scottish Rite of Freemasonry, Southern Jurisdiction, 1988), p.15, 247; Albert G. Mackey, *The Symbolism of Freemasonry* (New York: Clark and Maynard, 1869), p.192, 195, 196, 331, 361; J. S. M. Ward, *Freemasonry and the Ancient Gods* (London: Simpkin, Marshall, Hamilton, Kent and Company, Ltd., 1921), p.10; Steinmetz, *Freemasonry: Its Hidden Meaning, op. cit.,* p.62, 63, 87; *What? When? Where? Why? Who? in Freemasonry* (Silver Spring, Maryland: Masonic Service Association of the United States, 1956), p.74; A. T. C. Pierson, *The Traditions, Origin and Early History of Freemasonry* (New York: Masonic Publishing Company, 1865), p.379; Alain Danielou, *The Gods of India* (New York, New York: Inner Traditions International, Ltd., 1985), p.219, 352; J. E. Cirlot (Translated by Jack Sage), *A Dictionary of Symbols* (New York: Dorset Press, 1991 Edition), p.281, 351; George H. Steinmetz, *The Lost Word: Its Hidden Meaning* (New York: Macoy Publishing and Masonic Supply Company, 1953), p.148, 215; *Report from Concerned Christians* (May/June 1990), p.13; Gary Jennings, *Black Magic, White Magic* (Eau Claire, Wisconsin: The Dial Press, Inc., 1964), p.49; "The Significant Numbers,"

Short Talk Bulletin (September 1956; Vol. 34; No. 9), p.3; "Sanctum Sanctorum," *Short Talk Bulletin* (July 1944; Vol. 22, No. 7; Reprinted January 1982), p.5; Wes Cook, Editor, *Did You Know? Vignettes in Masonry from the Royal Arch Mason Magazine* (Missouri Lodge of Research, 1965), p.132; Henry C. Clausen, *Clausen's Commentaries on Morals and Dogma* (Supreme Council, 33rd Degree, Ancient and Accepted Scottish Rite of Freemasonry, Southern Jurisdiction, USA, 1974), p.72; R. P. Lawrie Krishna, *The Lamb Slain—Supreme Sacrifice*, Part 3 (Medway, Ohio: Manujothi Ashram Publications, n.d.), p.30; *Complete Occult Digest A to Z* (North Hollywood, California: International Imports, 1984), p.95; Albert Pike, *Morals and Dogma of the Ancient and Accepted Scottish Rite of Freemasonry* (Richmond, Virginia: L. H. Jenkins, Inc., 1871), p.323, 429, 632, 634, 782, 858, 861.

[5] *Ibid.*

[6] George H. Steinmetz, *Freemasonry: Its Hidden Meaning* (New York: Macoy Publishing and Masonic Supply Company, 1948), p.63, 67; George H. Steinmetz, *The Lost Word: Its Hidden Meaning* (New York: Macoy Publishing and Masonic Supply Company, 1953), p.148.

[7] Manly Palmer Hall, *The Lost Keys of Freemasonry* (Richmond, Virginia: Macoy Publishing and Masonic Supply Company, Inc., 1976; Originally published in 1923), p.92; See also: David L. Carrico quoting Manly Palmer Hall, *Manly P. Hall: The Honored Masonic Author* (Evansville, Indiana: Followers of Jesus Christ, 1992), p.5; Lynn F. Perkins, *Masonry in the New Age* (Lakemont, Georgia: CSA Press, 1971), p.101, 102.

[8] George H. Steinmetz, *The Lost Word: Its Hidden Meaning* (New York: Macoy Publishing and Masonic Supply Company, 1953), p.241-242; See also: David L. Carrico quoting George H. Steinmetz, *George Steinmetz: The Honored Masonic Author* (Evansville, Indiana: Followers of Jesus Christ, 1992), p.8-9.

[9] Joseph Fort Newton, *The Religion of Masonry: An Interpretation* (Richmond, Virginia: Macoy Publishing and Masonic Supply Company, Inc., 1969 Edition), p.37.

[10] A few Masonic books teaching the theme of godhood are as follows: Joseph Fort Newton, *The Religion of Masonry: An Interpretation* (Richmond, Virginia: Macoy Publishing and Masonic Supply Company, Inc., 1969 Edition), p.37; W. L. Wilmshurst, *The Masonic Initiation* (Ferndale, Michigan: Trismegistus Press, 1980; Originally published 1924), p.26, 27; Henry C. Clausen, *Emergence of the Mystical* (Washington, D.C.: Supreme Council, 1981, Second Edition), p.3; J. D. Buck, *Mystic Masonry* (Illinois: Indo-American Book Company, 1913, Sixth Edition), p.174, 247; Slipper, *The Symbolism of the Order of the Eastern Star, op. cit.*, p.21; Joseph Fort Newton, *The Builders: A Story and Study of Masonry* (Cedar Rapids, Iowa: The Torch Press, 1914), p.293; Charles H. Vail, *The Ancient Mysteries and Modern Masonry* (New York: Macoy Publishing and Masonic Supply Company, 1909), p.28, 33, 49, 68, 88-89, 125-126, 141, 190, 195; Arthur E. Powell, *The Magic of Freemasonry* (Baskerville Press, Ltd., 1924), p.17; Arthur H. Ward, *Masonic Symbolism and the Mystic Way* (London: Theosophical Publishing House, Ltd., 1923, Second Edition), p.130, 160-161; S. R. Parchment, *Ancient Operative Masonry* (San Francisco, California: San Francisco Center—Rosicrucian Fellowship, 1930), p.35, 36, 74; Steinmetz, *Freemasonry: Its Hidden Meaning, op. cit.*, p.67, 87; H. L. Haywood, *Symbolic Masonry: An Interpretation of the Three Degrees* (Washington, D.C.: Masonic Service Association of the United States, 1923), p.129, 263; R. Swinburne Clymer, *The Mysticism of Masonry* (Quakertown, Pennsylvania: The Philosophical Publishing Company, 1924), p.14, 16, 47; J. D. Buck, *The Genius of Free-Masonry and the Twentieth Century Crusade* (Chicago, Illinois: Indo-American Book Company, 1907), p.304-305; Steinmetz, *The Lost Word, op. cit.*, p.36; *The Scottish Rite Journal* (May 1992; Vol. 100, No. 5), p.17; Arthur Edward Waite, *The Secret Tradition in Freemasonry* (London: Rider and Company, 1937), p.483, 582; Arthur Edward Waite, *Emblematic Freemasonry and the Evolution of Its Deeper Issues* (London: William Rider and Son, Ltd., 1925), p.275. Other books quoting from Masonic sources are: Robert A. Morey, *The Origins and Teachings of Freemasonry* (Southbridge, Massachusetts: Crowne Publications, Inc., 1990), p.45; Malcolm Duncan, *Duncan's*

Ritual of Freemasonry (New York: David McKay Company, Inc., n.d., 3rd Edition), p.125; Larry Kunk quoting from Masonic sources, *What Is the Secret Doctrine of the Masonic Lodge and How Does It Relate to Their Plan of Salvation?* (1992, Unpublished manuscript), p.7, 9, 13, 14; David Carrico with Rick Doninger quoting J. D. Buck, *The Egyptian-Masonic-Satanic Connection* (Evansville, Indiana: Followers of Jesus Christ, 1991), p.16; David L. Carrico quoting George H. Steinmetz, *George Steinmetz: The Honored Masonic Author* (Evansville, Indiana: Followers of Jesus Christ, 1992), p.2-3.

[11] J. D. Buck, *Mystic Masonry* (Illinois: Indo-American Book Company, 1913, Sixth Edition), p.138.

[12] Arthur Edward Waite, *A New Encyclopedia of Freemasonry and of Cognate Instituted Mysteries: Their Rites, Literature and History* (New York: Weathervane Books, 1970 edition), p.421.

[13] Charles H. Vail, *The Ancient Mysteries and Modern Masonry* (New York: Macoy Publishing and Masonic Supply Company, 1909), p.25, 28.

[14] Arthur Edward Waite, *The Secret Tradition in Freemasonry* (London: Rider and Company, 1937), p.483, 582; *Ibid.,* p.189, p.33, 68; Arthur Edward Waite, *A New Encyclopedia of Freemasonry and of Cognate Instituted Mysteries, op. cit.,* p.421; W.L. Wilmshurst, *The Meaning of Masonry* (Bell Publishing Company, 1980 edition), p.147.

[15] Albert Churchward, *Signs and Symbols of Primordial Man* (London: George Allen and Company, Ltd., 1913, Second Edition), p.189, 309, 471.

[16] William Meyer, *The Order of the Eastern Star* (no other information available), p.20; See also: R. P. Lawrie Krishna, *The Lamb Slain—Supreme Sacrifice,* Part 3 (Medway, Ohio: Manujothi Ashram Publications, n.d.), p.30-32; J. S. M. Ward, *Freemasonry and the Ancient Gods* (London: Simpkin, Marshall, Hamilton, Kent and Company, Ltd., 1921), p.10-11.

[17] J. S. M. Ward, *Freemasonry and the Ancient Gods* (London: Simpkin, Marshall, Hamilton, Kent and Company, Ltd., 1921), p.10-11; See also: William Meyer, *The Order of the Eastern Star* (no other information available), p.20; Alain Danielou, *The Gods of India* (New York, New York: Inner Traditions International, Ltd., 1985), p.352.

[18] Anton Szandor LaVey, *The Satanic Bible* (New York: Avon Books, 1969), p.60, 145.

[19] Helena Petrovna Blavatsky, *Isis Unveiled,* Vol. I: Science (New York, New York: Trow's Printing and Bookbinding Company, 1877), p.578; See also: Texe Marrs, *Mystery Mark of the New Age: Satan's Design for World Domination* (Westchester, Illinois: Crossway Books, 1988), p.68.

[20] Alice A. Bailey, *Discipleship in the New Age* (Vol. II) (New York: Lucis Publishing Company, 1955), p.135-136.

[21] Benjamin Creme, *The Reappearance of the Christ and the Masters of Wisdom* (North Hollywood, California: Tara Center, 1980), p.5, 74, 75, 116; See also: Frank Gaynor, Editor, *Dictionary of Mysticism* (New York: Philosophical Library, 1953), p.167; Bailey, *op. cit.,* p.135-136. p.159; *Shamballa: Where the Will of God is Known* (New York, New York: Arcane School, n.d.), p.27; Catalog from All About Pyramids, p.19; *Shamballa: The Centre Where the Will of God Is Known* (New York, New York: World Goodwill, n.d., n.p.); *Magical Work of the Soul* (New York, New York: The Arcane School, n.d.), p.4, 5; Lynn F. Perkins, *Masonry in the New Age* (Lakemont, Georgia: CSA Press, 1971), p.56; *Transmission.* (April 1983, No. 1), p.2-3; *New Times* (March/April 1986; #862), p.23; John Godwin, *Occult America* (Garden City, New York: Doubleday and Company, Inc., 1972), p.294; Alice A. Bailey, *A Treatise on White Magic* (or *The Way of the Disciple*) (New York: Lucis Publishing Company, 1951), p.378-379; Frank Gaynor, Editor, *Dictionary of Mysticism* (New York: Philosophical Library, 1953), p.57-58.

[22] Bailey, *Discipleship in the New Age* (Vol. II), *op. cit.,* p.326.

[23] Alice A. Bailey, *Discipleship in the New Age* (Vol. I) (New York: Lucis Publishing Company, 1955), p.171.

[24] Lynn F. Perkins, *Masonry in the New Age* (Lakemont, Georgia: CSA Press, 1971), p.56.

[25] *Ibid.,* p.56-57.

[26] Kenneth R. H. MacKenzie, Editor, *The Royal Masonic Cyclopaedia of History, Rites, Symbolism, and Biography* (New York: J. W. Bouton, 1877), p.743.

[27] John Yarker, *The Arcane Schools: A Review of Their Origin and Antiquity: With a General History of Freemasonry and Its Relation to the Theosophic Scientific and Philosophic Mysteries* (Belfast, Ireland: William Tait, 1909), p.140.

[28] Ray V. Denslow, *Masonic Portraits* (Transactions of the Missouri Lodge of Research, Vol. #29, 1972), p.167-168.

[29] Alain Danielou, *The Gods of India* (New York, New York: Inner Traditions International Ltd., 1985), p.352.

[30] R. Swinburne Clymer, *The Mysteries of Osiris or Ancient Egyptian Initiation* (Quakertown, Pennsylvania: The Philosophical Publishing Company, 1951, Revised Edition), p.131.

[31] Catalog from Lizzie Brown/Pleiades (1993).

[32] Catalog from Syracuse Cultural Workers (1992), p.18.

[33] Texe Marrs, *Mystery Mark of the New Age: Satan's Design for World Domination* (Westchester, Illinois: Crossway Books, 1988), p.117.

Chapter 5: The Hexagram

[1] O. J. Graham, *The Six-Pointed Star* (New Puritan Library, 1988, Second Edition), p.32, 34; See also: William O. Peterson, Editor, *Masonic Quiz Book: "Ask Me Another, Brother"* (Chicago, Illinois: Charles T. Powner Company, 1950), p.277.

[2] Mary Ann Slipper, *Symbolism of the Eastern Star* (n.p., 1927), p.14; See also: Shirley Plessner, *Symbolism of the Eastern Star* (Cleveland, Ohio: Gilbert Publishing Company, 1956), p.125.

[3] Sarah H. Terry, *The Second Mile* (Corpus Christi, Texas: Christian Triumph Press, 1935), p.70.

[4] Graham, *op. cit.,* p.4, 11; Stewart Farrar, *What Witches Do: The Modern Coven Revealed* (Custer, Washington: Phoenix Publishing Company, 1983, Revised Edition), p.35.

[5] *Ibid.*

[6] E. L. Hawkins, *A Concise Cyclopaedia of Freemasonry* (EC: A. Lewis, 1908), p.124-125.

[7] Gary Jennings, *Black Magic, White Magic* (Eau Claire, Wisconsin: The Dial Press, Inc., 1964), p.51.; See also: Harry E. Wedeck, *Treasury of Witchcraft* (New York, New York: Philosophical Library, 1961), p.135.

[8] *Saints Alive in Jesus Newsletter* (March 1992), p.4.

[9] Jack T. Chick, *Spellbound* (Chino, California: Chick Publications, 1978), p.7.; See also: Eric Barger, *From Rock to Rock: The Music of Darkness Exposed!* (Lafayette, Louisiana: Huntington House, Inc., 1990), p.165; Texe Marrs, *Mystery Mark of the New Age: Satan's Design for World*

Domination (Westchester, Illinois: Crossway Books, 1988), p.118; David Carrico, *The Occult Meaning of the Great Seal of the United States* (Evansville, Indiana: Followers of Jesus Christ, 1991), p.25; Irene Arrington Park, *Modernized Paganism* (Tampa, Florida: Christ's Deliverance Ministries, 1983), p.8.

[10] Heinrich Zimmer with Joseph Campbell as Editor, *Myths and Symbols in Indian Art and Civilization* (New York: Harper and Row, 1962), p.147; See also: Alain Danielou, *The Gods of India* (New York, New York: Inner Traditions International, Ltd., 1985), p.352; Jeff Godwin, *Dancing with Demons: The Music's Real Master* (Chino, California: Chick Publications, 1988), p.312; Albert G. Mackey, *The Symbolism of Freemasonry* (New York: Clark and Maynard, 1869), p.195.

[11] *Ibid.;* See also: Alain Danielou, *The Gods of India* (New York, New York: Inner Traditions International, Ltd., 1985), p.352; Jeff Godwin, *Dancing with Demons: The Music's Real Master* (Chino, California: Chick Publications, 1988), p.312; Mackey, *The Symbolism of Freemasonry, op. cit.,* p.195.

[12] Wes Cook, Editor, *Did You Know? Vignettes in Masonry from the Royal Arch Mason Magazine* (Missouri Lodge of Research, 1965), p.132; See also: Texe Marrs, *Mystery Mark of the New Age: Satan's Design for World Domination* (Westchester, Illinois: Crossway Books, 1988), p.118; Graham, *op. cit.,* p.31-32; Thomas Albert Stafford, *Christian Symbolism in the Evangelical Churches* (Nashville, Tennessee: Abingdon Press, 1942), p.50; Albert Pike, *Morals and Dogma of the Ancient and Accepted Scottish Rite of Freemasonry* (Richmond, Virginia: L. H. Jenkins, Inc., 1871), p.13; Albert G. Mackey, *The Symbolism of Freemasonry* (New York: Clark and Maynard, 1869), p.195, 219, 361.

[13] Alain Danielou, *The Gods of India* (New York, New York: Inner Traditions International Ltd., 1985), p.219.

[14] Jeff Godwin quoting David J. Meyer, *Dancing with Demons: The Music's Real Master* (Chino, California: Chick Publications, 1988), p.278-279.

[15] E. A. Wallis Budge, *Amulets and Superstitions* (New York, New York: Dover Publications, Inc., 1978), p.432.

[16] Eric Barger, *From Rock to Rock: The Music of Darkness Exposed!* (Lafayette, Louisiana: Huntington House, Inc., 1990), p.166.

[17] J. S. M. Ward, *Freemasonry and the Ancient Gods* (London, England: Simpkin, Marshall, Hamilton, Kent and Company Ltd., 1921), p.10.

[18] *Ibid.,* p.12.

[19] Graham, *op. cit.,* p.91; See also: Godwin, *op. cit.,* p.279; *Saints Alive in Jesus Newsletter* (March 1992), p.4.

[20] Wes Cook, Editor, *Did You Know? Vignettes in Masonry from the Royal Arch Mason Magazine* (Missouri Lodge of Research, 1965), p.132.

[21] "The Significant Numbers," *Short Talk Bulletin* (September 1956; Vol. 34; No. 9), p.5; See also: Cook, *op. cit.,* p.34.

Chapter 6: The Pentagram

[1] Frank Gaynor, Editor, *Dictionary of Mysticism* (New York: Philosophical Library, 1953), p.136; See also: Stewart Farrar, *What Witches Do: The Modern Coven Revealed* (Custer, Washington: Phoenix Publishing Company, 1983, Revised Edition), p.18.

[2] Eric Barger, *From Rock to Rock: The Music of Darkness Exposed!* (Lafayette, Louisiana: Huntington House, Inc., 1990), p.143-144.

[3] David L. Carrico quoting Janet and Stewart Farrar, *The Pentagram, Freemasonry and the Goat* (Evansville, Illinois: Followers of Jesus Christ, 1992), p.7.

[4] Laurie Cabot with Tom Cowan, *Power of the Witch: The Earth, the Moon, and the Magical Path to Enlightenment* (New York, New York: Delacorte Press, 1989), p.90.

[5] Barger, *op. cit.,* p.118.

[6] *Llewellyn New Times* (September/October 1988; #885), p.77; *Magical Blend* (February/March/April 1988; Issue #18), p.39.

[7] Margot Adler, *Drawing Down the Moon: Witches, Druids, Goddess-Worshippers, and Other Pagans in America Today* (New York, New York: The Viking Press, 1979), p.46.

[8] Stewart Farrar, *What Witches Do: The Modern Coven Revealed* (Custer, Washington: Phoenix Publishing Company, 1983, Revised Edition), unnumbered page; Charles H. Vail, *The Ancient Mysteries and Modern Masonry* (New York: Macoy Publishing and Masonic Supply Company, 1909), p.189; S. R. Parchment, *Ancient Operative Masonry* (San Francisco, California: San Francisco Center—Rosicrucian Fellowship, 1930), p.43; "Symbolism," *Short Talk Bulletin* (March 1925; Vol. 3, No. 3; Reprinted May 1982), p.13; *Christian News* (April 17, 1989; Vol. 27, No. 16), p.12; Barger, *op. cit.,* p.163; Arthur Lyons, Jr., *The Second Coming: Satanism in America* (Dodd, Mead and Company, 1970), p.136; Arthur Edward Waite, *The Mysteries of Magic: A Digest of the Writings of Eliphas Levi* (Chicago, Illinois: De Laurence, Scott and Company, 1909), p.201, 202, 204, 295; Johanna Michaelsen, *Like Lambs to the Slaughter* (Eugene, Oregon: Harvest House Publishers, 1989), p.229-230; *Complete Occult Digest A to Z* (North Hollywood, California: International Imports, 1984), p.99, 106, 252; Editors of Time-Life Books, *Magical Arts* (Alexandria, Virginia: Time-Life Books, 1990), p.39; Arthur Edward Waite, *The Brotherhood of the Rosy Cross: Being Records of the House of the Holy Spirit in Its Inward and Outward History* (New Hyde Park, New York: University Books, 1961); p.578.

[9] Barger, *op. cit.,* p.144.

[10] Manly Palmer Hall, *The Secret Teachings of All Ages* (Los Angeles, California: The Philosophical Research Society Press, 1945, Seventh Edition), p.civ.

[11] J. Edward Decker, *Freemasonry: Satan's Door to America?* (Issaquah, Washington: Free the Masons Ministries, n.d.), p.3.

[12] CASH (brochure from Continental Association of Satan's Hope).

[13] *Ibid.*

[14] *Ibid.*

[15] Hall, *op. cit.,* p.civ; See also: Larry Kunk, *What Is the Secret Doctrine of the Masonic Lodge and How Does It Relate to Their Plan of Salvation?* (1992, Unpublished manuscript), p.16; Carrico, *op. cit.,* p.11.

[16] S. R. Parchment, *Ancient Operative Masonry* (San Francisco, California: San Francisco Center—Rosicrucian Fellowship, 1930), p.39-40.

[17] "Symbolism," *Short Talk Bulletin* (March 1925; Vol. 3, No. 3; Reprinted May 1982), p.13-14.

[18] Henry Leonard Stillson and William James Hughan, editors, *History of the Ancient and Honorable Fraternity of Free and Accepted Masons, and Concordant Orders* (Boston, Massachusetts: The Fraternity Publishing Company, 1895), p.49.

[19] John Lash, *The Seeker's Handbook: The Complete Guide to Spiritual Pathfinding* (New York: Harmony Books, 1990), p.341-342.

[20] Texe Marrs, *Mystery Mark of the New Age: Satan's Design for World Domination* (Westchester, Illinois: Crossway Books, 1988), p.95; See also: Rudolf Koch, *The Book of Signs* (New York, New York: Dover Publications, Inc., 1955 edition), p.6; John T. Lawrence, *The Perfect Ashlar* (London: A. Lewis, 1912), p.200; "Blazing Star" (Part 1), *Short Talk Bulletin* (March 1965; Vol. 43, No. 3), p.5; Mary Ann Slipper, *The Symbolism of the Order of the Eastern Star* (no other information available), p.15.

[21] Rudolf Koch, *The Book of Signs* (New York, New York: Dover Publications, Inc., 1955 edition), p.6.

[22] "Blazing Star" (Part 1), *Short Talk Bulletin* (March 1965; Vol. 43, No. 3), p.5, 8; See also: John T. Lawrence, *The Perfect Ashlar* (London: A. Lewis, 1912), p.200.

[23] Carrico quoting Janet and Stewart Farrar, *op. cit.*, p.1.

[24] Sybil Leek, *Numerology: The Magic of Numbers* (New York, New York: The MacMillan Company, 1969), p.21.

[25] *Circle Network News* (Summer 1987; Vol. 9, No. 2), p.12; See also: *Llewellyn New Times* (September/October 1988; #885), p.77; Brochure from The Magic Door, p.4; "Blazing Star," *Short Talk Bulletin, op. cit.*, p.8; John T. Lawrence, *The Perfect Ashlar* (London: A. Lewis, 1912), p.193.

[26] Leek, *op. cit.*, p.124; See also: Scott Cunningham, *Wicca: A Guide for the Solitary Practitioner* (St. Paul, Minnesota: Llewellyn Publications, 1989), p.33; *Self-Help Update: Create Your Own Reality* (1985, Issue #26), p.13; E. L. Hawkins, *A Concise Cyclopaedia of Freemasonry* (EC: A. Lewis, 1908), p.172; Carrico, *op. cit.*, p.1; Phil Phillips, *Turmoil in the Toybox* (Lancaster, Pennsylvania: Starburst Press, 1986), p.77.

[27] *Self-Help Update, op. cit.*

[28] Harry E. Wedeck, *Treasury of Witchcraft* (New York: Philosophical Library, 1961), p.59; See also: Barger, *op. cit.*, p.163; Gaynor, *op. cit.*

[29] *Complete Occult Digest A to Z*, 1984 catalog from International Imports, p.252; See also: W. J. McCormick, *Christ, the Christian and Freemasonry* (Belfast, Ireland: Great Joy Publications, 1984), p.91; J. E. Cirlot, *A Dictionary of Symbols* (New York, New York: Philosophical Library, Inc., 1972), p.309.

[30] *Ibid.*, p.117.

[31] *Ibid.*

[32] Gary Jennings, *Black Magic, White Magic* (Eau Claire, Wisconsin: The Dial Press, Inc., 1964), p.51.

[33] J. E. Cirlot (Translated by Jack Sage), *A Dictionary of Symbols* (New York: Dorset Press, 1991 Edition), p.143; See also: Arthur Edward Waite, *The Mysteries of Magic: A Digest of the Writings of Eliphas Levi* (Chicago, Illinois: De Laurence, Scott and Company, 1909), p.299.

[34] Percival George Woodcock, *Short Dictionary of Mythology* (Philosophical Library, 1953), p.93; See also: Eden Within (1994 Catalog), p.15.

[35] Brochure from Nuit Unlimited Imports, p.3.

[36] Catalog from The Occult Emporium (Summer 1990 to Summer 1991), p.45.

[37] Gaynor, Editor, *op. cit.*, p.24.

[38] Catalog from The Occult Emporium (Winter 1993 to Winter 1994), p.54.

[39] Catalog from The Occult Emporium (Mid 1990 to 1991), p.26.

[40] Brochure from Nuit Unlimited Imports, p.3; See also: *Ibid.;* Cirlot, *op. cit.,* p.80; Brochure from The Wicca describing a course in witchcraft; *Complete Occult Digest A to Z, op. cit.,* p.95, 106; Eric Maple, *The Complete Book of Witchcraft and Demonology* (Cranbury, New Jersey: A. S. Barnes and Company, Inc., 1966 Edition), Caption under picture facing p.145.

[41] Wanda Marrs, *New Age Lies to Women* (Austin, Texas: Living Truth Publishers, 1989), p.30.

[42] Arthur Lyons, Jr., *The Second Coming: Satanism in America* (Dodd, Mead and Company, 1970), p.53.

[43] D. Duane Winters, *A Search for Light in a Place of Darkness: A Study of Freemasonry* (no other information available), p.72.

[44] Arthur Edward Waite, *The Mysteries of Magic: A Digest of the Writings of Eliphas Levi* (Chicago, Illinois: De Laurence, Scott and Company, 1909), p.223; See also: D. Duane Winters, *A Search for Light in a Place of Darkness: A Study of Freemasonry* (no other information available), p.69.

[45] Eric Maple, *The Complete Book of Witchcraft and Demonology* (Cranbury, New Jersey: A. S. Barnes and Company, Inc., 1966 Edition), Picture facing p.145; See also: Brochure from Nuit Unlimited Imports, p.3; *Fate* (October 1990; Vol. 43, No. 9 [sic]), p.56; William Schnoebelen, *Masonry: Beyond the Light* (Chino, California: Chick Publications, 1991), p.169-170.

[46] Starhawk (Miriam Simos), *The Spiral Dance: A Rebirth of the Ancient Religion of the Great Goddess* (New York, New York: Harper-Collins Publishers, 1989 Edition), p.108.

[47] Waite, *The Mysteries of Magic, op. cit.,* p.487.

[48] *Ibid.,* p.202.

[49] *The F.A.T.A.L. Flaw* (Issaquah, Washington: Free the Masons Ministries, n.d.), p.5.

[50] *The World Book Encyclopedia,* 1961 Edition; Vol. 16, p.250; See also: Lyons, *The Second Coming, op. cit.,* p.23.

[51] Albert Churchward, *Signs and Symbols of Primordial Man* (London: George Allen and Company, Ltd., 1913, Second Edition), p.477; See also: Dave Hunt and T. A. McMahon, *America: The Sorcerer's New Apprentice: The Rise of New Age Shamanism* (Eugene, Oregon: Harvest House Publishers, 1988), p.239; E. A. Wallis Budge, *Amulets and Superstitions* (New York, New York: Dover Publications, Inc., 1978), p.141; Helena Petrovna Blavatsky, *Isis Unveiled,* Vol. I: Science (New York, New York: Trow's Printing and Bookbinding Company, 1877), p.554; Wedeck, *op. cit.,* p.89; Anton Szandor LaVey, *The Satanic Bible* (New York: Avon Books, 1969), p.60, 146.

[52] John Yarker, *The Arcane Schools: A Review of Their Origin and Antiquity: With a General History of Freemasonry and Its Relation to the Theosophic Scientific and Philosophic Mysteries* (Belfast, Ireland: William Tait, 1909), p.17.

[53] J. S. M. Ward, *Freemasonry and the Ancient Gods* (London: Simpkin, Marshall, Hamilton, Kent and Company, Ltd., 1921), p.64; See also: William J. Schnoebelen, *Twice the Child of Hell* (Issaquah, Washington: Saints Alive in Jesus, n.d.), p.9.

[54] *Adelphi Quarterly* (Third Quarter 1992), p.6; See also: *Voyage to the Source* (McMinnville, Oregon: The Aquarian Church of Universal Service, 1986), p.17.

[55] Anton Szandor LaVey, *The Satanic Bible* (New York: Avon Books, 1969), p.146.

[56] *Ibid.,* p.60; See also: J. Edward Decker, *Freemasonry: Satan's Door to America?* (Issaquah, Washington: Free the Masons Ministries, n.d.), p.3.

[57] Wedeck, *op. cit.,* p.89; See also: Josh McDowell and Don Stewart, *Understanding the Occult* (San Bernardino, California: Here's Life Publishers, Inc., 1982), p.128; Phil Phillips, *Saturday Morning Mind Control* (Nashville, Tennessee: Oliver-Nelson Books, 1991), p.196.

[58] Eklal Kueshana, *The Ultimate Frontier* (Quinlan, Texas: The Stelle Group, 1963), p.89.

[59] Helena Petrovna Blavatsky, *Isis Unveiled,* Vol. I: Science (New York, New York: Trow's Printing and Bookbinding Company, 1877), p.554, xxxiii.

[60] William J. Schnoebelen, *Twice the Child of Hell* (Issaquah, Washington: Saints Alive in Jesus, n.d.), p.9.

[61] *The F.A.T.A.L. Flaw, op. cit.*

[62] *New Larousse Encyclopedia of Mythology* (Prometheus Press, 1972 Edition), p.21; Veronica Ions, *Egyptian Mythology* (England: The Hamlyn Publishing Group, Ltd., 1965), p.63; M. Esther Harding, *Woman's Mysteries: Ancient and Modern* (New York: G. P. Putnam's Sons for the C. G. Jung Foundation for Analytical Psychology, 1971 Edition), p.172.

[63] Churchward, *op. cit.,* p.478.

[64] M. Esther Harding, *Woman's Mysteries: Ancient and Modern* (New York: G. P. Putnam's Sons for the C. G. Jung Foundation for Analytical Psychology, 1971 Edition), p.48.

[65] Arthur Lyons, *Satan Wants You: The Cult of Devil Worship in America* (New York, New York: The Mysterious Press, 1988), p.129.

[66] Harding, *op. cit.,* p.168; See also: *Circle Network News* (Summer 1984; Vol. 6, No. 2), p.3.

[67] *Ibid.,* p.168.

[68] Schnoebelen, *Twice the Child of Hell, op. cit.;* William and Sharon Schnoebelen, *Lucifer Dethroned* (Chino, California: Chick Publications, 1993), p.95.

[69] William Schnoebelen, *Masonry: Beyond the Light* (Chino, California: Chick Publications, 1991), p.106; See also: Lyons, *Satan Wants You, op. cit.,* p.126.

[70] Dave Hunt and T. A. McMahon, *America: The Sorcerer's New Apprentice: The Rise of New Age Shamanism* (Eugene, Oregon: Harvest House Publishers, 1988), p.236; Marrs, *Mystery Mark of the New Age, op. cit.,* p.182; William and Sharon Schnoebelen, *Lucifer Dethroned* (Chino, California: Chick Publications, 1993), p.93; Johanna Michaelsen, *Like Lambs to the Slaughter* (Eugene, Oregon: Harvest House Publishers, 1989), p.257; Schnoebelen, *Twice the Child of Hell, op. cit.,* p.8; Texe Marrs, *Texe Marrs Book of New Age Cults and Religions* (Austin, Texas: Living Truth Publishers, 1990), p.312.

[71] Marrs, *Mystery Mark of the New Age, op. cit.,* p.181; Johanna Michaelsen, *Like Lambs to the Slaughter* (Eugene, Oregon: Harvest House Publishers, 1989), p.257; Schnoebelen, *Twice the Child of Hell, op. cit.,* p.8, 9; *Constance Cumbey's New Age Monitor* (June 1986; Vol. 1, No. 2), p.7; Schnoebelen, *Masonry, op. cit.,* p.106; William and Sharon Schnoebelen, *Lucifer Dethroned* (Chino, California: Chick Publications, 1993), p.92; Texe Marrs, *Texe Marrs Book of New Age Cults and Religions* (Austin, Texas: Living Truth Publishers, 1990), p.312.

[72] Schnoebelen, *Twice the Child of Hell, op. cit.,* p.9; Johanna Michaelsen, *Like Lambs to the Slaughter* (Eugene, Oregon: Harvest House Publishers, 1989), p.257; Lyons, Jr., *The Second Coming, op. cit.,* p.172, 173; William and Sharon Schnoebelen, *Lucifer Dethroned* (Chino, California: Chick Publications, 1993), p.92; Lyons, *Satan Wants You, op. cit.,* p.109, 127-128.

[73] *Constance Cumbey's New Age Monitor* (June 1986; Vol. 1, No. 2), p.7; Marrs, *Mystery Mark of the New Age, op. cit.,* p.181; Hunt and McMahon, *America, op. cit.,* p.233; Texe Marrs, *Texe*

Marrs Book of New Age Cults and Religions (Austin, Texas: Living Truth Publishers, 1990), p.312.

[74] Hunt and McMahon, quoting Aquino, *America, op. cit.*

[75] *Ibid.,* p.238.

[76] Henry Leonard Stillson and William James Hughan, editors, *History of the Ancient and Honorable Fraternity of Free and Accepted Masons, and Concordant Orders* (Boston, Massachusetts: The Fraternity Publishing Company, 1895), p.101; See also: Waite, *The Mysteries of Magic, op. cit.,* p.202; Charles H. Vail, *The Ancient Mysteries and Modern Masonry* (New York: Macoy Publishing and Masonic Supply Company, 1909), p.189. Note: Charles H. Vail, a Mason and the former minister of the Pullman Memorial Church in Albion, New York, agrees with one difference—he states that the inverted pentagram represents Lucifer while the other authors claim that the pentagram with one point up represents Lucifer. He writes: "The Blazing Star also represents these two principles. If the point is turned upward it represents God; Good, Order, or the Lamb of Ormuzd and St. John; if the point is turned downward it denotes Lucifer, Evil, Disorder, or the accursed God of Mendes and the Mysteries."

Chapter 7: The Dream Net

[1] Frank Gaynor, Editor, *Dictionary of Mysticism* (New York: Philosophical Library, 1953), p.35.

[2] Selena Fox, "Amulets, Talismans & Charms: Past and Present," *Circle Network News* (Summer 1987, Vol. 9, No. 2), p.13; See also: *Pyramid Books and the New-Age Collection* Catalog (Winter/Spring 1993), p.46.

[3] Paper entitled "Legend of the Dream Catcher."

[4] John Lash, *The Seeker's Handbook: The Complete Guide to Spiritual Pathfinding* (New York: Harmony Books, 1990), p.268.

[5] *Ibid.*

[6] Catalog from Red Rose Collection (Holiday 1992), p.46.

Chapter 8: Elementals

[1] H. P. Blavatsky, *Isis Unveiled* Vol. I: Science (New York: Trow's Printing and Bookbinding Company, 1877), p.xxix-xxx; See also: John Lash, *The Seeker's Handbook: The Complete Guide to Spiritual Pathfinding* (New York: Harmony Books, 1990), p.262.

[2] *Discoveries Through Inner Quests* (Winter/Spring 1987), p.31; *Discoveries Through Inner Quests* (Spring 1989), p.33; *Discoveries Through Inner Quests* (1989), p.19.

[3] Samuel, "Helpers," *Connecting Link* (November/December 1989, Vol. 1, No. 5), p.4-5.

[4] "Treasure Trolls...The New Care Bears?", *Child Affects* (December 1992), p.4.

[5] "Treasure Trolls," *The Perilous Times* (June 1998), p.6.

[6] "Charms, Trolls, and Jesus Dolls," *The Front Page* (February 1993, Vol. 7, No. 2), p.7

[7] "Imagine If It Were a Cross!", *The Omega-Letter* (March 1990, Vol. 5, No. 3), p.3.

[8] *Ibid.*

[9] *Ibid.*

[10] "Treasure Trolls...", *Child Affects, op. cit.,* p.4.

[11] Berit Kjos, "Olympic Myths and Earthy Magic," *Christian News* (February 28, 1994, Vol. 32, No. 9), p.5.

[12] *Ibid.*

[13] John Lash, *The Seeker's Handbook: The Complete Guide to Spiritual Pathfinding* (New York: Harmony Books, 1990), p.262; See also: Frank Gaynor, Editor, *Dictionary of Mysticism* (New York: Philosophical Library, 1953), p.55.

[14] *Llewellyn New Times* (March/April 1986, Issue #862), p.61.

[15] Frank Gaynor, Editor, *Dictionary of Mysticism* (New York: Philosophical Library, 1953), p.55.

[16] J. Gordon Melton, Jerome Clark, and Aidan A. Kelly, *New Age Almanac* (Detroit, Michigan: Visible Ink, 1991), p.402; See also: Findhorn Community, *The Findhorn Garden* (New York, New York: Harper and Row, 1975), p.7-8, 17, 128; Paul Hawken, *The Magic of Findhorn* (New York, New York: Harper and Row, 1975), p.136-137.

[17] David Spangler, *Reflections on the Christ* (Scotland: Findhorn Publications, 1977), p. 43-44.

[18] *Ibid.,* p. 45.

[19] Laurie Cabot with Tom Cowan, *Power of the Witch: The Earth, the Moon, and the Magical Path to Enlightenment* (New York, New York: Delacorte Press, 1989), p.28.

[20] Susan Kauffman, "Great Gothic Gargoyles," *The News and Observer* (January 11, 1997), p.1E.

[21] Dennis L. Cuddy, *President Clinton Will Continue the New World Order* (Oklahoma City, Oklahoma: Southwest Radio Church, 1993), p.39.

[22] J. E. Cirlot (Translated by Jack Sage), *A Dictionary of Symbols* (New York: Dorset Press, 1991 Edition), p.115.

[23] *The News and Observer, op. cit.,* p.2E.

[24] *Ibid.*

[25] *Ibid.*

[26] *Ibid.*

[27] Texe Marrs (quoting from *The Gargoyle*), *Ravaged by the New Age: Satan's Plan to Destroy Our Kids* (Austin, Texas: Living Truth Publishers, 1989), p.150.

[28] Jolene L. Roehlkepartain, "Gargoyle Christmas," *Parents of Teenagers* (November/December 1992, Vol. 5, No. 2), p.47.

[29] Gaynor, *op. cit.,* p.29.

[30] *Ibid.,* p.75.

[31] *Ibid.,* p.63.

[32] *Ibid.,* p.177.

[33] *Ibid.*, p.192.

[34] *Ibid.*, p.70.

[35] *Ibid.*, p.89.

[36] *Ibid.*, p.160.

[37] *Ibid.*, p.72.

[38] *Ibid.*, p.24.

[39] *Ibid.*, p.76.

[40] *Ibid.*, p.78.

[41] *Ibid.*, p.71.

[42] *Ibid.*, p.82.

[43] *Ibid.*, p.162.

[44] *Ibid.*, p.164.

[45] *Ibid.*, p.139.

[46] *Ibid.*

[47] *Ibid.*, p.204.

[48] *Ibid.*, p.200.

[49] *Ibid.*, p.190.

[50] *Ibid.*, p.121.

[51] *Ibid.*, p.190.

[52] *Ibid.*, p.199.

[53] *Ibid.*, p.136.

[54] *Ibid.*, p.184.

[55] *Ibid.*, p.122.

[56] *Ibid.*, p.174.

[57] *Ibid.*

[58] *Ibid.*, p.172.

[59] *Ibid.*

[60] *Ibid.*, p.120.

[61] *Ibid.*, p.131.

[62] *Ibid.*, p.123.

[63] *Ibid.*, p.128.

[64] *Ibid.*, p.125-126.

[65] *Ibid.*, p.99.

[66] *Ibid.*, p.124.

[67] *Ibid.*

[68] *Ibid.*, p.95

[69] Eric Maple, *The Complete Book of Witchcraft and Demonology* (Cranbury, New Jersey: A. S. Barnes and Company, Inc., 1966 Edition), p.11 of Glossary.

[70] Gaynor, *op. cit.*, p.129.

[71] *Ibid.*, p.63.

[72] Maple, *op. cit.*, p.11-12 of Glossary.

Chapter 9: Tarot and Playing Cards

[1] J. Gordon Melton, Jerome Clark, and Aidan A. Kelly, *New Age Almanac* (Detroit, Michigan: Visible Ink, 1991), p.132-133.

[2] Frank Gaynor, Ed., *Dictionary of Mysticism* (New York: Philosophical Library, 1953), p.181.

[3] *The Llewellyn New Times* (May/June 1987, No. 873), p.40.

[4] Nat Freedland, *The Occult Explosion* (New York: G. P. Putnam's and Sons, 1972), p.134; See also: Colin Wilson, *The Occult: A History* (New York: Random House, 1971), p.115.

[5] *Ibid.*, p.136.

[6] *Ibid.*, p.135.

[7] Doris Chase Doane and King Keyes, *Tarot-Card Spread Reader* (West Nyack, New York: Parker Publishing Company, Inc., 1967), p.20; See also: Manly Palmer Hall, *The Secret Teachings of All Ages* (Los Angeles, California: The Philosophical Research Society Press, 1945, 7th Edition), p.cxxxii; *Devorss & Company New Publications Catalog*, 1989, p.12; Brochure from Life Spectrums announcing the 1987 Rainbow Experience, p.13.

[8] Stewart Farrar, *What Witches Do: The Modern Coven Revealed* (Custer, Washington: Phoenix Publishing Company, 1983, Revised Edition), p.103.

[9] Colin Wilson, *The Occult: A History* (New York: Random House, 1971), p.113-114.

[10] Charles G. Berger, *Our Phallic Heritage* (New York, New York: Greenwich Book Publishers, Inc., 1966), p. 179-180.

[11] "A Deck of Cards," *The Gospel Standard* (May 1991, Vol. 40, No. 11), p.3-4.

[12] William R. Denslow, *10,000 Famous Freemasons* (n.p., 1958), p.198.

Chapter 10: Humanist Symbols

[1] Claire Chambers, *The SIECUS Circle: A Humanist Revolution* (Belmont, Massachusetts: Western Islands, 1977), p.425.

[2] *Statement Affirming Evolution As a Principle of Science,* (Amherst, New York: American Humanist Association), p.2.

[3] S. R. Parchment, *Ancient Operative Masonry* (San Francisco, California: San Francisco Center—Rosicrucian Fellowship, 1930), p.126.

[4] Corliss Lamont, *The Philosophy of Humanism* (New York: Frederick Unger Publishing Company, 1965 Edition), p.154.

[5] *Ibid.*

[6] A. Ralph Epperson, *The Unseen Hand: An Introduction to the Conspiratorial View of History* (Tucson, Arizona: Publius Press, 1985), p.380.

[7] Paul Kurtz, *Humanist Manifestos I and II* (Buffalo, New York: Prometheus Books, 1973), p.3.

[8] *Ibid.*

[9] *Ibid.,* p.7.

[10] *Ibid.,* p.8-10.

[11] *Ibid.,* p.15.

[12] Johanna Michaelsen, *Like Lambs to the Slaughter* (Eugene, Oregon: Harvest House Publishers, 1989), p.31.

[13] Dennis Laurence Cuddy, *Now Is the Dawning of the New Age New World Order* (Oklahoma City, Oklahoma: Hearthstone Publishing Ltd., 1991, p.374-375.

[14] Lamont, *op. cit.,* p.52-54.

[15] Dennis Laurence Cuddy, "Public Schools Disseminating Humanistic Values," *An American Commentary* (Oklahoma City, Oklahoma, 1993), p.98.

[16] *Ibid.;* See also: Dennis Laurence Cuddy, *The Grab for Power: A Chronology of the NEA* (Marlborough, New Hampshire: Plymouth Rock Foundation, 1993), p.1; Dennis Laurence Cuddy, "Secular Humanism: Are Public School Texts Teaching It to Your Children?", *Christian World Report* (September 1989, Vol. 1, No. 7), p.17.

[17] *Ibid.*

[18] Kurtz, *op. cit.,* p.18.

[19] *Ibid.,* p.21.

[20] *Ibid.,* p.22.

[21] *Ibid.,* p.23.

[22] *Ibid.,* p.21.

[23] Ed Rowe, *New Age Globalism* (Herndon, Virginia: Growth Publishing, 1985), p.89.

[24] *Ibid.*

[25] Dennis Laurence Cuddy, "Secular Humanism: Are Public School Texts Teaching It to Your Children?", *Christian World Report* (September 1989, Vol. 1, No. 7), p.17.

[26] *Ibid.*

[27] Epperson, *op. cit.,* p.378.

[28] Cuddy, *An American Commentary, op. cit.;* See also: Cuddy, *Christian World Report, op. cit.;* "Humanists Confident They Will Overcome," *The Christian World Report* (December 1989, Vol. 1, No. 9), p.17.

[29] Epperson, *op. cit.*

[30] *Ibid.*

[31] Mel and Norma Gabler, quoting John Dunphy, *Humanism in Textbooks* (Longview, Texas, 1983), p.6; See also: Dennis Laurence Cuddy, *President Clinton Will Continue the New World Order* (Oklahoma City, Oklahoma: Southwest Radio Church, 1993), p.32; Texe Marrs *Dark Secrets of the New Age: Satan's Plan for a One World Religion* (Westchester, Illinois: Crossway Books, 1987), p.233-234.

[32] Cuddy, *Christian World Report, op. cit.*

[33] *Ibid.*

[34] Lamont, *op. cit.,* p.227.

[35] *Ibid.,* p.283.

[36] *Ibid.,* p.189.

[37] "Benjamin Creme Answers," *The Emergence* (June 1998, Vol. 16, No. 5), p.1.

[38] Peggy S. Cuddy, "Transformation Toward New Age Synthesis," *Distant Drums* (March 1986, Vol. 8, No. 1), p.4.

[39] Pat Means, *The Mystical Maze: A Guidebook Through the Mindfields of Eastern Mysticism* (Campus Crusade for Christ, Inc., 1976), p.212.

[40] Brochure from 3HO Foundation advertising their Summer Solstice, June 18-27, 1987; See also: Brochure from Joy of Living Health Vacations; Brochure from 3HO Kundalini Yoga Center.

[41] *Ibid.*

[42] Peggy S. Cuddy, *Distant Drums, op. cit.*

[43] *Encyclopedia of Associations* (Vol. 1, Part 2) (1998, 33rd Edition), p.2021.

[44] J. Gordon Melton, Jerome Clark, and Aidan A. Kelly, *New Age Almanac* (Detroit, Michigan: Visible Ink, 1991), p.153-154.

[45] http://www.3ho.org/3ho/pages.nsl/p/HomePage?Open Document

[46] *Ibid.*

[47] Donald M. Reynolds, "The Pursuit of the Sacred," *Imprimis* (June 1998, Vol. 27, No. 6), p.6-7.

[48] James Rizzutti, "The Gods of Olympus: The Thrill of Victory and the Agony of Defeat," *Midnight Call* (July 1998), p.28.

[49] *Ibid.,* quoting Terence D. McLean.

[50] *Ibid.*

[51] Kurtz, *op. cit.*

[52] Dennis Cuddy, *Chronology of Education with Quotable Quotes* (Highland City, Florida: Pro Family Forum, Inc., 1994, Updated, Bound Volume), p.37.

[53] James M. Parsons, *The Assault on the Family* (PRO Media Foundation, 1978), Appendix II, p.9.

[54] *Ibid.,* Appendix I, p.3.

[55] *Ibid.;* See also: Brochure from Elysium Book Nook; "Off the Newsstand," *Utne Reader* (March/April 1990, No. 38), p.138.

[56] Chambers, *op. cit.,* p.48-49.

[57] "Global Education: The Chinese Connection," *Distant Drums* (March 1981, Vol. 3, No. 1), p.10.

[58] Parsons, *op. cit.,* Appendix II, p.9.

[59] *Ibid.,* Appendix I, p.3.

[60] George Oliver, *Symbol of Glory Shewing the Object and End of Freemasonry* (New York: John W. Leonard and Company, 1855), p.193.

[61] Paul Hamlyn, *Greek Mythology* (London, England: Paul Hamlyn Limited, 1967), p.129.

[62] *Ibid.*

[63] Harry E. Wedeck, *Treasury of Witchcraft* (New York, New York: Philosophical Library, 1961), p.188.

[64] *Holistic Education Review* (Fall 1989, Vol. 2, No. 3).

[65] *Holistic Living* (December 1984/January 1985, Vol. 11, No. 2), p.3.

[66] "Youth for Christ Buys into Psychology," *Return to the Word* (June 1998), p.10.

[67] *Ibid.,* quoting from a letter from Sam Atiemo.

[68] *New Man* (July/August 1998), p.71.

[69] Chambers, *op. cit.,* p.425.

[70] *Ibid.*

[71] *Ibid.*

[72] *Ibid.*

[73] *Ibid.*

Chapter 11: Animals, Birds, and Insects

[1] John Lash, *The Seeker's Handbook: The Complete Guide to Spiritual Pathfinding* (New York: Harmony Books, 1990), p.257.

[2] J. E. Cirlot, *A Dictionary of Symbols* (New York, New York: Philosophical Library, Inc., 1972), p.60.

[3] *New Larousse Encyclopedia of Mythology* (Prometheus Press, 1972 Edition), p.150.

[4] Melissa Tignor, "Dionysus Offers Joyous Inspiration," *Circle Network News* (Spring 1986, Vol. 8, No. 1), p.11.

[5] J. S. M. Ward, *Who Was Hiram Abiff?* (London, England: The Baskerville Press, Limited, 1925), p.52.

[6] Percival George Woodcock, *Short Dictionary of Mythology* (New York: Philosophical Library, 1953), p.17.

[7] *Ibid.*, p.100.

[8] Joseph Campbell, *The Masks of God: Creative Mythology* (New York, New York: The Viking Press, 1968), p.204.

[9] Woodcock, *op. cit.*, p.100.

[10] Franz Sales Meyer, *Handbook of Ornament* (Dover), p.86.

[11] E. A. Wallis Budge, *From Fetish to God in Ancient Egypt* (London, England: Oxford University Press, 1934), p.76-77.

[12] Cirlot, *op. cit.*, p.84-85.

[13] J. Gordon Melton, Jerome Clark, and Aidan A. Kelly, *New Age Almanac* (Detroit, Michigan: Visible Ink, 1991), p.382.

[14] *Ibid.*, p.414.

[15] *Ibid.*, p.382.

[16] "Close Encounter with Dolphins Latest Fad," *The Omega-Letter* (October 1989, Vol. 4, No. 9), p.3.

[17] *Ibid.*

[18] Melton, Clark, and Kelly, *op. cit.*, p.383.

[19] *Ibid.*, p.384.

[20] "What Are They Teaching in Public Schools?", *The Phyllis Schlafly Report* (January 1994, Vol. 27, No. 6), p.1.

[21] Udo Becker, Editor, *The Continuum Encyclopedia of Symbols* (1994), p.130; See also: J. C. Cooper, *An Illustrated Encyclopedia of Traditional Symbols* (London, England: Thames and Hudson, 1982 reprint), p.75.

[22] Scott Cunningham, *Wicca: A Guide for the Solitary Practitioner* (St. Paul, Minnesota: Llewellyn Publications, 1989), p.12.

[23] Albert Churchward, *The Origin and Evolution of Freemasonry Connected with the Origin and Evolution of the Human Race* (London, England: George Allen and Unwin Ltd., 1920), p.76; H. P. Blavatsky, *The Secret Doctrine: The Synthesis of Science, Religion, and Philosophy* (Vol. I— Cosmogenesis) (Covina, California: Theosophical University Press, 1947, Fourth Edition), p.358.

[24] Thomas Milton Stewart, *The Symbolism of the Gods of the Egyptians and the Light They Throw on Freemasonry* (London, England: Baskerville Press, Limited, 1927), p.76; See also: *Ibid.* J. C. Cooper, *An Illustrated Encyclopedia of Traditional Symbols* (London, England: Thames and Hudson, 1982 reprint), p.75.

[25] Becker, *op. cit.*, p.94.

[26] *Ibid.*

[27] *Ibid.*

[28] Albert Pike, *Morals and Dogma of the Ancient and Accepted Scottish Rite of Freemasonry* (Richmond, Virginia: L. H. Jenkins, Inc., 1871), p.496.

[29] Harry E. Wedeck, *Treasury of Witchcraft* (Philosophical Library, 1961), p.18.

[30] J. C. Cooper, *An Illustrated Encyclopedia of Traditional Symbols* (London, England: Thames and Hudson, 1982 reprint), p.75.

[31] Shaun Willcock, *The Pagan Festivals of Christmas and Easter* (Pietermaritzburg, South Africa: Bible Based Ministries, 1992), p.19.

[32] Becker, *op. cit.,* p.242.

[33] Rex R. Hutchens, *A Bridge to Light* (Washington, D.C.: Supreme Council, 33° Ancient and Accepted Scottish Rite of Freemasonry, Southern Jurisdiction, 1988), p.201.

[34] *Siva's Cosmic Dance* (San Francisco, California: Himalayan Academy), p.4.

[35] Jean Chevalier and Alain Gheerbrant, *A Dictionary of Symbols* (Blackwell Publishers, 1994), p.140.

[36] *Ibid.*

[37] *Ibid.,* p.141.

[38] *Connecting Link* (November/December 1989, Vol. 1, No. 5), p.18.

[39] Johanna Michaelsen, *The Beautiful Side of Evil* (Eugene, Oregon: Harvest House Publishers, 1982), p.165.

[40] Dennis Laurence Cuddy, *Now Is the Dawning of the New Age New World Order* (Oklahoma City, Oklahoma: Hearthstone Publishing Ltd., 1991), p.10.

[41] *Ibid.,* p.280-281; Texe Marrs, *Millennium: Peace, Promises, and the Day They Take Our Money Away* (Austin, Texas: Living Truth Publishers, 1990), p.183-185.

[42] Manly Palmer Hall, *The Secret Destiny of America* (New York, New York: Philosophical Library, Inc., 1958), p.176-177; See also: Manly Palmer Hall, *The Lost Keys of Freemasonry* (Richmond, Virginia: Macoy Publishing and Masonic Supply Company, Inc., 1976 Edition), p.107-108; William T. Still, *New World Order: The Ancient Plan of Secret Societies* (Lafayette, Louisiana: Huntington House, Inc., 1990), p.65; J. S. M. Ward and W. G. Stirling, *The Hung Society or the Society of Heaven and Earth* (Vol. 1) (London, England: The Baskerville Press, Limited, 1925), p.44; Friedrich Rest, *Our Christian Symbols* (Philadelphia, Pennsylvania: The Christian Education Press, 1954), p.64; Richard Leviton, "Where Mind and Body Meet," *East West* (November 1989, Vol. 10, No. 11), p.53; *Man, Myth and Magic: The Illustrated Encyclopedia of Mythology, Religion and the Unknown* (North Bellmore, New York: Marshall Cavendish Corporation, 1994), p.2033.

[43] Manly Palmer Hall, *America's Assignment with Destiny* (Los Angeles, California: Philosophical Research Society, Inc., 1951), p.42.

[44] Hall, *The Secret Destiny of America, op. cit.,* p.177.

[45] Cuddy quoting Barbara Walker, *Now Is the Dawning, op. cit.,* p.281.

[46] William Schnoebelen, "Satan's Door Revisited," *Saints Alive in Jesus* (March 1992), p.4.

[47] William Schnoebelen, *Masonry: Beyond the Light* (Chino, California: Chick Publications, 1991), p.122.

[48] Cirlot, *op. cit.,* p.98.

[49] Budge, *op. cit.*, p.244; See also: Sir Wallis Budge, *Egyptian Magic* (Secaucus, New Jersey, Inc., n.d.), p.32-33; *Ritual National Imperial Court of the Daughters of Isis North and South America* (Ezra A. Cook Publications, Inc., n.d.), p.2.

[50] Joseph Fort Newton, *The Builders: A Story and Study of Masonry* (Cedar Rapids, Iowa: The Torch Press, 1914), p.13-14; See also: J. S. M. Ward and W. G. Stirling, *The Hung Society or the Society of Heaven and Earth* (Vol. 1) (London, England: The Baskerville Press, Limited, 1925), p.44, 102.

[51] Hutchens, *op. cit.*, p.318-319.

[52] Sharon Boyd, "Occult America: The U.S.: Founded on Occultism Not Christianity," *What Is* (1987, Vol. 1, No. 2), p.12.

[53] *Ibid.*

[54] *Holy Bible* (Wichita Kansas: Heirloom Bible Publishers, 1971), p.40; See also: George Oliver, *Signs and Symbols* (New York: Macoy Publishing and Masonic Supply Company, 1906), p.48; R. Swinburne Clymer, *The Mysteries of Osiris or Ancient Egyptian Initiation* (Quakertown, Pennsylvania: The Philosophical Publishing Company, 1951, Revised Edition), p.220; Kenneth R. H. MacKenzie, Editor, *The Royal Masonic Cyclopaedia of History, Rites, Symbolism, and Biography* (New York: J. W. Bouton, 1877), p.168; Lewis Spence, *Myths and Legends of Babylonia and Assyria* (London, England: George G. Harrap and Company, 1916), p.296.

[55] *Ibid.*

[56] Henry C. Clausen, *Clausen's Commentaries on Morals and Dogma* (The Supreme Council, 33°, Ancient and Accepted Scottish Rite of Freemasonry, Southern Jurisdiction, 1974), p.79, 167.

[57] *Self-Help Update* (Issue 27), p.13.

[58] Boyd, *op. cit.;* See also: Jim Tresner, "Wings of the Eagle, Wings on Our Feet," *Scottish Rite Journal* (July 1998), p.7-8.

[59] *Ibid.*

[60] A. Ralph Epperson, *The New World Order* (Tucson, Arizona: Publius Press, 1990), p.138.

[61] *Ibid.,* quoting Rex Hutchens, p.139

[62] Pike, *op. cit.*, p.291, 254; Albert Pike, *The Magnum Opus* (Kila, Montana: Kessinger Publishing Company, 1992), p.xviii.

[63] Manly Palmer Hall, *The Secret Teachings of All Ages* (Los Angeles, California: The Philosophical Research Society Press, 1945), p.lxxxix.

[64] *Ibid.;* Cirlot *op. cit.*, p.92; Walter McLeod, Editor, *Beyond the Pillars* (Grand Lodge A.F. & A.M. of Canada, 1973), p.100.

[65] Albert Churchward, *Signs and Symbols of Primordial Man: The Evolution of Religious Doctrine from the Eschatology of the Ancient Egyptians* (London, England: George Allen and Company, Ltd., 1913, Second Edition), p.459.

[66] Cirlot *op. cit.*, p.91.

[67] *Ibid.*, p.278.

[68] R. Swinburne Clymer, *The Mysteries of Osiris or Ancient Egyptian Initiation* (Quakertown, Pennsylvania: The Philosophical Publishing Company, 1951, Revised Edition), p.42.

[69] Cirlot *op. cit.,* p.92-93.

[70] Hutchens, *op. cit.,* p.284.

[71] Mustafa El-Amin, *Freemasonry: Ancient Egypt and the Islamic Destiny* (Jersey City, New Jersey: New Mind Productions, 1988), p.24.

[72] Jim Tresner, "Wings of the Eagle, Wings on Our Feet," *Scottish Rite Journal* (July 1998), p.7.

[73] Herbert F. Inman, *Masonic Problems and Queries* (London, England: A. Lewis Ltd., 1978), p.210; See also: Charles G. Berger, *Our Phallic Heritage* (New York, New York: Greenwich Book Publishers, Inc., 1966), p.204.

[74] Cirlot, *op. cit.,* p.286-288.

[75] Sandra L. Koch, *Combating the New Age Movement: A Christian Warfare Manual* (Boca Raton, Florida: Foundation Tabernacle Ministries, Inc., n.d.); See also: Robert S. Liichow, *The Two Roots of Today's Revival* (Kearney, Nebraska: Morris Publishing, 1997), p.209-212.

[76] Alain Danielou, *The Gods of India* (New York, New York: Inner Traditions International Ltd., 1985), p.217, 219.

[77] Lash, *op. cit.,* p.336.

[78] George Oliver, *Signs and Symbols* (New York: Macoy Publishing and Masonic Supply Company, 1906), p.36.

[79] *Ibid.,* p.33.

[80] Clymer, *op. cit.,* p.128.

[81] Rollin C. Blackmer, *The Lodge and the Craft: A Practical Explanation of the Work of Freemasonry* (St. Louis, Missouri: The Standard Masonic Publishing Company, 1923), p.249.

[82] Charles G. Berger, *Our Phallic Heritage* (New York, New York: Greenwich Book Publishers, Inc., 1966), p.31-32.

[83] Clymer, *op. cit.*

[84] Miranda Bruce-Mitford, *The Illustrated Book of Signs and Symbols* (1996), p.108.

[85] Frank Gaynor, Editor, *Dictionary of Mysticism* (New York: Philosophical Library, 1953), p.132.

[86] Clymer, *op. cit.,* p.134; *The New Age Magazine* (June 1973, Vol. 81, No. 6), p.17; Oliver, *op. cit.,* p.33; Hutchens, *op. cit.,* p.252.

[87] R. Swinburne Clymer, *The Mysteries of Osiris or Ancient Egyptian Initiation* (Quakertown, Pennsylvania: The Philosophical Publishing Company, 1951, Revised Edition), p.131.

[88] Oliver, *op. cit.,* p.27.

[89] Hall, *The Secret Teachings of All Ages, op. cit.,* p.lxxxviii.

[90] Lynn F. Perkins, *Masonry in the New Age* (Lakemont, Georgia: CSA Press, 1971), p.99.

[91] *Ibid.*

[92] *Ibid.,* p.100.

[93] Pike, *op. cit.,* p.734; See also: Hutchens, *op. cit.,* p.253

[94] Berger, *op. cit.,* p.60.

[95] Lash, *op. cit.,* p.224.

[96] Cirlot, *op. cit.,* p.22; See also: Thomas Bulfinch, *Bulfinch's Mythology: The Age of Fable or Stories of Gods and Heroes* (Garden City, New York: Doubleday and Company, Inc., 1948), p.338.

[97] Rebecca Carina, "The Bee and Sweetness of Life," *Lightworks* (January 1996).

[98] "The Bee Hive," *The Short Talk Bulletin* (September 1951, Vol. 29, No. 9), p.5.

[99] Kenneth R. H. MacKenzie, Editor, *The Royal Masonic Cyclopaedia of History, Rites, Symbolism, and Biography* (New York: J. W. Bouton, 1877), p.71.

[100] C. F. McQuaig, *The Masonic Report* (Norcross, Georgia: Answer Books and Tapes), p.53.

[101] Texe Marrs, *Circle of Intrigue* (Austin, Texas: Living Truth Ministries, 1995), p.219.

[102] H. L. Haywood, *Symbolic Masonry: An Interpretation of the Three Degrees* (Washington, D.C.: Masonic Service Association of the United States, 1923), p.287.

[103] *Ibid.*

[104] Norman MacKenzie, Editor, *Secret Societies* (1967), p.143.

[105] Willcock, *op. cit.*

[106] Arthur Edward Waite, *A New Encyclopedia of Freemasonry and of Cognate Instituted Mysteries: Their Rites, Literature and History* (Vol. I) (New York: Weathervane Books, 1970), p.61-61.

[107] John Yarker, *The Arcane Schools: A Review of Their Origin and Antiquity: With a General History of Freemasonry and Its Relation to the Theosophic Scientific and Philosophic Mysteries* (Belfast, Ireland: William Tait, 1909), p.267.

[108] William O. Peterson, Editor, *Masonic Quiz Book: "Ask Me Another, Brother"* (Chicago, Illinois: Charles T. Powner Company, 1950), p.32, 133; See also: William Adrian Brown, *Facts, Fables and Fantasies of Freemasonry* (New York, New York: Vantage Press, Inc., 1968), p.169.

[109] John T. Lawrence, *The Perfect Ashlar* (London: A. Lewis, 1912), p.295, updated language. The quotation actually reads: "At ye makeing of ye Toure of Babell, there was Masonrie first much esteemed of, and the King of Babilon yt was called Nimrod was a mason himself and loved well Masons."

[110] Kenneth MacKenzie, *op. cit.,* p.308.

[111] Helena Petrovna Blavatsky, *Isis Unveiled,* Vol. I: Science (New York, New York: Trow's Printing and Bookbinding Company, 1877), p.554, xxxiii.

[112] Becker, *op. cit.,* p.38; *The Authorized Standard Ritual of the Order of the Eastern Star* (New York: Press of Andrew H. Kellogg Company, 1916 Edition), p.203.

[113] Fritz Springmeier, *The Top 13 Illuminati Bloodlines* (Portland, Oregon: Fritz Springmeier), p.85.

[114] Dave Hunt, *The Cult Explosion* (Eugene, Oregon: Harvest House Publishers, 1980), p.77.

[115] "The Bee Hive," *The Short Talk Bulletin, op. cit.,* p.4-5.

[116] Texe Marrs, *How Will We Know the Antichrist? 21 Ways to Identify the Beast of Prophecy* (Austin, Texas: Living Truth Publishers, 1990), p.2.

[117] Eric Barger, *From Rock to Rock: The Music of Darkness Exposed!* (Lafayette, Louisiana: Huntington House, Inc., 1990), p.117.

[118] Berger, *op. cit.,* p.37; See also: Gaynor, *op. cit.,* p.163.

[119] Veronica Ions, *Egyptian Mythology* (Middlesex, England: The Hamlyn Publishing Group Ltd., 1965), p.26, 46.

[120] *Ibid.,* p.26.

[121] *Circle Network News* (Spring 1986, Vol. 8, No. 1), p.12; See also: Phil Phillips, *Saturday Morning Mind Control* (Nashville, Tennessee: Oliver-Nelson Books, 1991), p.190; Barger, *op. cit.,* p.117, 118.

[122] *New Larousse Encyclopedia of Mythology, op. cit.,* p.3; See also: *Circle Network News* (Spring 1986, Vol. 8, No. 1), p.12; Ions, *op. cit.,* p.24.

[123] Anton Szandor LaVey, *The Satanic Bible* (New: Avon Books, 1969), p.60; See also p.58.

[124] Orion, "Moonchild—Take Heart Scarab—Not Cancer—Thou Art," *Sphaera Imaginatio #16,* p.17.

[125] Autumn Moon, "Amulets of the Nile Gods," *Circle Network News* (Summer 1987, Vol. 9, No. 2), p.14; Sir Wallis Budge, *Egyptian Magic* (Secaucus, New Jersey: University Books, Inc., n.d.), p.36.

[126] Wedeck, *op. cit.,* p.134-135.

[127] Hutchens, *op. cit.,* p.213.

[128] Cirlot *op. cit.,* p.143; See also: Arthur Edward Waite, *The Mysteries of Magic: A Digest of the Writings of Eliphas Levi* (Chicago, Illinois: De Laurence, Scott and Company, 1909), p.299.

[129] Hall, *The Secret Teachings of All Ages, op. cit.,* p.xci.

[130] Alice A. Bailey, *Discipleship in the New Age* (Vol. II) (New York: Lucis Publishing Company, 1955), p.62; See also: Lash, *op. cit.,* p.279.

[131] Texe Marrs quoting Alice Bailey, *Millennium: Peace, Promises, and the Day They Take Our Money Away* (Austin, Texas: Living Truth Publishers, 1990), p.224.

[132] Cooper, *op. cit.*

[133] *The Living Unicorn* (Carver, Minnesota: The Living Unicorn, Inc., 1980), p.13. See also: Wanda Marrs, *New Age Lies to Women* (Austin, Texas: Living Truth Publishers, 1989), p.69.

[134] Al Dager, *The Unicorn: Fabled Beast of Myth and Magic* (Costa Mesa, California: Media Spotlight, n.d.), unnumbered page.

[135] *Ibid.;* See also: Phil Phillips, *Turmoil in the Toybox* (Lancaster, Pennsylvania: Starburst Publishers, 1986), p.79.

[136] *The Living Unicorn, op. cit.,* p.3.

[137] *Ibid.*

[138] *Ibid.,* p.5.

[139] Lash, *op. cit.,* p.394; See also: Maurice Bessy, *A Pictorial History of Magic and the Supernatural* (Hamlyn Publishing Group Limited, 1964), p.128; *Meditation* (Winter 1991, Vol. 6, No. 1), Back Cover.

[140] Texe Marrs, *Mystery Mark of the New Age: Satan's Design for World Domination* (Westchester, Illinois: Crossway Books, 1988), p.116.

[141] Catalog from Little Shop of Incense (Spring 1987).

[142] *The Llewellyn New Times* (January/February 1987, #871), p.68.

[143] Margot Adler, *Drawing Down the Moon: Witches, Druids, Goddess-Worshippers, and Other Pagans in America Today,* (New York, New York: The Viking Press, 1979), p.412

[144] *Llewellyn New Times, op. cit.* p.61.

[145] Laurie Cabot with Tom Cowan, *Power of the Witch: The Earth, the Moon, and the Magical Path to Enlightenment* (New York, New York: Delacorte Press, 1989), p.306, 308.

[146] Cuddy, *op. cit.,* p.317.

Chapter 12: Winged Symbols

[1] J. E. Cirlot (Translated by Jack Sage), *A Dictionary of Symbols* (New York: Dorset Press, 1991), p.374.

[2] Paul Hamlyn, *Greek Mythology* (London: Paul Hamlyn, Ltd., 1967), p.50-51; *The New Age Magazine* (June 1973, Vol. 81, No. 6), p.16; Albert E. Bedworth and David A. Bedworth, *Health for Human Effectiveness* (Englewood Cliffs, New Jersey: Prentice-Hall, Inc., 1982), p.6; Edith Hamilton, *Mythology* (Boston, Massachusetts: Little, Brown and Company, 1942), p.34; Richard Patrick, *All Color Book of Greek Mythology* (London, England: Octopus Books Limited, 1972), p.46; *The World Book Encyclopedia* (1961 Edition, Vol. 12), p.340; Thomas Bulfinch, *Bulfinch's Mythology: The Age of Fable or Stories of Gods and Heroes* (Garden City, New York: Doubleday and Company, Inc., 1948), p.7.

[3] Albert E. Bedworth and David A. Bedworth, *Health for Human Effectiveness* (Englewood Cliffs, New Jersey: Prentice-Hall, Inc., 1982), p.6

[4] Carl C. Jung, M.-L. von Franz, Joseph L. Henderson, Jolande Jacobe, Aniela Jaffe, *Man and His Symbols* (Garden City, New Jersey: Doubleday and Company, Inc., 1964), p.156.

[5] *The World Book Encyclopedia* (1961 Edition, Vol. 12), p.340; See also: *Health* (February 1986), p.80; Percival George Woodcock, *Short Dictionary of Mythology* (Philosophical Library, 1953), p.94; *New Larousse Encyclopedia of Mythology* (Prometheus Press, 1972 Edition), p.238; *Perceptions* (Summer 1993, Vol. 1, Issue 2), p.20; Frank Gaynor, Editor, *Dictionary of Mysticism* (New York: Philosophical Library, 1953), p.77; Thomas Bulfinch, *Bulfinch's Mythology: The Age of Fable or Stories of Gods and Heroes* (Garden City, New York: Doubleday and Company, Inc., 1948), p.7; Edith Hamilton, *Mythology* (Boston, Massachusetts: Little, Brown and Company, 1942), p.34; Thomas Bulfinch, *The Age of Fable or the Beauties of Mythology* (New York: The Heritage Press, 1942), p.9; Joseph Campbell, *The Masks of God: Creative Mythology* (New York, New York: The Viking Press, 1968), p.203.

[6] *Ibid.;* See also: "The Masonic Rod," *Short Talk Bulletin* (September 1957; Vol. 35, No. 9; Reprinted March 1986), p.6; Edith Hamilton, *Mythology* (Boston, Massachusetts: Little, Brown and Company, 1942), p.35; Percival George Woodcock, *Short Dictionary of Mythology* (Philosophical Library, 1953), p.94.

[7] *New Larousse Encyclopedia of Mythology* (Prometheus Press, 1972 Edition), p.238.

[8] Harry E. Wedeck, *Treasury of Witchcraft* (New York, New York: Philosophical Library, 1961), p.8.

[9] *Ibid.,* p.188.

[10] Bedworth and Bedworth, *op. cit.; The New Age Magazine* (June 1973, Vol. 81, No. 6), p.16; Campbell, *The Hero with a Thousand Faces, op. cit.,* p.72.

[11] Albert Pike, *Morals and Dogma of the Ancient and Accepted Scottish Rite of Freemasonry* (Richmond, Virginia: L. H. Jenkins, Inc., 1871), p.506.

[12] *Ibid.,* p.586.

[13] Catalog from Sounds True, Inside front cover; Edith Hamilton, *Mythology* (Boston, Massachusetts: Little, Brown and Company, 1942), p.44.

[14] *The New Age Magazine* (June 1973, Vol. 81, No. 6), p.16; See also: J. P. Brooke-Little, *An Heraldic Alphabet* (New York: Arco Publishing Company, Inc., 1973), p.57; Frank Gaynor, Editor, *Dictionary of Mysticism* (New York: Philosophical Library, 1953), p.31; Percival George Woodcock, *Short Dictionary of Mythology* (Philosophical Library, 1953), p.29; Thomas Bulfinch, *Bulfinch's Mythology: The Age of Fable or Stories of Gods and Heroes* (Garden City, New York: Doubleday and Company, Inc., 1948), p.7; Thomas Bulfinch, *The Age of Fable or the Beauties of Mythology* (New York: The Heritage Press, 1942), p.9; Charles G. Berger, *Our Phallic Heritage* (New York, New York: Greenwich Book Publishers, Inc., 1966), p.204; William O. Peterson, Editor, *Masonic Quiz Book: "Ask Me Another, Brother"* (Chicago, Illinois: Charles T. Powner Company, 1950), p.256.

[15] Percival George Woodcock, *Short Dictionary of Mythology* (New York: Philosophical Library, 1953), p.29; See also: *The New Age Magazine* (June 1973, Vol. 81, No. 6), p.16.

[16] Cirlot *op. cit.,* p.35-37.

[17] Pike, *op. cit.,* p.502; *Ibid.,* p.35.

[18] Laurie Cabot and Tom Cowan, *The Power of the Witch: The Earth, the Moon, and the Magical Path to Enlightenment* (New York, New York: Delacorte Press, 1989), p.114.

[19] David L. Carrico, *Lucifer—Eliphas Levi—Albert Pike and the Masonic Lodge* (Evansville, Indiana: Followers of Jesus Christ, 1991), p.18-22; J. D. Buck, *Mystic Masonry* (Illinois: Indo-American Book Company, 1913, Sixth Edition), p.xvi; Arthur Edward Waite, *The Holy Kabbalah* (London: Williams and Norgate Ltd., 1929), p. 553; Arthur Edward Waite, *The Secret Tradition in Freemasonry* (London: Rider and Company, 1937), p.619; Joseph Fort Newton, *The Builders: A Story and Study of Masonry* (Cedar Rapids, Iowa: The Torch Press, 1914), p.66; Arthur Edward Waite, *An Encyclopedia of Freemasonry and of Cognate Instituted Mysteries: Their Rites, Literature and History* (Vol. II) (New York: Weathervane Books, 1970), p.278; Rex R. Hutchens and Donald W. Monson, *The Bible in Albert Pike's Morals and Dogma* (Washington, D.C.: Supreme Council, 33rd Degree, 1992), p.19, 29, 42, 45, 63, 71, 101, 102, 103, 159, 170, 172, 174, 177, 178, 181, 243, 244; Robert A. Morey, *The Origins and Teachings of Freemasonry* (Southbridge, Massachusetts: Crowne Publications, Inc., 1990), p.37, 38, 49, 75.

[20] Lucien V. Rule, *Pioneering in Masonry: The Life and Times of Rob Morris, Masonic Poet Laureate, Together with Story of Clara Barton and the Eastern Star* (Louisville, Kentucky: Brandt and Connors Company, 1922), p.158.

[21] Arthur Edward Waite, *The Mysteries of Magic: A Digest of the Writings of Eliphas Levi* (Chicago, Illinois: De Laurence, Scott and Company, 1909), p.214.

[22] H. P. Blavatsky, *The Secret Doctrine: The Synthesis of Science, Religion, and Philosophy* (Vol. II—Anthropogenesis) (Covina, California: Theosophical University Press, 1947, Fourth Edition), p.364.

[23] "The Masonic Rod," *Short Talk Bulletin* (September 1957; Vol. 35, No. 9; Reprinted March 1986), p.3-4.

[24] William O. Peterson, Editor, *Masonic Quiz Book: "Ask Me Another, Brother"* (Chicago, Illinois: Charles T. Powner Company, 1950), p.256.

[25] Kenneth R. H. MacKenzie, Editor, "Caduceus," *The Royal Masonic Cyclopaedia of History, Rites, Symbolism, and Biography* (New York: J. W. Bouton, 1877), p.89.

[26] Peterson, *op. cit.*

[27] Pike, *op. cit.*, p.502-503.

[28] Count Goblet D'Alviella, *The Migration of Symbols* (Westminster: Archibald Constable and Company, 1894), p.230.

[29] Blavatsky, *op. cit.*, (Vol. I—Cosmogenesis), p.365.

[30] Charles Clyde Hunt, *Some Thoughts on Masonic Symbolism* (New York: Macoy Publishing and Masonic Supply Company, 1930), p.123.

[31] Pike, *op. cit.*, p.496.

[32] *The New Age Magazine* (June 1973, Vol. 81, No. 6), p.17; See also: Peterson, *op. cit.*, p.83.

[33] George Oliver, *Signs and Symbols* (New York: Macoy Publishing and Masonic Supply Company, 1906), p.33.

[34] Pike, *op. cit.*, p.500.

[35] Fritz Springmeier, *The Watchtower and the Masons* (Portland, Oregon, 1992), p.xi.

[36] *Ibid.*, p.115.

[37] Frank Gaynor, Editor, *Dictionary of Mysticism* (New York: Philosophical Library, 1953), p.102.

[38] Eric Barger, *From Rock to Rock: The Music of Darkness Exposed!* (Lafayette, Louisiana: Huntington House, Inc., 1990), p.117.

[39] *Ibid.*, p.117, 156.

[40] S. R. Parchment, *Ancient Operative Masonry* (San Francisco, California: San Francisco Center—Rosicrucian Fellowship, 1930), p.125.

[41] Pike, *op. cit.*, p.850-851.

[42] John Yarker, *The Arcane Schools: A Review of Their Origin and Antiquity; with a General History of Freemasonry, and Its Relation to the Theosophic, Scientific, and Philosophic Mysteries* (Belfast, Ireland: William Tait, 1909), p.208.

[43] John Sebastian Marlow Ward, *The Sign Language of the Mysteries* (New York: Land's End Press, 1969), p.185-186.

[44] Rex R. Hutchens, *A Bridge to Light* (Washington, D.C.: Supreme Council, 33° Ancient and Accepted Scottish Rite of Freemasonry, Southern Jurisdiction, 1988), p.201.

[45] *Ibid.*, p.300-301.

[46] Jacques Duchesne-Guillemin, Edited by Ruth Nanda Anshen, *Symbols and Values in Zoroastrianism: Their Survival and Renewal* (New York, New York: Harper and Row, 1966, p.17.

[47] Springmeier, *op. cit.*, p.153.

[48] Texe Marrs, *Texe Marrs Book of New Age Cults and Religions* (Austin, Texas: Living Truth Publishers, 1990), p.228.

[49] Cirlot *op. cit.,* 82.

[50] *New Larousse Encyclopedia of Mythology, op. cit.,* p.21; See also: Veronica Ions, *Egyptian Mythology* (Middlesex, England: The Hamlyn Publishing Group Ltd., 1965), p.68; Henry Ridgely Evans, "Egyptian Decorations of Naval Lodge No. 4, Washington, D.C.," *The New Age Magazine* (May 1948, Vol. 56, No. 5).

[51] Charles F. Pfeiffer, Editor, *The Biblical World: A Dictionary of Biblical Archaeology* (New York: Bonanza Books, 1966), p.206.

[52] Veronica Ions, *Egyptian Mythology* (Middlesex, England: The Hamlyn Publishing Group Ltd., 1965), p.24.

[53] Geoffrey Parringer, Editor, *World Religions: From Ancient History to the Present* (New York, New York: Facts on File Publications, 1983), p.116.

[54] *New Larousse Encyclopedia of Mythology, op. cit.,* p.57; Lewis Spence, *Myths and Legends of Babylonia and Assyria* (London, England: George G. Harrap and Company, 1916), p.206-208; Gaynor, *op. cit.,* p.17.

[55] Springmeier, *op. cit.,* p.111, 127.

[56] *Ibid.,* p.ii-iii.

[57] J. S. M. Ward, *Freemasonry and the Ancient Gods* (London, England: Simpkin, Marshall, Hamilton, Kent and Company Ltd., 1921), p.64.

[58] Manly Palmer Hall, *America's Assignment with Destiny* (Los Angeles, California: Philosophical Research Society, Inc., 1951), p.31-32.

[59] Henry Ridgely Evans, "Egyptian Decorations of Naval Lodge No. 4, Washington, D.C.," *The New Age Magazine* (May 1948, Vol. 56, No. 5).

[60] *New Larousse Encyclopedia of Mythology* (Prometheus Press, 1972 Edition), p.22.

[61] *Ibid.,* p.29; See also: Evans, *op. cit.,* p.284.

[62] Catalog from Dancing Dragon Designs (Summer 1990), p.2.

[63] Phil Phillips, *Saturday Morning Mind Control* (Nashville, Tennessee: Oliver-Nelson Books, 1991), p.115.

[64] *Ibid.*

[65] Phil Phillips, *Turmoil in the Toybox* (Lancaster, Pennsylvania: Starburst Publishers, 1986), p. 78-79; See also: Albert James Dager, *Dragonraid: Can Fantasy Role-Playing Games Be "Christianized"?,* unnumbered page; *National Enquirer* (May 27, 1986), p.61.

[66] Texe Marrs, *Mystery Mark of the New Age: Satan's Design for World Domination* (Westchester, Illinois: Crossway Books, 1988), p.116.

[67] Hamlyn, *op. cit.,* p.142.

[68] *New Larousse Encyclopedia of Mythology, op. cit.* p.135.

[69] Pike, *op. cit.,* p.15, 597; *Ibid.,* p.13; George Oliver, *Signs and Symbols* (New York: Macoy Publishing and Masonic Supply Company, 1906), p.94; *The World Book Encyclopedia,* (1961 Edition, Vol. 16), p.129; Thomas Bulfinch, *Bulfinch's Mythology* (New York: Thomas Y. Crowell Company, Inc., 1970), p.967; Arthur Coon, *The Theosophical Seal* (no other info available), p.190; Cirlot *op. cit.,* p.67, 278; A. T. C. Pierson, *The Traditions, Origin and Early History of Freemasonry*

(New York: Masonic Publishing Company, 1865), p.221; Aleister Crowley, *Seven, Seven, Seven* (no other information available), p.73; R. Swinburne Clymer, *The Mysteries of Osiris or Ancient Egyptian Initiation* (Quakertown, Pennsylvania: The Philosophical Publishing Company, 1951, Revised Edition), p.111; 278; M. Esther Harding, *Woman's Mysteries: Ancient and Modern* (New York: G. P. Putnam's Sons for the C. G. Jung Foundation for Analytical Psychology, 1971 Edition), p.94.

[70] *The World Book Encyclopedia* (1961 Edition, Vol. 16), p.129.

[71] *Ibid.;* Thomas Bulfinch, *Bulfinch's Mythology* (New York: Thomas Y. Crowell Company, Inc., 1970), p.920, 967; Woodcock, *op. cit.,* p.35; Thomas Bulfinch, *Bulfinch's Mythology: The Age of Fable or Stories of Gods and Heroes* (Garden City, New York: Doubleday and Company, Inc., 1948), p.9; Charles G. Berger, *Our Phallic Heritage* (New York, New York: Greenwich Book Publishers, Inc., 1966), p.40; Gustav Schwab, *Gods and Heroes: Myths and Epics of Ancient Greece* (New York: Pantheon Books, 1946), p.36; Thomas Bulfinch, *Bulfinch's Mythology* (New York: Thomas Y. Crowell Company, Inc., 1970), p.967; Arthur Coon, *The Theosophical Seal* (no other info available), p.190; Edith Hamilton, *Mythology* (Boston, Massachusetts: Little, Brown and Company, 1942), p.21, 51; Helena Petrovna Blavatsky, *Isis Unveiled,* Vol. I: Science (New York, New York: Trow's Printing and Bookbinding Company, 1877), p.263; Clifton L. Fowler, *Santa Claus and Christmas* (Knoxville, Tennessee: Evangelist of Truth, 1982), p.28; Hamlyn, *op. cit.,* p.7.

[72] Ward, *op. cit.,* p.232; See also: Texe Marrs, *Mystery Mark of the New Age: Satan's Design for World Domination* (Westchester, Illinois: Crossway Books, 1988), p.69.

[73] Waite, *op. cit.,* p.214.

[74] Texe Marrs, *Mystery Mark of the New Age: Satan's Design for World Domination* (Westchester, Illinois: Crossway Books, 1988), p.68.

[75] Woodcock, *op. cit.,* p.135.

[76] Robert Macoy, *A Dictionary of Freemasonry: A Compendium of Masonic History, Symbolism, Rituals, Literature, and Myth* (New York: Bell Publishing Company, n.d.), p.65.

[77] Helena Petrovna Blavatsky, *Isis Unveiled,* Vol. I: Science (New York, New York: Trow's Printing and Bookbinding Company, 1877), p.263, 578.

[78] William Schnoebelen, *Masonry: Beyond the Light* (Chino, California: Chick Publications, 1991), p.158.

[79] *The World Book Encyclopedia* (1961 Edition, Vol. 16), p.250.

[80] Charles G. Berger, *Our Phallic Heritage* (New York, New York: Greenwich Book Publishers, Inc., 1966), p.40, 80; Cirlot, *op. cit.,* p.279; Clifton L. Fowler, *Santa Claus and Christmas* (Knoxville, Tennessee: Evangelist of Truth, 1982), p.28; Al Dager, *Origins of Christmas Traditions* (Costa Mesa, California: Media Spotlight, 1985 Special Report), unnumbered page; *CIB Bulletin* (December 1989; Vol. 5, No. 12), p.1; Anthony Frewin, *The Book of Days* (St. James Place, London: William Collins Sons and Company, Ltd., 1979), p.384; "Babel Becomes One," *The Omega-Letter* (April 1990, Vol. 5, No. 4), p.7; Ralph Edward Woodrow, *Babylon Mystery Religion: Ancient and Modern* (Riverside, California: Ralph Woodrow Evangelistic Association, Inc., 1990 Edition), p.143; Peter Lalonde, *One World Under Antichrist* (Eugene, Oregon: Harvest House Publishers, 1991), p.59; Woodcock, *op. cit.,* p.134; Dave Hunt, *Whatever Happened to Heaven?* (Eugene, Oregon: Harvest House Publishers, 1988), p.113.

[81] Al Dager, *Origins of Christmas Traditions* (Costa Mesa, California: Media Spotlight, 1985 Special Report), unnumbered page.

[82] Clifton L. Fowler, *Santa Claus and Christmas* (Knoxville, Tennessee: Evangelist of Truth, 1982), p.28.

[83] Anton Szandor LaVey, *The Satanic Bible* (New York: Avon Books, 1969), p.98; Henry C. Clausen, *Clausen's Commentaries on Morals and Dogma* (Supreme Council, 33rd Degree, Ancient and Accepted Scottish Rite of Freemasonry, Southern Jurisdiction, USA, 1974), p.142, Joseph Fort Newton, *The Builders: A Story and Study of Masonry* (Cedar Rapids, Iowa: The Torch Press, 1914), p.183; George H. Steinmetz, *Freemasonry: Its Hidden Meaning* (New York: Macoy Publishing and Masonic Supply Company, 1948), p.93-94; *What? When? Where? Why? Who? in Freemasonry* (Silver Spring, Maryland: Masonic Service Association of the United States, 1956), p.67-68; Allen E. Roberts, *The Craft and Its Symbols: Opening the Door to Masonic Symbolism* (Richmond, Virginia: Macoy Publishing and Masonic Supply Company, Inc., 1974), p.36; W. L. Wilmshurst, *The Masonic Initiation* (Ferndale, Michigan: Trismegistus Press, 1980; Originally published 1924), p.95, 187-188; "Sts. Johns' Days," *Short Talk Bulletin* (December 1933; Vol. 11, No. 12; Reprinted July 1986), p.5-6, 8; Texe Marrs, *Millennium: Peace, Promises, and the Day They Take Our Money Away* (Austin, Texas: Living Truth Publishers, 1990), p.50; Albert G. Mackey, *A Manual of the Lodge* (New York: Charles E. Merrill Company, 1870), p.57; Charles H. Vail, *The Ancient Mysteries and Modern Masonry* (New York: Macoy Publishing and Masonic Supply Company, 1909), p.51-52, 135-136, 186; Colin F. W. Dyer, *Symbolism in Craft Freemasonry* (England: A Lewis, Ltd., 1976), p.98, 100-101; Albert G. Mackey, *The Symbolism of Freemasonry* (New York: Clark and Maynard, 1869), p.115; J. D. Buck, *Mystic Masonry* (Illinois: Indo-American Book Company, 1913, Sixth Edition), p.86; Albert Churchward, *Signs and Symbols of Primordial Man* (London: George Allen and Company, Ltd., 1913, Second Edition), p.289.

[84] Waite, *The Mysteries of Magic, op. cit.,* p.217; Woodcock, *op. cit.,* p.135; Cirlot *op. cit.,* p.281; *The World Book Encyclopedia* (1961 Edition, Vol. 16), p.129; Berger, *op. cit.,* p.41.

[85] Cirlot *op. cit.,* p.281; See also: George Oliver, *Signs and Symbols* (New York: Macoy Publishing and Masonic Supply Company, 1906), p.82; Charles Scott, *The Analogy of Ancient Craft Masonry to Natural and Revealed Religion* (Philadelphia, Pennsylvania: E. H. Butler and Company, 1857), p.311.

[86] George Oliver, *Signs and Symbols* (New York: Macoy Publishing and Masonic Supply Company, 1906), p.82; Charles Scott, *The Analogy of Ancient Craft Masonry to Natural and Revealed Religion* (Philadelphia, Pennsylvania: E. H. Butler and Company, 1857), p.311; *Pocket Masonic Dictionary* (Silver Spring, Maryland: The Masonic Service Association of the United States, February 1988), p.25; Berger, *op. cit.,* p.41.

[87] *Pocket Masonic Dictionary* (Silver Spring, Maryland: The Masonic Service Association of the United States, February 1988), p.27.

[88] Waite, *The Mysteries of Magic, op. cit.,* p.217.

[89] Woodcock, *op. cit.,* p.41.

[90] *New Larousse Encyclopedia of Mythology, op. cit.,* p.132; See also: Hamlyn, *op. cit.,* 1967).

[91] G. O. Marx, "Why I Don't Want to Be Your Valentine," *The Voice in the Wilderness* (February 1992), p.14.

[92] Paul R. Cannon, "Venereal Disease," *The World Book Encyclopedia* (1961 Edition, Vol. 18), p.239.

[93] Cirlot *op. cit.,* p.31.

Chapter 13: Organizational Logos

[1] H. Spencer Lewis, *Rosicrucian Manual* (Vol. No. 8), (San Jose, California: Supreme Grand Lodge of AMORC, 1966), p.137-138.

[2] Laurie Cabot with Tom Cowan, *Power of the Witch: The Earth, the Moon, and the Magical Path* (New York, New York: Delacorte Press, 1989), Inside front cover.

[3] *Ibid.,* p.149-150.

[4] Rex R. Hutchens, *A Bridge to Light* (Washington, D.C.: Supreme Council, 33° Ancient and Accepted Scottish Rite of Freemasonry, Southern Jurisdiction, 1988), p.250; See also: J. E. Cirlot (Translated by Jack Sage), *A Dictionary of Symbols* (New York: Dorset Press, 1991 Edition), p.6; John Maxson Stillman, *The Story of Alchemy and Early Chemistry* (New York, New York: Dover Publications, Inc., 1960), p.151.

[5] Helena Petrovna Blavatsky, *Isis Unveiled,* Vol. I: Science (New York, New York: Trow's Printing and Bookbinding Company, 1877), p.554, xxxiii.

[6] *Mysteries of Mind, Space and Time: The Unexplained* (Vol. 1) (Westport, Connecticut: H.S. Stuttman, Inc., 1992), p.41-42; See also: William Schnoebelen, *Masonry: Beyond the Light* (Chick Publications, 1991), p.176-177.

[7] Frank Gaynor, Editor, *Dictionary of Mysticism* (New York: Philosophical Library, 1953), p.77; See also: Harry E. Wedeck, *Treasury of Witchcraft* (New York: Philosophical Library, 1961), picture caption between p.40 and 41.

[8] Maurice Bessy, *A Pictorial History of Magic and the Supernatural* (Hamlyn Publishing Group Limited, 1964), p.87.

[9] Wolfgang Hochheimer quoting Carl Jung, *The Psychotherapy of C. G. Jung* (G. P. Putnam's Sons, 1969), p.70.

[10] Colin Wilson, *The Occult: A History* (New York, Random House, 1971), p.249.

[11] *Ibid.*

[12] Gaynor, *op.cit.,* p.172.

[13] *Ibid.,* p.199.

[14] Arthur Edward Waite, *The Mysteries of Magic: A Digest of the Writings of Eliphas Levi* (Chicago, Illinois: De Laurence, Scott and Company, 1909), p.48.

[15] John Maxson Stillman, *The Story of Alchemy and Early Chemistry* (New York, New York: Dover Publications, Inc., 1960), p.367.

[16] *New Times* (July/August 1988; #884), p.28.

[17] Editors of Time-Life Books, *Magical Arts* (Alexandria, Virginia: Time-Life Books, 1990), p.54.

[18] Gaynor, *op. cit.,* p.92.

[19] Dennis Laurence Cuddy (quoting from *The Rosicrucian Digest),* Now Is the Dawning of the New Age New World Order (Oklahoma City, Oklahoma: Hearthstone Publishing Ltd., 1991), p.120-121.

[20] Catalog from The Occult Emporium (Winter 1993 to Winter 1994), p.1.

[21] *Ibid.*, p.4.

[22] *Ibid.*, p.54.

[23] Kimberly Snoddy, "Symbol of Unity," *CPWR Journal* (November 1993, Vol. 5, No. 6), p.3.

[24] John Blofeld, *The Tantric Mysticism of Tibet* (Boston, Massachusetts: Shambhala Publications, Inc., 1970), p.102.

[25] "Guidelines: The Mandala," *Crescendo: The Newsletter of the Institute for Music and Imagery* (July 1987, Vol. 7, No. 2), p.2; See also: Carl G. Jung, M.-L. von Franz, Joseph L. Henderson, Jolande Jacobi, Aniela Jaffe, *Man and His Symbols* (Garden City, New York: Doubleday and Company, Inc., 1964), p.213; Nancy Wilson Ross, *Three Ways of Asian Wisdom* (New York, New York: Simon and Schuster, 1966), p.59; Robert Hieronimus, *America's Secret Destiny: Spiritual Vision and the Founding of a Nation* (Rochester, Vermont: Destiny Books, 1989), p.68; Joseph Campbell with Bill Moyers, Betty Sue Flowers, Editor, *The Power of Myth* (New York, New York: Doubleday, 1988), p.216; Johanna Michaelsen, *Like Lambs to the Slaughter* (Eugene, Oregon: Harvest House Publishers, 1989), p.104-105.

[26] 1986 Catalog of Events from Joy Lake Mountain Seminar Center, p.21.

[27] Catalog from the Theosophical Publishing House.

[28] Howard Kent, *A Color Guide to Yoga* (Intercontinental Book Productions, 1980), p.58.

[29] *Ibid.*, p.59.

[30] Cabot *op. cit.*, p.93.

[31] Alan Morrison, *The Serpent and the Cross: Religious Corruption in an Evil Age* (Birmingham, England: K & M Books, 1994), p.261.

[32] David L. Carrico with Rick Doninger, *The Egyptian-Masonic-Satanic Connection* (Evansville, Indiana: Followers of Jesus Christ, 1991), p.12, 13; Texe Marrs, *Texe Marrs Book of New Age Cults and Religions* (Austin, Texas: Living Truth Publishers, 1990), 199, 238.

[33] William Schnoebelen, *Masonry: Beyond the Light* (Chino, California: Chick Publications, 1991), p.205; *Battle Cry* (March/April 1991), p.4; Constance Cumbey, *The Hidden Dangers of the Rainbow: The New Age Movement and Our Coming Age of Barbarism* (Shreveport, Louisiana: Huntington House, Inc., Revised Edition, 1983), p.49.

[34] David Carrico, *The Occult Meaning of the Great Seal of the United States* (Evansville, Indiana: Followers of Jesus Christ, 1991), p.83.

[35] Foster Bailey, "A New Age Symbol," *The Beacon* (January/February 1993), p.4-5.

[36] Cover of *Lucifer* magazine.

[37] Texe Marrs, *Texe Marrs Book of New Age Cults and Religions* (Austin, Texas: Living Truth Publishers, 1990), p.299.

[38] M. Temple Richmond, *Sirius* (Mariposa, California: Source Publications, 1997), p.29.

[39] Joseph Campbell, *The Hero with a Thousand Faces* (Princeton, New Jersey: Princeton University Press, 1968, Second Edition), p.213.

[40] *The World Book Encyclopedia* (1961 Edition, Vol. 18), p.251; *Webster's Seventh New Collegiate Dictionary,* 1967, p.502; H. P. Blavatsky, *The Secret Doctrine: The Synthesis of Science, Religion, and Philosophy* (Vol. II—Anthropogenesis) (Covina, California: Theosophical University Press, 1947, Fourth Edition), p.759.

[41] Marrs, *op. cit.,* p.299.

[42] *Ibid.,* p.186; David Spangler, "Finding Heaven on Earth, *New Age Journal* (January/February 1988, Vol. 4, Issue 1); *Is the Antichrist in the World Today?,* Interview with Constance Cumbey (Oklahoma City, Oklahoma: Southwest Radio Church, 1982); David Spangler, *Emergence: The Rebirth of the Sacred* (New York: Dell Publishing, 1984), p.32; "Earth and Spirit: The Spiritual Dimension of the Environmental Crisis," Chinook Learning Center, p.6; Texe Marrs, *Dark Secrets of the New Age: Satan's Plan for a One World Religion* (Westchester, Illinois: Crossway Books, 1987), p.37; Catalog from the Flower Essence Society, p.17; David Spangler, *Links with Space* (Marina Del Rey, California: DeVorss and Company, 1971), p.13; David Spangler, *Revelation: The Birth of a New Age* (Middleton, Wisconsin: The Lorian Press, 1976), p.11; Constance Cumbey, *The Hidden Dangers of the Rainbow: The New Age Movement and Our Coming Age of Barbarism* (Shreveport, Louisiana: Huntington House, Inc., Revised Edition, 1983), p.51.

[43] Arthur Edward Waite, *A New Encyclopedia of Freemasonry and of Cognate Instituted Mysteries: Their Rites, Literature and History* (Vol. I) (New York: Weathervane Books, 1970), p.ix; See also: Waite, *The Mysteries of Magic, op. cit.,* p.202, 206, 212, 442; Joseph Carr, *The Lucifer Connection* (Lafayette, Louisiana: Huntington House, Inc., 1987), p.139; John Sebastian Marlow Ward, *The Sign Language of the Mysteries* (Land's End Press, 1969), p.86; Hutchens, *op. cit.,* p.81; Albert Churchward, *Signs and Symbols of Primordial Man* (London: George Allen and Company, Ltd., 1913, Second Edition), p.469; *The World Book Encyclopedia* (1961 Edition, Vol. 18), p.251; Geoffrey Parrinder, Editor, *World Religions: From Ancient History to the Present* (New York, New York: Facts on File, 1971), p.117; Ward, *Freemasonry and the Ancient Gods, op. cit.,* p. before p.111; Starhawk (Miriam Simos), *The Spiral Dance: A Rebirth of the Ancient Religion of the Great Goddess* (New York, New York: Harper-Collins Publishers, 1989 Edition), p.92; John T. Lawrence, *The Perfect Ashlar* (London: A. Lewis, 1912), p.164; Rex R. Hutchens and Donald W. Monson, *The Bible in Albert Pike's Morals and Dogma* (Washington, D.C.: Supreme Council, 33rd Degree, 1992), p.102; Gaynor, *op. cit.,* p.101; Manly Palmer Hall, *America's Assignment with Destiny* (Los Angeles, California: Philosophical Research Society, Inc., 1951), p.19; *Llewellyn New Times* (January/February 1988, #881), p.36; R. Swinburne Clymer, *The Mysteries of Osiris or Ancient Egyptian Initiation* (Quakertown, Pennsylvania: The Philosophical Publishing Company, 1951, Revised Edition), p.124; John J. Robinson, *A Pilgrim's Path: One Man's Road to the Masonic Temple* (New York: New York: M. Evans and Company, Inc., 1993), p.48; Percival George Woodcock, *Short Dictionary of Mythology* (Philosophical Library, 1953), p.87.

[44] H. P. Blavatsky, *The Secret Doctrine: The Synthesis of Science, Religion, and Philosophy* (Vol. II—Anthropogenesis) (Covina, California: Theosophical University Press, 1947, Fourth Edition), p.759.

[45] David L. Carrico, *Manly P. Hall: The Honored Masonic Author* (Evansville, Indiana: Followers of Jesus Christ, 1992), p.12.

[46] E. M. Butler, *The Myth of the Magus* (New York: MacMillan Company, 1948), p.259.

[47] Gary Kah, *En Route to Global Occupation* (Lafayette, Louisiana: Huntington House Publishers, 1992), p.89; John Yarker, *The Arcane Schools: A Review of Their Origin and Antiquity: With a General History of Freemasonry and Its Relation to the Theosophic Scientific and Philosophic Mysteries* (Belfast, Ireland: William Tait, 1909), p.486; Schnoebelen, *Masonry, op. cit.,* p.204; *Battle Cry* (March/April 1991), p.4.

[48] G. A. Riplinger quoting Helena Petrovna Blavatsky, *New Age Bible Versions* (Munroe Falls, Ohio: A. V. Publications, 1993), p.121.

[49] Albert Pike, *Morals and Dogma of the Ancient and Accepted Scottish Rite of Freemasonry* (Richmond, Virginia: L. H. Jenkins, Inc., 1871), p.734.

[50] Hutchens, *op. cit.,* p.253.

[51] Waite, *The Mysteries of Magic, op. cit.,* p.68, 453.

[52] Pike, *op. cit.,* p.321; See also: *Ibid.,* p.442.

[53] Blavatsky, *The Secret Doctrine, op. cit.,* p.513; See also: Israel Regardie quoting Helena Petrovna Blavatsky, *The Golden Dawn* (St. Paul, Minnesota: Llewellyn Publications, 1986), p.34.

[54] *Ibid.,* p.235.

[55] *Ibid.,* p.387.

[56] *Ibid.*

[57] Manly P. Hall, *America's Assignment with Destiny* (Los Angeles, California: Philosophical Research Society, Inc., 1951), p.19.

[58] Manly Palmer Hall, *Initiates of the Flame* (Los Angeles, California: The Phoenix Press, 1934), p.20.

[59] Blavatsky, *The Secret Doctrine, op. cit.,* p.378.

[60] Lynn F. Perkins, *Masonry in the New Age* (Lakemont, Georgia: CSA Press, 1971), p.144.

[61] "How to Build Your Own Washington Monument" punch out.

[62] Cuddy quoting from *The Rosicrucian Digest, op. cit.,* p.52.

[63] Dwight L. Kinman quoting Robert Muller, *The World's Last Dictator* (Woodburn, Oregon: Solid Rock Books, Inc. 1995), p. 81.

[64] *Blueprint for Building the New World Order* (Dearborn, Michigan: The Omega-Letter/Christian World Report), p.21.

[65] Robert Muller, *New Genesis: Shaping a Global Spirituality* (Garden City, New York: Image Books, 1984), p.75.

[66] *The Rainbow Connection* (April 1995), p.3.

[67] Brochure from the Temple of Understanding, Received March 12, 1991, p.2.

[68] *Breakthrough* (Winter/Summer 1990, Vol. 11, No.2-4), p.2; See also: Rosamond C. Rodman, Editor, *The United Nations in an Interdependent World: Past, Present, Future* (New York, New York: Global Education Associates, 1995), p.2.

[69] Letter from Planetary Citizens dated April 17, 1985.

[70] Robert Sessler, *To Be God of One World: The French Revolution Globalized* (Merlin, Oregon: Let There Be Light Publications, 1992), p.63.

[71] Robert Muller, *Framework for Preparation for the Year 2000, The 21st Century* (Hamden, Connecticut: Albert Schweitzer Institute/Quinnipiac College Press, 1994), p.8.

[72] Robert Muller, *A World Core Curriculum* (n.d., n.p.), Front Cover.

[73] Constance Cumbey, *A Planned Deception: The Staging of a New Age "Messiah"* (East Detroit, Michigan: Pointe Publishing, Inc., 1985), p.34.

[74] Dennis Laurence Cuddy, *Chronology of Education with Quotable Quotes* (Highland City, Florida: Pro Family Forum, Inc., 1994, Updated, Bound Volume), p.77; Cuddy, *Now Is the Dawning, op. cit.,* p.217, 272; Peggy S. Cuddy, "Transformation Toward New Age Synthesis," *Distant Drums*

(May 1986, Vol. 8, No. 2), p.2; "Dr. Paul Cedar Pulls Endorsement from *Star of 2000*," Report from Broadcasters United for Revival and Reformation, p.2; *Don Bell Reports* (January 10, 1986), Vol. 33, No.2., p.3.

[75] *Ibid.;* Cuddy, *Now Is the Dawning, op. cit.,* p.272; Peggy S. Cuddy, "Transformation Toward New Age Synthesis," *Distant Drums* (May 1986, Vol. 8, No. 2), p.2; *Flashpoint* (January 1990), p.1.

[76] Texe Marrs, "New Agers Meet to Plan World Takeover," *Flashpoint* (January 1990), p.1; Rhea Fulmer, Teri Jeter, and Wanda Riner, "Robert Muller's Vision for 2000 A.D.," *The Christian Conscience* (May 1995, Vol. 1, No. 5.), p.35.

[77] Muller, *New Genesis, op. cit.,* p.183.

[78] Brochure from the Center for the Dances of Universal Peace.

[79] "About Our Logo," *Dance Network News* (January/February 1989, Vol. 1, No. 4), p.4.

[80] Brochure from the Center for the Dances of Universal Peace.

[81] *Ibid.*

[82] Pamphlet from Spiritual Unity of Religions entitled "Introducing S.U.N.," Front Cover.

[83] John Cotter, *A Study in Syncretism* reprinted in *Despatch* (March 1993, Vol. 5, No. 1), p.12.

[84] Cuddy, *Chronology of Education, op. cit.,* p.50; Cuddy, *Now Is the Dawning, op. cit.,* p.120, 146.

[85] Cuddy (quoting from Caryl Matrisciana's book), *Now Is the Dawning, op. cit.,* p.147.

[86] *Ibid.,* p.35.

[87] http//globalvisions.org/cl/udcworld/about.html

[88] *Ibid.*

[89] *Ibid.*

[90] Material received April 2, 1996 entitled *The Three Meditation Festivals of Spring: A World Religion for the New Age* (Ojai, California: Group for Creative Meditation), p.3-4; See also: *The Full Moon Story* (Manhattan Beach, California: Rams' Dell Press, 1974 Revision), p.32-33.

[91] *Ibid.,* p.3-4.

[92] Tom Carney, "Calling All Servers," *Thoughtline* (June 1995), p.3.

[93] Leland P. Stewart, "Synthesis and the Meaning of Unity-and-Diversity," *Thoughtline* (June 1998), p.1-2.

[94] *Change Works* (Spring/Summer 1998), p.33.

[95] Cuddy, *Now Is the Dawning, op. cit.,* p.256.

[96] *Ibid.,* p.257.

[97] *Ibid.,* p.286.

[98] *San Francisco Chronicle* (January 23, 1996).

[99] Sonni Efron, "Yeltsin Turns to Nation's Czarist Past for Eagle Seal to Reflect New Russia," *The News Tribune* (December 2, 1993), p.A2.

[100] http://home.earthlink.net/-hyphenate/oneworld.html

[101] *Ibid.*

[102] *Ibid.*

[103] *The Whole Earth Papers: Christian Voice on World Order* (1978, Vol. 1, No. 10), Back Cover.

[104] A. Ralph Epperson, *The Unseen Hand: An Introduction to the Conspiratorial View of History* (Tucson, Arizona: Publius Press, 1985), p. 197.

[105] *Ibid.*

[106] Texe Marrs, *Circle of Intrigue* (Austin, Texas: Living Truth Ministries, 1995), p.203.

[107] Cuddy, *Now Is the Dawning, op. cit.,* p.433.

[108] Henry C. Clausen, *Masons Who Helped Shape Our Nation* (The Supreme Council, 33°, Ancient and Accepted Scottish Rite of Freemasonry Southern Jurisdiction, 1976), p.71.

[109] Letter received February 17, 1993 from Barry Lynn, Executive Director of Americans United for Separation of Church and State.

[110] Hutchens, *op. cit.,* p.250; *Mysteries of Mind, Space and Time, op. cit.;* Maurice Bessy, *A Pictorial History of Magic and the Supernatural* (Hamlyn Publishing Group Limited, 1964), p.87.

[111] Maurice Bessy, *A Pictorial History of Magic and the Supernatural* (Hamlyn Publishing Group Limited, 1964), p.87.

[112] Bill Wilson, *As Bill Sees It: The A.A. Way of Life* (New York, New York: Alcoholics Anonymous World Services, Inc., p.307.

[113] *Ibid.*

[114] Sandra L. Koch, *Combating the New Age Movement: A Christian Warfare Manual* (Boca Raton, Florida: Foundation Tabernacle Ministries, Inc., n.d.).

[115] *Ibid.*

[116] Pamphlet from the California Institute of Integral Studies entitled "East West Graduate Education."

[117] Texe Marrs, "Devil Companies, Devil Products, Devil Logos?," *Flashpoint* (December 1997), p.1-2.

[118] *Ibid.,* p.2.

[119] "New UFO Sex Cult Thrives," *Flashpoint* (September 1992), p.3.

[120] "Editors' Introduction," *Addiction and Consciousness Journal* (September 1988, Vol. 3, No. 3), p.2.

[121] "The Triscele," *Addiction and Consciousness Journal* (September 1988, Vol. 3, No. 3), p.12; See also: *The Brookridge Forum* (Winter 1987-88, Vol. 3, No. 1).

[122] *What Is* (1987, Vol. 1, No. 2), p.2; See also: *Self-Help Update: Create Your Own Reality* (1985, Issue #28), p.9.

[123] "Hunter Shane Sutphen," *Master of Life* (1986, Issue 32), p.5

[124] *Master of Life* (1986, Issue 32), p.5.

[125] "Hunter Shane Sutphen," *op. cit.*

[126] *What Is* (Summer 1986, Vol. 1, No. 1).

[127] Francois Ribadeau Dumas (Translated by Elisabeth Abbott), *Cagliostro: Scoundrel or Saint?* (New York: The Orion Press, 1967), p.45.

[128] J. D. Buck, *Mystic Masonry* (Chicago, Illinois: Indo-American Book Company, 1913, Sixth Edition), p.244-245.

[129] Catalog from DASO, p.3.

[130] "What Happened to George Bush That Mysterious Night at the Tomb?", *Flashpoint* (Special Edition), p.2.

[131] J. Gordon Melton, *The Encyclopedia of American Religions* (Vol. 2) (Wilmington, North Carolina: McGrath Publishing Company, 1978), p.256.

[132] M. Temple Richmond, *Sirius* (Mariposa, California: Source Publications, 1997), p.194.

Chapter 14: Hand Signals

[1] Malcolm Duncan, *Duncan's Ritual of Freemasonry* (New York: David McKay Company, Inc., n.d., 3rd Edition), p.94; Jim Shaw and Tom McKenney, *The Deadly Deception* (Lafayette, Louisiana: Huntington House, Inc., 1988), p.137; Stephen Knight, *The Brotherhood* (Briarcliff Manor, New York: Stein and Day, 1984), p.234.

[2] *Ibid.,* p.230.

[3] Jim Shaw and Tom McKenney, *The Deadly Deception* (Lafayette, Louisiana: Huntington House, Inc., 1988), p.137.

[4] *Ibid.,* quoting Edmond Ronayne.

[5] Scott Cunningham, *Wicca: A Guide for the Solitary Practitioner* (St. Paul, Minnesota: Llewellyn Publications, 1989), p.41-45.

[6] Udo Becker, *The Continuum Encyclopedia of Symbols* (New York: Continuum, 1994).

[7] Jeff Godwin, *The Devil's Disciples: The Truth About Rock* (Chino, California: Chick Publications, 1985), p.134.

[8] Jeff Godwin, *Dancing with Demons: The Music's Real Master* (Chino, California: Chick Publications, 1988), p.308.

[9] Godwin, *The Devil's Disciples, op. cit.*

[10] *Ibid.,* p.39.

[11] Eric Barger, *From Rock to Rock: The Music of Darkness Exposed!* (Lafayette, Louisiana: Huntington House, Inc., 1990), p.103.

[12] Godwin, *The Devil's Disciples, op. cit.,* p.134.

[13] Barger, *op. cit.,* p.104.

[14] Anton Szandor LaVey, *The Satanic Bible* (New York: Avon Books, 1969), p.60, 145.

[15] J. S. M. Ward, *Freemasonry and the Ancient Gods* (London, England: Simpkin, Marshall, Hamilton, Kent and Company Ltd., 1921), p.15.

[16] Alain Danielou, *The Gods of India* (New York, New York: Inner Traditions International Ltd., 1985), p.211; See also: *New Larousse Encyclopedia of Mythology* (Prometheus Press, 1972 Edition), p.374.

[17] Stewart Farrar, *What Witches Do: The Modern Coven Revealed* (Custer, Washington: Phoenix Publishing Company, 1983 Revised Edition), p.104.

[18] S. R. Parchment, *Ancient Operative Masonry* (San Francisco, California: San Francisco Center—Rosicrucian Fellowship, 1930), p.43.

[19] John Lash, *The Seeker's Handbook: The Complete Guide to Spiritual Pathfinding* (New York: Harmony Books, 1990), p.324-325; See also: Gary Doore, Compiler and Editor, *Shaman's Path: Healing, Personal Growth and Empowerment* (Boston, Massachusetts: Shambhala, 1988), p.66.

[20] Frank Gaynor, Editor, *Dictionary of Mysticism* (New York: Philosophical Library, 1953), p.116.

[21] Danielou, *op. cit.,* p.362.

[22] "Peace Symbols: The Truth About Those Strange Designs," *American Opinion,* p.12.

[23] Bill Schnoebelen, *Straight Talk #10 on the Peace Sign Gesture* (Dubuque, Iowa: With One Accord Ministries, 1995), p.2.

[24] *Ibid.,* p.2-4.

[25] "Peace Symbols," *op. cit.,* p.11, 13.

[26] Sandra L. Koch, *Combating the New Age Movement: A Christian Warfare Manual* (Boca Raton, Florida: Foundation Tabernacle Ministries, Inc., n.d.).

[27] "Peace Symbols," *op. cit.* p.12.

[28] Schnoebelen, *op. cit.,* p.2, 6.

[29] *Ibid.,* p.6.

[30] "Peace Symbols," *op. cit.* p.13.

[31] Barger, *op. cit.,* p.162.

[32] "Peace Symbols," *op. cit.,* p.16.

[33] *Ibid.,* p.4.

[34] *Ibid.,* p.6-7.

[35] Rudolf Koch, *The Book of Signs* (New York, New York: Dover Publications, Inc., 1955 edition), p.5.

[36] "Peace Symbols," *op. cit.,* p.7.

[37] *Ibid.,* p.7, 10.

[38] Texe Marrs, *Mystery Mark of the New Age: Satan's Design for World Domination* (Westchester, Illinois: Crossway Books, 1988), p.109.

[39] *Last Trumpet Newsletter* (July 1986, Vol. 5, Issue 7), p.2.

[40] *New Larousse Encyclopedia of Mythology* (Prometheus Press, 1972 Edition), p.205.

[41] Percival George Woodcock, *Short Dictionary of Mythology* (New York: Philosophical Library, 1953), p.152; *Ibid.*

[42] J. E. Cirlot (Translated by Jack Sage), *A Dictionary of Symbols* (New York: Dorset Press, 1991), p.362.

[43] Woodcock, *op. cit.*, p.150-151.

[44] Albert G. Mackey, *The Symbolism of Freemasonry* (New York: Clark and Maynard, 1869), p.15, 361, 362.

[45] William P. Peterson, Editor, *Masonic Quiz Book: "Ask Me Another, Brother"* (Chicago, Illinois: Charles T. Powner Company, 1950), p.18, 88, 131, 213; John Yarker, *The Arcane Schools: A Review of Their Origin and Antiquity: With a General History of Freemasonry and Its Relation to the Theosophic Scientific and Philosophic Mysteries* (Belfast, Ireland: William Tait, 1909), p.30; A. R. Chambers, Editor, *Questions and Answers* (1972), p.237; Duncan, *op. cit.*, p.97.

[46] Interfaith Witness Department, *A Study of Freemasonry* (Atlanta, Georgia: Home Mission Board, Southern Baptist Convention, n.d.), p.32; See also: Mustafa El-Amin, *Freemasonry: Ancient Egypt and the Islamic Destiny* (Jersey City, New Jersey: New Mind Productions, 1988), p.20.

[47] Manly Palmer Hall, *The Lost Keys of Freemasonry* (Richmond, Virginia: Macoy Publishing and Masonic Supply Company, Inc., 1976 Edition), p.48.

[48] William Schnoebelen, *Masonry: Beyond the Light* (Chino, California: Chick Publications, 1991), p.123-124; See also: Mustafa El-Amin, *Freemasonry: Ancient Egypt and the Islamic Destiny* (Jersey City, New Jersey: New Mind Productions, 1988), p.20.

[49] "Peace Symbols," *op. cit.*, p.3.

[50] John Yarker, *The Arcane Schools: A Review of Their Origin and Antiquity: With a General History of Freemasonry and Its Relation to the Theosophic Scientific and Philosophic Mysteries* (Belfast, Ireland: William Tait, 1909), p.146; Vail, *op. cit.*, p.190.

[51] *Pocket Masonic Dictionary* (Silver Spring, Maryland: The Masonic Service Association of the United States, 1988), p.17, 18, 24; *What? When? Where? Why? Who? in Freemasonry* (Silver Spring, Maryland: Masonic Service Association of the United States, 1956), p.39; Albert G. Mackey, *A Manual of the Lodge* (New York: Charles E. Merrill Company, 1870), p.40; R. Swinburne Clymer, *The Mysticism of Masonry* (Quakertown, Pennsylvania: The Philosophical Publishing Company, 1924), p.146; Daniel Sickles, Editor, *The Freemason's Monitor* (New York: Macoy Publishing and Masonic Supply Company, 1901), p.38; George Oliver, *The Historical Landmarks and Other Evidences of Freemasonry, Explained* (Vol. I & II) (New York: John W. Leonard and Company, 1855), p.132; Duncan, *op. cit.*, p.50; W. J. McCormick, *Christ, the Christian and Freemasonry* (Belfast, Ireland: Great Joy Publications, 1984), p.89, etc.

[52] Albert G. Mackey, *A Manual of the Lodge* (New York: Charles E. Merrill Company, 1870), p.40-41; See also: Daniel Sickles, Editor, *The Freemason's Monitor* (New York: Macoy Publishing and Masonic Supply Company, 1901), p.38; Edmond Ronayne, *The Master's Carpet (Mah-Hah-Bone)* (n.p., 1879), p.276, quoting A. T. C. Pierson, and p.276-277, quoting Albert Mackey; See also: R. Swinburne Clymer quoting Daniel Sickles, *The Mysticism of Masonry* (Quakertown, Pennsylvania: The Philosophical Publishing Company, 1924), p.146.

[53] Duncan, *op. cit.*, p.50.

Chapter 15: A Medley of Symbols

[1] Thomas Albert Stafford, *Christian Symbolism in the Evangelical Churches* (Nashville, Tennessee: Abingdon Press, 1942), p.75; See also: J. C. Cooper, *An Illustrated Encyclopedia of Traditional Symbols* (London, England: Thames and Hudson, 1978), p.181.

[2] J. C. Cooper, *An Illustrated Encyclopedia of Traditional Symbols* (London, England: Thames and Hudson, 1978), p.181.

[3] 1989 Catalog from Papa Jim, Inc., p.60

[4] Catalog entitled *The Pyramid Collection* (Late Summer 1997), p.49.

[5] *The Brookridge Forum* (Winter 1987-88, Vol. 3, No. 1), p.1.

[6] Count Goblet D'Alviella, *The Migration of Symbols* (Westminster: Archibald Constable and Company, 1894), p.xi.

[7] *The Pyramid Collection, op. cit.,* p.25.

[8] Isis Catalog, p.40.

[9] William and Sharon Schnoebelen, *Lucifer Dethroned* (Chino, California: Chick Publications, 1993), p.235.

[10] *Ibid.,* p.236; See also: Scott Cunningham, *Wicca: A Guide for the Solitary Practitioner* (St. Paul, Minnesota: Llewellyn Publications, 1989), p.29-30.

[11] R. Swinburne Clymer, *The Mysticism of Masonry* (Quakertown, Pennsylvania: The Philosophical Publishing Company, 1924), p.125; A. T. C. Pierson, *The Traditions, Origin and Early History of Freemasonry* (New York: Masonic Publishing Company, 1865), p.232.

[12] Patricia, "New Year New Moon Chant," *Circle Network News* (Winter 1980-1981), p.3.

[13] Edith Hamilton, *Mythology* (Boston, Massachusetts: Little, Brown and Company, 1942), p.32; See also: Laurie Cabot with Tom Cowan, *Power of the Witch: The Earth, the Moon, and the Magical Path to Enlightenment* (New York, New York: Delacorte Press, 1989), p.32; Percival George Woodcock, *Short Dictionary of Mythology* (Philosophical Library, 1953), p.20; J. E. Cirlot (Translated by Jack Sage), *A Dictionary of Symbols* (New York: Dorset Press, 1991), p.81, 143; Harry E. Wedeck, *Treasury of Witchcraft* (New York, New York: Philosophical Library, 1961), p.39, 72.

[14] Laurie Cabot with Tom Cowan, *Power of the Witch: The Earth, the Moon, and the Magical Path to Enlightenment* (New York, New York: Delacorte Press, 1989), p.32; See also: Harry E. Wedeck, *Treasury of Witchcraft* (New York, New York: Philosophical Library, 1961), p.39, 72; Eden Within (1994 Catalog), p.12.

[15] Thomas Bulfinch, *Bulfinch's Mythology* (New York: Thomas Y. Crowell Company, Inc., 1970), p.934; G. A. Riplinger, *New Age Bible Versions* (Munroe Falls, Ohio: A. V. Publications, 1993), p.125; Frank Gaynor, Editor, *Dictionary of Mysticism* (New York: Philosophical Library, 1953), p.76; Editors of Time-Life Books, *Magical Arts* (Alexandria, Virginia: Time-Life Books, 1990), p.22.

[16] *Is the Antichrist in the World Today?,* Interview with Constance Cumbey (Oklahoma City, Oklahoma: Southwest Radio Church, 1982), p.2, 27.

[17] *Ibid.,* p.27.

[18] *Ibid.,* p.2.

[19] *The Forum* (January/February 1987).

[20] *Tampa Tribune* (October 31, 1988).

[21] *Ibid.*

[22] *Ibid.*

[23] *Circle Network News* (Summer 1987, Vol. 9, No. 2), p.12.

[24] Scott Cunningham, *Wicca: A Guide for the Solitary Practitioner* (St. Paul, Minnesota: Llewellyn Publications, 1989), p.12.

[25] *Ibid.*, p.59.

[26] Catalog from Lizzie Brown/Pleiades, received September 13, 1997.

[27] *Necronomicon* (New York, New York: Avon Books, 1977), p.7, 30.

[28] J. S. M. Ward, *Who Was Hiram Abiff?* (London, England: The Baskerville Press, Ltd., 1925), p.48.

[29] J. E. Cirlot, *A Dictionary of Symbols* (New York, New York: Philosophical Library, Inc., 1972), p.21-22; See also: Geoffrey Parrinder, Editor, *World Religions: From Ancient History to the Present* (New York, New York: Facts on File Publications, 1983), p.63.

[30] J. S. M. Ward, *Freemasonry and the Ancient Gods* (London, England: Simpkin, Marshall, Hamilton, Kent and Company, Ltd., 1921), p.241.

[31] *Ibid.*, p.215-216, 235, 238; See also: Peter Partner, *The Knights Templar and Their Myth* (Rochester, Vermont: Destiny Books, 1990, Revised Edition), p.140; Stafford, *op. cit.*, p.68; George Oliver, *The Historical Landmarks and Other Evidences of Freemasonry, Explained* (Vol. I & II) (New York: John W. Leonard and Company, 1855), p.67.

[32] John Sebastian Marlow Ward, *The Sign Language of the Mysteries* (New York: Land's End Press, 1969), p.156.

[33] Godfrey Higgins, *Anacalypsis, An Attempt to Draw Aside the Veil of the Saitic Isis* (London, England: n.p., 1874), p.373; See also: John Yarker, *The Arcane Schools: A Review of Their Origin and Antiquity with a General History of Freemasonry, and Its Relation to the Theosophic, Scientific, and Philosophic Mysteries* (Belfast, Ireland: William Tait, 1909), p.146.

[34] William Schnoebelen, *Masonry: Beyond the Light* (Chino, California: Chick Publications, 1991), p.119; See also: "Babel Becomes One," *The Omega-Letter* (April 1990, Vol. 5, No. 4), p.8.

[35] Frank Gaynor, Editor, *Dictionary of Mysticism* (New York: Philosophical Library, 1953), p.182.

[36] Texe Marrs, *Mystery Mark of the New Age: Satan's Design for World Domination* (Westchester, Illinois: Crossway Books, 1988), p.91, 182; John Lust, *The Herb Book* (New York, New York: Bantam Books, Inc., 1974), p.592, 607; George Oliver, *Signs and Symbols* (New York: Macoy Publishing and Masonic Supply Company, 1906), p.14; Percival George Woodcock, *Short Dictionary of Mythology* (New York: Philosophical Library, 1953), p.144; W. Wynn Westcott, *Numbers: Their Occult Power and Mystic Virtues* (London, England: Theosophical Publishing Society, 1902, Second Edition), p.41; Gaynor, *op. cit.*, p.186; Geoffrey Parrinder, Editor, *World Religions: From Ancient History to the Present* (New York, New York: Facts on File Publications, 1983), p.111; *New Larousse Encyclopedia of Mythology* (Prometheus Press, 1972 Edition), p.258; 1989 Catalog from Papa Jim, Inc., p.44; Bulfinch, *op. cit.*, p.355; Editors of Time-Life Books, *Magical Arts* (Alexandria, Virginia: Time-Life Books, 1990), p.28; John T. Lawrence, *The Perfect Ashlar* (London, England: A. Lewis, 1912), p.196; Cirlot, *op. cit.*, p.342; Phil Phillips, *Turmoil in the Toybox* (Lancaster, Pennsylvania: Starburst Publishers, 1986), p.79.

[37] Max Wood, *Rock and Roll: An Analysis of the Music* (n.p., n.d.), p.30.

[38] *Ibid.,* p.31.

[39] Jeff Godwin, *The Devil's Disciples: The Truth About Rock* (Chino, California: Chick Publications, 1985), p.133.

[40] *Ibid.;* See also: Eric Barger, *From Rock to Rock: The Music of Darkness Exposed!* (Lafayette, Louisiana: Huntington House, Inc., 1990), p.161.

[41] *Ibid.,* p.257.

[42] Cirlot, *op. cit.,* p.342.

[43] D'Alviella, *op. cit.,* p.99.

[44] Anton Szandor LaVey, *The Satanic Bible* (New York: Avon Books, 1969), p.60, 145; See also: Joseph Campbell, *The Masks of God: Creative Mythology* (New York, New York: The Viking Press, 1968), p.204, 411.

[45] W. Wynn Westcott, *Numbers: Their Occult Power and Mystic Virtues* (London, England: Theosophical Publishing Society, 1902, Second Edition), p.41.

[46] D'Alviella, *op. cit.,* p.225.

[47] John T. Lawrence, *The Perfect Ashlar* (London, England: A. Lewis, 1912), p.196; Westcott, *op. cit.*

[48] *Ibid.,* p.196-197.

[49] *Ibid.,* p.351, 81.

[50] Joseph Campbell, *The Masks of God: Creative Mythology* (New York, New York: The Viking Press, 1968), p.204, 410, 411.

[51] *Ibid.,* p.411.

[52] *Ibid.,* p.17.

[53] Cooper, *op. cit.,* p.180.

[54] John Lash, *The Seeker's Handbook: The Complete Guide to Spiritual Pathfinding* (New York: Harmony Books, 1990), p.297.

[55] H. P. Blavatsky, *The Secret Doctrine: The Synthesis of Science, Religion, and Philosophy* (Vol. II—Anthropogenesis) (Covina, California: Theosophical University Press, 1947, Fourth Edition), p.580.

[56] Cunningham, *op. cit.,* p.176.

[57] Texe Marrs, *Texe Marrs Book of New Age Cults and Religions* (Austin, Texas: Living Truth Publishers, 1990), p.116.

[58] "Zondervan Takes Prompt Action," *Flashpoint* (October/November 1988), p.3.

[59] Stewart Farrar, *What Witches Do: The Modern Coven Revealed* (Custer, Washington: Phoenix Publishing Company, 1983, Revised Edition), p.104; Arthur Edward Waite, *The Mysteries of Magic: A Digest of the Writings of Eliphas Levi* (Chicago, Illinois: De Laurence, Scott and Company, 1909), p.294, 298.

[60] Starhawk, *The Spiral Dance: A Rebirth of the Ancient Religion of the Great Goddess* (New York, New York: Harper-Collins Publishers, 1989), p.35-36.

[61] Francois Ribadeau Dumas (Translated by Elisabeth Abbott), *Cagliostro: Scoundrel or Saint?* (New York: The Orion Press, 1967), p.46.

[62] Catalog from Macoy Publishing and Masonic Supply Company, Inc. (September 1991, No. 107), p.119.

[63] William J. Whalen, *Handbook of Secret Organizations* (Milwaukee, Wisconsin: Bruce Publishing Company, 1966), p.118.

[64] *Pocket Masonic Dictionary* (Silver Spring, Maryland: The Masonic Service Association of the United States, 1988), p.27.

[65] Alain Danielou, *The Gods of India* (New York, New York: Inner Traditions International Ltd., 1985), p.219, 354; Michael Jordan, *Encyclopedia of Gods: Over 2,500 Deities of the World* (New York, New York: Facts on File, 1993), p.239.

[66] Arthur Edward Waite, *The Mysteries of Magic: A Digest of the Writings of Eliphas Levi* (Chicago, Illinois: De Laurence, Scott and Company, 1909), p.222-223.

[67] Cunningham, *op. cit.;* p.65, 198; See also: De-Anna Alba, "A Candlemas Purification and Self-Dedication Rite," *Circle Network News* (Winter 1980-81, Vol. 2, No. 4), p.7.

[68] Cirlot *op. cit.,* p.249; See also: *Complete Occult Digest A to Z* (North Hollywood, California: International Imports, 1984), p.115; *What? When? Where? Why? Who? in Freemasonry* (Silver Spring, Maryland: Masonic Service Association of the United States, 1956), p.37; LaVey, *op. cit.,* p.59, 145; Thomas Bulfinch, *Bulfinch's Mythology: The Age of Fable or Stories of Gods and Heroes* (Garden City, New York: Doubleday and Company, Inc., 1948), p.181; Bulfinch, *op. cit.,* p.957.

[69] Charles G. Berger, *Our Phallic Heritage* (New York, New York: Greenwich Book Publishers, Inc., 1966), p.32; See also: Thomas Bulfinch, *Bulfinch's Mythology: The Age of Fable or Stories of Gods and Heroes* (Garden City, New York: Doubleday and Company, Inc., 1948), p.181.

[70] LaVey, *op. cit.,* p.59.

[71] Farrar, *op. cit.,* p.33.

[72] Starhawk, "Ritual to Rebuild Community," *Utne Reader* (November/December 1987), p.70.

[73] Scott Cunningham, *Magical Herbalism: The Secret Craft of the Wise* (St. Paul, Minnesota: Llewellyn Publications, 1982), p.43; See also: Schnoebelen, *Lucifer Dethroned, op. cit.,* p.329; "Festivals and Sabbats," *Christian Parent Alert* (October 1991, Vol. 1, No. 3), p.13; Eric Maple, *The Compete Book of Witchcraft and Demonology* (Cranbury, New Jersey: A. S. Barnes and Company, Inc., 1966), p.175.

[74] Farrar, *op. cit.,* p.82; See also: M. Esther Harding, *Woman's Mysteries: Ancient and Modern* (G. P. Putnam's Sons, 1971 Edition), p.130.

[75] Ralph Edward Woodrow, *Babylon Mystery Religion: Ancient and Modern* (Riverside, California: Ralph Woodrow Evangelistic Association, 1990 Edition), p.146.

[76] Cirlot *op. cit.,* p.143; Maria Leach, Editor, *Funk and Wagnalls Standard Dictionary of Folklore, Mythology and Legend* (Vol. 1) (New York: Funk and Wagnalls, 1949), p.487.

[77] Percival George Woodcock, *Short Dictionary of Mythology* (New York: Philosophical Library, 1953), p.38.

[78] *Ibid.,* p.73; Berger, *op. cit.,* p.46.

[79] Thomas Bulfinch, *Bulfinch's Mythology: The Age of Fable or Stories of Gods and Heroes* (Garden City, New York: Doubleday and Company, Inc., 1948), p.4.

[80] H. P. Blavatsky, *Isis Unveiled* Vol. 1: Science (New York: Trow's Printing and Bookbinding Company, 1877), p.125.

[81] *New Larousse Encyclopedia of Mythology* (Prometheus Press, 1972 Edition), p.163.

[82] *Ibid.,* p.143.

[83] Albert Pike, *Morals and Dogma of the Ancient and Accepted Scottish Rite of Freemasonry* (Richmond, Virginia: L. H. Jenkins, Inc., 1871), p.434.

[84] *New Larousse Encyclopedia of Mythology, op. cit.,* p.144.

[85] *The World Book Encyclopedia* (1961 Edition, Vol. 18), p.251; *Webster's Seventh New Collegiate Dictionary,* 1967, p.502; Eliphas Levi (Translated by Arthur Edward Waite), *The History of Magic Including a Clear and Precise Exposition of Its Procedure, Its Rites and Its Mysteries* (London, England: William Rider and Son, Limited, 1992), p.192.

[86] Marrs quoting Edouard Schure, *Mystery Mark of the New Age, op. cit.,* p.240.

[87] Arthur H. Ward, *Masonic Symbolism and the Mystic Way,* (London: Theosophical Publishing House, Ltd., 1923, Second Edition), p.149-150.

[88] Manly Palmer Hall, *Freemasonry of the Ancient Egyptians to Which Is Added an Interpretation of the Crata Repoa Initiation Rite* (Los Angeles, California: The Philosophers Press, 1937), p.122.

[89] *The Rainbow Bridge Newsletter* (October/November 1984, Vol. 1, No. 4), p.1-2.

[90] Kenneth R. H. MacKenzie, Editor, *The Royal Masonic Cyclopaedia of History, Rites, Symbolism, and Biography* (New York: J. W. Bouton, 1877), p.308.

[91] *Ibid.,* p.580.

[92] Berit Kjos, "Olympic Myths and Earthy Magic," *Christian News* (February 28, 1994, Vol. 32, No. 9), p.5.

[93] Texe Marrs, *Dark Majesty: The Secret Brotherhood and the Magic of a Thousand Points of Light* (Austin, Texas: Living Truth Publishers, 1992), p.212.

[94] D'Alviella, *op. cit.,* p.27.

[95] Oliver, *op. cit.,* p.124; R. Swinburne Clymer, *The Mysteries of Osiris or Ancient Egyptian Initiation* (Quakertown, Pennsylvania: The Philosophical Publishing Company, 1951, Revised Edition), p.185; See also: Udo Becker, Editor, *The Continuum Encyclopedia of Symbols* (1994), p.243.

[96] Marrs, *Mystery Mark of the New Age, op. cit.,* p.97.

[97] Edith Hamilton, *Mythology* (Boston, Massachusetts: Little, Brown and Company, 1942), p.459; *New Larousse Encyclopedia of Mythology, op. cit.,* p.249, 268; Blavatsky, *Isis Unveiled, op. cit.,* p.161; Edmond Ronayne, *The Master's Carpet (Mah-Hah-Bone)* (n.p., 1879), p.323.

[98] R. Swinburne Clymer, *The Mysteries of Osiris or Ancient Egyptian Initiation* (Quakertown, Pennsylvania: The Philosophical Publishing Company, 1951, Revised Edition), p.185.

[99] *Ibid.*

[100] Udo Becker, Editor, *The Continuum Encyclopedia of Symbols* (1994), p.243.

[101] *Ibid.*

[102] *Ibid.,* p.244.

[103] For example, see: *The New Age Movement—Age of Aquarius—Age of Antichrist,* Interview with Constance Cumbey (Oklahoma City, Oklahoma: Southwest Radio Church, 1982), p.5; Phil Phillips, *Turmoil in the Toybox* (Lancaster, Pennsylvania: Starburst Press, 1986), p.83; Johanna Michaelsen, *Like Lambs to the Slaughter* (Eugene, Oregon: Harvest House Publishers, 1989), p.218; Phil Phillips, *Saturday Morning Mind Control* (Nashville, Tennessee: Oliver-Nelson Books, 1991), p.111.

[104] For instance, see: Alice A. Bailey, *Discipleship in the New Age* (Vol. II) (New York: Lucis Publishing Company, 1955), p.268, 408; *Shamballa: Where the Will of God is Known* (New York, New York: Arcane School, n.d.), p.19; *The Beacon* (July/August 1985, Vol. 51, No. 4), p.119-120; *Spiritual Mothering Journal* (Winter 1986, Vol. 6, No. 4), p.22; Alice A. Bailey, *Education in the New Age* (New York: Lucis Publishing Company, 1954), p.96-97; Alice A. Bailey, *Discipleship in the New Age* (Vol. I) (New York: Lucis Publishing Company, 1972); Alice A. Bailey, *The Soul: Quality of Life* (New York: Lucis Publishing Company, 1974), p.243; Pamphlet from Energy Systems Parameters, p.2-3; Brochure from Harmony Horizons, Inc.; *Thoughtline* (August 1990), p.3; Lynn F. Perkins, *Masonry in the New Age* (Lakemont, Georgia: CSA Press, 1971), p.241, 307; Brochure from Sancta Sophia Seminary, p.5; Gary Doore, Editor and Compiler, *Shaman's Path: Healing, Personal Growth and Empowerment* (Boston, Massachusetts: Shambhala, 1988), p.66-71; *New Teachings for an Awakening Humanity* (Santa Clara, California: S. E. E. Publishing Company, n.d.), p.1; Wendell C. Beane and William G. Doty, *Myths, Rites, Symbols: A Mircea Eliade Reader* (Vol. II) (New York, New York: Harper Colophon Books, 1975), p.409-411; Colin Wilson, *The Occult: A History* (New York, Random House, 1971), p.207; *New Larousse Encyclopedia of Mythology, op. cit.* p.249, 268; Gaynor, *op. cit.,* p.12; Lash, *op. cit.,* p.63. Books written from a Christian perspective that warn about the occult teachings of the rainbow are: Marrs, *Mystery Mark of the New Age, op. cit.,* p.97-98; Texe Marrs, *Ravaged by the New Age: Satan's Plan to Destroy Our Kids* (Austin, Texas: Living Truth Publishers, 1989), p.63; *The New Age Movement—Age of Aquarius—Age of Antichrist,* Interview with Constance Cumbey (Oklahoma City, Oklahoma: Southwest Radio Church, 1982), p.5.

[105] Dennis L. Cuddy, "The Deceptive New Age 'Service' and 'Light,'" *The Christian World Report* (February 1991, Vol. 3, No. 2), p.8.

[106] Lynn F. Perkins, *Masonry in the New Age* (Lakemont, Georgia: CSA Press, 1971), p.307.

[107] Marrs, *Mystery Mark of the New Age, op. cit.;* See also: Phil Phillips, *Saturday Morning Mind Control* (Nashville, Tennessee: Oliver-Nelson Books, 1991), p.111-112.

[108] *Llewellyn New Times* (September/October 1987, #875), p.72.

[109] Norma Milanovich and Shirley McCune, *The Light Shall Set You Free* (Athena Publishing), p.94.

[110] Letter on file from David J. Meyer, dated September 5, 1993.

[111] *Transmission* (April 1983, No. 1), p.3.

[112] Benjamin Creme, *The Reappearance of the Christ and the Masters of Wisdom* (North Hollywood, California: Tara Center, 1980), p.5.

[113] Dennis Carpenter, "A Special Place in Nature, *Circle Network News* (Spring 1988, Vol. 10, No. 1), p.12.

[114] Van Ault, "Lazaris," *Magical Blend* (February/March/April 1988, Issue #18), p.77.

[115] Summit University Press (30th Anniversary Sale), p.6.

[116] Milanovich and McCune, *op. cit.,* p.29.

[117] For instance, see the following: Newton, *The Religion of Masonry, op. cit.,* p.82; Shirley MacLaine, *Dancing in the Light* (New York, New York: Bantam Books, Inc., 1985), p.36-37; Carla L. Rueckert, *A Channeling Handbook* (Amherst, Wisconsin: Palmer Publications, Inc., 1987), p.21; *Master of Life* (1987, Issue #37), p.17; *Master of Life: Tools and Teachings to Create Your Own Reality* (1986, Issue #32), p.42, 43, 44, 47; *Master of Life: Tools and Teachings to Create Your Own Reality* (1986, Issue #33), p.21; *Master of Life: Tools and Teachings to Create Your Own Reality* (1987, Issue #35), p.8, 11, 13; Don Elkins, Carla Rueckert, and James Allen McCarty *The Ra Material* (Norfolk, Virginia: The Donning Company, 1984), p.30-31; Bernard Gunther, *Energy Ecstasy and Your Seven Vital Chakras* (Van Nuys, California: Newcastle Publishing Company, Inc., 1978), p.6, 91; *Siva's Cosmic Dance* (San Francisco, California: Himalayan Academy, n.d.), p.17; Dave Hunt and T. A. McMahon, *America: The Sorcerer's New Apprentice: The Rise of New Age Shamanism* (Eugene, Oregon: Harvest House Publishers, 1988), p.64-65; p.108, quoting from the Creativity in Business course offered by Stanford Graduate School of Business; Scott Malcolmson, "Sex and Death in Key West," *Mother Jones* (February/March 1988, Vol. 13, No. 2), p.45, 31; Agnes Sanford, *The Healing Light: The Art and Method of Spiritual Healing* (St. Paul, Minnesota: MacAlester Park Publishing Company, 1947), p.146; *Prophecy Newsletter* quoting Benjamin Creme (Vol. 1, No. 6), p.12-13; Kirstine Tomasik, "Your Body, Your Self," *Jr. High Ministry* (September/October 1986, Vol. 1, No.5), p.69-70; Esalen (January-June 1985 Catalog), p.17; Kenneth Ring interview with *Psychic Guide* (March/April/May 1985), p.17; Psychic BookShop, p.8; *Complete Occult Digest A to Z* (North Hollywood, California: International Imports, 1984), p.207; *Self-Help Update: Create Your Own Reality* (1985, Issue #26), p.21, 45, 49, 50, 51, 52; David Spangler, *Emergence: The Rebirth of the Sacred* (New York, New York: Dell Publishing, 1984), p.62; Johanna Michaelsen, *The Beautiful Side of Evil* (Eugene, Oregon: Harvest House Publishers, 1982), p.103; *Self-Help Update: Create Your Own Reality* (Issue #30), p.11; *Self-Help Update: Create Your Own Reality* (Issue #31), p.32; Summit University Press (30th Anniversary Sale), p.6, 21; *Llewellyn New Times* (July/August 1986, #864), p.51; Baraka Bashad, "Trance of the Meeting of Magickal Energies East and West," *Circle Network News* (Spring 1988, Vol. 10, No. 1), p.10; Michael Harismides, "Basic Tree Meditation," p.11, and Selena Fox, "Pennsylvania Dutch Hex Signs," *Circle Network News* (Summer 1987, Vol. 9, No. 2), p.11; Gerald Tros, *New Age Notes* (IBM disk); Maureen Murdock, *Spinning Inward: Using Guided Imagery with Children for Learning, Creativity and Relaxation* (Boston, Massachusetts: Shambhala Publications, Inc., 1987, Revised and Expanded Edition), p.22; "Changing Our Reality," Rita Lynne interview with *Aquarian Voices* (August 1989), p.10; Martin and Deidre Bobgan quoting Bill Wilson, *12 Steps to Destruction: Codependency/Recovery Heresies* (Santa Barbara, California: EastGate Publishers, 1991), p.98; *Pass It On: The Story of Bill Wilson and How the A.A. Message Reached the World* (New York, New York: Alcoholics Anonymous World Services, Inc., 1984), p.120-121; Lily Dale Summer Workshop (Catalog), p.8; Texe Marrs quoting Elizabeth Clare Prophet, *America Shattered* (Austin, Texas: Living Truth Publishers, 1991), p.70; "Teaching Children to Contact Evil Spirits?," compiled from a report issued by the National Association of Christian Educators in *"God's Watchman"* and the Hope of Israel (Vol. 18, No. 1), p.14-15, etc.

[118] J. Gordon Melton, *The Encyclopedia of American Religions* (Vol. 2) (Wilmington, North Carolina: McGrath Publishing Company, 1978), p.262.

[119] *Circle Network News* (Summer 1987, Vol. 9, No. 2), p.20.

[120] Melton, *op. cit.*

[121] Blavatsky, *The Secret Doctrine, op. cit.* (Vol. I—Cosmogenesis), p.379.

[122] Manly Palmer Hall, *Initiates of the Flame* (Los Angeles, California: The Phoenix Press, 1934), p.32.

[123] Berger, *op. cit.,* p.47; Charles Clyde Hunt, *Some Thoughts on Masonic Symbolism* (New York: Macoy Publishing and Masonic Supply Company, 1930), p.219.

[124] Henry Ridgely Evans, "Egyptian Decorations of Naval Lodge No. 3, Washington, D.C.," *The New Age Magazine* (May 1948, Vol. 56, No. 5) p.285.

[125] Autumn Moon, "Amulets of the Nile Gods," *Circle Network News* (Summer 1987, Vol. 9, No. 2), p.14.

[126] Hall, *op. cit.,* p.33.

[127] Albert Pike, *The Magnum Opus* (Kila, Montana: Kessinger Publishing Company, 1992), p.xviii.

[128] Manly Palmer Hall, *The Secret Teachings of All Ages* (Los Angeles, California: The Philosophical Research Society Press, 1945), p.xciii.

[129] Marrs, *Mystery Mark of the New Age, op. cit.,* p.114.

[130] Cirlot, *op. cit.,* p.193.

[131] *Ibid.,* p.199.

[132] M. Esther Harding, *Woman's Mysteries: Ancient and Modern* (G. P. Putnam's Sons, 1971 Edition), p.224.

[133] Sybil Leek, *Numerology: The Magic of Numbers* (New York, New York: The MacMillan Company, 1969), p.110-111; See also: Geoffrey Parrinder, Editor, *World Religions: From Ancient History to the Present* (New York, New York: Facts on File Publications, 1983), p.302.

Chapter 16: Zodiac Signs

[1] John Ellis Sech, "The Fears of Babylon," *Fate* (September 1990, Vol. 43, No. 9, Issue 486), p.37.

[2] Wilson D. Wallis, "Occult," *The World Book Encyclopedia* (1961 Edition, Vol. 13), p.487.

[3] Bart J. Bok, "Astrology," *The World Book Encyclopedia* (1961 Edition, Vol. 1), p.675.

[4] *The World Book Encyclopedia* (1961 Edition, Vol. 12), p.47.

[5] Nat Freedland, *The Occult Explosion* (New York: G. P. Putnam's and Sons, 1972), p.111.

[6] *Ibid.,* p.15.

[7] Harry E. Wedeck, *Treasury of Witchcraft* (New York: Philosophical Library, 1961), p.219.

[8] Frank Gaynor, Editor, *Dictionary of Mysticism* (New York: Philosophical Library, 1953), p.72.

[9] Kenneth R. H. MacKenzie, Editor, *The Royal Masonic Cyclopaedia of History, Rites, Symbolism, and Biography* (New York: J. W. Bouton, 1877), p.266.

[10] F. De P. Castells, *Antiquity of the Holy Royal Arch: The Supreme Degree in Freemasonry* (London, England: A. Lewis, 1927), p.154-155.

[11] *Ibid.,* p.155; See also: S. R. Parchment, *Ancient Operative Masonry* (San Francisco, California: San Francisco Center—Rosicrucian Fellowship, 1930), p.16; R. Swinburne Clymer, *The Mysteries of Osiris or Ancient Egyptian Initiation* (Quakertown, Pennsylvania: 1951, Revised Edition), p.147; F. de P. Castells, *Origin of the Masonic Degrees* (London, England: A. Lewis, 1928), p.188.

[12] Harold Waldwin Percival, *Masonry and Its Symbols in the Light of "Thinking and Destiny"* (New York, New York: The Word Foundation, Inc., 1952), p.58.

[13] George H. Steinmetz, *The Lost Word: Its Hidden Meaning: A Correlation of the Allegory and Symbolism of the Bible with That of Freemasonry and an Exposition of the Secret Doctrine* (New York: Macoy Publishing and Masonic Supply Company, 1953), p.224, 226.

[14] *Charisma and Christian Life* (November 1991, Vol. 17, No. 4), p.57.

[15] D. James Kennedy, *The Gospel in the Stars* (Fort Lauderdale, Florida: Coral Ridge Ministries, n.d.), p.9; See also: D. James Kennedy, *The Real Meaning of the Zodiac: Capricornus* (Fort Lauderdale, Florida: Coral Ridge Ministries, n.d.), p.2.

[16] *Ibid.*, p.2.

[17] "D. James Kennedy," Rick Miesel, *BDM Letter* (November 1992, Vol. 1, No. 9), p.3.

[18] Texe Marrs, *Mystery Mark of the New Age: Satan's Design for World Domination* (Westchester, Illinois: Crossway Books, 1988), p.86; See also: Texe Marrs, *Dark Majesty: The Secret Brotherhood and the Magic of a Thousand Points of Light* (Austin, Texas: Living Truth Publishers, 1992), p.41.

[19] Texe Marrs, *Texe Marrs Book of New Age Cults and Religions* (Austin, Texas: Living Truth Publishers, 1990), p.139-140.

[20] *Yoga International* (March/April 1994, Vol. 3, No. 5), p.69.

[21] Martin and Deidre Bobgan, *Four Temperaments, Astrology, and Personality Testing* (Santa Barbara, California: EastGate Publishers, 1992), p.115-116.

Chapter 17: Talismans

[1] E. A. Wallis Budge, *Amulets and Superstitions* (New York, New York: Dover Publications, Inc., 1978), p.14.

[2] Catalog, p.112.

[3] Arthur Edward Waite, *The Mysteries of Magic: A Digest of the Writings of Eliphas Levi* (Chicago, Illinois: De Laurence, Scott and Company, 1909), p.217.

[4] Catalog ad.

[5] Catalog ad.

[6] Catalog entitled *The Pyramid Collection* (Late Summer 1997), p.34.

[7] *Pyramid Books and New-Age Collection* Catalog (Received March 21, 1992), p.13.

[8] Jeff Godwin, *What's Wrong with Christian Rock?* (Chino, California: Chick Publications, 1990), p.47.

[9] Jeff Godwin, *Dancing with Demons: The Music's Real Master* (Chino, California: Chick Publications, 1988), p.251.

[10] *The World Book Encyclopedia* (1961 Edition, Vol. 15), p.481.

[11] *Ibid.* See also: *Llewellyn New Times* (July/August 1990, #904, p.8; *New Larousse Encyclopedia of Mythology* (Prometheus Press, 1972 Edition), p.255; Thomas Bulfinch, *Bulfinch's Mythology: The Age of Fable or Stories of Gods and Heroes* (Garden City, New York, 1948), p.381.

[12] Catalog from Esalen (January-June 1985), p.10.

[13] *Circle Network News* (Summer 1987, Vol. 9, No. 2), p.13; Holistic Health Catalog, p.22; Mother Owl's Aquarian Age Information Network Catalog, p.7; Omega Institute (Summer 1986), p.34.

[14] *Magical Arts* (Alexandria, Virginia: Time-Life Books, 1990), p.27.

[15] Godwin, *What's Wrong with Christian Rock?, op. cit.*

[16] Catalog from The Occult Emporium (Winter 1993 to Winter 1994), p.34; Catalog from The Occult Emporium (Mid 1990 to 1991), p.27.

[17] Eric Barger, *From Rock to Rock: The Music of Darkness Exposed!* (Lafayette, Louisiana: Huntington House, Inc., 1990), p.169.

[18] Catalog from The Occult Emporium (Winter 1993 to Winter 1994), p.36.

Chapter 18: Jewelry

[1] Scott Cunningham, *Cunningham's Encyclopedia of Crystal, Gem and Metal Magic* (St. Paul, Minnesota: Llewellyn Publications, 1988), p.55; See also: M. C. Poinsot, *The Occult Sciences* (New York: Robert M. McBride and Company, 1972), p.319.

[2] Laurie Cabot with Tom Cowan, *Power of the Witch: The Earth, the Moon, and the Magical Path to Enlightenment* (New York, New York: Delacorte Press, 1989), p.133.

[3] Bernard E. Jones, *Freemasons' Book of the Royal Arch* (London, England: George G. Harrap and Company Ltd., 1957), p.230; See also: Bernard E. Jones, *Freemasons' Guide and Compendium* (New York: Macoy Publishing and Masonic Supply Company), p.406-407.

[4] Sybil Leek, *Numerology: The Magic of Numbers* (New York, New York: The MacMillan Company, 1969), p.117; See also: Joseph R. Chambers, *Jewelry, Paganism and the New Age* (Charlotte, North Carolina: Paw Creek Ministries, n.d.), p.2.

[5] *Ibid.,* p.118.

[6] *Light Speed* (1993, Issue 13), p.15.

[7] *Self-Help Update: Create Your Own Reality* (1985, Issue #29), p.63.

[8] Catalog from Prisma, p.5.

[9] M. C. Poinsot, *The Occult Sciences* (New York: Robert M. McBride and Company, 1972), p.319.

[10] Catalog from Christian Book Distributors (Summer 1998), p.62.

[11] Scott Cunningham, *Wicca: A Guide for the Solitary Practitioner* (St. Paul, Minnesota: Llewellyn Publications, 1989), p.51.

[12] Jeff Godwin, *Dancing with Demons: The Music's Real Master* (Chino, California: Chick Publications, 1988), p.111.

[13] Tanya Turner, *New Age Emphasis on Stones and Gems: A Revival of Paganism* (Charlotte, North Carolina: Paw Creek Ministries, n.d.), p.4.

[14] *Ibid.,* p.1.

[15] Catalog from Prisma, p.6.

[16] Cunningham, *Cunningham's Encyclopedia of Crystal, Gem and Metal Magic, op. cit.,* p.128-129.

[17] Catalog from Prisma, p.6.

[18] Cunningham, *Cunningham's Encyclopedia of Crystal, Gem and Metal Magic, op. cit.,* p.121.

[19] *Ibid.*

[20] *Ibid.,* p.121-122.

[21] Catalog from Prisma, p.6.

[22] Cunningham, *Cunningham's Encyclopedia of Crystal, Gem and Metal Magic, op. cit.,* p.69-70.

[23] Catalog from Prisma, p.12.

[24] Cunningham, *Cunningham's Encyclopedia of Crystal, Gem and Metal Magic, op. cit.* p.56-57.

[25] Udo Becker, *The Continuum Encyclopedia of Symbols* (New York: Continuum, 1994).

[26] Charles G. Berger, *Our Phallic Heritage* (New York, New York: Greenwich Book Publishers, Inc., 1966), p.176.

[27] Manly Palmer Hall, *The Secret Teachings of All Ages* (Los Angeles, California: The Philosophical Research Society Press, 1945, Seventh Edition), p.c.

[28] M. C. Poinsot, *The Occult Sciences* (New York: Robert M. McBride and Company, 1972), p.320.

[29] Maurice Bessy, *A Pictorial History of Magic and the Supernatural* (New York: Hamlyn Publishing Group Limited, 1964), p.56; See also: Joseph Wallman, *The Kabalah: From Its Inception to Its Evanescence* (Brooklyn, New York: Theological Research Publishing Company, 1958), p.1, 162.

[30] Joseph Wallman, *The Kabalah: From Its Inception to Its Evanescence* (Brooklyn, New York: Theological Research Publishing Company, 1958), p.162; Frank Gaynor, Editor, *Dictionary of Mysticism* (New York: Philosophical Library, 1953), p.134; *The World Book Encyclopedia* (1961 Edition, Vol. 14), p.91; Kurt Koch, Translated by Michael Freeman, *Occult ABC* (Germany: Literature Mission Aglasterhausen Inc., 1978), p.103.

[31] Rossell Hope Robbins, *The Encyclopedia of Witchcraft and Demonology* (New York, New York: Crown Publishers, Inc., 1966); Frank Gaynor, Editor, *Dictionary of Mysticism* (New York: Philosophical Library, 1953), p.36.

[32] Frank Gaynor, Editor, *Dictionary of Mysticism* (New York: Philosophical Library, 1953), p.36.

[33] *The World Book Encyclopedia* (1961 Edition, Vol. 14), p.91.

[34] Cunningham, *Cunningham's Encyclopedia of Crystal, Gem and Metal Magic, op. cit.,* p.57.

[35] J. E. Cirlot, *A Dictionary of Symbols* (New York, New York: Philosophical Library, Inc., 1972), p.227.

[36] Irene Arrington Park, *What Every Christian Should Know About Symbols, Signs and Emblems* (Tampa, Florida: Christ's Deliverance Ministries, 1982), p.3.

[37] *Ibid.*

[38] Eric Barger, *From Rock to Rock: The Music of Darkness Exposed!* (Lafayette, Louisiana: Huntington House, Inc., 1990), p.171.

[39] *Last Trumpet Newsletter* (July 1986, Vol. 5, Issue 7), p.3.

[40] Betty Miller, *Exposing Satan's Devices* (Dewey, Arizona: Christ Unlimited Ministries, Inc., 1980), p.34.

[41] Park, *op. cit.,* p.4.

[42] Editor of Time-Life Books, *Magical Arts* (Alexandria, Virginia, 1990), p.118.

[43] Cunningham, *Cunningham's Encyclopedia of Crystal, Gem and Metal Magic, op. cit.,* p.57-58.

[44] *Last Trumpet Newsletter* (October 1994, Vol. 13, Issue 10), p.3.

[45] Cunningham, *Cunningham's Encyclopedia of Crystal, Gem and Metal Magic, op. cit.,* p.57.

[46] Cabot *op. cit.,* p.245-246.

[47] *Ibid.,* p.245.

[48] *Ibid.,* p.245-246.

[49] "Superstitions Get Some Started in Witchcraft," *Shepherdsfield Update* (Spring 1989, No. 22), p.20.

[50] Nels Pedersen, "The Painted Face," *The Satisfying Portion* (March/April 1991, Vol. 18, No. 1), p.5.

Chapter 19: Masonic and Eastern Star Symbols

[1] Arthur Edward Waite, *The Mysteries of Magic: A Digest of the Writings of Eliphas Levi* (Chicago, Illinois: De Laurence, Scott and Company, 1909), p.217.

[2] *The World Book Encyclopedia* (1961 Edition, Vol. 18), p.251; *Webster's Seventh New Collegiate Dictionary,* 1967, p.502; Joseph Carr, *The Lucifer Connection* (Lafayette, Louisiana: Huntington House, Inc., 1987), p.139; Manly Palmer Hall, *America's Assignment with Destiny* (Los Angeles, California: Philosophical Research Society, Inc., 1951), p.19; H. P. Blavatsky, *The Secret Doctrine: The Synthesis of Science, Religion, and Philosophy* (Vol. II—Anthropogenesis) (Covina, California: Theosophical University Press, 1947, Fourth Edition), p.759.

[3] Waite, *op. cit.,* p.205; Rex R. Hutchens, *A Bridge to Light* (Washington, D.C.: Supreme Council, 33° Ancient and Accepted Scottish Rite of Freemasonry, Southern Jurisdiction, 1988), p.201, 205.

[4] M. Temple Richmond, *Sirius* (Mariposa, California: Source Publications, 1997), p.209.

[5] Albert Pike, *Morals and Dogma of the Ancient and Accepted Scottish Rite of Freemasonry* (Richmond, Virginia: L. H. Jenkins, Inc., 1871), p.632.

[6] William Schnobelen, *Masonry: Beyond the Light* (Chino, California: Chick Publications, 1991), p.121.

[7] Jean M'Kee Kenaston, Compiler, *History of the Order of the Eastern Star* (Cedar Rapids, Iowa: The Torch Press, 1917), p.664; *Pocket Masonic Dictionary* (Silver Spring, Maryland: The Masonic Service Association of the United States, 1988), p.9; *What? When? Where? Why? Who? in*

Freemasonry (Silver Spring, Maryland: Masonic Service Association of the United States, 1956), p.11; Robert Macoy (Arranged by), *Adoptive Rite Ritual* (Virginia: Macoy Publishing and Masonic Supply Company, 1897), p.114-115; W. J. McCormick, *Christ, the Christian and Freemasonry* (Belfast, Ireland: Great Joy Publications, 1984), p.87; F. A. Bell, *Bell's Eastern Star Ritual* (P. R. C. Publications, Inc., 1988 Revised Edition), p.89.

[8] *Pocket Encyclopedia of Masonic Symbols* (Silver Spring, Maryland: The Masonic Service Association of the United States, 1953), p.15; See also: *What? When? Where? Why? Who? in Freemasonry* (Silver Spring, Maryland: Masonic Service Association of the United States, 1956), p.11.

[9] Joseph Fort Newton, *The Builders: A Story and Study of Masonry* (Cedar Rapids, Iowa: The Torch Press, 1914), p.9.

[10] "The Broken Column," *Short Talk Bulletin* (February 1956, Vol. 34, No. 2; Reprinted January 1985), p.6-7; See also: Edmond Ronayne, *The Master's Carpet (Mah-Hah-Bone)* (n.p., 1879), p.387-388; W. J. McCormick, *Christ, the Christian and Freemasonry* (Belfast, Ireland: Great Joy Publications, 1984), p.87; Malcolm Duncan, *Duncan's Ritual of Freemasonry* (New York: David McKay Company, Inc., n.d., 3rd Edition), p.125; Harold Waldwin Percival, *Masonry and Its Symbols in the Light of "Thinking and Destiny"* (New York, New York: The Word Foundation, Inc., 1952), p.35; *What? When? Where? Why? Who? in Freemasonry* (Silver Spring, Maryland: Masonic Service Association of the United States, 1956), p.80.

[11] William Schnoebelen, *Masonry: Beyond the Light* (Chino, California: Chick Publications, 1991), p.158; See also: Percival George Woodcock, *Short Dictionary of Mythology* (Philosophical Library, 1953), p.145; Charles G. Berger, *Our Phallic Heritage* (New York, New York: Greenwich Book Publishers, Inc., 1966), p.40; J. E. Cirlot (Translated by Jack Sage), *A Dictionary of Symbols* (New York: Dorset Press, 1991 Edition), p.278.

[12] A. T. C. Pierson, *The Traditions, Origin and Early History of Freemasonry* (New York: Masonic Publishing Company, 1865), p.232.

[13] J. S. M. Ward, *Freemasonry and the Ancient Gods* (London: Simpkin, Marshall, Hamilton, Kent and Company, Ltd., 1921), p.232; See also: Texe Marrs, *Mystery Mark of the New Age: Satan's Design for World Domination* (Westchester, Illinois: Crossway Books, 1988), p.69.

[14] J. E. Cirlot, *A Dictionary of Symbols* (New York, New York: Philosophical Library, Inc., 1972), p.278.

[15] Waite, *op. cit.,* p.217; Percival George Woodcock, *Short Dictionary of Mythology* (Philosophical Library, 1953), p.135; *Ibid.,* p.281.

[16] Cirlot *op. cit.,* p.281; See also: George Oliver, *Signs and Symbols* (New York: Macoy Publishing and Masonic Supply Company, 1906), p.82; Charles Scott, *The Analogy of Ancient Craft Masonry to Natural and Revealed Religion* (Philadelphia, Pennsylvania: E. H. Butler and Company, 1857), p.311.

[17] Veronica Ions, *Egyptian Mythology* (England: The Hamlyn Publishing Group, Ltd., 1965), p.85.

[18] *Ibid.,* p.58, 75, 85, 91; *New Larousse Encyclopedia of Mythology* (Prometheus Press, 1972 Edition), p.19; E. A. Wallis Budge, *Amulets and Superstitions* (New York, New York: Dover Publications, Inc., 1978), p.xix.

[19] Frank Gaynor, Editor, *Dictionary of Mysticism* (New York: Philosophical Library, 1953), p.87.

[20] William T. Still, *New World Order: The Ancient Plan of Secret Societies* (Lafayette, Louisiana: Huntington House, Inc., 1990), p.24.

[21] R. Swinburne Clymer, *The Mysteries of Osiris or Ancient Egyptian Initiation* (Quakertown, Pennsylvania: The Philosophical Publishing Company, 1951, Revised Edition), p.63.

[22] Waite, *op. cit.*

[23] Clifton L. Fowler, *Santa Claus and Christmas* (Knoxville, Tennessee: Evangelist of Truth, 1982), p.28.

[24] John Yarker, *The Arcane Schools: A Review of Their Origin and Antiquity: With a General History of Freemasonry and Its Relation to the Theosophic Scientific and Philosophic Mysteries* (Belfast, Ireland: William Tait, 1909), p.267.

[25] Kenaston, *op. cit.;* Willis D. Engle, *A General History of the Order of the Eastern Star* (Indianapolis, Indiana: Willis D. Engle, 1901), p.71; Robert Macoy (Arranged by), *Adoptive Rite Ritual* (Virginia: Macoy Publishing and Masonic Supply Company, 1897), p.127; Shirley Plessner, *Symbolism of the Eastern Star* (Cleveland, Ohio: Gilbert Publishing Company, 1956), p.101; Carl H. Claudy, *Masonic Harvest* (Washington, D.C.: The Temple Publishers, 1948), p.234-235; W. L. Wilmshurst, *The Masonic Initiation* (Ferndale, Michigan: Trismegistus Press, 1980; Originally published 1924), 52-53; Albert G. Mackey, *The Symbolism of Freemasonry* (New York: Clark and Maynard, 1869), p.253, 261; "Veiled in Allegory and Illustrated by Symbols," *Short Talk Bulletin* (November 1974; Vol. 52, No. 11), p.3; Arthur Edward Waite, *The Secret Tradition in Freemasonry* (London: Rider and Company, 1937), p.646, 650; *Masonic Vocabulary* (Silver Spring, Maryland: Masonic Service Association of the United States, 1955), p.4; *What? When? Where? Why? Who? in Freemasonry* (Silver Spring, Maryland: Masonic Service Association of the United States, 1956), p.2; Schnoebelen, *op. cit.; Pocket Encyclopedia of Masonic Symbols* (Silver Spring, Maryland: The Masonic Service Association of the United States, 1953), p.5; *Pocket Masonic Dictionary* (Silver Spring, Maryland: The Masonic Service Association of the United States, 1988), p.6, 14; Manly Palmer Hall, *An Encyclopedic Outline of Masonic, Hermetic, Qabbalistic and Rosicrucian Symbolical Philosophy: Being an Interpretation of the Secret Teachings Concealed Within the Rituals, Allegories and Mysteries of All Ages* (San Francisco, California: H. S. Crocker Company, Inc., 1928), p.36; John J. Robinson, *Born in Blood: The Lost Secrets of Freemasonry* (New York, New York: M. Evans and Company, 1989), p.222, 270, 271.

[26] Albert G. Mackey, *The Symbolism of Freemasonry* (New York: Clark and Maynard, 1869), p.259-260 in correlation with p.261.

[27] *Pocket Encyclopedia of Masonic Symbols, op. cit.,* p.5; See also: *What? When? Where? Why? Who? in Freemasonry* (Silver Spring, Maryland: Masonic Service Association of the United States, 1956), p.2.

[28] Texe Marrs, *Mystery Mark of the New Age: Satan's Design for World Domination* (Westchester, Illinois: Crossway Books, 1988), p.65; Helena Petrovna Blavatsky, *Isis Unveiled,* Vol. I: Science (New York, New York: Trow's Printing and Bookbinding Company, 1877), p.263, 578.

[29] Albert G. Mackey, *A Manual of the Lodge* (New York: Charles E. Merrill Company, 1870), p.56; See also: Mackey, *The Symbolism of Freemasonry, op. cit.,* p.60.

[30] Mary Ann Slipper, *The Symbolism of the Eastern Star* (n.p., 1927), p.36.

[31] J. D. Buck, *Mystic Masonry* (Illinois: Indo-American Book Company, 1913, Sixth Edition), p.244; Harold Waldwin Percival, *Masonry and Its Symbols in the Light of "Thinking and Destiny"* (New York, New York: The Word Foundation, Inc., 1952), p.50; C. F. McQuaig quoting J. D. Buck, *The Masonic Report* (Norcross, Georgia: Answer Books and Tapes, 1976), p.51.

[32] Jim Shaw and Tom McKenney, *The Deadly Deception* (Lafayette, Louisiana: Huntington House, Inc., 1988), p.143-144; See also: Pike, *op. cit.,* p.850-851 for more explanation of these symbols.

[33] Schnoebelen, *op. cit.,* p.146.

[34] Mackey, *The Symbolism of Freemasonry, op. cit.,* p.294.

[35] *Ibid.,* p.164.

[36] *Ibid.*

[37] Albert Churchward, *Signs and Symbols of Primordial Man: The Evolution of Religious Doctrine from the Eschatology of the Ancient Egyptians* (London, England: George Allen and Company, Ltd., 1913, Second Edition), p.289, 303.

[38] Newton, *op. cit.,* p.28.

[39] *History of the Order of the Eastern Star* (General Grand Chapter in the U. S. A., 1989), p.21.

[40] Laurie Cabot with Tom Cowan, *Power of the Witch: The Earth, the Moon, and the Magical Path to Enlightenment* (New York, New York: Delacorte Press, 1989), p.95.

[41] Pike, *op. cit.,* p.459.

[42] Cirlot *op. cit.,* p.173.

[43] Morning Glory and Otter G'Zell, *Who on Earth Is the Goddess?* (Berkeley, California: Covenant of the Goddess, n.d.), p.2.

[44] Slipper, *op. cit.,* p.137.

[45] John Lash, *The Seeker's Handbook: The Complete Guide to Spiritual Pathfinding* (New York: Harmony Books, 1990), p.307.

[46] *Ibid.*

[47] *Watchman Mini-Expositor* (March 1997), p.2.

[48] Dennis Laurence Cuddy, *Now Is the Dawning of the New Age New World Order* (Oklahoma City, Oklahoma: Hearthstone Publishing Ltd., 1991), p.206.

[49] *Ibid.,* p.205-206.

[50] James S. Fritz, "Alchemy," *The World Book Encyclopedia* (1961 Edition, Vol. 1), p.468; See also: *Chrysalis* (Autumn 1987, Vol. 2, Issue 3), p.252.

[51] Richmond, *op. cit.,* p.119.

[52] *Circle Network News* (Summer 1987, Vol. 9, No. 2), p.15.

[53] Pike, *op. cit.,* p.376, 378; See also: "Mosaic Pavement and Blazing Star," *Short Talk Bulletin* (April 1951, Vol. 29, No. 4; Reprinted April 1990), p.7-8; Churchward, *op. cit.,* p.206.

[54] Pike, *op. cit.,* p.430; See also: The Rim Institute (1989 Catalog of Summer Programs), p.16; Gaynor, *op. cit.,* p.13; Thomas Bulfinch, *Bulfinch's Mythology* (New York: Thomas Y. Crowell Company, Inc., 1970), p.907; Fritz, *op. cit.,* p.468.

[55] Ions, *op. cit.,* p.83.

[56] Pike, *op. cit.; New Larousse Encyclopedia of Mythology* (Prometheus Press, 1972 Edition), p.25; *Ibid.;* Geoffrey Parrinder, Editor, *World Religions: From Ancient History to the Present* (New York, New York: Facts on File, 1971), p.141; *Circle Network News* (Summer 1987), *op. cit.,* p.14; Percival George Woodcock, *Short Dictionary of Mythology* (Philosophical Library, 1953), p.16; Gaynor, *op. cit.,* p.13; Cabot *op. cit.,* p.48; Fritz, *op. cit.,* p.468.

[57] *New Larousse Encyclopedia of Mythology* (Prometheus Press, 1972 Edition), p.27; Campbell, *The Hero with a Thousand Faces, op. cit.,* p.72; Editors of Time-Life Books, *Magical Arts* (Alexandria, Virginia: Time-Life Books, 1990), p.53; Charles F. Pfeiffer, Editor, *The Biblical World: A Dictionary of Biblical Archaeology* (New York: Bonanza Books, 1966), p.218, 482; Brochure from Wise Woman Center, unnumbered page; Ions, *op. cit.,* p.86-87; Gaynor, *op. cit.,* p.186; Carl C. Jung, M.-L. von Franz, Joseph L. Henderson, Jolande Jacobe, Aniela Jaffe, *Man and His Symbols* (Garden City, New Jersey: Doubleday and Company, Inc., 1964), p.156; *The World Book Encyclopedia* (1961 Edition, Vol. 17), p.206; Cirlot, *op. cit.,* p.155.

[58] *The World Book Encyclopedia* (1961 Edition, Vol. 16), p.250.

[59] Ions, *op. cit.,* p.63.

[60] Brochure from Wise Woman Center, unnumbered page; Catalog from Abyss, p.39; Geoffrey Parrinder, Editor, *World Religions: From Ancient History to the Present* (New York, New York: Facts on File, 1971), p.141; Ions, *op. cit.,* p.21, 86.

[61] Catalog from Sounds True, Inside Front Cover; *The World Book Encyclopedia* (1961 Edition, Vol. 14), p.93.

[62] Catalog from Abyss, p.39.

[63] Frederic Portal (Translated by John W. Simons), *A Comparison of Egyptian Symbols with Those of the Hebrews* (New York: Masonic Publishing and Manufacturing Company, 1866), p.50-51; See also: *Last Trumpet Newsletter* (April 1993, Vol. 12, Issue 4), p.2; John B. Harrison and Richard E. Sullivan, *A Short History of Western Civilization* (New York: Alfred A. Knopf, 1960), p.13-14; Gaynor, *op. cit.,* p.103; Geoffrey Parrinder, Editor, *World Religions: From Ancient History to the Present* (New York, New York: Facts on File, 1971), p.181.

[64] *Last Trumpet Newsletter* (April 1993, Vol. 12, Issue 4), p.2.

[65] Shaw and McKenney, *op. cit.,* p.85; Rex Hutchens, *A Bridge to Light* (Washington, D.C.: Supreme Council, 33° Ancient and Accepted Scottish Rite of Freemasonry, Southern Jurisdiction, 1988), p.300-301.

[66] Rex R. Hutchens, *A Bridge to Light* (Washington, D.C.: Supreme Council, 33° Ancient and Accepted Scottish Rite of Freemasonry, Southern Jurisdiction, 1988), p.300-301.

[67] Sarah H. Terry, *The Second Mile* (Corpus Christi, Texas: Christian Triumph Press, 1935), p.73; See also: George Oliver, *Signs and Symbols* (New York: Macoy Publishing and Masonic Supply Company, 1906), p.14; Yarker, *op. cit.,* p.222; Thomas Bulfinch, *Bulfinch's Mythology* (New York: Thomas Y. Crowell Company, Inc., 1970), p.972.

[68] Gaynor, *op. cit.,* p.186.

[69] Pike, *op. cit.,* p.13, 552; See also: W. L. Wilmshurst, *The Masonic Initiation* (Ferndale, Michigan: Trismegistus Press, 1980; Originally published 1924), p.92; Charles H. Vail, *The Ancient Mysteries and Modern Masonry* (New York: Macoy Publishing and Masonic Supply Company, 1909), p.67; *Pocket Encyclopedia of Masonic Symbols* (Silver Spring, Maryland: The Masonic Service Association of the United States, 1953), p.51; Hutchens, *op. cit.,* p.231; Percival George Woodcock, *Short Dictionary of Mythology* (Philosophical Library, 1953), p.144; Gaynor, *op. cit.*

[70] Pike, *op. cit.,* p.15.

[71] *Ibid.,* p.368.

[72] Stephen Knight, *The Brotherhood: The Secret World of the Freemasons* (Briarcliff Manor, New York: Stein and Day, 1984), p.236.

[73] Pike, *op. cit.*

[74] Einar Haugen, "Thor," *The World Book Encyclopedia* (1961 Edition, Vol. 17), p.204.

[75] *The World Book Encyclopedia* (1961 Edition, Vol. 17), p.204; See also: *Pocket Encyclopedia of Masonic Symbols* (Silver Spring, Maryland: The Masonic Service Association of the United States, 1953), p.51; Gaynor, *op. cit.;* George Oliver, *Signs and Symbols* (New York: Macoy Publishing and Masonic Supply Company, 1906), p.14; Percival George Woodcock, *Short Dictionary of Mythology* (Philosophical Library, 1953), p.144; Thomas Bulfinch, *Bulfinch's Mythology* (New York: Thomas Y. Crowell Company, Inc., 1970), p.972.

[76] Ward, *op. cit.,* p.238.

[77] *Ibid.,* p.241.

[78] Godfrey Higgins, *Anacalypsis, An Attempt to Draw Aside the Veil of the Saitic Isis* (London, England: J. Burns, 1874), p.373; See also: Yarker, *op. cit.,* p.146; Thomas Albert Stafford, *Christian Symbolism in the Evangelical Churches* (Nashville, Tennessee: Abingdon Press, 1942), p.68; Catalog entitled *The Pyramid Collection* (Late Summer 1997), p.7.

[79] Henry Ridgely Evans, "Egyptian Decorations of Naval Lodge No 4, Washington, D.C.," *The New Age Magazine* (May 1948, Vol. 56, No. 5), p.283, 284; Herbert F. Inman, *Masonic Problems and Queries* (London, England: A. Lewis Ltd., 1978), p.37; Ray V. Denslow, *Masonic Portraits* (Transactions of the Missouri Lodge of Research, Vol. #29, 1972), p.7; E. A. Wallis Budge, *Amulets and Superstitions* (New York, New York: Dover Publications, Inc., 1978), p.134; Churchward, *op. cit.,* p.368; Marrs, *Mystery Mark of the New Age, op. cit.,* p.112; Thomas Milton Stewart, *The Symbolism of the Gods of the Egyptians and the Light They Throw on Freemasonry* (London, England: Baskerville Press, Ltd., 1927), p.84; Catalog from Occult Emporium (Winter 1993 to Winter 1994), p.34.

[80] Gaynor, *op. cit.,* p.12.

[81] Count Goblet D'Alviella, *The Migration of Symbols* (Westminster: Archibald Constable and Company, 1894), p.188.

[82] Rollin C. Blackmer, *The Lodge and the Craft: A Practical Explanation of the Work of Freemasonry* (St. Louis, Missouri: The Standard Masonic Publishing Company, 1923), p.249. See also: Yarker, *op. cit.,* p.23; Kenneth R. H. MacKenzie, Editor, *The Royal Masonic Cyclopaedia of History, Rites, Symbolism, and Biography* (New York: J. W. Bouton, 1877), p.142; E. A. Wallis Budge, *Amulets and Superstitions* (New York, New York: Dover Publications, Inc., 1978), p.134; Churchward, *op. cit.,* p.368; Margot Adler, *Drawing Down the Moon: Witches, Druids, Goddess-Worshippers, and Other Pagans in America Today* (New York, New York: The Viking Press, 1979), p.125; Thomas Milton Stewart, *The Symbolism of the Gods of the Egyptians and the Light They Throw on Freemasonry* (London, England: Baskerville Press, Ltd., 1927), p.118.

[83] Ed and Mary Tarkowski, "What Is the Occult? A Glossary of Occult Terms," *The Origins, Practices and Traditions of Halloween* (Erie, Pennsylvania: Guardians of the Heart, n.d.), p.7.

[84] Irene Arrington Park, *What Every Christian Should Know About Symbols, Signs and Emblems* (Tampa, Florida: Christ's Deliverance Ministries, 1982), p.2.

[85] Herbert F. Inman, *Masonic Problems and Queries* (London, England: A. Lewis Ltd., 1978), p.37.

[86] H. P. Blavatsky, *The Secret Doctrine: The Synthesis of Science, Religion, and Philosophy* (Vol. II—Anthropogenesis) (Covina, California: Theosophical University Press, 1947, Fourth Edition), p.587.

[87] Kenneth R. H. MacKenzie, Editor, *The Royal Masonic Cyclopaedia of History, Rites, Symbolism, and Biography* (New York: J. W. Bouton, 1877), p.352-353; See also: *New Larousse Encyclopedia of Mythology, op. cit.,* p.257.

[88] E. A. Wallis Budge, *Amulets and Superstitions* (New York, New York: Dover Publications, Inc., 1978), p.333.

[89] Yarker, *op. cit.,* p.222.

[90] Dennis Laurence Cuddy, *Chronology of Education with Quotable Quotes* (Highland City, Florida: Pro Family Forum, Inc., 1994, Updated, Bound Volume), p.51.

[91] Churchward, *op. cit.,* p.465.

[92] *Ibid.,* p.353, 465.

[93] J. Edward Decker, Editor, *The Dark Side of Freemasonry* (Lafayette, Louisiana: Huntington House Publishers, 1994), p.204.

[94] Newton, *op. cit.,* p.24.

[95] *Hinduism Today* (February 1992, Vol. 14, No. 2), p.13. "The information in this article draws primarily from a 300-page US government study of the swastika researched under the auspices of the Smithsonian Institution, published in 1984." See also: John Blofeld, *The Tantric Mysticism of Tibet* (Boston, Massachusetts: Shambhala Publications, Inc., 1970), p.102.

[96] M. Esther Harding, *Woman's Mysteries: Ancient and Modern* (New York: G. P. Putnam's Sons for the C. G. Jung Foundation for Analytical Psychology, 1971 Edition), p.223. See also: Ward, *op. cit.,* p.11; Budge, *Amulets and Superstitions, op. cit.,* p.332.

[97] Gaynor, *op. cit.,* p.177. See also: Cirlot, *op. cit.,* p.322-323; A. Ralph Epperson, *The New World Order* (Tucson, Arizona: Publius Press, 1990), p.132; Thomas Albert Stafford, *Christian Symbolism in the Evangelical Churches* (Nashville, Tennessee: Abingdon Press, 1942), p.74.

[98] A. Ralph Epperson, *The New World Order* (Tucson, Arizona: Publius Press, 1990), p.132; Joseph J. Carr, *The Twisted Cross* (Shreveport, Louisiana: Huntington House Inc., 1985), p.103; Texe Marrs, *Dark Secrets of the New Age: Satan's Plan for a One World Religion* (Westchester, Illinois: Crossway Books, 1987), p.252.

[99] Cuddy, *Now Is the Dawning, op. cit.,* p.46, 111; Texe Marrs, *Texe Marrs Book of New Age Cults and Religions* (Austin, Texas: Living Truth Publishers, 1990), p.318; Joseph J. Carr, *The Twisted Cross* (Shreveport, Louisiana: Huntington House Inc., 1985), p.103, 282.

[100] *Ibid.,* p.111.

[101] Blavatsky, *The Secret Doctrine* (Vol. I—Cosmogenesis), *op. cit.,* p.5.

[102] *Ibid.* (Vol. II—Anthropogenesis), p.98.

[103] "Behavior Changes Clue to Parents," *The Tampa Tribune* (October 31, 1988).

[104] Marrs, *Mystery Mark of the New Age, op. cit.,* p.112.

[105] William Hutchinson, *The Spirit of Masonry,* revised by Rev. George Oliver (New York: Bell Publishing Company, 1982; originally published in 1775), p.195.

[106] Churchward, *op. cit.,* p.189.

[107] Joseph Campbell, *The Masks of God: Creative Mythology* (New York, New York: The Viking Press, 1968), p.17.

[108] F. de P. Castells, *The Apocalypse of Freemasonry: A Constructive Scheme of Interpretation of the Symbolism of the Masonic Lodge* (Dartford, England: Snowden Brothers, 1924), p.73; Walter McLeod, Editor, *Beyond the Pillars* (Grand Lodge A.F. and A.M. of Canada, 1973), p.148; , Carl H. Claudy, *Introduction to Freemasonry: Entered Apprentice, Fellowcraft, and Master Mason Complete in One Volume* (Washington, D.C.: The Temple Publishers, 1931), p.108-109; Malcolm Duncan, *Duncan's Ritual of Freemasonry* (New York: David McKay Company, Inc., n.d.), p.99; *What? When? Where? Why? Who? in Freemasonry* (Silver Spring, Maryland: Masonic Service Association of the United States, 1956), p.22; John T. Lawrence, *The Perfect Ashlar* (London, England: A. Lewis, 1912), p.52; MacKenzie, *op. cit.,* p.34; *Pocket Masonic Dictionary* (Silver Spring, Maryland: The Masonic Service Association of the United States, 1988), p.13; *Pocket Encyclopedia of Masonic Symbols* (Silver Spring, Maryland: The Masonic Association of the United States, 1953), p.23, 35; *The Pennsylvania Freemason* (November 1989, Vol. 36, No. 4), p.13; "Sun, Moon and Stars," *Short Talk Bulletin* (March 1930, Vol. 8, No. 3), p.10, 11.

[109] *Last Trumpet Newsletter* (July 1986, Vol. 5, Issue 7), p.3.

[110] Walter McLeod, Editor, *Beyond the Pillars* (Grand Lodge A.F. & A.M. of Canada, 1973), p.148.

[111] Carl H. Claudy, *Introduction to Freemasonry: Entered Apprentice, Fellowcraft, and Master Mason Complete in One Volume* (Washington, D.C.: The Temple Publishers, 1931), p.108-109. See also: "Sun, Moon and Stars," *Short Talk Bulletin* (March 1930, Vol. 8, No. 3), p.10-11; *What? When? Where? Why? Who? in Freemasonry* (Silver Spring, Maryland: Masonic Service Association of the United States, 1956), p.22; John T. Lawrence, *The Perfect Ashlar* (London, England: A. Lewis, 1912), p.52; MacKenzie, *op. cit.,* p.34; *Pocket Encyclopedia of Masonic Symbols* (Silver Spring, Maryland: The Masonic Association of the United States, 1953), p.23, 35.

[112] Charles G. Berger, *Our Phallic Heritage* (New York, New York: Greenwich Book Publishers, 1966), p.60.

[113] Cirlot, *op. cit.,* p.62.

[114] *The Pennsylvania Youth Foundation* (Elizabethtown, Pennsylvania: The Pennsylvania Youth Foundation, n.d.), p.4.

[115] *Pocket Masonic Dictionary* (Silver Spring, Maryland: The Masonic Service Association of the United States, 1988), p.23; *Pocket Encyclopedia of Masonic Symbols* (Silver Spring: Maryland: The Masonic Service Association of the United States, 1953), p.47; *What? When? Where? Why? Who? in Freemasonry* (Silver Spring, Maryland: Masonic Service Association of the United States, 1956), p.60; H. L. Haywood, *Introduction to Freemasonry* (Des Moines, Iowa: Research Lodge Number 2, n.d.), p.36; F. de P. Castells, *The Apocalypse of Freemasonry: A Constructive Scheme of Interpretation of the Symbolism of the Masonic Lodge* (Dartford, England: Snowden Brothers, 1924), p.73.

[116] John T. Lawrence, *The Perfect Ashlar* (London, England: A. Lewis, 1912), p.101; See also: H. L. Haywood, *Symbolic Masonry: An Interpretation of the Three Degrees* (Washington, D.C.: Masonic Service Association of the United States, 1923), p.211.

[117] Blackmer, *op. cit.,* p.50.

[118] "Overcoming Fragmentation," *Breakthrough* (Winter/Summer 1990, Vol. 11, No. 2-4), p.56.

[119] David Spangler, *Reflections on the Christ* (Scotland: Findhorn Publications, 1977), p.116.

[120] David Spangler, *Emergence: The Rebirth of the Sacred* (New York: Dell Publishing, 1984), p.51-52.

[121] Wanda Marrs, *New Age Lies to Women* (Austin, Texas: Living Truth Publishers, 1989), p.20; *Bold Truth* (April 1993), p.12.

[122] George Oliver, *The Historical Landmarks and Other Evidences of Freemasonry, Explained* (Vol. I & II) (New York: John W. Leonard and Company, 1855), p.324; See also: Pierson, *op. cit.,* p.101-102.

[123] *Ibid.*

[124] Epperson, *op. cit.,* p.97.

[125] Newton, *op. cit.,* p.28.

[126] H. L. Haywood, *Symbolic Masonry: An Interpretation of the Three Degrees* (Washington, D.C.: Masonic Service Association of the United States, 1923), p.207; "Two Pillars," *Short Talk Bulletin* (September 1935, Vol. 13, No. 9; Reprinted September 1978), p.7; Claudy, *op. cit.,* p.81; Charles Clyde Hunt, *Some Thoughts on Masonic Symbolism* (New York: Macoy Publishing and Masonic Supply Company, 1930), p.101, 116; William Adrian Brown, *Facts, Fables and Fantasies of Freemasonry* (New York, New York: Vantage Press, Inc., 1968), p.40.

[127] Evans, *op. cit.,* p.285.

[128] W. Wynn Westcott, *Numbers: Their Occult Power and Mystic Virtues* (London, England: Theosophical Publishing Society, 1902, Second Edition), p.33.

[129] Haywood, *op. cit.,* p.206-207.

[130] Blackmer, *op. cit.,* p.94.

[131] Berger, *op. cit.,* p.34. See also: John George Gibson, *The Masonic Problem: The Purpose and Meaning of Freemasonry* (n.p., 1912), p.43; Ralph Edward Woodrow, *Babylon Mystery Religion: Ancient and Modern* (Riverside, California: Ralph Woodrow Evangelistic Association, Inc., 1990 Edition), p.35; Willy Peterson, *The Leavening: A New Age Primer for Christian Parents* (Linwood, Kansas, 1995), p.183.

[132] *Ibid.,* p.46.

[133] *Last Trumpet Newsletter* (June 1986, Vol. 5, Issue 6), p.2.

[134] Ralph Edward Woodrow, *Babylon Mystery Religion: Ancient and Modern* (Riverside, California: Ralph Woodrow Evangelistic Association, Inc., 1990 Edition), p.32.

[135] *Ibid.* p.33-34; See also: Epperson, *op. cit.,* p.97.

[136] Tad Tuleja, "Red-Letter Days: On the Origins of Holiday Rituals," *Utne Reader* (November/December 1987), p.79-80.

[137] Berger, *op. cit.,* p.171.

[138] Cabot, *op. cit.,* p.124-125.

[139] Naomi R. Goldenberg, *Changing of the Gods: Feminism and the End of Traditional Religions* (Boston, Massachusetts: Beacon Press, 1979), p.104; See also: John J. Robinson, *Born in Blood: The Lost Secrets of Freemasonry* (New York, New York: M. Evans and Company, 1989), p.195; Churchward, *op. cit.,* p.362; Francine du Plessix Gray, "Women's Rites," *Utne Reader* (November/December 1987), p.62.

[140] *Clubhouse Jr.* (May 1995, Vol. 8, No. 5), p.16.

[141] Cabot, *op. cit.,* p.124.

[142] James B. Walker, "Masonic Symbols in a $1 Bill," *The New Age* (April 1960, Vol. 68, No. 4), p.17.

[143] William Schnoebelen, "Satan's Door Revisited," *Saints Alive in Jesus* (March 1992), p.4; See also: Epperson, *op. cit.,* p.139-140.

[144] Ray V. Denslow, *Masonic Portraits* (Transactions of the Missouri Lodge of Research, Vol. #29), p.7.

[145] C. F. McQuaig, *The Masonic Report* (Norcross, Georgia: Answer Books and Tapes, 1976), p.34.

[146] Schnoebelen, *Masonry, op. cit.,* p.119-120.

[147] Fritz Springmeier, *The Watchtower and the Masons* (Portland, Oregon: Fritz Springmeier, 1990), p.ii.

[148] *Ibid.,* p.90.

[149] Robert Sessler, *To Be God of One World: The French Revolution Globalized* (Merlin, Oregon: Let There Be Light Publications, 1992), p.147.

[150] Jan Karel Van Baalen, *The Chaos of Cults* (Grand Rapids, Michigan: Wm. B. Eerdsmans Publishing Company, 1962 Edition), p.62.

[151] Alan Morrison, *The Serpent and the Cross: Religious Corruption in an Evil Age* (Birmingham, England: K & M Books, 1994), p.104.

[152] Colin Wilson, *The Occult: A History* (New York: Random House, 1971), p.330.

[153] Howard Kerr and Charles L. Crow, Editors, *The Occult in America: New Historical Perspectives* (Urbana, Illinois: University of Illinois Press, 1983), p.143.

[154] Springmeier, *op. cit.,* p.14.

[155] William R. Denslow, *10,000 Famous Freemasons* (Vol. I) (1957), p.177, 198, 302, 320; William R. Denslow, *10,000 Famous Freemasons* (Vol. II) (1958), p.31, 114, 192, 211; William R. Denslow, *10,000 Famous Freemasons* (Vol. III) (1959), p.133, 181, 229.

[156] *Ibid.,* (Vol. II), p.114, 211.

Chapter 20: The All-Seeing Eye

[1] Ralph Anderson, "Freemasonry: Yesterday, Today and Tomorrow," *Arcana Workshops* (June 1985), p.4-6; See also: *The Full Moon Story* (Manhattan Beach, California: Rams' Dell Press, 1974 Revised Edition), p.15-16; Dennis L. Cuddy, *President Clinton Will Continue the New World Order* (Oklahoma City, Oklahoma: Southwest Radio Church, 1993), p.18; Alice A. Bailey, *The Externalisation of the Hierarchy* (New York, New York: Lucis Publishing Company, 1957), p. 511.

[2] J. Edward Decker, Jr., *The Question of Freemasonry* (Issaquah, Washington: Free the Masons Ministries, n.d.), p.12; A. T. C. Pierson, *The Traditions, Origin and Early History of Freemasonry* (New York: Masonic Publishing Company, 1865), p.42.

[3] Albert Pike, *Morals and Dogma of the Ancient and Accepted Scottish Rite of Freemasonry* (Richmond, Virginia: L. H. Jenkins, Inc., 1871), p.15-16.

[4] *Ibid.,* p.477; See also: Albert Pike, *The Magnum Opus* (Kila, Montana: Kessinger Publishing Company, 1992), p.xxv; A. Ralph Epperson, *The New World Order* (Tucson, Arizona: Publius Press, 1990), p.141.

[5] Carl H. Claudy, *Introduction to Freemasonry: Entered Apprentice, Fellowcraft, and Master Mason Complete in One Volume* (Washington, D.C.: The Temple Publishers, 1931), p.148; See also: Charles H. Vail, *The Ancient Mysteries and Modern Masonry* (New York, New York: Macoy Publishing and Masonic Supply Company, 1909), p.189.

[6] Albert G. Mackey, *The Symbolism of Freemasonry: Illustrating and Explaining Its Science and Philosophy, Its Legends, Myths, and Symbols* (New York: Clark and Maynard, 1869), 334-335, 190-192; See also: *Pocket Encyclopedia of Masonic Symbols* (Silver Spring, Maryland: The Masonic Service Association of the United States, 1953), p.7; Thomas Albert Stafford, *Christian Symbolism in the Evangelical Churches* (Nashville, Tennessee: Abingdon Press, 1942), p.35; Rex R. Hutchens, *A Bridge to Light* (Washington, D.C.: Supreme Council, 33° Ancient and Accepted Scottish Rite of Freemasonry, Southern Jurisdiction, 1988), p.18; W. J. McK. McCormick, *Christ, The Christian, and Freemasonry* (Belfast, Ireland: Great Joy Publications, 1984), p.84.

[7] Robert Hieronimus, *America's Secret Destiny: Spiritual Vision and the Founding of a Nation* (Rochester, Vermont: Destiny Books, 1989), p.81; See also: Veronica Ions, *Egyptian Mythology* (Middlesex, England: The Hamlyn Publishing Group Ltd., 1965), p.24; E. A. Wallis Budge, *Amulets and Superstitions* (New York, New York: Dover Publications, Inc., 1978), p.141; Lucie Lamy, *Egyptian Mysteries* (1981), p.16.

[8] *New Larousse Encyclopedia of Mythology* (Prometheus Press, 1972 Edition), p.14; See also: Veronica Ions, *Egyptian Mythology* (Middlesex, England: The Hamlyn Publishing Group Ltd., 1965), p.41.

[9] Veronica Ions, *Egyptian Mythology* (Middlesex, England: The Hamlyn Publishing Group Ltd., 1965), p.41.

[10] Pike, *op. cit.*, p.732.

[11] Albert Pike, *The Magnum Opus* (Kila, Montana: Kessinger Publishing Company, 1992), p.28; See also: C. F. McQuaig, *The Masonic Report* (Norcross, Georgia: Answer Books and Tapes, 1976), p.45.

[12] Paul Hamlyn, *Greek Mythology* (London, England: Paul Hamlyn Limited, 1967), p.109, 114.

[13] *Ibid.*, p.112.

[14] Herbert F. Inman, *Masonic Problems and Queries* (London, England: A. Lewis Ltd., 1978), p.172; William O. Peterson, Editor, *Masonic Quiz Book: "Ask Me Another, Brother"* (Chicago, Illinois: Charles T. Powner Company, 1950), p.163; See also: George H. Steinmetz, *Freemasonry: Its Hidden Meaning* (New York: Macoy Publishing and Masonic Supply Company, 1948), p.92; Pike, *Morals and Dogma, op. cit.*, p.15.

[15] Albert G. Mackey, *A Manual of the Lodge* (New York: Charles E. Merrill Company, 1870), p.56; See also: Edmond Ronayne quoting Albert Mackey, *The Master's Carpet (Mah-Hah-Bone)* (n.p., 1879), p.324-326; Alain Danielou, *The Gods of India* (New York, New York: Inner Traditions International Ltd., 1985), p.223; Rollin C. Blackmer, *The Lodge and the Craft: A Practical Explanation of the Work of Freemasonry* (St. Louis, Missouri: The Standard Masonic Publishing Company, 1923), p.94.

[16] Pike, *Morals and Dogma, op. cit.*, p.401; See also: A. T. C. Pierson, *The Traditions, Origin and Early History of Freemasonry* (New York: Masonic Publishing Company, 1865), p.87.

[17] Albert Churchward, *Signs and Symbols of Primordial Man* (London, England: George Allen and Company, Ltd., 1913), p.326.

[18] "The All-Seeing Eye," *The Short Talk Bulletin* (December 1932, Vol. 10, No. 12), p.9.

[19] Hieronimus, *op. cit.*

[20] Alice A. Bailey, *Discipleship in the New Age* (Volume II) (New York: Lucis Publishing Company, 1955), p.265.

[21] *Ibid.* (Volume II), p.265.

[22] A. T. C. Pierson, *The Traditions, Origin and Early History of Freemasonry* (New York: Masonic Publishing Company, 1865), p.232.

[23] Charles H. Vail, *The Ancient Mysteries and Modern Masonry* (New York City, New York: Macoy Publishing and Masonic Supply Company, 1909), p.189.

[24] J. D. Buck, *Mystic Masonry* (Chicago, Illinois: Indo-American Book Company, 1896), p.182, 180-181; See also: Texe Marrs, *Mystery Mark of the New Age: Satan's Design for World Domination* (Westchester, Illinois: Crossway Books, 1988), p.104.

[25] Hieronimus, *op. cit.*, p.82; See also: Alexander Cannon, *The Power of Karma: In Relation to Destiny* (E. P. Dutton and Company, Inc., 1937), p.88-89; Darshan Singh, *Helping Factors on the Spiritual Path* (Delhi, India: n.p.), p.2-3; J. E. Cirlot, *A Dictionary of Symbols* (New York, New York: Philosophical Library, Inc., 1972), p.100; Lucie Lamy, *Egyptian Mysteries* (1981), p.16.

[26] Catalog from Samuel Weiser (1989/1990), p.66.

[27] Desmond Dunne, *Yoga Made Easy* (Englewood Cliffs, New Jersey: Prentice-Hall, Inc., 1961), p.54, 97.

[28] Catalog from Bantam/Doubleday/Dell (Spring/Summer 1988), p.17; See also: Johanna Michaelsen, *Like Lambs to the Slaughter* (Eugene, Oregon: Harvest House Publishers, 1989), p.101; Sri Chinmoy, *Spiritual Power, Occult Power and Will Power* (Jamaica, New York: Agni Press, 1976), p.59.

[29] Jane Gumprecht quoting Alice Bailey, *New Age Health Care: Holy or Holistic* (Orange, California: Promise Publishing, 1988), p.190.

[30] Alice A. Bailey, *The Soul: Quality of Life* (New York: Lucis Publishing Company, 1974), p.201; See also: Alice A. Bailey, *A Treatise on White Magic or the Way of the Disciple* (New York: Lucis Publishing Company, 1951), p.213.

[31] Laurie Cabot with Tom Cowan, *Power of the Witch: The Earth, the Moon, and the Magical Path* (New York, New York: Delacorte Press, 1989), p.176.

[32] *Ibid.*, p.246.

[33] Thomas Milton Stewart, *The Symbolism of the Gods of the Egyptians and the Light They Throw on Freemasonry* (London, England: Baskerville Press, Limited, 1927), p.5.

[34] William Schnoebelen, *Masonry: Beyond the Light* (Chino, California: Chick Publications, 1991), p.197.

[35] Alexander Cannon, *The Power of Karma: In Relation to Destiny* (E. P. Dutton and Company, Inc., 1937), p.78.

[36] *Ibid.*, p.81.

[37] *Ibid.*

[38] *Ibid.*

[39] *Ibid.*, p.83.

[40] Pike, *Morals and Dogma, op. cit.*, p.16.

[41] *Ibid.*, p.506.

[42] Dennis Laurence Cuddy, *Now Is the Dawning of the New Age New World Order* (Oklahoma City, Oklahoma: Hearthstone Publishing, Ltd., 1991), p.383.

[43] Texe Marrs, *Mystery Mark of the New Age: Satan's Design for World Domination* (Westchester, Illinois: Crossway Books, 1988), p.53.

[44] Cabot, *op. cit.,* p.245.

[45] *Ibid.*

[46] *Ibid.,* p.246.

[47] Eric Maple, *The Complete Book of Witchcraft and Demonology* (Cranbury, New Jersey: A. S. Barnes and Company, Inc., 1966), p.11.

[48] Therese Ruth Revesz, *Witches* (New York, New York: Contemporary Perspectives, Inc., 1977), p.44.

[49] Catalog from The Occult Emporium (Winter 1993 to Winter 1994), p.34.

[50] E. A. Wallis Budge, *Amulets and Superstitions* (New York, New York: Dover Publications, Inc., 1978), p.15.

[51] *Ibid.,* p.468-469; See also: J. S. M. Ward and W. G. Stirling, *The Hung Society or the Society of Heaven and Earth* (Vol. I) (London, England: The Baskerville Press, Limited, 1925), p.118; John Sebastian Marlow Ward, *The Sign Language of the Mysteries* (New York: Land's End Press, 1969), p.3-4; Cecile Donner and Jean-Luc Caradeau (Translated by Richard LeFanu), *Dictionary of Superstitions* (New York, New York: Henry Holt and Company, Inc., 1984), p.63; Scott Cunningham, *Wicca: A Guide for the Solitary Practitioner* (St. Paul, Minnesota: Llewellyn Publications, 1989), p.42; Jeff Godwin, *The Devil's Disciples: The Truth About Rock* (Chino, California: Chick Publications, 1985), p.134.

[52] Cabot, *op. cit.,* p.66.

[53] John Sebastian Marlow Ward, *The Sign Language of the Mysteries* (New York: Land's End Press, 1969), p.56, 163; See also: J. S. M. Ward, *Freemasonry and the Ancient Gods* (London, England: Simpkin, Marshall, Hamilton, Kent and Company Ltd., 1921), page following p.14.

[54] Jeff Godwin, *The Devil's Disciples: The Truth About Rock* (Chino, California: Chick Publications, 1985), p.134.

[55] Selena Fox, "Pennsylvania Dutch Hex Signs," *Circle Network News* (Summer 1987, Vol. 9, No. 2), p.11.

[56] O. J. Graham, *The Six-Pointed Star* (New Puritan Library, 1988 Edition), p.29.

[57] Fox, *op. cit.*

[58] *Ibid.*

[59] J. Gordon Melton, *The Encyclopedia of American Religions* (Vol. 2) (Wilmington, North Carolina: McGrath Publishing Company, 1978), p.271.

[60] Frank Gaynor, Editor, *Dictionary of Mysticism* (New York: Philosophical Library, 1953), p.73.

[61] John Lash, *The Seeker's Handbook: The Complete Guide to Spiritual Pathfinding* (New York: Harmony Books, 1990), p.283.

[62] Robert A. Morey, *Islam Unveiled: The True Desert Storm* (Shermans Dale, Pennsylvania: The Scholars Press, 1991), p.39; *Circle Network News* (Summer 1987, Vol. 9, No. 2), p.13; Godfrey

Higgins, *Anacalypsis, An Attempt to Draw Aside the Veil of the Saitic Isis* (London, England: n.p., 1874), p.129; Wade Davis, "The Power to Heal," *Newsweek* (September 24, 1990, Vol. 116, No. 13), p.40; "Superstitions Get Some Started in Witchcraft," *Shepherdsfield Update* (Spring 1989, No. 22), p.20; Harry E. Wedeck, *Treasury of Witchcraft* (New York: Philosophical Library, 1961), p.15.

[63] "Blazing Star" (Part 1), *The Short Talk Bulletin* (March 1965, Vol. 43, No. 3), p.12.

[64] William T. Still, *New World Order: The Ancient Plan of Secret Societies* (Lafayette, Louisiana: Huntington House, Inc., 1990), p.24.

[65] Marrs, *op. cit.,* p.102.

[66] Cuddy, *op. cit.,* p.195.

[67] Dennis L. Cuddy, *President Clinton Will Continue the New World Order* (Oklahoma City, Oklahoma: Southwest Radio Church, 1993), p.98.

[68] Jeff Godwin, *Rock and Roll Religion* (Bloomington, Indiana: The Rock Ministries, 1995), p.93.

[69] "Jesus Junk (Another Jesus)" *The Perilous Times* (January 1996, Vol. 17, No. 11). p.6.

[70] "The Coors Connection," *Christian News* (August 7, 1995, Vol. 33, No. 32), p.11.

[71] *Council on Foreign Relations 1993* (Annual Report July 1, 1992 to June 30, 1993), p.128.

[72] *New American Schools Development Corporation* (Annual Report 1994/1995), p.32.

[73] *1994 Annual Report* from Points of Light Foundation, p.18.

[74] Texe Marrs, *Dark Majesty: The Secret Brotherhood and the Magic of a Thousand Points of Light* (Austin, Texas: Living Truth Publishers, 1992), p.81.

[75] Cuddy, *Now Is the Dawning, op. cit.,* p.10-11.

[76] Francis Huxley, *The Eye: The Seer and the Seen* (London, England: Thames and Hudson, 1990), p.40.

[77] S. R. Parchment, *Ancient Operative Masonry* (San Francisco, California: San Francisco Center—Rosicrucian Fellowship, 1930), p.52.

Chapter 21: Symbols in Brief

[1] Frank Gaynor, Editor, *Dictionary of Mysticism* (New York: Philosophical Library, 1953), p.132.

[2] *Ibid.,* p.199.

[3] Texe Marrs, *Mystery Mark of the New Age: Satan's Design for World Domination* (Westchester, Illinois: Crossway Books, 1988), p.116.

[4] Hugh A. Moran and David H. Kelley, *The Alphabet and the Ancient Calendar Signs* (Palo Alto, California: Daily Press, 1969), p.24.

[5] Catalog entitled *The Pyramid Collection* (Late Summer 1997), p.46.

[6] *Pyramid Books and the New-Age Collection* Catalog (Winter/Spring 1993), p.54.

[7] *Pyramid Books and the New-Age Collection* Catalog (Received March 21, 1992), p.66.

[8] *Pyramid Books and the New-Age Collection* Catalog (Winter/Spring 1993), p.52.

[9] Harry E. Wedeck, *Treasury of Witchcraft* (New York: Philosophical Library, 1961), p.97.

[10] *Pyramid Books and the New-Age Collection* Catalog (Received March 21, 1992), p.57.

[11] J. E. Cirlot, *A Dictionary of Symbols* (New York, New York: Philosophical Library, Inc., 1972), p.100.

[12] Arthur Edward Waite, *The Secret Tradition in Freemasonry* (Vol. 2) (1911 Edition), p.430-431.

[13] *Ibid.,* p.431.

[14] *Meditation* (Winter 1991, Vol. 6, No. 1), p.45.

[15] John Lash, *The Seeker's Handbook: The Complete Guide to Spiritual Pathfinding* (New York: Harmony Books, 1990), p.390.

[16] *Pyramid Books and the New-Age Collection* Catalog (Winter/Spring 1993), p.67.

[17] Catalog ad.

[18] *Last Trumpet Newsletter* (July 1986, Vol. 5, Issue 7), p.2.

[19] Catalog ad.

[20] Catalog ad.

[21] Catalog ad.

[22] Robert A. Morey, *Islam Unveiled: The True Desert Storm* (Shermans Dale, Pennsylvania: The Scholars Press, 1991), p.48-49.

[23] *Ibid.,* p.46.

[24] Irene Arrington Park, *What Every Christian Should Know About Symbols, Signs and Emblems* (Tampa, Florida: Christ's Deliverance Ministries, 1982), p.3.

[25] Jeremy Kingston, *Healing Without Medicine* (Doubleday and Company, Inc., 1976), p.32-33.

[26] Manly Palmer Hall, *Initiates of the Flame* (Los Angeles, California: The Phoenix Press, 1934), p.45.

BIBLIOGRAPHY

(The following is a partial listing of the reference materials that were used in preparing this book.)

1994 Annual Report from Points of Light Foundation.

"3—5—7." *Short Talk Bulletin* (June 1925, Vol. 3, No. 6; Reprinted December 1990).

"Acacia Leaves and Easter Lilies." *Short Talk Bulletin* (April 1929, Vol. 7, No. 4; Reprinted March 1985).

Addiction and Consciousness Journal (September 1988, Vol. 3, No. 3).

Adelphi Quarterly (Third Quarter 1992).

Adler, Margot. *Drawing Down the Moon: Witches, Druids, Goddess-Worshippers, and Other Pagans in America Today* (New York, New York: The Viking Press, 1979).

"Albert Gallatin Mackey." *Short Talk Bulletin* (February 1936, Vol. 14, No. 2; Reprinted July 1980).

"Albert Pike." *Short Talk Bulletin* (July 1923, Vol. 1, No. 7; Reprinted December 1988).

"All-Seeing Eye, The." *Short Talk Bulletin* (December 1932, Vol. 10, No. 12; Reprinted January 1982).

"Altar Is Born, The." *Short Talk Bulletin* (January 1955, Vol. 33 No. 1).

"Apron, The." *Short Talk Bulletin* (June 1932, Vol. 10, No. 6; Reprinted March 1986).

Aquarian Voices (August 1989).

Arcana Workshops (June 1985).

Authorized Standard Ritual of the Order of the Eastern Star of New York, The (New York, Press of Andrew H. Kellogg Company, 1876, Twentieth Edition, 1916).

Baigent, Michael and Leigh, Richard. *The Temple and the Lodge* (New York: Arcade Publishing, Inc., 1989).

Bailey, Alice A. *A Treatise on White Magic* (or *The Way of the Disciple*) (New York: Lucis Publishing Company, 1951).

Bailey, Alice A. *Discipleship in the New Age* (Vol. I) (New York: Lucis Publishing Company, 1972).

Bailey, Alice A. *Discipleship in the New Age* (Vol. II) (New York: Lucis Publishing Company, 1955).

Bailey, Alice A. *Education in the New Age* (New York: Lucis Publishing Company, 1954).

Bailey, Alice A. *The Externalisation of the Hierarchy* (New York, New York: Lucis Publishing Company, 1957).

Bailey, Alice A. *The Soul: Quality of Life* (New York: Lucis Publishing Company, 1974).

Bailey, Foster, "A New Age Symbol." *The Beacon* (January/February 1993).

Barger, Eric. *From Rock to Rock: The Music of Darkness Exposed!* (Lafayette, Louisiana: Huntington House, Inc., 1990).

Battle Cry (March/April 1991).

BDM Letter (November 1992, Vol. 1, No. 9).

Beacon, The (July/August 1985, Vol. 51, No. 4).

Beane, Wendell C., and Doty, William G. *Myths, Rites, Symbols: A Mircea Eliade Reader* (Vol. II) (New York, New York: Harper Colophon Books, 1975).

Becker, Udo, Editor. *The Continuum Encyclopedia of Symbols* (1994).

Bedworth, Albert E. and Bedworth, David A. *Health for Human Effectiveness* (Englewood Cliffs, New Jersey: Prentice-Hall, Inc., 1982).

"Bee Hive, The." *Short Talk Bulletin* (September 1951, Vol. 29, No. 9; Reprinted April 1990).

"Behind the Symbol." *Short Talk Bulletin* (July 1954, Vol. 32, No. 7).

Bell, F. A. *Bell's Eastern Star Ritual* (P. R. C. Publications, Inc., 1988 Revised Edition).

Berger, Charles G. *Our Phallic Heritage* (New York, New York: Greenwich Book Publishers, Inc., 1966).

Bessy, Maurice. *A Pictorial History of Magic and the Supernatural* (New York: Hamlyn Publishing Group Limited, 1964).

Blackmer, Rollin C. *The Lodge and the Craft: A Practical Explanation of the Work of Freemasonry* (St. Louis, Missouri: The Standard Masonic Publishing Company, 1923).

Blavatsky, Helena Petrovna. *Isis Unveiled,* Vol. I: Science (New York, New York: Trow's Printing and Bookbinding Company, 1877).

Blavatsky, H. P. *The Secret Doctrine: The Synthesis of Science, Religion, and Philosophy* (Vol. I—Cosmogenesis) (Covina, California: Theosophical University Press, 1947, Fourth Edition).

Blavatsky, H. P. *The Secret Doctrine: The Synthesis of Science, Religion, and Philosophy* (Vol. II—Anthropogenesis) (Covina, California: Theosophical University Press, 1947, Fourth Edition).

"Blazing Star" (Part 1). *Short Talk Bulletin* (March 1965, Vol. 43, No. 3).

Blofeld, John. *The Tantric Mysticism of Tibet* (Boston, Massachusetts: Shambhala Publications, Inc., 1970).

Blueprint for Building the New World Order (Dearborn, Michigan: The Omega-Letter/Christian World Report).

Bobgan, Martin and Deidre. *12 Steps to Destruction: Codependency/Recovery Heresies* (Santa Barbara, California: EastGate Publishers, 1991).

Bobgan, Martin and Deidre. *Four Temperaments, Astrology, and Personality Testing* (Santa Barbara, California: EastGate Publishers, 1992).

Bold Truth (April 1993).

Breakthrough (Winter/Summer 1990, Vol. 11, No. 2-4).

Brookridge Forum, The (Winter 1987-88, Vol. 3, No. 1).

"Broken Column, The." *Short Talk Bulletin* (February 1956, Vol. 3, No. 2; Reprinted January 1985).

Brooke-Little, J. P. *An Heraldic Alphabet* (New York: Arco Publishing Company, Inc., 1973).

Brown, William Adrian. *Facts, Fables and Fantasies of Freemasonry* (New York, New York: Vantage Press, Inc., 1968).

Bruce-Mitford, Miranda. *The Illustrated Book of Signs and Symbols* (1996).

Buck, J. D. *Mystic Masonry* (Illinois: Indo-American Book Company, 1913, Sixth Edition).

Buck, J. D. *The Genius of Free-Masonry and the Twentieth Century Crusade* (Chicago, Illinois: Indo-American Book Company, 1907).

Budge, E. A. Wallis. *Amulets and Superstitions* (New York, New York: Dover Publications, Inc., 1978).

Budge, E. A. Wallis. *From Fetish to God in Ancient Egypt* (London, England: Oxford University Press, 1934).

Budge, Sir Wallis. *Egyptian Magic* (Secaucus, New Jersey: University Books, Inc., n.d.).

Bulfinch, Thomas. *Bulfinch's Mythology: The Age of Fable or Stories of Gods and Heroes* (Garden City, New York: Doubleday and Company, Inc., 1948).

Bulfinch, Thomas. *Bulfinch's Mythology* (New York: Thomas Y. Crowell Company, Inc., 1970).

Bulfinch, Thomas. *The Age of Fable or the Beauties of Mythology* (New York: The Heritage Press, 1942).

Butler, E. M. *The Myth of the Magus* (New York: MacMillan Company, 1948).

Cabot, Laurie with Cowan, Tom. *Power of the Witch: The Earth, the Moon, and the Magical Path to Enlightenment* (New York, New York: Delacorte Press, 1989).

Campbell, Joseph, Editor. *Philosophies of India* (Princeton, New Jersey: Princeton University Press, 1951).

Campbell, Joseph. *The Hero with a Thousand Faces* (Princeton, New Jersey: Princeton University Press, 1968, Second Edition).

Campbell, Joseph. *The Masks of God: Creative Mythology* (New York: New York: The Viking Press, 1968).

Campbell, Joseph with Moyers, Bill; Flowers, Betty Sue, Editor, *The Power of Myth* (New York, New York: Doubleday, 1988).

Cannon, Alexander. *The Power of Karma: In Relation to Destiny* (E. P. Dutton and Company, Inc., 1937).

Carr, Joseph. *The Lucifer Connection* (Lafayette, Louisiana: Huntington House, Inc., 1987).

Carr, Joseph J. *The Twisted Cross* (Shreveport, Louisiana: Huntington House, Inc., 1985).

Carrico, David L. *George Steinmetz: The Honored Masonic Author* (Evansville, Indiana: Followers of Jesus Christ, 1992).

Carrico, David L. *Lucifer—Eliphas Levi—Albert Pike and the Masonic Lodge* (Evansville, Indiana: Followers of Jesus Christ, 1991).

Carrico, David L. *Manly P. Hall: The Honored Masonic Author* (Evansville, Indiana: Followers of Jesus Christ, 1992).

Carrico, David L. *The Occult Meaning of the Great Seal of the United States* (Evansville, Indiana: Followers of Jesus Christ, 1991).

Carrico, David L. *The Pentagram, Freemasonry and the Goat* (Evansville, Illinois: Followers of Jesus Christ, 1992).

Carrico, David L. with Doninger, Rick. *The Egyptian-Masonic-Satanic Connection* (Evansville, Indiana: Followers of Jesus Christ, 1991).

Case, Paul Foster. *The Masonic Letter G* (Los Angeles, California: Builders of the Adytum, Ltd., 1981).

CASH (Continental Association of Satan's Hope, n.d.).

Castells, F. De P. *Antiquity of the Holy Royal Arch: The Supreme Degree in Freemasonry* (London, England: A. Lewis, 1927).

Castells, F. De P. *Genuine Secrets in Freemasonry Prior to A.D. 1717* (London: A. Lewis, 1930).

Castells, F. De P. *The Apocalypse of Freemasonry: A Constructive Scheme of Interpretation of the Symbolism of the Masonic Lodge* (Dartford, England: Snowden Brothers, 1924).

Catalog from Abyss.

Catalog from All About Pyramids.

Catalog from Bantam/Doubleday/Dell (Spring/Summer 1988).

Catalog from Christian Book Distributors (Summer 1998).

Catalog from Dancing Dragon Designs (Summer 1990).

Catalog from DASO.

Catalog from Eden Within (1994).

Catalog from Esalen (January-June 1985).

Catalog from Isis.

Catalog from JBL.

Catalog from Joy Lake Mountain Seminar Center (1986).

Catalog from Lily Dale Summer Workshop.

Catalog from Little Shop of Incense (Spring 1987).

Catalog from Lizzie Brown/Pleiades (1993).

Catalog from Macoy Publishing and Masonic Supply Company, Inc. (September 1991, No. 107).

Catalog from Nuit Unlimited Imports.

Catalog from Papa Jim, Inc. (1989).

Catalog from Prisma.

Catalog from Pyramid Books and the New-Age Collection (Winter/Spring 1993).

Catalog from Red Rose Collection (Holiday 1992).

Catalog from Samuel Weiser (1989/1990).

Catalog from Sounds True.

Catalog from Syracuse Cultural Workers (1992).

Catalog from the Flower Essence Society.

Catalog from The Occult Emporium (Mid 1990 to 1991).

Catalog from The Occult Emporium (Summer 1990 to Summer 1991).

Catalog from The Occult Emporium (Winter 1993 to Winter 1994).

Catalog from The Pyramid Collection (Late Summer 1997).

Catalog from The Rim Institute (1989).

Catalog from the Theosophical Publishing House.

Catalog from Wayfarer Publications, n.p., n.d.

Chambers, A. R., Editor. *Questions & Answers* (n.p., 1972).

Chambers, Claire. *The SIECUS Circle: A Humanist Revolution* (Belmont, Massachusetts: Western Islands, 1977).

Chambers, Joseph R. *Jewelry, Paganism and the New Age* (Charlotte, North Carolina: Paw Creek Ministries, n.d.).

Change Works (Spring/Summer 1998).

Charisma and Christian Life (November 1991, Vol. 17, No. 4).

Chernin, Dennis and Manteuffel, Gregory. *Health: A Holistic Approach* (Wheaton, Illinois: Theosophical Publishing House).

Chevalier, Jean and Gheerbrant, Alain. *A Dictionary of Symbols* (Blackwell Publishers, 1994).

Chick, Jack T. *Spellbound* (Chino, California: Chick Publications, 1978).

Child Affects (December 1992).

Chinmoy, Sri. *Spiritual Power, Occult Power and Will Power* (Jamaica, New York: Agni Press, 1976).

Christian Conscience, The (June 1998, Vol. 4, No. 5.).

Christian Conscience, The (May 1995, Vol. 1, No. 5.).

Christian News (April 17, 1989, Vol. 27, No. 16).

Christian News (August 7, 1995, Vol. 33, No. 32).

Christian News (February 28, 1994, Vol. 32, No. 9).

Christian Parent Alert (October 1991, Vol. 1, No. 3).

Christian World Report, The (December 1989, Vol. 1, No. 9).

Chrysalis (Autumn 1987, Vol. 2, Issue 3).

Churchward, Albert. *Signs and Symbols of Primordial Man: The Evolution of Religious Doctrine from the Eschatology of the Ancient Egyptians* (London, England: George Allen and Company, Ltd., 1913, Second Edition).

Churchward, Albert. *The Origin and Evolution of Freemasonry Connected with the Origin and Evolution of the Human Race* (London, England: George Allen and Unwin Ltd., 1920).

CIB Bulletin (December 1989, Vol. 5, No. 12).

Circle Network News (Spring 1986, Vol. 8, No. 1).

Circle Network News (Spring 1988, Vol. 10, No. 1).

Circle Network News (Summer 1984, Vol. 6, No. 2).

Circle Network News (Summer 1987, Vol. 9, No. 2).

Circle Network News (Winter 1980-1981).

Cirlot, J. E. *A Dictionary of Symbols* (New York, New York: Philosophical Library, Inc., 1972).

Cirlot, J. E. (Translated by Jack Sage). *A Dictionary of Symbols* (New York: Dorset Press, 1991 Edition).

Claudy, Carl H. *Introduction to Freemasonry: Entered Apprentice, Fellowcraft, and Master Mason Complete in One Volume* (Washington, D.C.: The Temple Publishers, 1931).

Claudy, Carl H. *Masonic Harvest* (Washington, D.C.: The Temple Publishers, 1948).

Clausen, Henry C. *Clausen's Commentaries on Morals and Dogma* (Supreme Council, 33rd Degree, Ancient and Accepted Scottish Rite of Freemasonry, Southern Jurisdiction, USA, 1974).

Clausen, Henry C. *Emergence of the Mystical* (Washington, D.C.: Supreme Council, 1981, Second Edition).

Clausen, Henry C. *Masons Who Helped Shape Our Nation* (The Supreme Council, 33°, Ancient and Accepted Scottish Rite of Freemasonry Southern Jurisdiction, 1976).

Clubhouse Jr. (May 1995, Vol. 8, No. 5).

Clymer, R. Swinburne. *The Mysteries of Osiris or Ancient Egyptian Initiation* (Quakertown, Pennsylvania: The Philosophical Publishing Company, 1951, Revised Edition).

Clymer, R. Swinburne. *The Mysticism of Masonry* (Quakertown, Pennsylvania: The Philosophical Publishing Company, 1924).

Complete Occult Digest A to Z (North Hollywood, California: International Imports, 1984).

Connecting Link (November/December 1989, Vol. 1, No. 5).

Constance Cumbey's New Age Monitor (June 1986, Vol. 1, No. 2).

Cook, Wes, Editor. *Did You Know? Vignettes in Masonry from the Royal Arch Mason Magazine* (Missouri Lodge of Research, 1965).

Coon, Arthur. *The Theosophical Seal* (no other info available).

Cooper, J. C. *An Illustrated Encyclopedia of Traditional Symbols* (London, England: Thames and Hudson, 1982 reprint).

Cotter, John. *A Study in Syncretism* reprinted in *Despatch* (March 1993, Vol. 5, No. 1).

Council on Foreign Relations 1993 (Annual Report July 1, 1992 to June 30, 1993).

CPWR Journal (November 1993, Vol. 5, No. 6).

Creme, Benjamin. *The Reappearance of the Christ and the Masters of Wisdom* (North Hollywood, California: Tara Center, 1980).

Crescendo: The Newsletter of the Institute for Music and Imagery (July 1987, Vol. 7, No. 2).

Crowley, Aleister. *Seven, Seven, Seven* (no other information available).

Cuddy, Dennis Laurence. *Chronology of Education with Quotable Quotes* (Highland City, Florida: Pro Family Forum, Inc., 1994, Updated, Bound Volume).

Cuddy, Dennis Laurence. *Now Is the Dawning of the New Age New World Order* (Oklahoma City, Oklahoma: Hearthstone Publishing, Ltd., 1991).

Cuddy, Dennis Laurence. *President Clinton Will Continue the New World Order* (Oklahoma City, Oklahoma: Southwest Radio Church, 1993).

Cuddy, Dennis Laurence, "Public Schools Disseminating Humanistic Values." *An American Commentary* (Oklahoma City, Oklahoma, 1993).

Cuddy, Dennis Laurence, "Secular Humanism: Are Public School Texts Teaching It to Your Children?" *Christian World Report* (September 1989, Vol. 1, No. 7).

Cuddy, Dennis Laurence, "The Deceptive New Age 'Service' and 'Light.'" *The Christian World Report* (February 1991, Vol. 3, No. 2).

Cuddy, Dennis Laurence. *The Grab for Power: A Chronology of the NEA* (Marlborough, New Hampshire: Plymouth Rock Foundation, 1993).

Cuddy, Peggy S., "Exploris: Creating a New National Prototype." *The Florida Forum* (Spring 1998).

Cuddy, Peggy S., "Transformation Toward New Age Synthesis." *Distant Drums* (March 1986, Vol. 8, No. 1).

Cuddy, Peggy S., "Transformation Toward New Age Synthesis." *Distant Drums* (May 1986, Vol. 8, No. 2).

Cumbey, Constance. *A Planned Deception: The Staging of a New Age "Messiah"* (East Detroit, Michigan: Pointe Publishing, Inc., 1985).

Cumbey, Constance. *The Hidden Dangers of the Rainbow: The New Age Movement and Our Coming Age of Barbarism* (Shreveport, Louisiana: Huntington House, Inc., Revised Edition, 1983).

Cunningham, Scott. *Cunningham's Encyclopedia of Crystal, Gem and Metal Magic* (St. Paul, Minnesota: Llewellyn Publications, 1988).

Cunningham, Scott. *Magical Herbalism: The Secret Craft of the Wise* (St. Paul, Minnesota: Llewellyn Publications, 1982).

Cunningham, Scott. *Wicca: A Guide for the Solitary Practitioner* (St. Paul, Minnesota: Llewellyn Publications, 1989).

D'Alviella, Count Goblet. *The Migration of Symbols* (Westminster: Archibald Constable and Company, 1894).

Da Costa, Hippolyto Joseph. *The Dionysian Artificers* (Los Angeles, California: The Philosophical Research Society Press, 1936).

Dager, Albert James. *Acupuncture: Magic or Medical Science* (Redmond, Washington: Media Spotlight, 1985).

Dager, Albert James. *Dragonraid: Can Fantasy Role-Playing Games Be "Christianized"?*

Dager, Albert James. *Origins of Christmas Traditions* (Costa Mesa, California: Media Spotlight, 1985 Special Report).

Dager, Albert James. *The Unicorn: Fabled Beast of Myth and Magic* (Costa Mesa, California: Media Spotlight, n.d.).

Dance Network News (January/February 1989, Vol. 1, No. 4).

Danielou, Alain. *The Gods of India* (New York, New York: Inner Traditions International, Ltd., 1985).

De Riencourt, Amaury. *The Eye of Shiva: Eastern Mysticism and Science* (New York, New York: William Morrow and Company, Inc., 1980).

Decker, J. Edward. *Freemasonry: Satan's Door to America?* (Issaquah, Washington: Free the Masons Ministries, n.d.).

Decker, J. Edward, Editor. *The Dark Side of Freemasonry* (Lafayette, Louisiana: Huntington House Publishers, 1994).

Decker, J. Edward, Jr. *The Question of Freemasonry* (Issaquah, Washington: Free the Masons Ministries, n.d.).

Decker, J. Edward, Jr., *The Question of Freemasonry* (Lafayette, Louisiana: Huntington House Publishers, 1992).

Denslow, Ray V. *Masonic Portraits* (Transactions of the Missouri Lodge of Research, Vol. #29, 1972).

Denslow, William R. *10,000 Famous Freemasons* (Vol. I) (1957).

Denslow, William R. *10,000 Famous Freemasons* (Vol. II) (1958).

Denslow, William R. *10,000 Famous Freemasons* (Vol. III) (1959).

Denslow, William R. *10,000 Famous Freemasons* (Vol. IV) (1961).

Desautels, Paul E. *The Gem Kingdom* (New York: Random House, Inc., n.d.).

Devorss & Company New Publications Catalog (1989).

"Diane Stein Balances Yin and Yang in an I Ching for the New Age." *New Times* (March/April 1986).

Discoveries Through Inner Quests (1989).

Discoveries Through Inner Quests (Spring 1989).

Discoveries Through Inner Quests (Winter/Spring 1987).

Divine Principle, The (New York, New York: Holy Spirit Association for the Unification of World Christianity).

Distant Drums (March 1981, Vol. 3, No. 1).

Doane, Doris Chase and Keyes, King. *Tarot-Card Spread Reader* (West Nyack, New York: Parker Publishing Company, Inc., 1967).

Don Bell Reports (January 10, 1986), Vol. 33, No.2.

Donner, Cecile, and Caradeau, Jean-Luc (Translated by Richard LeFanu). *Dictionary of Superstitions* (New York, New York: Henry Holt and Company, Inc., 1984).

Doore, Gary, Compiler and Editor. *Shaman's Path: Healing, Personal Growth and Empowerment* (Boston, Massachusetts: Shambhala, 1988).

"Dr. Paul Cedar Pulls Endorsement from *Star of 2000,*" Report from Broadcasters United for Revival and Reformation.

Duchesne-Guillemin, Jacques. Edited by Ruth Nanda Anshen, *Symbols and Values in Zoroastrianism: Their Survival and Renewal* (New York, New York: Harper and Row, 1966.

Dumas, Francois Ribadeau (Translated by Elisabeth Abbott). *Cagliostro: Scoundrel or Saint?* (New York: The Orion Press, 1967).

Duncan, Malcolm. *Duncan's Ritual of Freemasonry* (New York: David McKay Company, Inc., n.d., Third Edition).

Dunne, Desmond. *Yoga Made Easy* (Englewood Cliffs, New Jersey: Prentice-Hall, Inc., 1961).

Dyer, Colin F. W. *Symbolism in Craft Freemasonry* (England: A Lewis, Ltd., 1976).

"Earth and Spirit: The Spiritual Dimension of the Environmental Crisis," Chinook Learning Center.

East West (November 1989, Vol. 10, No. 11).

Editors of Time-Life Books. *Magical Arts* (Alexandria, Virginia: Time-Life Books, 1990).

Eisenberg, David, "Encounters with Qi: A Harvard Doctor Explores the Ancient Chinese Concept of 'Vital Energy.'" *The New Age Journal* (January/February 1987, Vol. 3, Issue 1).

El-Amin, Mustaga. *Freemasonry: Ancient Egypt and the Islamic Destiny* (Jersey City, New Jersey: New Mind Productions, 1988).

Elkins, Don; Rueckert, Carla; and McCarty, James Allen. *The Ra Material* (Norfolk, Virginia: The Donning Company, 1984).

Emergence, The (June 1998, Vol. 16, No. 5).

Encyclopedia of Associations (Vol. 1, Part 2), 1998, 33rd Edition.

Engle, Willis D. *A General History of the Order of the Eastern Star* (Indianapolis, Indiana: Willis D. Engle, 1901).

Epperson, A. Ralph. *The Unseen Hand: An Introduction to the Conspiratorial View of History* (Tucson, Arizona: Publius Press, 1985).

F.A.T.A.L. Flaw, The (Issaquah, Washington: Free the Masons Ministries, n.d.).

Farrar, Stewart. *What Witches Do: The Modern Coven Revealed* (Custer, Washington: Phoenix Publishing Company, 1983, Revised Edition).

Fate (October 1990, Vol. 43, No. 9 [sic]).

Fate (September 1990, Vol. 43, No. 9, Issue 486).

Ferguson, Marilyn. *The Aquarian Conspiracy: Personal and Social Transformation in the 1980s* (Los Angeles, California: J. P. Tarcher, Inc., 1980).

Findhorn Community, *The Findhorn Garden* (New York, New York: Harper and Row, 1975).

Flashpoint (April/May 1991).

Flashpoint (January 1990).

Flashpoint (October/November 1988).

Flashpoint (September 1992).

Flashpoint (Special Edition).

Florida Forum, The (Spring 1998).

For Full Moon Workers (Manhattan Beach, California: Arcana Workshops, n.d.).

Forum, The (January/February 1987).

Fowler, Clifton L. *Santa Claus and Christmas* (Knoxville, Tennessee: Evangelist of Truth, 1982).

Freedland, Nat. *The Occult Explosion* (New York: G. P. Putnam's and Sons, 1972).

Frewin, Anthony. *The Book of Days* (St. James Place, London: William Collins Sons and Company, Ltd., 1979).

Fritz, James S., "Alchemy." *The World Book Encyclopedia,* 1961 Edition; Vol. 1.

"From Whence Came We?" *Short Talk Bulletin* (October 1932, Vol. 10, No. 10; Reprinted December 1983).

Front Page, The (February 1993, Vol. 7, No. 2).

Full Moon Story, The (Manhattan Beach, California: Rams' Dell Press, July 1967; Revised September 1974).

Gabler, Mel and Norma. *Humanism in Textbooks* (Longview, Texas, 1983).

Gaynor, Frank, Editor. *Dictionary of Mysticism* (New York: Philosophical Library, 1953).

Gibson, John George. *The Masonic Problem: The Purpose and Meaning of Freemasonry* (n.p., 1912).

"Globes." *Short Talk Bulletin* (July 1967, Vol. 45, No. 7).

Glory, Morning and G'Zell, Otter. *Who on Earth is the Goddess?* (Berkeley, California: Covenant of the Goddess, n.d.).

"God's Watchman" and the Hope of Israel (Vol. 18, No. 1).

Godwin, Jeff. *Dancing with Demons: The Music's Real Master* (Chino, California: Chick Publications, 1988).

Godwin, Jeff. *Rock and Roll Religion* (Bloomington, Indiana: The Rock Ministries, 1995).

Godwin, Jeff. *The Devil's Disciples: The Truth About Rock* (Chino, California: Chick Publications, 1985).

Godwin, Jeff. *What's Wrong with Christian Rock?* (Chino, California: Chick Publications, 1990).

Godwin, John. *Occult America* (Garden City, New York: Doubleday and Company, Inc., 1972).

Goldenberg, Naomi R. *Changing of the Gods: Feminism and the End of Traditional Religions* (Boston, Massachusetts: Beacon Press, 1979).

Gospel Standard, The (May 1991, Vol. 40, No. 11).

Graham, O. J. *The Six-Pointed Star* (New Puritan Library, 1988, Second Edition).

Gumprecht, Jane. *New Age Health Care: Holy or Holistic* (Orange, California: Promise Publishing, 1988).

Gunther, Bernard. *Energy Ecstasy and Your Seven Vital Chakras* (Van Nuys, California: Newcastle Publishing Company, Inc., 1978).

Hall, Manly Palmer. *America's Assignment with Destiny* (Los Angeles, California: Philosophical Research Society, Inc., 1951).

Hall, Manly Palmer. *An Encyclopedic Outline of Masonic, Hermetic, Qabbalistic and Rosicrucian Symbolical Philosophy: Being an Interpretation of the Secret Teachings Concealed Within the Rituals, Allegories and Mysteries All Ages* (San Francisco, California: H. S. Crocker Company, Inc., 1928).

Hall, Manly Palmer. *Freemasonry of the Ancient Egyptians to Which Is Added an Interpretation of the Crata Repoa Initiation Rite* (Los Angeles, California: The Philosophers Press, 1937).

Hall, Manly Palmer. *Initiates of the Flame* (Los Angeles, California: The Phoenix Press, 1934).

Hall, Manly Palmer. *The Lost Keys of Freemasonry* (Richmond, Virginia: Macoy Publishing and Masonic Supply Company, Inc., 1976; Originally published in 1923).

Hall, Manly Palmer. *The Secret Destiny of America* (New York, New York: Philosophical Library, Inc., 1958).

Hall, Manly Palmer. *The Secret Teachings of All Ages* (Los Angeles, California: The Philosophical Research Society Press, 1945, Seventh Edition).

Hamilton, Edith. *Mythology* (Boston, Massachusetts: Little, Brown and Company, 1942).

Hamlyn, Paul. *Greek Mythology* (London: Paul Hamlyn, Ltd., 1967).

Harding, M. Esther. *Woman's Mysteries: Ancient and Modern* (New York: G. P. Putnam's Sons for the C. G. Jung Foundation for Analytical Psychology, 1971 Edition).

Harrison, John B. and Sullivan, Richard E. *A Short History of Western Civilization* (New York: Alfred A. Knopf, 1960).

Hawken, Paul. *The Magic of Findhorn* (New York, New York: Harper and Row, 1975).

Hawkins, E. L. *A Concise Cyclopaedia of Freemasonry* (EC: A. Lewis, 1908).

Haywood, H. L. *Introduction to Freemasonry* (Des Moines, Iowa: Research Lodge Number 2, n.d.).

Haywood, H. L. *Symbolic Masonry: An Interpretation of the Three Degrees* (Washington, D.C.: Masonic Service Association of the United States, 1923).

Haywood, H. L. *The Great Teachings of Masonry* (New York: George H. Doran Company, 1923).

Health (February 1986).

Hieronimus, Robert. *America's Secret Destiny: Spiritual Vision and the Founding of a Nation* (Rochester, Vermont: Destiny Books, 1989).

Higgins, Godfrey. *Anacalypsis, An Attempt to Draw Aside the Veil of the Saitic Isis* (London, England: n.p., 1874).

Hinduism Today (February 1992, Vol. 14, No. 2).

History of the Order of the Eastern Star (General Grand Chapter in the U. S. A., 1989).

Hochheimer, Wolfgang. *The Psychotherapy of C. G. Jung* (G. P. Putnam's Sons, 1969).

Holistic Education Review (Fall 1989, Vol. 2, No. 3).

Holistic Health Catalog.

Holistic Living (December 1984/January 1985, Vol. 11, No. 2).

Holy Bible (Wichita Kansas: Heirloom Bible Publishers, 1971).

"Holy Saints John, The." *Short Talk Bulletin* (December 1975, Vol. 53, No. 12).

"How to Build Your Own Washington Monument."

Hunt, Charles Clyde. *Some Thoughts on Masonic Symbolism* (New York: Macoy Publishing and Masonic Supply Company, 1930).

Hunt, Dave. *The Cult Explosion* (Eugene, Oregon: Harvest House Publishers, 1980).

Hunt, Dave. *Whatever Happened to Heaven?* (Eugene, Oregon: Harvest House Publishers, 1988).

Hunt, Dave and Decker, Ed. *The God Makers: A Shocking Expose of What the Mormon Church Really Believes* (Eugene, Oregon: Harvest House Publishers, 1984).

Hunt, Dave and McMahon, T. A. *America: The Sorcerer's New Apprentice: The Rise of New Age Shamanism* (Eugene, Oregon: Harvest House Publishers, 1988).

Hutchens, Rex R. *A Bridge to Light* (Washington, D.C.: Supreme Council, 33° Ancient and Accepted Scottish Rite of Freemasonry, Southern Jurisdiction, 1988).

Hutchens, Rex R. and Monson, Donald W. *The Bible in Albert Pike's Morals and Dogma* (Washington, D.C.: Supreme Council, 33rd Degree, 1992).

Hutchinson, William. *The Spirit of Masonry,* revised by Rev. George Oliver, originally published in 1775 (New York: Bell Publishing Company, 1982).

Huxley, Francis. *The Eye: The Seer and the Seen* (London, England: Thames and Hudson, 1990).

"Illustrated by Symbols." *Short Talk Bulletin* (March 1941, Vol. 19; No. 3; Reprinted January 1989).

Imprimis (June 1998, Vol. 27, No. 6).

"In the Beginning, God." *Short Talk Bulletin* (January 1967, Vol. 45, No. 1; Reprinted January 1982).

Inman, Herbert F. *Masonic Problems and Queries* (London, England: A. Lewis Ltd., 1978).

Interfaith Witness Department, *A Study of Freemasonry* (Atlanta, Georgia: Home Mission Board, Southern Baptist Convention, n.d.).

"Introducing S.U.N."

Ions, Veronica. *Egyptian Mythology* (England: The Hamlyn Publishing Group, Ltd., 1965).

Is the Antichrist in the World Today?, Interview with Constance Cumbey (Oklahoma City, Oklahoma: Southwest Radio Church, 1982).

Jennings, Gary. *Black Magic, White Magic* (Eau Claire, Wisconsin The Dial Press, Inc., 1964).

Jones, Bernard E. *Freemasons' Book of the Royal Arch* (London, England: George G. Harrap and Company Ltd., 1957).

Jordan, Michael. *Encyclopedia of Gods: Over 2,500 Deities of the World* (New York, New York: Facts on File, 1993).

Jr. High Ministry (September/October 1986, Vol. 1, No.5).

Jung, Carl; Von Franz, M.-L.; Henderson, Joseph L.; Jacobi, Jolande; and Jaffe, Aniela. *Man and His Symbols* (Garden City, New York: Doubleday and Company, Inc., 1964).

Kah, Gary. *En Route to Global Occupation* (Lafayette, Louisiana: Huntington House Publishers, 1992).

Kah, Gary H. *The Demonic Roots of Globalism* (Lafayette, Louisiana: Huntington House Publishers, 1995).

Kenaston, Jean M'Kee, Compiler. *History of the Order of the Eastern Star* (Cedar Rapids, Iowa: The Torch Press, 1917).

Kennedy, D. James. *The Gospel in the Stars* (Fort Lauderdale, Florida: Coral Ridge Ministries, n.d.).

Kennedy, D. James. *The Real Meaning of the Zodiac: Aquarius* (Fort Lauderdale, Florida: Coral Ridge Ministries, n.d.).

Kennedy, D. James. *The Real Meaning of the Zodiac: Aries* (Fort Lauderdale, Florida: Coral Ridge Ministries, n.d.).

Kennedy, D. James. *The Real Meaning of the Zodiac: Cancer* (Fort Lauderdale, Florida: Coral Ridge Ministries, n.d.).

Kennedy, D. James. *The Real Meaning of the Zodiac: Capricornus* (Fort Lauderdale, Florida: Coral Ridge Ministries, n.d.).

Kennedy, D. James. *The Real Meaning of the Zodiac: Gemini* (Fort Lauderdale, Florida: Coral Ridge Ministries, n.d.).

Kennedy, D. James. *The Real Meaning of the Zodiac: Leo* (Fort Lauderdale, Florida: Coral Ridge Ministries, n.d.).

Kennedy, D. James. *The Real Meaning of the Zodiac: Libra* (Fort Lauderdale, Florida: Coral Ridge Ministries, n.d.).

Kennedy, D. James. *The Real Meaning of the Zodiac: Pisces* (Fort Lauderdale, Florida: Coral Ridge Ministries, n.d.).

Kennedy, D. James. *The Real Meaning of the Zodiac: Sagittarius* (Fort Lauderdale, Florida: Coral Ridge Ministries, n.d.).

Kennedy, D. James. *The Real Meaning of the Zodiac: Scorpio* (Fort Lauderdale, Florida: Coral Ridge Ministries, n.d.).

Kennedy, D. James. *The Real Meaning of the Zodiac: Taurus* (Fort Lauderdale, Florida: Coral Ridge Ministries, n.d.).

Kennedy, D. James. *The Real Meaning of the Zodiac: Virgo* (Fort Lauderdale, Florida: Coral Ridge Ministries, n.d.).

Kent, Howard. *A Color Guide to Yoga* (Intercontinental Book Productions, 1980).

Kerr, Howard and Crow, Charles L., Editors. *The Occult in America: New Historical Perspectives* (Urbana, Illinois: University of Illinois Press, 1983).

Kingdom Voice (August 1990).

Kingdom Voice (May 1989).

Kingston, Jeremy. *Healing Without Medicine* (Doubleday and Company, Inc., 1976).

Kinman, Dwight L. *The World's Last Dictator* (Woodburn, Oregon: Solid Rock Books, Inc. 1995).

Knight, Stephen. *The Brotherhood* (Briarcliff Manor, New York: Stein and Day, 1984).

Koch, Kurt (Translated by Michael Freeman). *Occult ABC* (Germany: Literature Mission Aglasterhausen Inc., 1978).

Koch, Rudolf (Translated by Dyvyan Holland). *The Book of Signs* (New York, New York: Dover Publications, 1955).

Koch, Sandra L. *Combating the New Age Movement: A Christian Warfare Manual* (Boca Raton, Florida: Foundation Tabernacle Ministries, Inc., n.d.).

Krishna, R. P. Lawrie. *The Lamb Slain—Supreme Sacrifice,* Part 3 (Medway, Ohio: Manujothi Ashram Publications, n.d.).

Kueshana, Eklal. *The Ultimate Frontier* (Quinlan, Texas: The Stelle Group, 1963).

Kunk, Larry. *What Is the Secret Doctrine of the Masonic Lodge and How Does It Relate to Their Plan of Salvation?* (1992, Unpublished manuscript).

Kurtz, Paul. *Humanist Manifestos I and II* (Buffalo, New York: Prometheus Books, 1973).

Lai, Whalen W., "Before the Yin-Yang Circle Was Created: Individuation in a Soto Zen Circle Series." *Anima* (Spring Equinox 1984, Vol. 10, No. 2).

Lalonde, Peter. *One World Under Antichrist* (Eugene, Oregon: Harvest House Publishers, 1991).

Lamont, Corliss. *The Philosophy of Humanism* (New York: Frederick Unger Publishing Company, 1965 Edition).

Lamy, Lucie. *Egyptian Mysteries* (1981).

Lash, John. *The Seeker's Handbook: The Complete Guide to Spiritual Pathfinding* (New York: Harmony Books, 1990).

Last Trumpet Newsletter (April 1993, Vol. 12, Issue 4).

Last Trumpet Newsletter (July 1986, Vol. 5, No. 7).

Last Trumpet Newsletter (June 1986, Vol. 5, Issue 6).

Last Trumpet Newsletter (October 1994, Vol. 13, Issue 10).

LaVey, Anton Szandor. *The Satanic Bible* (New York: Avon Books, 1969).

Lawrence, John T. *The Perfect Ashlar* (London: A. Lewis, 1912).

Leach, Maria, Editor. *Funk and Wagnalls Standard Dictionary of Folklore, Mythology and Legend* (Vol. 1) (New York: Funk and Wagnalls, 1949).

Leek, Sybil. *Numerology: The Magic of Numbers* (New York, New York: The MacMillan Company, 1969).

Leek, Sybil. *Reincarnation: The Second Chance* (Briarcliff Manor New York: Stein and Day, 1974).

"Legend of the Dream Catcher."

"Legend of the Lost Word, The." *Short Talk Bulletin* (May 1928, Vol. 6; No. 5; Reprinted March 1986).

"Letter 'G,' The." *Short Talk Bulletin* (June 1933, Vol. 11, No. Reprinted April 1986).

"Letters." *Whole Life Times* (Mid-November/December 1984).

Levi, Eliphas (Translated by Arthur Edward Waite). *The History of Magic Including a Clear and Precise Exposition of Its Procedure, Its Rites and Its Mysteries* (London, England: William Rider and Son, Limited, 1992).

Lewis, H. Spencer. *Rosicrucian Manual* (Vol. No. 8), (San Jose, California: Supreme Grand Lodge of AMORC, 1966).

Lightworks (January 1996).

Light Speed (1993, Issue 13).

Liichow, Robert S. *The Two Roots of Today's Revival* (Kearney, Nebraska: Morris Publishing, 1997).

Living Unicorn, The (Carver, Minnesota: The Living Unicorn, Inc. 1980).

Llewellyn New Times (January/February 1987, #871).

Llewellyn New Times (January/February 1988, #881).

Llewellyn New Times (July/August 1986, #864).

Llewellyn New Times (July/August 1990, #904).

Llewellyn New Times (March/April 1986, Issue #862).

Llewellyn New Times (May/June 1987, No. 873).

Llewellyn New Times (September/October 1987, #875).

Llewellyn New Times (September/October 1988, #885).

"Lost Word, The." *Short Talk Bulletin* (November 1955, Vol. 33, No. 11).

Lucifer magazine.

Lust, John. *The Herb Book* (New York, New York: Bantam Books, Inc., 1974).

Lyons, Arthur, Jr., *The Second Coming: Satanism in America* (Dodd, Mead and Company, 1970).

Lyons, Arthur. *Satan Wants You: The Cult of Devil Worship in America* (New York, New York: The Mysterious Press, 1988).

Mackenzie, Kenneth R. H., Editor. *The Royal Masonic Cyclopaedia* (England: The Aquarian Press, 1987; First published in 1877).

MacKenzie, Norman, Editor. *Secret Societies* (Holt, Rinehart and Winston, 1967).

Mackey, Albert G. *A Manual of the Lodge* (New York: Charles E. Merrill Company, 1870).

Mackey, Albert G. *An Encyclopedia of Freemasonry and Its Kindred Science* (Chicago, Illinois: The Masonic History Company, 1924).

Mackey, Albert G. *Encyclopedia of Freemasonry* (Vol. 1) (Chicago, Illinois: The Masonic History Company, 1909).

Mackey, Albert G. *The Symbolism of Freemasonry: Illustrating and Explaining Its Science and Philosophy, Its Legends, Myths, and Symbols* (New York: Clark and Maynard, 1869).

MacLaine, Shirley. *Dancing in the Light* (New York, New York: Bantam Books, Inc., 1985).

MacNulty, W. Kirk. *Freemasonry: A Journey Through Ritual and Symbol* (London, England: Thames and Hudson, Inc., 1991).

Macoy, Robert. *A Dictionary of Freemasonry: A Compendium of Masonic History, Symbolism, Rituals, Literature, and Myth* (New York: Bell Publishing Company, n.d.).

Macoy, Robert (Arranged by). *Adoptive Rite Ritual* (Virginia: Macoy Publishing and Masonic Supply Company, 1897).

Magical Blend (February/March/April 1988, Issue #18).

Magical Work of the Soul (New York, New York: The Arcane School, n.d.).

Man, Myth and Magic: The Illustrated Encyclopedia of Mythology, Religion and the Unknown (North Bellmore, New York: Marshall Cavendish Corporation, 1994).

Maple, Eric. *The Complete Book of Witchcraft and Demonology* (Cranbury, New Jersey: A. S. Barnes and Company, Inc., 1966 Edition).

Marrs, Texe. *America Shattered* (Austin, Texas: Living Truth Publishers, 1991).

Marrs, Texe. *Circle of Intrigue* (Austin, Texas: Living Truth Ministries, 1995).

Marrs, Texe. *Dark Majesty: The Secret Brotherhood and the Magic of Thousand Points of Light* (Austin, Texas: Living Truth Publishers, 1992).

Marrs, Texe. *Dark Secrets of the New Age: Satan's Plan for a One World Religion* (Westchester, Illinois: Crossway Books, 1987).

Marrs, Texe, "Devil Companies, Devil Products, Devil Logos?" *Flashpoint* (December 1997).

Marrs, Texe. *How Will We Know the Antichrist? 21 Ways to Identify the Beast of Prophecy* (Austin, Texas: Living Truth Publishers, 1990).

Marrs, Texe. *Millennium: Peace, Promises, and the Day They Take Our Money Away* (Austin, Texas: Living Truth Publishers, 1990).

Marrs, Texe. *Mystery Mark of the New Age: Satan's Design for World Domination* (Westchester, Illinois: Crossway Books, 1988).

Marrs, Texe. *Ravaged by the New Age: Satan's Plan to Destroy Our Kids* (Austin, Texas: Living Truth Publishers, 1989).

Marrs, Texe. *Texe Marrs Book of New Age Cults and Religions* (Austin, Texas: Living Truth Publishers, 1990).

Marrs, Wanda. *New Age Lies to Women* (Austin, Texas: Living Truth Publishers, 1989).

"Masonic Firmament, The." *Short Talk Bulletin* (January 1945, Vol. 23, No. 1; Reprinted March 1985).

"Masonic Goat, The." *Short Talk Bulletin* (November 1936, Vol. 14, No. 11).

"Masonic Rod, The." *Short Talk Bulletin* (September 1957, Vol. 35, No. 9; Reprinted March 1986).

Masonic Vocabulary (Silver Spring, Maryland: Masonic Service Association of the United States, 1955).

Master of Life: Tools and Teachings to Create Your Own Reality (1986, Issue #32).

Master of Life: Tools and Teachings to Create Your Own Reality (1986, Issue #33).

Master of Life: Tools and Teachings to Create Your Own Reality (1987, Issue #35).

Master of Life: Tools and Teachings to Create Your Own Reality (1987, Issue #37).

McCormick, W. J. *Christ, the Christian and Freemasonry* (Belfast, Ireland: Great Joy Publications, 1984).

McDowell, Josh and Stewart, Don. *Understanding the Occult* (San Bernardino, California: Here's Life Publishers, Inc., 1982).

McLeod, Walter, Editor. *Beyond the Pillars* (Grand Lodge A.F.& A.M. of Canada, 1973).

McQuaig, C. F., *The Masonic Report* (Norcross, Georgia: Answer Books and Tapes, 1976).

Meadows, Kenneth. *Earth Medicine: Revealing Hidden Teachings of the Native American Medicine Wheel* (Rockport, Massachusetts: Element, 1991).

Means, Pat. *The Mystical Maze: A Guidebook Through the Mindfields of Eastern Mysticism* (Campus Crusade for Christ, Inc., 1976).

Meditation (Winter 1991, Vol. 6, No. 1).

Melton, J. Gordon. *The Encyclopedia of American Religions* (Vol. 2) (Wilmington, North Carolina: McGrath Publishing Company, 1978).

Melton, J. Gordon; Clark, Jerome; and Kelly, Aidan A. *New Age Almanac* (Detroit, Michigan: Visible Ink, 1991).

Meyer, Franz Sales. *Handbook of Ornament* (Dover).

Meyer, William. *The Order of the Eastern Star* (no other information available).

Michaelsen, Johanna. *Like Lambs to the Slaughter* (Eugene, Oregon: Harvest House Publishers, 1989).

Michaelsen, Johanna. *The Beautiful Side of Evil* (Eugene, Oregon: Harvest House Publishers, 1982).

Midnight Call (July 1998).

Milanovich, Norma, and McCune, Shirley. *The Light Shall Set You Free* (Athena Publishing).

Miller, Betty. *Exposing Satan's Devices* (Dewey, Arizona: Christ Unlimited Ministries, Inc., 1980).

MoonStar, "Casting the Stalks for Understanding and Guidance." *Circle Network News* (Spring 1985, Vol. 7, No. 1).

Moran, Hugh A. and Kelley, David H. *The Alphabet and the Ancient Calendar Signs* (Palo Alto, California: Daily Press, 1969, Second Edition).

Morey, Robert A. *Islam Unveiled: The True Desert Storm* (Shermans Dale, Pennsylvania: The Scholars Press, 1991).

Morey, Robert A. *The Origins and Teachings of Freemasonry* (Southbridge, Massachusetts: Crowne Publications, Inc., 1990).

Morning Glory and G'Zell, Otter. *Who on Earth Is the Goddess?* (Berkeley, California: Covenant of the Goddess, n.d.).

Morrison, Alan. *The Serpent and the Cross: Religious Corruption in an Evil Age* (Birmingham, England: K & M Books, 1994).

"Mosaic Pavement and Blazing Star." *Short Talk Bulletin* (April 1951, Vol. 29, No. 4; Reprinted April 1990).

Mother Jones (February/March 1988, Vol. 13, No. 2).

Mother Owl's Aquarian Age Information Network Catalog.

Muller, Robert. *A World Core Curriculum* (n.d., n.p.).

Muller, Robert. *Framework for Preparation for the Year 2000, The 21st Century* (Hamden, Connecticut: Albert Schweitzer Institute/Quinnipiac College Press, 1994).

Muller, Robert. *New Genesis: Shaping a Global Spirituality* (Garden City, New York: Image Books, 1984).

Murdock, Maureen. *Spinning Inward: Using Guided Imagery with Children for Learning, Creativity and Relaxation* (Boston, Massachusetts: Shambhala Publications, Inc., 1987, Revised and Expanded Edition).

Mysteries of Mind Space and Time: The Unexplained (Vol. 1) (Westport, Connecticut: H. S. Stuttman, Inc., 1992).

"Mystic Tie, The." *Short Talk Bulletin* (October 1940, Vol. 28, No. 10; Reprinted March 1982).

National Enquirer (May 27, 1986).

"Nature of Symbols, The." *Short Talk Bulletin* (July 1957, Vol. 3, No. 7; Reprinted May 1982).

Necronomicon (New York, New York: Avon Books, 1977).

New Age Journal (January/February 1988, Vol. 4, Issue 1).

New Age, The (April 1960, Vol. 68, No. 4).

New Age Magazine, The (June 1973, Vol. 81, No. 6).

New Age Magazine, The (May 1948, Vol. 56, No. 5.

New Age Movement—Age of Aquarius—Age of Antichrist, The. Interview with Constance Cumbey (Oklahoma City, Oklahoma: Southwest Radio Church, 1982).

New American Schools Development Corporation (Annual Report 1994/1995).

New Larousse Encyclopedia of Mythology (Prometheus Press, 1972 Edition).

New Man (July/August 1998).

New Teachings for an Awakening Humanity (Santa Clara, California: S. E. E. Publishing Company, n.d.).

New Times (July/August 1988, #884).

New Times (March/April 1986, #862).

News and Observer, The (January 11, 1997).

News Tribune, The (December 2, 1993).

Newsweek (September 24, 1990, Vol. 116, No. 13).

Newton, Joseph Fort. *The Builders: A Story and Study of Masonry* (Cedar Rapids, Iowa: The Torch Press, 1914).

Newton, Joseph Fort. *The Religion of Masonry: An Interpretation* (Richmond, Virginia: Macoy Publishing and Masonic Supply Company, Inc., 1969 Edition).

"Numerology of Masonry." *Short Talk Bulletin* (June 1946, Vol. 2, No. 6; Reprinted November 1984).

Oliver, George. *Signs and Symbols* (New York: Macoy Publishing and Masonic Supply Company, 1906).

Oliver, George. *Symbol of Glory Shewing the Object and End of Freemasonry* (New York: John W. Leonard and Company, American Masonic Agency, 1855).

Oliver, George. *The Historical Landmarks and Other Evidences of Freemasonry, Explained* (Vol. I & II) (New York: John W. Leonard and Company, 1855).

Omega Institute (Summer 1986).

Omega-Letter, The (April 1990, Vol. 5, No. 4).

Omega-Letter, The (August 1990, Vol. 5, No. 6 [sic]).

Omega-Letter, The (March 1990, Vol. 5, No. 3).

Omega-Letter, The (October 1989, Vol. 4, No. 9).

Palos, Stephan. *The Chinese Art of Healing* (New York, New York: Herder and Herder, Inc., 1971).

Parchment, S. R. *Ancient Operative Masonry* (San Francisco, California: San Francisco Center—Rosicrucian Fellowship, 1930).

Parents of Teenagers (November/December 1992, Vol. 5, No. 2).

Park, Irene Arrington. *Modernized Paganism* (Tampa, Florida: Christ's Deliverance Ministries, 1983).

Park, Irene Arrington. *What Every Christian Should Know About Symbols, Signs and Emblems* (Tampa, Florida: Christ's Deliverance Ministries, 1982).

Parrinder, Geoffrey, Editor. *World Religions: From Ancient History to the Present* (New York, New York: Facts on File, 1971).

Parsons, James M. *The Assault on the Family* (PRO Media Foundation, 1978), Appendix II.

Partner, Peter. *The Knights Templar and Their Myth* (Rochester, Vermont: Destiny Books, 1990, Revised Edition).

Pass It On: The Story of Bill Wilson and How the A.A. Message Reach the World (New York, New York: Alcoholics Anonymous World Services, Inc. 1984).

Patrick, Richard. *All Color Book of Greek Mythology* (London, England: Octopus Books Limited, 1972).

"Peace Symbols: The Truth About Those Strange Designs," *American Opinion,*

Pennsylvania Freemason, The (November 1989, Vol. 36, No. 4).

Pennsylvania Youth Foundation, The (Elizabethtown, Pennsylvania: The Pennsylvania Youth Foundation, n.d.).

Perceptions (Summer 1993, Vol. 1, Issue 2).

Percival, Harold Waldwin. *Masonry and Its Symbols in the Light of "Thinking and Destiny"* (New York, New York: The Word Foundation, Inc., 1952).

Perilous Times, The (January 1996, Vol. 17, No. 11).

Perilous Times, The (June 1998).

Perkins, Lynn F. *Masonry in the New Age* (Lakemont, Georgia: CSA Press, 1971).

Personal Energy Patterns: How They Affect Your Personality, Health, and Relationships (Albany, California: Taoist Healing Centre, n.d.).

Petersen, William J. *Those Curious New Cults* (New Canaan, Connecticut: Keat Publishing, Inc., 1973).

Peterson, William O., Editor. *Masonic Quiz Book: "Ask Me Another, Brother"* (Chicago, Illinois: Charles T. Powner Company, 1950).

Peterson, Willy. *The Leavening: A New Age Primer for Christian Parents* (Linwood, Kansas, 1995).

Pfeiffer, Charles F., Editor. *The Biblical World: A Dictionary of Biblical Archaeology* (New York: Bonanza Books, 1966).

Phillips, Phil. *Saturday Morning Mind Control* (Nashville, Tennessee: Oliver-Nelson Books, 1991).

Phillips, Phil. *Turmoil in the Toybox* (Lancaster, Pennsylvania: Starburst Press, 1986).

Phyllis Schlafly Report, The (January 1994, Vol. 27, No. 6).

Pierson, A. T. C. *The Traditions, Origin and Early History of Freemasonry* (New York: Masonic Publishing Company, 1865).

Pike, Albert. *Morals and Dogma of the Ancient and Accepted Scottish Rite of Freemasonry Prepared for the Supreme Council of the Thirty-Third Degree, for the Southern Jurisdiction of the United States, and Published by Its Authority* (Richmond, Virginia: L. H. Jenkins, Inc., 1871, Reprinted 1944).

Pike, Albert. *The Magnum Opus* (Kila, Montana: Kessinger Publishing Company, 1992).

Plessner, Shirley. *Symbolism of the Eastern Star* (Cleveland, Ohio: Gilbert Publishing Company, 1956).

Pocket Encyclopedia of Masonic Symbols (Silver Spring, Maryland: The Masonic Service Association of the United States, 1953).

Pocket Masonic Dictionary (Silver Spring, Maryland: The Masonic Service Association of the United States, 1988).

Poinsot, M. C. *The Occult Sciences* (New York: Robert M. McBride and Company, 1972).

"Point Within a Circle." *Short Talk Bulletin* (August 1931, Vol. 9, No. 8; Reprinted July 1990).

Portal, Frederic (Translated by John W. Simons). *A Comparison of Egyptian Symbols with Those of the Hebrews* (New York: Masonic Publishing and Manufacturing Company, 1866).

Powell, Arthur E. *The Magic of Freemasonry* (Baskerville Press, Ltd., 1924).

Prophecy Newsletter (Vol. 1, No. 6).

Psychic BookShop.

Psychic Guide (March/April/May 1985).

Rainbow Bridge Newsletter, The (October/November 1984, Vol. 1, No. 4).

Rainbow Connection, The (April 1995).

Rays from the Rose Cross (April/May 1988).

Regardie, Israel. *The Golden Dawn* (St. Paul, Minnesota: Llewellyn Publications, 1986).

Report from Concerned Christians (May/June 1990).

Rest, Friedrich. *Our Christian Symbols* (Philadelphia, Pennsylvania: The Christian Education Press, 1954).

Return to the Word (June 1998).

Revesz, Terese Ruth. *Witches* (New York, New York: Contemporary Perspectives, Inc., 1977).

Richmond, M. Temple, *Sirius* (Mariposa, California: Source Publications, 1997).

Riplinger, G. A. *New Age Bible Versions* (Munroe Falls, Ohio: A. V. Publications, 1993).

"Ritual in Freemasonry." *Short Talk Bulletin* (August 1990, Vol. 68, No. 8).

"Ritual Is Important, The." *Short Talk Bulletin* (July 1965, Vol. 43; No. 7; Reprinted April 1983).

Ritual National Imperial Court of the Daughters of Isis North and South America (Ezra A. Cook Publications, Inc., n.d.).

Robbins, Rossell Hope. *The Encyclopedia of Witchcraft and Demonology* (New York, New York: Crown Publishers, Inc., 1966).

Roberts, Allen E. *The Craft and Its Symbols: Opening the Door to Masonic Symbolism* (Richmond, Virginia: Macoy Publishing and Masonic Supply Company, Inc., 1974).

Robinson, John J. *A Pilgrim's Path: One Man's Road to the Masonic Temple* (New York: New York: M. Evans and Company, Inc., 1993).

Robinson, John J. *Born in Blood: The Lost Secrets of Freemasonry* (New York, New York: M. Evans and Company, 1989).

Rodman, Rosamond C., Editor. *The United Nations in an Interdependent World: Past, Present, Future* (New York, New York: Global Education Associates, 1995).

Ronayne, Edmond. *The Master's Carpet (Mah-Hah-Bone)* (n.p., 1879).

Rosicrucian Manual (Prepared under the supervision of H. Spence Lewis with revision by Ralph M. Lewis) (San Jose, California: Grand Lodge of AMORC, 1987, 27th Edition).

Ross, Nancy Wilson. *Three Ways of Asian Wisdom* (New York, New York: Simon and Schuster, 1966).

Rowe, Ed. *New Age Globalism* (Herndon, Virginia: Growth Publishing, 1985).

Rueckert, Carla L. *A Channeling Handbook* (Amherst, Wisconsin: Palmer Publications, Inc., 1987).

Rule, Lucien V. *Pioneering in Masonry: The Life and Times of Rob Morris, Masonic Poet Laureate, Together with Story of Clara Barton and the Eastern Star* (Louisville, Kentucky: Brandt and Connors Company, 1922).

Saints Alive in Jesus Newsletter (March 1992).

San Francisco Chronicle (January 23, 1996).

"Sanctum Sanctorum." *Short Talk Bulletin* (July 1944, Vol. 22, No. 7, Reprinted January 1982).

Sanford, Agnes. *The Healing Light: The Art and Method of Spiritual Healing* (St. Paul, Minnesota: MacAlester Park Publishing Company, 1947).

Satisfying Portion, The (March/April 1991, Vol. 18, No. 1).

Schnoebelen, William. *Masonry: Beyond the Light* (Chino, California: Chick Publications, 1991).

Schnoebelen, William, "Satan's Door Revisited." *Saints Alive in Jesus* (March 1992).

Schnoebelen, William. *Straight Talk #10 on the Peace Sign Gesture* (Dubuque, Iowa: With One Accord Ministries, 1995).

Schnoebelen, William. *Twice the Child of Hell* (Issaquah, Washington: Saints Alive in Jesus, n.d.).

Schnoebelen, William and Sharon. *Lucifer Dethroned* (Chino, California: Chick Publications, 1993).

Schwab, Gustav. *Gods and Heroes: Myths and Epics of Ancient Greece* (New York: Pantheon Books, 1946).

Scott, Charles. *The Analogy of Ancient Craft Masonry to Natural and Revealed Religion* (Philadelphia, Pennsylvania: E. H. Butler and Company, 1857).

Scottish Rite Journal, The (July 1998).

Scottish Rite Journal, The (May 1992, Vol. 100, No. 5).

"Secrecy in Symbolism." *Short Talk Bulletin* (July 1981, Vol. 50 No. 7).

Seeger, Elizabeth. *Eastern Religions* (New York: Thomas Y. Cromwell Company, 1973).

Self-Help Update: Create Your Own Reality (1985, Issue #26).

Self-Help Update: Create Your Own Reality (1985, Issue #28).

Self-Help Update: Create Your Own Reality (1985, Issue #29).

Self-Help Update: Create Your Own Reality (Issue #30).

Self-Help Update: Create Your Own Reality (Issue #31).

Sessler, Robert. *To Be God of One World: The French Revolution Globalized* (Merlin, Oregon: Let There Be Light Publications, 1992).

Shamballa: The Centre Where the Will of God Is Known (New York, New York: World Goodwill, n.d.).

Shamballa: Where the Will of God is Known (New York, New York: Arcane School, n.d.).

Shaw, Jim and McKenney, Tom. *The Deadly Deception* (Lafayette, Louisiana: Huntington House, Inc., 1988).

"Shekinah." *Short Talk Bulletin* (June 1942, Vol. 22, No. 6).

Shepherdsfield Update (Spring 1989, No. 22).

Sickles, Daniel, Editor. *The Freemason's Monitor* (New York: Macoy Publishing and Masonic Supply Company, 1901).

"Significant Numbers, The." *Short Talk Bulletin* (September 1956, Vol. 34; No. 9).

"Signs." *Short Talk Bulletin* (August 1937, Vol. 15, No. 8; Reprinted March 1989).

Singh, Darshan. *Helping Factors on the Spiritual Path* (Delhi, India: n.p.).

Siva's Cosmic Dance (San Francisco, California: Himalayan Academy, n.d.).

Slipper, Mary Ann. *The Symbolism of the Order of the Eastern Star* (no other information available).

Slipper, Mary Ann. *The Symbolism of the Eastern Star* (n.p., 1927).

"So Mote It Be." *Short Talk Bulletin* (June 1927, Vol. 5, No. 6; Reprinted September 1981).

Spangler, David. *Emergence: The Rebirth of the Sacred* (New York, New York: Dell Publishing, 1984).

Spangler, David, "Finding Heaven on Earth." *New Age Journal* (January/February 1988; Vol. 4, Issue 1).

Spangler, David. *Links with Space* (Marina Del Rey, California: DeVorss and Company, 1971).

Spangler, David. *Reflections on the Christ* (Scotland: Findhorn Publications, 1977).

Spangler, David. *Revelation: The Birth of a New Age* (Middleton, Wisconsin: The Lorian Press, 1976).

Spear, William, "Ancient Chinese Philosophy, Astrology and the I Ching." *Rowe Conference Center* (Spring 1989).

Spence, Lewis. *Myths and Legends of Babylonia and Assyria* (London, England: George G. Harrap and Company, 1916).

Sphaera Imaginatio #16.

Spiritual Mothering Journal (Winter 1986, Vol. 6, No. 4).

Springmeier, Fritz. *The Top 13 Illuminati Bloodlines* (Portland, Oregon: Fritz Springmeier).

Springmeier, Fritz. *The Watchtower and the Masons* (Portland, Oregon, 1992).

Stafford, Thomas Albert. *Christian Symbolism in the Evangelical Churches* (Nashville, Tennessee: Abingdon Press, 1942).

Stamps, Jeffrey S.*Holonomy: A Human Systems Theory* (Intersystems Publications).

Starhawk (Miriam Simos). *The Spiral Dance: A Rebirth of the Ancient Religion of the Great Goddess* (New York, New York: Harper-Collins Publishers, 1989 Edition).

Statement Affirming Evolution As a Principle of Science, (Amherst, New York: American Humanist Association).

Steinmetz, George H. *Freemasonry: Its Hidden Meaning* (New York: Macoy Publishing and Masonic Supply Company, 1948).

Steinmetz, George H. *The Lost Word: Its Hidden Meaning: A Correlation of the Allegory and Symbolism of the Bible with That of Freemasonry and an Exposition of the Secret Doctrine* (New York: Macoy Publishing and Masonic Supply Company, 1953).

Stewart, Thomas Milton. *The Symbolism of the Gods of the Egyptians and the Light They Throw on Freemasonry* (London, England: Baskerville Press, Limited, 1927).

Still, William T. *New World Order: The Ancient Plan of Secret Societies* (Lafayette, Louisiana: Huntington House, Inc., 1990).

Stillman, John Maxson. *The Story of Alchemy and Early Chemistry* (New York, New York: Dover Publications, Inc., 1960).

Stillson, Henry Leonard and Hughan, William James, Editors. *History of the Ancient and Honorable Fraternity of Free and Accepted Masons, and Concordant Orders* (no other information available).

"Sts. Johns' Days." *Short Talk Bulletin* (December 1933, Vol. 11, No. 12; Reprinted July 1986).

"Sun, Moon and Stars." *Short Talk Bulletin* (March 1930, Vol. 8, No. 3).

"Symbolism." *Short Talk Bulletin* (March 1925, Vol. 3, No. 3; Reprinted May 1982).

Tampa Tribune (October 31, 1988).

Tarkowski, Ed and Mary. *The Origins, Practices and Traditions of Halloween* (Erie, Pennsylvania: Guardians of the Heart, n.d.).

Tarkowski, Ed and Mary, "What Is the Occult? A Glossary of Occult Terms." *The Origins, Practices and Traditions of Halloween* (Erie, Pennsylvania: Guardians of the Heart, n.d.).

Terry, Sarah H., Compiler. *History of the Order of the Eastern Star* (n.p., 1914).

Terry, Sarah H. *The Second Mile* (Corpus Christi, Texas: Christian Triumph Press, 1935).

Thoughtline (August 1990).

Thoughtline (June 1995).

Thoughtline (June 1998).

Three Meditation Festivals of Spring: A World Religion for the New Age, The (Ojai, California: Group for Creative Meditation).

Tierra, Michael. *The Way of Herbs* (New York, New York: Washington Square Press, 1980).

Time-Life Books, Editors. *Magical Arts* (Alexandria, Virginia: Time-Life Books, 1990).

Transmission. (April 1983, No. 1).

Tros, Gerald. *New Age Notes* (IBM disk).

Turner, Tanya. *New Age Emphasis on Stones and Gems: A Revival of Paganism* (Charlotte, North Carolina: Paw Creek Ministries, n.d.).

"Two Pillars." *Short Talk Bulletin* (September 1935, Vol. 13, No. 9; Reprinted September 1978).

Utne Reader (March/April 1990, No. 38).

Utne Reader (November/December 1987).

Vail, Charles H. *The Ancient Mysteries and Modern Masonry* (New York: Macoy Publishing and Masonic Supply Company, 1909).

Van Baalen, Jan Karel. *The Chaos of Cults* (Grand Rapids, Michigan: Wm. B. Eerdsmans Publishing Company, 1962 Edition).

"Veiled in Allegory and Illustrated by Symbols." *Short Talk Bulletin* (November 1974, Vol. 52, No. 11).

"Veiled in Allegory." *Short Talk Bulletin* (September 1949, Vol. 27, No. 9; Reprinted April 1986).

Voice in the Wilderness, The (February 1992).

Voyage to the Source (McMinnville, Oregon: The Aquarian Church of Universal Service, 1986).

Waite, Arthur Edward. *A New Encyclopedia of Freemasonry and of Cognate Instituted Mysteries: Their Rites, Literature and History* (New York: Weathervane Books, 1970 edition).

Waite, Arthur Edward. *An Encyclopedia of Freemasonry and of Cognate Instituted Mysteries: Their Rites, Literature and History,* Vol. I (New York: Weathervane Books, 1970).

Waite, Arthur Edward. *An Encyclopedia of Freemasonry and of Cognate Instituted Mysteries: Their Rites, Literature and History,* Vol. II (New York: Weathervane Books, 1970).

Waite, Arthur Edward. *Emblematic Freemasonry and the Evolution of Its Deeper Issues* (London: William Rider and Son, Ltd., 1925).

Waite, Arthur Edward. *The Brotherhood of the Rosy Cross: Being Records of the House of the Holy Spirit in Its Inward and Outward History* (New Hyde Park, New York: University Books, 1961).

Waite, Arthur Edward. *The Holy Kabbalah* (London: Williams and Norgate Ltd., 1929).

Waite, Arthur Edward. *The Mysteries of Magic: A Digest of the Writings of Eliphas Levi* (Chicago, Illinois: De Laurence, Scott and Company, 1909).

Waite, Arthur Edward. *The Secret Tradition in Freemasonry* (London: Rider and Company, 1937).

Wallman, Joseph. *The Kabalah: From Its Inception to Its Evanescence* (Brooklyn, New York: Theological Research Publishing Company 1958).

Ward, Arthur H. *Masonic Symbolism and the Mystic Way* (London: Theosophical Publishing House, Ltd., 1923, Second Edition).

Ward, John Sebastian Marlow. *Freemasonry and the Ancient Gods* (London: Simpkins, Marshall, Hamilton, Kent and Company, Ltd., 1921).

Ward, John Sebastian Marlow. *The Sign Language of the Mysteries* (Land's End Press, 1969).

Ward, John Sebastian Marlow. *Who Was Hiram Abiff?* (London, England: The Baskerville Press, Limited, 1925).

Ward, John Sebastian Marlow and Stirling, W. G. *The Hung Society or the Society of Heaven and Earth* (Vol. 1) (London, England: The Baskerville Press, Limited, 1925).

Watchman Mini-Expositor (March 1997).

Wedeck, Harry E. *Treasury of Witchcraft* (New York, New York: Philosophical Library, 1961).

Westcott, W. Wynn. *Numbers: Their Occult Power and Mystic Virtues* (London, England: Theosophical Publishing Society, 1902, Second Edition).

Whalen, William J. *Handbook of Secret Organizations* (Milwaukee, Wisconsin: The Bruce Publishing Company, 1966).

What? When? Where? Why? Who? in Freemasonry (Silver Spring, Maryland: Masonic Service Association of the United States, 1956).

What Is (1987, Vol. 1, No. 2).

What Is (Summer 1986, Vol. 1, No. 1).

Whole Earth Papers: Christian Voice on World Order, The (1978, Vol. 1, No. 10).

Willcock, Shaun. *The Pagan Festivals of Christmas and Easter* (Pietermaritzburg, South Africa: Bible Based Ministries, 1992).

Wilmshurst, W. L. *The Masonic Initiation* (Ferndale, Michigan: Trismegistus Press, 1980; Originally published 1924).

Wilmshurst, W. L. *The Meaning of Masonry* (Bell Publishing Company, Reprint of fifth edition published in 1927).

Wilson, Bill. *As Bill Sees It: The A.A. Way of Life* (New York, New York: Alcoholics Anonymous World Services, Inc..

Wilson, Colin. *The Occult: A History* (New York, Random House, 1971).

"Winding Stairs, The." *Short Talk Bulletin* (January 1932, Vol. 1, No. 1; Reprinted July 1991).

Winters, D. Duane. *A Search for Light in a Place of Darkness: A Study of Freemasonry* (no other information available).

Wood, Max. *Rock and Roll: An Analysis of the Music* (n.p., n.d.).

Woodcock, Percival George. *Short Dictionary of Mythology* (Philosophical Library, 1953).

Woodrow, Ralph Edward. *Babylon Mystery Religion: Ancient and Modern* (Riverside, California: Ralph Woodrow Evangelistic Association, Inc., 1990 Edition).

World Book Encyclopedia, The (1961 Edition).

Yarker, John. *The Arcane Schools: A Review of Their Origin and Antiquity: With a General History of Freemasonry and Its Relation to the Theosophic Scientific and Philosophic Mysteries* (Belfast, Ireland: William Tait, 1909).

Yoga International (March/April 1994, Vol. 3, No. 5).

Your Masonic Capital City (Silver Spring, Maryland: The Masonic Service Association of the United States, n.d.).

Zimbardo, Philip G. and Ruch, Floyd L., Editors. *Psychology and Life* (Glenview, Illinois: Scott, Foresman and Company, 1977, Ninth Edition).

Zimmer, Heinrich with Campbell, Joseph as Editor, *Myths and Symbols in Indian Art and Civilization* (New York: Harper and Row, 1962).

Index

Mormonism, Masonry, and Godhood

Dr. Cathy Burns

Can Angels Be Trusted?

The Church o f Jesus Christ of Latter-day Saints (Mormons) began on April 6, 1830. In this book Dr. Burns covers many of key Mormon doctrines as well as looking closely at Mormon's founder, Joseph Smith.

This **well-documented** book answers questions such as the following:

— What **talisman** was found on Joseph Smith when he died?
— Was Joseph Smith involved in **magical and occultic practices?**
— Is there a **Masonic connection?**
— What takes place inside the Mormon Temple?
— Was God once a man?
— Is **polygamy** necessary to attain heaven?
— How can a Mormon attain **godhood?**
— What does Mormonism teach about **baptism for the dead?**
— Was Jesus married?
— Was Jesus crucified because He was a polygamist?

132 pages • $6.95 plus $1.25 postage • ISBN: 1-891117-01-7

SECURE IN CHRIST

In this most fascinating and Scripturally-oriented book you will find approximately 1000 Bible verses to meditate upon. It will enlighten you as you search the Scriptures and will encourage a closer walk with the Lord.

This book will also strengthen your spiritual outlook on life as you see how the Lord wants you to cast all your care upon Him and walk hand in hand in fellowship with Him as He leads you into the deep truth of His Word.

"Now unto Him that is able to keep you from falling, and to present you faultless before the presence of His glory with exceeding joy" (Jude 1:24).

For your gift of $6.95 plus $1.25 postage and handling.

136 pages • ISBN: 1-891117-10-6

Dr. Cathy Burns

ALCOHOLICS
UNMASKED
ANONYMOUS
Deception and Deliverance

Where do the 12 steps lead?

- Who is the Higher Power of AA?
- Were AA's founders Christians or occultists?
- How is the New Age involved?
- How successful is AA's treatment program?
- Is alcoholism a sin or a disease?

Don't you think it's time to learn about Bill Wilson's adulterous affairs, LSD experimentation, as well as his and Dr. Bob Smith's interest in seances and spiritualism?

128 pages • $5.95 • ISBN 1-56043-449-X

A ONE WORLD ORDER IS COMING

"Peace, peace, we must have peace at any cost," is the cry being heard from every quarter today. If we don't soon agree to have a peaceful world, we may all die in a nuclear holocaust. So, what will it take to have a peaceful coexistence? The answer given is the establishment of a one world government. In addition to a one world government, there will be a one world religion and a one world economy. What is also needed in a one world government is a leader. Who will this leader be?

In spite of many plans for this one world government, there is still one obstacle in the way. What—or **WHO**—is this obstacle?

Each of these topics are discussed in detail in this book and then compared to the Bible to see how prophecy is being fulfilled.

For your gift of $5.95 plus $1.25 postage and handling.
116 pages • ISBN: 1-891117-00-9

A SCRIPTURAL VIEW OF HELL

Dr. Cathy Burns

Does the Bible teach soul sleep?
Is Hell eternal?
Is Hell the grave?
Are the wicked annihilated?
Is there fire in Hell?
Is Hell a place of torment?
All of these questions are answered Scripturally in this small book.

For your gift of $4.95 plus $1.05 postage and handling.

40 pages • ISBN: 1-891117-11-4